JUST THE FACTS

TRUE TALES OF COPS AND CRIMINALS

PRO SE PRESS

JUST THE FACTS: TRUE TALES OF COPS AND CRIMINALS
A Pro Se Press Publication

Edited by - H. David Blalock and Mark Beaulieu
Editor in Chief, Pro Se Productions - Tommy Hancock
Submissions Editor - Barry Reese
Director of Corporate Operations - Morgan Minor
Publisher & Pro Se Productions, LLC-Chief Executive Officer - Fuller Bumpers

Cover Art by Jeff Hayes
Print Production and Book Design by Percival Constantine
E-Book Design by Russ Anderson
New Pulp Logo Design by Sean E. Ali
New Pulp Seal Design by Cari Reese

Pro Se Productions, LLC
133 1/2 Broad Street
Batesville, AR, 72501
870-834-4022

proseproductions@earthlink.net
www.prose-press.com

The following chapters were first published in *Mystery Readers Journal;* some have been revised for this publication.

"The Angels You Listen To," *MRJ* Vol. 22, No.3, Fall 2006, Academic Mysteries 101.
"Bill Tilghman, Cross-Genre-ational Crime-Fighter," *MRJ* Vol. 15, No. 1, Spring 1999, Cross-Genre Mysteries.
"The Case of the Terrified Tenor," *MRJ* Vol. 19, No. 3, Fall 2003, Music and Mysteries, Part II.
"Chocolate-Covered Murder Weapons," *MRJ* Vol. 18, No. 2, Summer 2002, Culinary Crime, First Course.

PRO SE ⚖ PRESS

"The Cigar Girl and the Storyteller," *MRJ* Vol. 15, No. 3, Fall 1999, The Short Mystery Story.

"Death Imitates Art," *MRJ* Vol. 20, No. 4, Winter 2004-05, Murder Down Under.

"The Dry Guys," *MRJ* Vol. 17, No. 2, Summer 2001, Partners in Crime I: Sleuthing Partners.

"Espionage Chic," *MRJ* Vol. 17, No. 4, Winter 2001–2002, Oxbridge Mysteries.

"Eye for an Eye, Tooth for a Tooth," *MRJ* Vol. 17, No. 1, Spring 2001, New England Mysteries.

"Final Appeal," *MRJ* Vol. 19, No. 1, Spring 2003, Mysteries South of the Mason- Dixon Line, Part II.

"The First Suicide Bomber," *MRJ*, Vol. 25, No. 3, Fall 2009, Los Angeles Mysteries II.

"A Fool for a Client," *MRJ* Vol.22, No. 2, Summer 2012, Legal Mysteries I.

"The Forgotten Man," *MRJ* Vol. 16, No. 4, Winter 2000–2001, Southwestern Mysteries.

"Gunfighter," *MRJ* Vol. 29, No. 2, Summer 2013, Chicago Mysteries.

"The Innovative Traditionalist," *MRJ* Vol. 18, No. 1, Spring 2002, Pacific Northwest Mysteries.

"Mole to Manhunter," *MRJ,* Vol. 24, No. 2, Summer 2008, Irish Mysteries.

"Playing Through the Pain," *MRJ* Vol. 15, No. 4, Winter 1999–2000, Florida Mysteries.

"The 'Ragged Stranger' Murders," *MRJ* Vol. 17, No. 3, Fall 2001, Partners in Crime II: Writing Partners.

"Something He Ate," *MRJ* Vol. 18, No. 3, Fall 2002, Culinary Crime, Second Seating.

"Truth Beneath a Tattered Coat," *MRJ* Vol. 27, No. 1, Spring 2011, London Mysteries I.

"Unsung for Sixty Years," *MRJ* Vol. 16, No. 3, Fall 2000, The Senior Sleuth.

"The Windiest Cop in the Windy City," *MRJ* Vol. 15, No. 2, Summer 1999, Chicago Mysteries.

For back issues and subscriptions, contact the *Mystery Readers Journal*, P.O. Box 8116, Berkeley, CA 94707, or see www.mysteryreaders.org.

Collection originally published by Deadly Serious Press.

Bill Tilghman, legendary Oklahoma lawman and town-tamer from the Territorial era to the Roaring Twenties. Richard Crafts, an airline pilot who killed his stewardess wife and fed her frozen body into a rented woodchipper. Hawaiian Policeman Chang Apana, the real Chinese-American detective who inspired Earl Derr Biggers to create Charlie Chan. Their stories and many more are brought to life by Jim Doherty, "Just the Facts" columnist for *Mystery Readers Journal.*

"This is a well researched, addictive collection of true case studies, some sensational, others little known, all intensely interesting. And one, 'The Mad Doctor and The Untouchable,' will no doubt become a terrific movie." —Joseph Wambaugh

"Jim Doherty combines the cool eye of a law enforcement professional (which he is) with the fiery enthusiasm of a fan (which he also is) in a superb collection of essays detailing the true-crime back-stories of some of mystery fiction's greatest yarns. These crisp, no-nonsense accounts are hypnotically readable, and the Eliot Ness chapter alone is worth the price of admission."
—Max Allan Collins, author of *Road To Perdition*

"With his stories of crime and crime-fighters in Chicago and nearby, Jim Doherty told me things about old-time Chicago that I never knew, even though I've lived here thirty years. Well-written, well-researched and fascinating!"
—Barbara D'Amato, author of *The Doctor, the Murder, the Mystery*

PULP
STUDIES

JUST THE FACTS

TRUE TALES OF COPS AND CRIMINALS

BY JIM DOHERTY

PRO SE PRESS

To Mom,
Who showed me the love of books and reading;

To Dad,
Who showed me the love of story-telling;

And to Katy,
First reader, chief editor, dearest friend,
most trusted confidante, lifetime romantic partner,
who showed me the meaning of love.

CONTENTS

FOREWORD

Oddly, the inspiration for this collection of non-fiction articles about various and sundry real-life crimes, was a pair of novels. Historical novels, to be sure. Novels based on actual people and events, but novels, nevertheless. Pieces of fiction.

I was temporarily stationed in San Antonio, Texas, taking a month-long course on traffic enforcement and accident investigation/reconstruction. I wasn't regularly a reader of westerns, though neither was I an infrequent one. And it's hard to be in Texas for very long and not get caught up in the cowboy ethos, so, to get into the spirit of things, I picked up a novel by award-winning frontier writer Matt Braun entitled *Outlaw Kingdom* (St. Martin's, 1995), which was based on the real-life pursuit of Oklahoma bandit Bill Doolin by Oklahoma peace officer Bill Tilghman.

I found the book immensely enjoyable, and found the character of Bill Tilghman immensely interesting. Here was a frontier lawman who really *was* a lawman. Unlike better-known figures, such as Wyatt Earp or Bat Masterson, who dabbled in the profession then went on to more profitable pursuits, Tilghman made law enforcement his life's work. Over the next few months I sought out and read a number of biographies of Tilghman, and I read about the outlaw-plagued Oklahoma and Indian Territories he and others policed in the closing days of the 19th century.

A few years later, Braun wrote a sequel, *One Last Town* (St. Martin's, 1997). Set close to the end of Tilghman's life, it fictionalized the marshal's last law enforcement assignment, when he was called out of retirement to tame a gangster-plagued boom-town in the years following World War I. Where *Outlaw Kingdom* had been a western, in the tradition of Zane Grey and *The Riders of the Purple Sage* (Harper, 1912), *One Last Town* was a Roaring '20s gangster novel, in the tradition of W.R. Burnett and *Little Caesar* (Dial, 1939). Yet they both featured the same main character, and that main character had actually lived the adventures Braun was fictionalizing.

At just about that same time, Janet Rudolph, founder, owner, publisher, and editor-in-chief of *Mystery Readers Journal*, announced that one of the upcoming issues would be devoted to cross-genre mysteries, that is mysteries that were also romances, or science fiction stories, or supernatural horror stories.

Or westerns.

And it occurred to me that Bill Tilghman, by starting his career in the era of Wyatt Earp and Billy the Kid and ending it in the era of Eliot Ness and Al Capone, had also started it in the era of Owen Wister and ended it in the era of Dashiell Hammett. He was a real-life cross-genre character. I thought to myself that it was too bad that the *Journal* didn't take true-crime articles, because if it did, an article on Tilghman would be a natural.

Now if you're not familiar with the *Journal,* you should know that each issue is devoted to a particular theme. Mysteries set in a particular locale, mysteries featuring detectives who are also clergypersons, mysteries having a gay or lesbian theme, etc. Articles about the history of the chosen theme in the larger history of crime fiction, articles about favorite examples of mysteries within that theme, articles by professional writers about why they chose to write in that theme, may all be part of a given issue.

And it suddenly occurred to me that there was no reason that a true-crime article about a real-life example of the theme couldn't also be included. And if it could be included in one issue, why not in every issue? It could be a regular column in the magazine.

So I approached Janet with the idea, and was pleasantly surprised when she liked it. The article on Tilghman became the first entry in the new column, which, partly to differentiate it from articles about fictional treatments of a given theme, and partly to evoke a certain based-on-fact TV-radio series that has been influential on my particular choice of professions (policeman and crime writer), I decided to call *Just the Facts.*

And after four years, there were almost enough columns to fill a book. Almost, but not quite.

So when Kate Derie, the Internet's "ClueLass," and the founder, owner, and publisher of Deadly Serious Press (and incidentally, Janet's associate editor on *Mystery Readers Journal*), suggested collecting them in a book, we decided that such a book should be rounded out by additional chapters, devoted to themes that had been covered in the *Journal* before the column began. So the first collection of "Just the Facts" columns, there were five extra, never-before-published chapters, four on themes that I never got a chance to write about, and one on a theme that I actually covered, but out of which I didn't think I'd really gotten the full potential.

Looking back, I notice that a lot more of my articles are devoted to the people who solve crimes than to the people who commit them, which may make *Just the Facts* a bit unusual as true-crime books go. I'm reminded of something the great historical mystery novelist Ellis Peters once said, that good people fascinated her more than evil ones, a rather refreshing viewpoint in an era where it's increasingly hard to find novels that contain a single admirable character. I might offer the paraphrase that heroism interests me more than villainy. I've never read about a criminal whose story tempted me to take that same road, but I've read about lots of police officers who've made me proud to be in the same profession, and I guess that, unconsciously, that attitude is reflected in the kind of stories I've chosen to write about from issue to issue.

Another similarity that many of the stories have, but one which was, at least at first, just as unconscious, is that many of the cases described here were later used as the raw material of various fictional treatments. Often I chose a case that had been made into a novel or movie I admired. Other times a case I was researching sparked a memory of a book or movie I'd enjoyed years earlier without realizing that it had a real-life basis.

Soon, it began to seem as though every true-life crime I was writing about had a fictional counterpart. Indeed, one chapter is basically the story of how a real-life crime came to be used as the basis for a fictional treatment. In any event, it began happening often enough that, before too long, in addition to mentioning sources readers could go to for more detailed information about the case, I started adding a section listing the fictional treatments of the case (hey, these articles were written for mystery readers, after all). That's not unheard of in true-crime journalism, but it is, perhaps, another point that sets this book apart from the mainstream.

There are many people I'd like to thank for making *Just the Facts* possible. Janet for agreeing that her magazine could use a true-crime column. Kate for suggesting that they should be collected in a book. And, of course, all the many true-crime writers whose books and articles I turned to in researching these stories; this book, in many ways, just piggybacks off their hard work. Researching and reading was always the best part of writing every column, and, in the end, there was usually little left for me to do except to put the stories in my own words.

I'd also like to thank Tommy Hancock, of Pro Se Productions, who, after reading the book, said he'd love to reprint it. My column in *Mys-*

tery Readers Journal continued after the collection was first published in 2004, so, for this new edition, some new chapters, from issues of the *Journal* that appeared after the publication of the original Deadly Serious Press edition, have been added, along with three that appear here for the first time, based on *Journal* themes I didn't get a chance to write about for the magazine.

I hope you'll all enjoy reading those words as much as I've enjoyed writing them.

—JIM DOHERTY

BILL TILGHMAN, CROSS-GENRE-ATIONAL CRIME-FIGHTER

Cross-Genre Mysteries

Not too long ago, the US Postal Service put out a commemorative stamp series honoring well-known figures from America's frontier era. Four of the stamps depicted a group of the Old West's most celebrated lawmen: James Butler "Wild Bill" Hickok, William Barclay "Bat" Masterson, Wyatt Berry Stapp Earp, and William Matthew Tilghman, Jr.

Thanks to Hollywood, the first three legendary peace officers are quite well-known to the general public, but, unless you're a student of frontier history, you may not have heard of the fourth. And that's ironic, because Bill Tilghman was, without doubt, the best of them. Masterson himself called Tilghman "the greatest of us all." In fact, in a very real sense, in the sense of approaching law enforcement as a profession, he was the only truly *professional* lawman in that group.

In those days, packing a badge wasn't necessarily a job one sought out. It was a job one fell into while looking for something else to do. Earp, for example, held various law enforcement posts in Illinois, Kansas, and Arizona, yet his years as a peace officer don't amount to more than a half-dozen of the 90 or so he spent on earth. He considered himself a businessman more than a lawman. The years Masterson spent policing the West were even fewer than Earp's; his real ambition was to be a newspaperman, and he eventually wound up as a sportswriter in New York City.

Tilghman, on the other hand, was a vocational lawman. It was the profession he aspired to as a boy, one he trained and prepared for. And, after pinning on a badge for the first time at 19, there were very few years between then and the end of his life that he spent without one.

His career spanned a half century, beginning in the era of Wild Bill Hickok, Jesse James, and dime novelist Ned Buntline, and ending in the era of Eliot Ness, Al Capone, and pulp writer Dashiell Hammett. When he started, his antagonists were drunken cowboys out on a spree, horse thieves, cattle rustlers, and train robbers. When he finished, he was deal-

5

ing with corporate-style urban gangsters, bootleggers, drug smugglers, and corrupt public officials.

He was something of an anomaly among frontier peace officers. One of the deadliest gunfighters in the West, he had a reputation for going to great lengths to take a man alive. At a time when many who wore a star had little or no knowledge of the law, Tilghman made a point of studying the statutes he was charged with enforcing. In contrast to many of his loner colleagues, Tilghman was a devoted family man, a faithful husband, and a loving father. In an era when one of the measures of a man was the amount of liquor he could hold, Tilghman was an abstainer.

Bill Tilghman met George M. Cohan's definition of a Yankee Doodle Dandy, being born on the Fourth of July, 1854, in Fort Dodge, Iowa, to William Tilghman, Sr., the sutler at the fort, and his wife, the former Amanda Shepherd. By the time young Bill was six, his father had given up his sutler's contract, and settled his family on a homestead in the Territory of Kansas. At the age of eight, Bill found himself the man of the house when, with the Civil War raging, his father and older brother went for soldiers in the Union Army. He showed an early aptitude for marksmanship, hunting for food to sustain his mother and younger siblings. It was during this time, captivated by reports of the heroic exploits of Wild Bill Hickok, that he resolved to make law enforcement his career.

Before fulfilling that childhood ambition, Bill would work as a buffalo hunter, an Army scout, a cowboy, and a homesteader. He would also fall in love with a pretty young widow named Flora Robinson (nee Kendall) and marry her in 1877, adopting her infant child. Shortly thereafter, newly-elected Ford County Sheriff Bat Masterson offered him a position in his office.

Dodge City, the seat of Ford County, was known as "the toughest cowtown in the West," where "they ate peace officers for breakfast." Four years earlier, Tilghman had been sworn in as a "special deputy" for Masterson's predecessor, Charlie Bassett, but that had been a temporary commission to perform a specific task (the tracking of a livestock thief), which ended when that task was completed. Now he was really a professional lawman. For the next eight years, first as Undersheriff for Masterson, then in the same position for Masterson's successor, Pat Sughrue, and finally as Dodge City Marshal, Tilghman earned a well-deserved reputation for firm, fair, but most of all, *lawful* peacekeeping. It was Tilghman, not Wyatt Earp as legend has it, who suggested, and then enforced, the "no guns within city limits" ordinance that had such a pacifying influence on the town. It was Tilghman, not Earp, who faced, and survived, a series of gun battles. It was, in short, Tilghman, not Masterson or Earp, who tamed "the queen of the cowtowns."

By 1886, Tilghman decided to give up law work and devote himself full-time to his family and his ranch. With the Santa Fe Railroad pushing farther west into Colorado, Dodge was losing its main role as a shipping point for cattle and the unruly and/or criminal element that the cattle business naturally attracted was seeking greener pastures. He had satisfied his youthful ambition. Now it was time to make a better life for his family.

Nature had other plans. A vicious blizzard hit the area in the winter of 1887. When the snow finally cleared, it left the grass roots beneath the ground dead. It would take years for the range grass to be restored. In the meantime, there was nothing for Tilghman to do except move his family elsewhere.

Tilghman was one of the thousands who took part in the great "Oklahoma Land Rush" of 1889, and the later rush in 1891, establishing commercial sites from which he could draw rent in the newly formed township of Guthrie, and a new ranch site just outside the infant township of Chandler.

Tilghman apparently had no intention of ever again assuming the duties of a peace officer but his reputation followed. Oklahoma's newly formed "boom towns" were giving new meaning to the phrase "wild and woolly" and the need for experienced lawmen was acute. Within days of Guthrie's official incorporation and election of a municipal government, Tilghman was approached to take on the job of pacifying the town.

At this point, Guthrie was still a tent city. No survey had been made prior to the rush, so no one knew whether the parcels to which they were staking their claims would ultimately be determined to be a lot or a street. When the survey was completed, it became necessary for someone to clear the areas set aside for roadways. That was the potentially dangerous assignment that the city government wanted Tilghman to undertake. Those who had staked out property later determined to be a street had done so in good faith and would not take kindly to being ordered to pull out.

The method Tilghman and his deputy, Jim Masterson (brother of Bat), chose to accomplish their task was rough but effective. They took a piece of timber with a length approximately equal to the proposed width of a street and attached a chain to either end. Both chains were then tethered to a pair of horses. An announcement was made that the street would be cleared at a particular time. When the time arrived, Tilghman and Masterson mounted the horses and, with their rifles held at port arms, slowly dragged the piece of timber from one end of the town to the other. Anything that hadn't been moved out of their path was simply mowed down. When they got to the other end of the town, they'd left a cleared thruway behind them.

Once it was apparent that they meant business, additional streets were cleared less dramatically. Simply by creating pathways that made it possible for Guthrie to be properly gridded, Tilghman tamed the town before it had a chance to get wild. This suited Tilghman fine. Clearing the streets was to be his swan song as a peacekeeper. He had no intention of getting involved in policing Guthrie on a long-term basis. He had a ranch to build and a family to raise.

In the 1890s, the Oklahoma Territory was a breeding ground for outlawry of every kind. Dozens of criminal gangs roamed at will, unimpeded by the disorganized, uncoordinated law enforcement that existed in the still sparsely settled area. The most famous of these was the Dalton Gang, but they were by no means unique. The only centrally organized force capable of patrolling the still-developing region was the staff of deputies appointed by the Territorial United States Marshal.

In 1891, though he had intended to leave law enforcement behind, Tilghman was persuaded to accept an appointment as a Deputy US Marshal. In fact, persuading him probably wasn't all that difficult. He was coming to realize law enforcement was the trade he was born for. For the rest of that century, first under Marshal William Grimes, then under Evett Dumas Nix, and finally under William Fossett, Tilghman policed the Oklahoma Territory and the Cherokee Strip as a federal officer.

Tilghman was probably the best-known of the Oklahoma deputies, but there were others who had achieved almost as impressive a reputation. Heck Thomas and Chris Madsen, two men with whom Tilghman would form lifelong friendships, were also among those chosen for this force.

At various times in his career, Thomas had been a city policeman in Atlanta, Georgia, an express company guard, a Texas Ranger, a private detective, and a Deputy US Marshal in the Indian Territory under the famous "Hanging Judge," Isaac Parker. In one of his most celebrated feats of crime-fighting, Thomas had played a major role in ending the rampage of Texas train robber Sam Bass and his gang.

8

Scandinavian immigrant Madsen, a professional soldier, had served in the Danish Army, the French Foreign Legion, and the US Cavalry prior to giving up military life for police work.

The trio of deputies soon became known as "The Three Guardsmen of Oklahoma."

Perry, another of the Territory's newly-formed townships, was one of the first places Tilghman was sent after his federal appointment. In the few short months since the area had been settled, more than a hundred saloons had opened and the free flow of liquor had turned the community into a wild, dangerous place. Tilghman's assignment was to perform the particular function that had become his law enforcement specialty: towntaming.

Alongside Thomas and Madsen, he accomplished the task efficiently, with the force of his personality when possible, with his skill as a gunfighter when necessary. When Perry was incorporated a few months after Tilghman's arrival, he was offered the job of town marshal. Tilghman was not willing to accept this post on a permanent basis, but he did agree to take a leave of absence from his federal job for a few months until a permanent replacement could be hired.

The most famous case undertaken by the Three Guardsmen was undoubtedly the pursuit of Bill Doolin, who took over the remnants of the Dalton Gang after that crew was largely decimated during an attempted bank holdup in Coffeyville, Kansas. Doolin was a natural-born leader who planned his robberies with meticulous, almost military precision. Banks, trains, whole towns, were plundered seemingly at will by the wily bandit's expanded gang, now known as the Wild Bunch. During a chase that lasted four years, Tilghman, Thomas, and Madsen tracked down and captured many of Doolin's henchmen, but the leader of the pack stayed frustratingly out of reach. Finally, early in 1896, Tilghman traced the outlaw to the resort town of Eureka Springs, Arkansas. There, disguised as a clergyman, he was able to take Doolin by surprise, peacefully subduing the long-time fugitive.

Tilghman personally escorted Doolin back to Guthrie. However, the chase was not over yet. Just before his trial started, Doolin managed to break jail. He was eventually tracked down a second time by Thomas and killed in the ensuing shoot-out. Tilghman, counting on the reward money the arrest and conviction of Doolin would bring him, received a mere pittance for his masterful capture of the outlaw.

But, by this time, it mattered little to him. He and Flora had begun to drift apart. Tilghman was not cut out to be anything but a lawman but Flora was not cut out to be a lawman's wife. They separated and were even investigating the possibility of divorce when Flora contracted tuberculosis. Illness reconciled the couple briefly. When she quietly passed away, Bill, stricken with grief and guilt, left active service with the Marshal's Office to devote his time to his business interests and to his four motherless children.

Though his businesses prospered, he couldn't quite resist the tug of his true vocation. In 1900, he was elected Sheriff of Lincoln County, serving two peaceful terms. During this time, he met, fell in love with, and married his second wife, the former Zoe Stratton, a 23-year-old graduate of the newly-established University of Oklahoma, who would later make a name for herself as an accomplished poet and journalist.

Leaving the post of Sheriff in 1904, Tilghman undertook a variety of projects. His family, ranch, and business interests continued to keep him busy. He had three more children with Zoe. He raised crops, race-horses (including one Kentucky Derby winner), and gamecocks. He operated race-tracks, gaming establishments, picnic grounds, and fairgrounds.

He had also discovered a new interest: politics. He was elected a delegate to the Democratic National Convention in 1904, President of the Chandler Town Council (equivalent to mayor) in 1909, and Oklahoma State Senator in 1910.

During this whole time, Tilghman had retained his Deputy US Marshal's commission (though he'd gone from active to standby status with the death of Flora and his election as Lincoln County's Sheriff), and whenever a particularly difficult job of law enforcement came up, he was always ready to accept a special assignment. It was on just such an assignment that, at the personal request of President Theodore Roosevelt, he traveled into Mexico in pursuit of an international fugitive named Fitzpatrick, who had fled south of the border after embezzling funds from his employer.

On another occasion, he undertook an assignment from Governor Charles Haskell to find and arrest one Chitto Harjo, an Indian activist who had taken refuge in the hills of Oklahoma after allegedly murdering two sheriff's deputies (though Tilghman's investigation indicated that this charge was probably spurious). Harjo was never found. He may have been the only fugitive ever pursued by the marshal about whom this could be said. On the other hand, Tilghman, who made no secret of his doubts about the case against Harjo, never seemed particularly upset by his failure to bring him in, despite the blotch it made on his near-perfect record.

On July 4, 1911, his 57th birthday, Tilghman returned to full-time law enforcement as Oklahoma City's Chief of Police. Times were changing and Tilghman was no longer a lone figure on horseback bringing law and order to scattered rural settlements. Now he was running a big-city police force, where his job, in theory, would be more administrative than operational. Not surprisingly, however, Tilghman proved to be a hands-on chief. Partnered with his best plainclothes investigator, Detective Johnny Cassidy, he personally investigated and solved a series of safe burglaries that had plagued the states of Texas and Oklahoma for nearly a year. Some months later, when local dry-cleaner T.J. Gentry was found murdered, Chief Tilghman personally conducted the interrogations of the prime suspects, Mrs. Gentry, her brother, and her lover, obtaining signed confessions and corroborating evidence within 24 hours of the crime's discovery.

Tilghman drew some public criticism, however, for his insistence that state and local Prohibition laws be strictly enforced. When his arrest of a dozen bootleggers was questioned, Tilghman replied that, "If the people of Oklahoma City don't like their town dry, they can vote it wet. Until they do, however, I'll enforce the law as now written." Impeccable logic, of course, but the people of Oklahoma City, stubbornly illogical, apparently wanted both Prohibition and booze, and Tilghman took some heat for not seeing it their way. Oklahoma's early, ill-advised experiment with dry laws did little except to give bootleggers in that state the inside track when the Eighteenth Amendment and the accompanying Volstead Act were passed years later.

Tilghman resigned from the Oklahoma City Police in February of 1913, leaving behind a lowered crime rate and heightened officer morale, to seek the post of Chief US Marshal for the State of Oklahoma. Though popular and respected, he failed to win the appointment. Tilghman was clearly the most qualified applicant for the job, but the position of US Marshal was and is a political, not a merit appointment, and in the arena of politics common sense doesn't always carry the day. The job went to Dr. J.Q. Newell, a physician with not a whit of law enforcement experience but all kinds of clout.

With a return to federal service closed off, Tilghman became a special trouble-shooting investigator for the Governor of Oklahoma, performing a variety of special assignments. On one occasion he was ordered to track down and arrest fugitive parole violators. On another, to gather up a convict work gang whose members were planning to make a break and transport them back to prison. On still another, to look into criminal activity in the coal fields of eastern Oklahoma.

His most dramatic law enforcement activity during this time was acting as the bodyguard of Governor J.B.A. Robertson during a trip to the Klan-dominated town of Okmulgee. Robertson, an outspoken foe of the KKK, had appeared in town to answer charges of malfeasance in his administration of the State Banking Commission. The charges were spurious, designed solely for the embarrassment of the governor, who insisted on meeting his accusers personally.

On the steps of the County Courthouse, Robertson was confronted by mob of Klansmen led by one Roy Bool. When the confrontation between Bool and Robertson suddenly came to blows, the mob started to surge forward. Tilghman quickly stepped between the governor and Bool, held up his hand and quietly advised the mob that they'd gone far enough. The forward surge stopped. Tilghman had prevented a riot with nothing more than his reputation and a display of intestinal fortitude that humbled the crowd. The KKK's power in Oklahoma was not broken that day, but it did begin to subside. While it would continue to wield influence for several more years, its influence steadily declined thanks to the courageous stand of a single, determined lawman who'd managed to stare them all down. Some years after this confrontation, the Klan achieved a small measure of revenge when they sabotaged Tilghman's campaign for the position of Sheriff of Oklahoma County. But the net effect of keeping Tilghman out of the Sheriff's Office was to keep him in state service, which, in retrospect, seems a Pyrrhic victory.

In between state assignments, Tilghman tended to his business interests, joined fraternal organizations, and even produced, wrote, directed, and starred in a movie based on his career, *The Passing of the Oklahoma Outlaws*. Would there ever be another call to serve the cause of law and order?

By July 1924, Bill Tilghman had reached his seventieth birthday. He had worn one badge or another almost continuously for over a half-century. He had served in law enforcement at the municipal, county, state, and federal levels. He had worked in rural areas where he was the only peace officer around. He had commanded a large metropolitan police force. He had single-handedly stood down a mob of vicious white supremacists. He had tamed the towns of Dodge City, Guthrie, and Perry. He had earned many times over a peaceful, happy, and prosperous retirement. But the bugle was about to blow one more time and, like an ancient cavalry horse, Tilghman would hasten to answer that call.

Technological progress was the wave of the future. The machinery that drove that progress needed oil and Oklahoma just happened to be sitting on top of an ocean of the stuff. Oil boom towns had sprung up all over the state and criminal elements had followed closely behind. These were not rowdy cowboys looking for a high time after a long trail drive. These were organized, big-city gangsters, empowered by the nationwide imposition of Prohibition, ruthlessly operating their criminal enterprises along business lines.

Cromwell, in Seminole County, was possibly the most notorious of these boom towns, a community held fast in the grip of urbanized hoodlums. The townspeople formed a committee to request that Tilghman set things straight. Though they were not yet incorporated and consequently not authorized to appoint peace officers, a man of Tilghman's eminence should surely be able to secure some sort of official appointment. Would he please come out of retirement one last time, tame one last town?

Tilghman, once more commissioned by the governor, accepted the offer. The local sheriff wasn't happy about Tilghman's presence, but in the face of that state commission, he was bound to give at least surface cooperation. With reluctance, he also deputized Tilghman. When Cromwell was officially incorporated a few weeks after Tilghman's arrival, the newly-elected council made it a law enforcement trifecta by appointing Tilghman the town's first police chief. Tilghman quickly set about making changes. He was conspicuous in his walking patrols of the town. He organized a Volunteer Fire Company. He started an ambulance service after convincing one of the oil companies to donate a truck for the purpose. He arranged for a traveling clergyman to make Cromwell a regular stop. Criminals who tried to shoot it out and lost, like the pair of hijackers who Tilghman caught in a stolen car, or the racketeers who became the targets of Tilghman's liquor, gambling, prostitution, and drug raids, could no longer operate freely. But these were surface changes. Tilghman knew the real showdown was still to come. And when it came he'd probably face it alone.

Men he should have been able to count on for backup were unreliable. The assistant he'd hired, Hugh Sawyer, was willing and eager but young and inexperienced. The local sheriff, while not necessarily on the take, had made his displeasure at Tilghman's appointment apparent, and his initial hesitation to give Tilghman a deputy Sheriff's commission indicated that he was unwilling to become embroiled in a dangerous confrontation between the marshal and the gangster faction. The only other major law enforcement presence in Cromwell was Federal Agent Wiley Lynn, in charge of investigating Prohibition violations in the area, a thoroughly untrustworthy individual whom Tilghman suspected of being the mobsters' inside man in police circles.

On Hallowe'en night, acting on information received through an anonymous phone tip, Tilghman and Sawyer staked out an oil field where a narcotics drop was scheduled to be made. Crouched in hiding, they heard a plane overhead. The plane dropped to tree-top height and a package was dropped from the cockpit. Tilghman and Sawyer waited all night for the pickup, but it was never made. A car pulled to the edge of the field, but never came in. Possibly information of the surveillance had leaked. Possibly Tilghman and Sawyer weren't as well-hidden as they'd thought. Possibly the pick-up man had just been spooked. In any case they were not able to make an arrest. But they *had* kept the dope out of the hands of the gang.

The next evening, November 1, 1924, Wiley Lynn appeared on the streets of Cromwell, drunk and shooting off his gun. Tilghman quickly approached him. Sawyer, off-duty and perhaps a drink or two past sobriety himself, followed. Quickly disarming Lynn, Tilghman ordered him to go home and sleep it off. He hadn't counted on Lynn's packing a hidden back-up piece. As Tilghman started to walk him away from the scene, Lynn jerked his arm away, drew his concealed pistol, pumped three rounds into the lawman's stomach, and fled in his car while Sawyer stood there shocked and helpless.

Bill Tilghman had faced dozens of desperadoes in his career and had always come out on top, but in the end it was, with tragic irony, a brother officer who finished him off. At the orders of Governor Martin Trapp, Tilghman lay in state for three days under the rotunda of Oklahoma's Capitol Building, an honor never before accorded a slain policeman. "He died for the state he helped create," said Trapp. "He set an example of modesty and courage that few could match, yet he made us all better men for trying."

Lynn, in the meantime, had been apprehended and brought to trial, but, thanks to intimidated witnesses and unconscionable incompetence on the part of the prosecuting attorneys (and, possibly, some jury tampering on the part of Lynn's organized crime contacts, though this was never proven), what should have been a slam-dunk conviction wound up an acquittal.

Justice finally collected on Wiley Lynn's marker in 1932, but at the cost of another cop's life. Special Agent Crockett Long of the Oklahoma State Crime Bureau died in an exchange of gunfire with the corrupt Prohibition Officer, but not before firing the shots that finally brought Lynn down. Ironically, it was Tilghman, at one time the State of Oklahoma's lone criminal investigator, who suggested the need for a full-time state-wide criminal investigation unit. Shortly after Tilghman's murder, this suggestion was finally acted upon. Fitting though it was that Tilghman's murderer was finally made to pay by a member of the agency that had been conceived by, and in a sense founded by, Tilghman himself, it was tragic that such a heavy sacrifice was required to claim the debt.

Joe Hagen, the young sheriff of neighboring Okfuskee County, was hired to take Tilghman's place in Cromwell. When he arrived, he found he had precious little to do. The townspeople, responding to the murder of Tilghman as they might to a natural disaster, were drawn together to help each other through the crisis and felt suddenly emboldened by the realization that their numbers were so great. The grafters, pimps, bootleggers, and dope dealers, their power to intimidate waning, either drifted out of town on their own, were driven out, or were burned out.

"Bill cleaned up this place from his grave," Hagen later remarked. Though at a terribly high cost, Tilghman had gone out a winner. He had tamed one last town.

FURTHER READING

Tilghman has been the subject of a number of fine biographies. The best is undoubtedly *Guardian of the Law* (Eakin, 1988) by the late Glenn Shirley, a retired policeman who became perhaps the most highly respected of all true-crime writers specializing in Old West subjects. Copiously researched and well-written, *Guardian of the Law* is indispensable reading for anyone interested in learning more about Tilghman. Shirley is also the author of several other books which, though not specifically about Tilghman, provide further insight into the legendary marshal's career. *Six Gun and Silver Star* (University of New Mexico, 1955), for example, is about the taming of the Oklahoma Territory in general and the hunt for Bill Doolin and his Wild Bunch in particular. More than 20 years later, Shirley, armed with an additional two decades of research, wrote a second, more comprehensive book on the same subject, *West of Hell's Fringe* (University of Oklahoma, 1990). *Gunfight at Ingalls* (Western, 1990), a shorter book describing a single incident from the Doolin case, tells the story of the most ferocious shootout in frontier history. Shirley also wrote *Heck Thomas – Frontier Marshal* (Chilton, 1962), a biography of another "Oklahoma Guardsman" who became one of Tilghman's closest friends.

After *Guardian of the Law*, the most comprehensive Tilghman biography is *Marshal of the Last Frontier* (Clark, 1949) by Tilghman's widow, Zoe. Mrs. Tilghman, with a background in journalism, made a valiant attempt to present her husband's life objectively, but she was a woman who loved her spouse deeply, and this came through despite her best efforts. Floyd Miller's *Bill Tilghman* (Doubleday, 1968) is also a valuable source of information about the storied peace officer. *Fast-Draw Tilghman* (Messner, 1959) is a biography for young adults by Dale White, but is well-written enough to be of interest to adults as well. The author has won multiple Golden Spur awards for juvenile frontier literature from the Western Writers of America. Ron W. Fischer's self-published *The Last Great Frontier Marshall* [sic] (Fischer Enterprises, 2001) is a more recent Tilghman biography.

Not specifically about Tilghman, but providing lots of interesting first-hand details about the early fight against crime following Oklahoma's 1889 Land Rush, and particularly about the Doolin case, is *Oklahombres, Particularly the Wilder Ones* (Eden, 1929) by Evett Dumas Nix (the US Marshal under whom Tilghman served as deputy) with Gordon Hines. Chris Madsen, the third member of the Three Guardsmen, is the subject of Homer Croy's *Trigger Marshal* (Duell, 1958). Another useful book is Ron Owens's *Oklahoma Justice* (Turner, 1995), a superb history of the Oklahoma City Police Department, from its founding in the weeks following the Rush, to the bombing of the Murrah Federal Building in 1995. Crisply written, and copiously illustrated, it gives a detailed account of Tilghman's tenure as OKCPD's chief. A wonderful small-press magazine called *Oklahombres Journal*, in honor of Marshal Nix's book, has published many fine articles that would be of interest to anyone wishing to learn more about Tilghman specifically, or the taming of Oklahoma in general. Some of those articles are reproduced on their website at www.oklahombres.org.

For a less flattering portrait of the Marshal and his colleagues, you might, in the interests of "equal time," want to read Nancy B. Samuleson's *Shoot from the Lip: Lives, Legends, and Lies of "The Three Guardsmen of Oklahoma" and US Marshal Nix* (Shooting Star, 1998).

BILL TILGHMAN IN FICTION

Tilghman himself is responsible for what is perhaps the first fictional treatment of his career, the silent western movie *The Passing of the Oklahoma Outlaws* (Eagle Films, 1915), which he wrote, co-produced, directed, and portrayed himself in. Heck Thomas had already passed away by the time this film was made, so his part was taken by another actor. However, Chris Madsen, Evett Nix, and at least one member of Doolin's outlaw band, "Arkansas Tom" Daugherty, were all portrayed by the actual real-life figures. The complete film no longer exists, but a large fragment is stored at the Library of Congress, and a videocassette made from those available reels has been shown to the public at venues such as the Cowboy Hall of Fame in Oklahoma City.

More than three decades later, Randolph Scott starred in a far more fictionalized treatment of the taming of Oklahoma Territory, *Return of the Bad Men* (RKO, 1948) directed by Ray Enright from a script by Jack Natteford, Charles O'Neal, and Luci Ward. Bill Doolin, portrayed by Robert Armstrong, leads a criminal gang that, in addition to the formidable outlaws who comprised the Oklahoma Wild Bunch in real life, also includes the Younger brothers, Billy the Kid, and Wyoming Wild Bunch leaders Butch Cassidy and the Sundance Kid. It's a veritable "who's who" of frontier criminality. Vance Cordell, the federal marshal portrayed by Scott, may be taken as a composite character comprising traits of all three of the Guardsmen as well as Wyoming lawmen Joe LeFors and Tim Keliher, the implacable pursuers of Cassidy, Sundance, and their cohorts.

A year later, in *The Doolins of Oklahoma* (Columbia, 1949), Scott changed sides and took on the role of Bill Doolin. Directed by Gordon Douglas and written by Kenneth Gamet, the film portrayed Doolin as a noble outlaw who tries to go straight for the sake of his wife, but is drawn, against his will, back into a life of crime by his former associates. Robert Barrat plays a supporting role as "The Marshal," who, like Cordell in *Return of the Bad Men*, is probably meant to be a composite character.

Robert Ward's novel, *Cattle Annie and Little Britches* (Morrow, 1978), looks at life in the Doolin gang from the point of view of two teen-aged girls who, captivated by the romance of outlaw life, run away from home and become Wild Bunch hangers-on. A 1981 Universal film version, directed by Lamont Johnson and written by Ward and David Eyre, featured a somewhat overage Burt Lancaster as Doolin, a terribly miscast Rod Steiger as Tilghman (physically, at least, Steiger would have been better-suited for the role of the rotund Chris Madsen), and Diane Lane and Amanda Plummer as the titular juvenile delinquents.

Western novelist Matt Braun has, perhaps, made the most frequent fictional use of Tilghman's life and career. Tilghman actually appears as a minor character in Braun's multi-generational historical novel, *The Kincaids* (Putnam, 1976), which won a well-deserved Spur Award from the WWA. Many of the feats performed by Tilghman in real life, however, such as the tracking down of the Oklahoma Wild Bunch, the pursuit of international fugitive Fitzpatrick into Mexico, and the taming of Cromwell, are assigned, in this book, to a fictional stand-in, Owen Kincaid. Perhaps to atone for "hijacking" Tilghman's deeds and attributing them to an imaginary character, Braun returned, years later, to the pursuit of Doolin and his Wild Bunch in *Outlaw Kingdom* (St. Martin's, 1995), this time giving credit where it was due. Telescoping time down to a much shorter period, and re-ordering some events for dramatic purposes (e.g. the death of Flora takes place before Tilghman's move to Oklahoma, leaving him free to simultaneously romance Zoe and chase bandits), *Outlaw Kingdom* is, nevertheless, a reasonably accurate and thoroughly enjoyable fictional treatment of one of the most dramatic manhunts in frontier annals.

Where *Outlaw Kingdom* depicts a Tilghman in the prime of young adulthood, totally at home in the untamed frontier, Braun's sequel, *One Last Town* (St. Martin's, 1997), about the Marshal's heroic final stand in Cromwell, shows him in old age, finding it difficult to adjust to a world dominated by oil, automobiles, airplanes, and big-city gangsters. *One Last Town* was adapted into an excellent made-for-TV film, *You Know My Name* (TNT, 1999), written and directed by John Kent Harrison, and starring a masterfully-cast Sam Elliott, in possibly his finest performance, as the legendary peace officer. Some editions of Braun's novel were published under the movie title. Another Braun book, *The Last Stand* (St. Martin's, 1998), though not specifically about Tilghman, seems to have been loosely inspired by, if not directly based on, Tilghman's investigation of the Chitto Harjo affair.

Braun's comments about the man whose real life inspired his fiction provide an appropriate close to this chapter. "Bill Tilghman stood tall above the rest. His record as a lawman needs no exaggeration.... He was without equal among men who wore a badge."

PLAYING THROUGH THE PAIN

Florida Mysteries

"The FBI should only have the 1930's happen to them all over again!"

Any number of crime journalists studying the history of the Federal Bureau of Investigation have made that observation. A combination of circumstances that had never existed before; Prohibition, Depression, the alarming rise in violent crime, the landslide election of Franklin Roosevelt and the adoption of his New Deal, the consequent growth of federal bureaucracy in both size and in importance to the everyday life of the average American citizen—all coalesced in a manner that transformed a small, relatively unknown branch of the US Department of Justice into the nation's premier police agency, and its chief, the indomitable J. Edgar Hoover, into the nation's top cop.

Any book dealing with the Bureau's most famous cases is going to be heavily weighted with stories from the '30s. Armed with FDR-backed legislation that greatly expanded its power and authority, it faced some of its best-known foes: colorful desperadoes like "Pretty Boy" Floyd, Alvin "Old Creepy" Karpis, Ma Barker and her sons, the psychopathic "Baby-Face" Nelson, and most famously, John Dillinger.

Suddenly, kids weren't just playing "cops-and-robbers" anymore, they were playing "G-men-and-robbers." Suddenly, Hollywood began a love affair with the Bureau, one that has waxed and waned in subsequent years but never really ended. Suddenly Hoover, previously a fairly anonymous bureaucrat in a fairly anonymous bureaucracy, was the most famous law enforcement official in the world, routinely listed as one of the Most Admired Men in America.

Obviously, the FBI's done some quality work in the ensuing 60-odd years, but it hasn't necessarily been the stuff of which Jimmy Cagney films are made. In fact, it's been suggested that the Bureau instituted its "Ten Most Wanted" list in the early '50s not so much to gather information that would lead to the arrest of criminal fugitives as to generate the kind of publicity that it enjoyed in years past by adding to latter-day hoodlums the kind of color and dash that their predecessors had.

If that *was* the unstated purpose, the Bureau's Top 10 list was a bust. How many of you can even name one of the fugitives currently on the list? On the other hand, how many of you have ever heard of Dillinger or Floyd? I rest my case.

There's no getting around it. The '30s were the Bureau's glory years, but the '30s are over, never to return. On the balmy spring morning of Friday, April 11, 1986, however, on a sunny street in South Miami, Florida, the '30s *did* return. With a vengeance.

It all started some 15 months earlier when a rash of bank robberies, armored car hold-ups, and car-jackings, characterized by the extraordinary viciousness of the offenders began in the southern part of Dade County. FBI agents and local police joined in the search for the two gangsters.

Like the Depression-era outlaws of the Midwest on which the Bureau's fame was built, the men they were looking for, William Matix, 34, and Michael Platt, 32, hailed from America's heartland. Matix's home town was Lewisburg, Ohio, while Platt was born and raised in Bloomington, Indiana. They had met and become friends while on military duty in Korea approximately a decade earlier.

After his discharge from the Army, Matix married Patty Buchanan. Apparently a sober, church-going couple, Matix and his wife seemed to be happy. In December, 1983, just two months after giving birth to a daughter, Patty Matix and a co-worker were found stabbed to death in the medical research lab in Columbus, Ohio, where they were employed. The murders were never solved.

At the urging of Platt, Matix moved to Miami where the two Army buddies started a lawn-care/tree-trimming business called the Yankee Clipper. Shortly after Matix's arrival in Florida, Platt's wife Regina was found dead from an apparently self-inflicted shotgun blast.

The gruesome coincidence of the business partners' wives both dying in violent, suspicious circumstances went unnoticed. The two young widowers went about their apparently respectable business, raising their motherless children and eventually re-marrying. They seemed to be leading a thoroughly ordinary, even dull, suburban lifestyle.

Behind closed doors things were different. Matix became a parishioner at Miami's Riverside Baptist Church where he met, courted, and in May 1985 married another member of the congregation. Two weeks after the wedding, however, Christy Matix found that her new husband had suddenly become temperamental and mercurial, given to ugly bursts of anger. Christy assumed that the problem was monetary, since by this time the Yankee Clipper business had been dissolved. She had no idea what was really going on and by the time she found out, she had already moved back with her parents and filed for divorce.

Money was not Matix's problem at all. He'd netted $350,000 in insurance money following his first wife's murder and he and his partner had found a new source of income. Matix and Platt may have been responsible for more than a dozen different robberies in the Miami area. Eventually, they were definitely tied to six.

On October 16, 1985, two armed men in ski masks attacked a Wells Fargo truck parked at a South Miami supermarket. Shots were fired and one of the guards was severely wounded but the robbers failed to get any money.

Later that month, a 25-year-old man told his family he was going target shooting in a nearby rock quarry. Except for some skeletal remains that eventually turned up in that quarry, he was never seen again. The car he was driving that day was.

On November 8, 1985, two separate bank robberies occurred in the same general area as the attempted armored car hold-up.

On January 10, 1986, two armed men in ski masks approached a Brink's guard as he was opening the back of his armored truck. One shot him in the back with a shotgun. As the guard lay in the street bleeding, the other shot him in the groin with a rifle. Miraculously the guard survived, and was able to describe the car the two bandits used. It was the same car the target shooter from the rock quarry had been driving. The two bandits were later seen abandoning the car for a white pick-up truck.

Early in March, 1986, as José Colazzo was target-shooting in a remote corner of the Everglades, he was approached by two men who shot him four times in the back, left him for dead in a shallow pond, then made off with his black Chevrolet Monte Carlo. The marksmanship of the two car-jackers was deficient. Colazzo lived to describe his attackers. They'd been driving the same white pick-up truck that the Brinks robbers had been seen entering after abandoning their stolen getaway car.

On April 14, Special Agent Gordon McNeill, 43, in charge of the FBI squad responsible for running down the bandits, thought it likely that the two outlaws would hit one of several banks in South Miami and authorized a rolling stakeout of the town to try to spot the stolen Monte Carlo. McNeill would later say it was "both the luckiest and the unluckiest hunch I've ever had."

In one of the five FBI cars was Special Agent Ben Grogan, 53, a veteran of 24 years, and his partner, Special Agent Jerry Dove, 30, who'd been with the Bureau for four. Both were regarded as top-flight lawmen. Grogan had been eligible for retirement for three years but had elected to stay on, even managing to get himself appointed as head of the Miami Field Office's elite SWAT team. Dove was also a SWAT veteran, having been assigned to security at the 1984 Olympics.

At 9:20 a.m., Dove and Grogan spotted the stolen Monte Carlo rolling down Southwest 82nd Avenue and radioed for back-up. Two more FBI cars joined them, following the suspects for a few blocks while waiting for further reinforcements. When the Monte Carlo was within a block of the heavily traveled South Dixie Highway, McNeill, in one of the back-up cars, suddenly saw a rifle barrel rise up in the front seat.

"They're loading up!" McNeill radioed to his squad.

Now knowing for certain that the suspects were armed, it became imperative to minimize the public danger by keeping them off the South Dixie. The FBI cars converged on the black Chevy, forcing it off the road and into a tree just as two more FBI cars arrived at the scene. Platt and Matix immediately rolled out of their car, combat-style, and opened up on the agents with a 12-gauge shotgun and a Ruger Mini-14 rifle, beginning one of the bloodiest gun battles in the Bureau's history.

Special Agent John Hanlon, 48, was one of the first to be wounded by the outlaw's gunfire. "My hand exploded," he later said, "and I flopped over on my back and looked to my left hand and saw the guy standing by the car. Then he came around and shot me again on the ground in the groin. There was a lot of machine gun fire and all the casings came down on me."

Grogan and Dove were also among the first to be hit. "I heard Ben go 'Oh, my God,' but I didn't feel him fall down," said Hanlon. "Then Jerry Dove fell down right next to me . . . his eyes were closed and the guy who I think shot me, shot Jerry in the back of the head. Executed him."

Grogan and Dove had just become the 28th and 29th FBI agents to be killed in the line of duty.

Hanlon's partner, Special Agent Edmundo Mireles, 33, was wounded in the left arm as he attempted to take cover behind McNeill's car. "It felt like someone had hit me with a sledgehammer," he later recalled. "I looked at my arm. It was completely shattered. I thought, 'They're going to have to amputate.' All hell was breaking loose. I could hear shots to my right and shots to my left."

McNeill was shot in the hand, but managed to empty his revolver at Matix and Platt. His wound made it difficult to reload. He reached into the back seat for a shotgun when another volley of rifle fire hit him, one of the rounds nicking his spine and temporarily paralyzing him.

Agents Dick Manauzzi and Gilbert Orrantia, who'd been in the car that actually forced the Monte Carlo off the road, were the next to fall to the withering fire of Platt and Matix. In a space of just a few seconds, the two gunmen had killed two federal agents and incapacitated five others.

All this time, normal traffic continued to flow down Southwest 82nd Avenue. The agents, armed with shotguns or medium caliber handguns, had to hold their fire whenever a civilian wandered into their field of vision. Platt and Matix had no such scruples. Passersby later said that they assumed an episode of *Miami Vice* was being filmed. There was a sudden let-up in the shooting as Platt and Matix, their own car disabled, jumped into Grogan's and Dove's FBI vehicle to make their escape. Mireles, in the meantime, had grabbed a pump-style 12-gauge and had managed to crawl around the car to see what was happening. He spied Platt and Matix desperately trying to get the FBI vehicle started.

Mireles rested his shotgun on the rear bumper of the car and fired at the two cop-killers. The powerful blast of the weapon sent shivers of agony down his left arm, but Mireles persevered. Ducking back behind cover, he painfully racked the shotgun by bracing it between his legs and working the pump with his one good arm. In this manner he managed to fire at his antagonists five times.

Platt and Matix continued to try to get the FBI car started. Mireles, suffering from blood loss and enduring incredible pain, could feel himself starting to fade, but his brother agents were still sprawled on the street behind the car that Matix and Platt were trying to start. They'd be run over if the suspects managed to get the car started and backed out.

His pump-gun empty, Agent Mireles had only his six-shot .357 Magnum revolver with which to face two desperate, heavily-armed killers.

In sports, the athletes who earn our greatest admiration are the ones who "play through the pain." The pitcher who wins games despite an arthritic shoulder; the gymnast who vaults her team to an Olympic gold medal despite a painful ankle sprain; the running back who rushes for crucial extra yardage despite a broken wrist; the sprinter who wins races despite severe asthma; the battered prizefighter, acting on sheer heart, who manages to stay on his feet and go the distance; these are the sports heroes whose deeds fire our imagination. In the sport of manhunting, Ed Mireles was about to put them all to shame.

Pushing himself up to a standing position with his good right hand, he drew his revolver, stepped out from behind cover, and advanced on the getaway car. Another agent yelled for Mireles to get back, but Mireles continued on his course. As he approached the car, he opened fire on the occupants, emptying his weapon.

Mireles's super-human effort paid off. Platt and Matix lay dead in the vehicle. The agents laying helpless behind the car were safe. The whole battle had lasted less than four minutes.

In the wake of the gunfight, numerous questions were raised. Was it a tactical blunder to force the suspect vehicle off the road at that moment? Were FBI weapons adequate against the superior firepower of the criminals? The biggest questions, however, and the ones that remained forever unanswered, were the ones revolving around Matix and Platt.

With no police records, no particular money worries, and no history to indicate a predilection for this kind of *professional* criminality, why did Matix and Platt turn outlaw? Subsequent investigation indicated no ties to organized crime, to the drug trade, or to white supremacist paramilitary groups. They were mavericks, totally independent from the established underworld community with nothing in their past to point the police in their direction when they took up a life of crime. Like the professional thief of fiction, cloaking his misdeeds behind the facade of a placid, everyday life, Matix and Platt seemed less like real-life figures than characters from a crime novel.

Donald Westlake, in his Richard Stark persona, once described his series gangster character, Parker, as "Dillinger mythologized into a machine." On another occasion, he said that he'd stopped writing the Parker novels because, "try as I might, I just couldn't seem to find any more stories about Dillinger in the papers," which I take to be a Westlakean way of saying that he found Parker too much of an anachronism. Recently, however, after a hiatus of more than two decades, Westlake resurrected Parker in *Comeback* (Mysterious, 1997) and *Backflash* (Mysterious, 1998). One wonders whether the saga of Matix and Platt might have had something to do with Westlake's decision.

Criticism of the agents' decision to make the suspect vehicle stop when they did, a decision that had to be made in seconds before the car turned onto the South Dixie, seemed churlish in light of the heroism displayed that day.

Criticism of the weaponry with which they were equipped was taken more seriously, since both suspects had sustained a number of hits without being stopped. The standard FBI sidearms at that time were either .38 revolvers, .357 Magnum revolvers, or 9 mm semi-automatics, all of which fire projectiles which are, give or take a few thousandths of an inch, the same size. All the agents assigned to the rolling stakeout were equipped with one of those kinds of handguns, along with the pump-action 12-gauges.

Although it was Mireles's low-tech six-shooter that finally ended the fight, seemingly a pretty strong endorsement for the weapon, the South Miami shootout was one of the benchmarks that signaled the end of the wheel-gun as the standard police weapon in this country. Now most American police forces, whether federal, state, county, or municipal, have transitioned to semi-automatic pistols.

The FBI was already well on the way to making that transition in 1986, but the deaths of two agents indicated that perhaps something more than medium caliber was called for. On the other hand, the .45 caliber, the most popular and most effective big bore weapon, was and is difficult for small-framed persons to handle. With more and more women entering the police service and height and weight restrictions being eliminated, something in-between had to be developed.

A number of innovations were put on the market in response to the FBI's search for the perfect handgun round. The 10 mm, for example, had a brief vogue, particularly when Don Johnson's character on *Miami Vice*, Metro Dade County Detective James "Sonny" Crockett, started packing one. The FBI finally went with the .40 caliber. Larger and more powerful than the .38 and its brethren, but smaller and easier to shoot (and to train with) than the .45, it seemed the best compromise. Soon the .40 caliber was carried, not only by FBI agents, but by members of the Secret Service, the various enforcement branches of Immigration and Naturalization, the DEA, and the Federal Protective Service. The Battle of South Miami had changed the face of not only the FBI but also most of federal law enforcement.

The International Association of Chiefs of Police, in conjunction with *Parade* magazine, gives an annual award that is widely regarded as the most prestigious in American law enforcement: the coveted title of Police Officer of the Year. On October 7, 1986, that title was conferred upon FBI Agent Ed Mireles, the rugged Texan who "played through the pain" to apprehend two vicious felons and protect his brother officers. As one Miami policeman remarked to Mireles's supervisor, Gordon McNeill, "What Mireles did you can't teach."

THE SOUTH MIAMI SHOOTOUT IN FICTION

Like many dramatic real-life crimes, the Battle of South Miami has inspired fictionalizations. The first of NBC's "In the Line of Duty" presentations, an irregularly scheduled series of well-made TV-movies dramatizing real-life cases in which police officers have been killed, was entitled *The FBI Murders* (1988), and featured David Soul and Michael Gross as the two gunmen.

A few years later, ABC's short-lived weekly anthology series, *FBI – The Untold Stories* (1991-93), in which real-life agents narrated dramatizations of their cases, aired an episode on the South Miami shootout.

Michael Mann's epic cop movie, *Heat* (Warners, 1995), though said to be based on a case investigated by Chicago Police Sergeant Chuck Adamson (a frequent screenwriting collaborator of Mann's), also seems to have been derived, at least in part, from the Platt/Matix story.

But, as is so often the case, the fiction doesn't stand up to the real story.

THE DRY GUYS

Partners in Crime – Sleuthing Partners

If ever there was a law that citizens were disinclined to observe, it was the national ban on alcoholic beverages. It's difficult to say just how widespread the breach was. After all, since booze was illegal, it wasn't as if anyone was keeping accurate corporate records on its production and people who were swilling the stuff weren't admitting it to any official recording agency. Still, some available statistics seem to indicate that the average American drank far more alcohol during Prohibition than he or she did either before its enactment or after its repeal.

Not too surprisingly, the investigators charged with enforcing this unpopular law weren't held in particularly high regard either. In fact they got it coming and going. If they did their duty and enforced the law, they were castigated for persecuting otherwise law-abiding citizens for enjoying what had been a perfectly legal commodity only a few years earlier. If they looked the other way, they were criticized for being venal, corrupt grafters.

Generally, agents of the US Bureau of Prohibition were more likely to be censured for falling into the latter category than the former. The Volstead Act of 1920 provided for enforcement of the Prohibition amendment and the newly-formed agency, in its haste to get some kind of force out into the field, hired 1500 agents. Character references weren't required. Neither was previous experience in police work. Many of the agents hired turned out to have criminal records. Many others became corrupt after they were hired. Still others proved to be just plain incompetent. Ultimately, nearly 900 of the 1500 officers initially hired were fired for bribery, extortion, and drunkenness. By 1929, nearly 18,000 Prohibition Agents had been hired and nearly 14,000 of those had been dismissed. Police corruption was all too common during the Dry Years, but "Prohis" were in a class all by themselves.

Still, for all the dirt and stink that clung to the agency, there were Prohibition Agents who made excellent, even legendary records. For example, Frank Hamer, possibly the finest American policeman ever to wear a badge, though best-remembered as a Texas Ranger, spent a year keeping the Mexican border clean as a federal dry agent. The famous

Windy City lawman Pat Roche, in between stints as a Chicago police officer and as a DA's investigator for Cook County, spent a few years "enforcing Prohibition for Uncle Sam," as he put it. And, thanks to TV and movies, a young fellow named Eliot Ness, placed in charge of a small, elite squad of Prohibition Agents assigned to do whatever it took to get Al Capone became, arguably, the most famous cop of the 20th Century. These men, ruggedly good-looking, hard-edged, two-fisted, gun-slinging professional crime-fighters, fit the popular heroic image of tough, incorruptible law enforcement.

But the team of "Prohis" who made the best record in the short but tempestuous history of the Eighteenth Amendment was about as far from that image as it was possible to get. Short, heavy-set (well, let's not mince words; they were fat), balding, and homely, their unimpressive appearance, far from impeding their success, was the key to it.

The senior partner of the duo, Isidor Einstein, known to his friends as Izzy, was a Jewish immigrant from Austria whose father had hoped he would seek a vocation as a rabbi. Up to 1920, however, he had supported his wife and four sons first as a salesman then as a postal clerk in NYC. In January of that year he applied for a transfer from the Post Office Department to the Treasury Department. He'd decided that he was the perfect candidate for the job of enforcing the Volstead Act. The salary of $40 a week represented a major jump in his income.

James Sheldon, chief agent of the Prohibition Unit's Southern New York District, was reluctant to accept the 5-foot 5-inch, 225-pound, 40-year-old as an investigator. "You don't look the type," he said.

That, replied Einstein, was precisely why he'd be perfect for the job. "A type like me," he insisted, "that would never be spotted as a sleuth could get results that the regular plainclothesman couldn't." Besides, he was multi-lingual, speaking German, Yiddish, Hungarian, and Polish, an enviable talent for a copper working in the ethnic stew that was New York City in the '20s.

Sheldon accepted Einstein's application conditionally. Directing him to a Manhattan speakeasy that the Unit had been unable to develop a case against, Sheldon told Einstein that the job was his permanently if he could obtain enough evidence to shut the place down.

Izzy proceeded to prove that no one would ever believe he was a G-Man in the most convincing way imaginable. He walked into the bar, slapped his badge on the counter, and said, "How about a pint of whiskey for a thirsty Prohibition Agent?" The bartender burst out laughing, poured Izzy a drink, and asked him where he'd gotten such a realistic-looking shield. Izzy replied that the tin had actually been issued by the Government and that he was closing down the premises and taking the barkeep in for violating the dry laws. That unfortunate speakeasy proprietor became the first of nearly 5000 arrests made by Izzy in his law enforcement career.

After a few months, Izzy convinced his boss to take on a new recruit, his old pal Moe Smith. Moe, who'd been running a cigar store prior to entering the Unit, was, at 33, seven years younger than Izzy, three or four inches taller, and at least 30 pounds heavier. The two friends would work side by side for the next few years, knocking over speaks, busting stills, confiscating oceans of illegal booze, and becoming the darlings of the press as the Tweedle-Dee and Tweedle-Dum of federal policing.

As their fame spread, taverns all over town started putting their pictures up on the walls as sort of reverse "wanted" fliers. "Don't serve these men," the caption beneath the photos warned. "They are Izzy and Moe and they are poison!" It didn't cramp the team's style in the least. They simply came up with a dazzling array of disguises to shroud their identities.

Once they posed as mud-caked football players demanding entrance to a speak across the street from a city park. Pounding on the door, they shouted, "Let us in! We won the game and we want to celebrate." They were admitted and promptly closed the joint down.

At a Manhattan nightclub, Izzy, who actually could play a few musical instruments after a fashion, posed as the club band's fiddler. His rendition of "How Dry I Am" was the cue for Moe, waiting outside with a squad of agents, to begin the raid.

At a swanky, high-class private club in the suburbs, they posed as Eastern European noblemen.

At "The Assembly", an upper-crust Manhattan speak frequented by judges, they posed as magistrates.

Staking out a delicatessen in Harlem that had a sideline in hooch, they wore black-face for nearly a week while they gathered their evidence.

At the 1924 Democratic Convention, they posed as delegates, Izzy sporting the goatee of a Southern colonel, and Moe the cowboy boots and Stetson of a Texas rancher.

At the Woodlawn Cemetery, across the street from a warehouse suspected of being a storage facility for bootleg liquor, they posed as gravediggers on whom the warehousemen took pity, offering them a few pints at "cut-rate prices."

On another occasion, Izzy posed as a marathon swimmer, and Moe as his trainer. Izzy submerged himself in the frigid waters of the Atlantic until he turned a convincing shade of blue. Rushing his moist buddy to a nearby speak, Moe called for a drink on humanitarian grounds. "Quickly," he cried, "before he freezes to death." As soon as the "medicinal" drink was produced, Izzy announced, "There's sad news here. You're pinched."

For sheer volume, their most successful masquerade was their impersonation of a pair of Broadway street-cleaners. They not only cleaned up the litter on the Great White Way, but, in a single 24-hour period, they made 71 collars, a career record.

The sheer number of arrests made by Izzy and Moe was staggering, but even more impressive was the 95% conviction rate that went along with that arrest record. They had a singular knack for combining quantity with quality.

Soon other cities were asking for the services of Izzy and Moe, and the team was loaned to District Offices all over the country. Izzy liked to record how much time passed in any given town between the time of their arrival and their first arrest. It took them a half hour in Cleveland, which is all the time they needed to locate and shut down the most popular bar in town. They needed only 20 minutes in Atlanta, where they spotted a candy store owner selling hooch along with more innocent wares. In New Orleans they made their first bust in less than a minute when the driver of the cab they entered offered to sell them a pint. In Chicago and St. Louis they never even got as far as the cab stands, locating and shutting down speakeasies operating openly right in the train depots.

Even more amazingly, in all the time he carried a badge, Izzy never carried a gun. Moe did occasionally but Izzy had no use for weapons. "I used the name of the law," he would proudly write in his memoirs, "and not a blackjack." Admirable as the attitude may have been, it was risky, perhaps even foolhardy. Dozens of federal agents were killed enforcing the dry laws during the '20s and '30s and hundreds of local and state police also fell to criminal gunfire, either directly as a result of Prohibition or from the peripheral violence that it generated. It was the most dangerous time in American history to be a cop, particularly an honest one. Despite this and despite the fact that guns were, in fact, pulled on him on at least two occasions, Izzy refused to pack.

In fact, he later would claim that the most dangerous thing that ever happened to him was not looking down the barrel of a 'legger's gun but being served a ham sandwich. Izzy had entered a speak hoping to make an arrest and it turned out to be one of the few times he was actually spotted as a Fed. The bartender, believing he recognized him from the pictures plastered all over town, braced him. When Izzy denied being the dreaded dry agent, the barkeep demanded proof. What kind of proof, Izzy wanted to know. The barkeep served him the unkosher sandwich, knowing that the real Izzy, who was widely renowned for strict devotion to his Jewish faith, would never eat it. As soon as the barkeep's back was turned, Izzy slid the ham out from between the two pieces of bread, stuck it in a pocket, gobbled up the rest of the sandwich, got his evidence in the form of a shot of whiskey, and made his bust.

There were over 150 dry officers in the Southern New York office and Izzy and Moe, the two of them comprising less than 1.5% of the District's entire roster of enforcement personnel, were responsible for 20% of all the cases made in that District. This was proving embarrassing to the Prohibition Unit's hierarchy, who were envious of the pair's continually receiving more headlines than they did. Many of their brother agents also resented the team's productivity.

In 1925, in an effort to clean house, the Treasury Department summarily dismissed the entire workforce of the Prohibition Unit. A select number of agents of demonstrated integrity were reinstated but Izzy and Moe were not among them. Some sources say they were never rehired because of the animus their success had engendered. Others say they were offered their jobs back but that the offers were contingent on their acceptance of a permanent reassignment to the Midwest, which Izzy and Moe declined. In either case, the colorful law enforcement career of the Prohibition Bureau's most effective two-man team was over.

Moe went into the insurance business and soon found a job in the firm for his old friend Izzy. For the rest of their lives, the business cards they carried as insurance agents noted that they were formerly agents "with the US Govt. Prohibition."

In 1938, Izzy died from complications following a leg amputation. He was 58. Moe died in 1960 at the age of 73, after a long illness. Though his federal career had ended more than three and a half decades earlier, his death certificate read "Revenue Agent" under "occupation."

FURTHER READING

The most comprehensive account of the career of Izzy and Moe is Izzy's own autobiography *Prohibition Agent No. 1* (Stokes, 1932), an entertaining, breezily written collection of anecdotes from their five years of suppressing bootleggers and moonshiners. The book is chiefly interesting for two reasons. One is Izzy's "expert" prediction that Prohibition would never be repealed in the foreseeable future, perhaps not in the lifetimes of anyone alive at the time of his writing. It was, of course, repealed one year after the book hit the stands.

The other interesting point about Izzy's memoirs is that nowhere in them is there a mention of Moe. There are occasional, vague references to "another agent" or "a partner I was working with at the time," but Moe Smith is never referred to by name. Some people assumed that the two old buddies had experienced a falling out and one or two standard reference books state this as a fact. Actually, Izzy refrained from mentioning Moe at Moe's own request. "Maybe," Izzy said in an interview to publicize the publication of his opus, "Moe will write his own book."

Izzy's autobiography is very difficult to find nowadays, but almost any book about America's "Noble Experiment" will contain at least a passing reference to the "Dry Guys." Jay Robert Nash's massive *Encyclopedia of World Crime* (CrimeBooks, 1990) has a very good article on the pair. "Izzy & Moe," a magazine piece by Iyna Bort Caruso, appears in the February 2001 issue of *American History* and is also a great source of information.

THE DRY GUYS IN FICTION

Such a colorful, theatrical team of sleuths would seem to be subjects ripe for fictionalization, but I'm aware of only two.

When Kip Tarleton, a committed believer in absolute temperance who is the hero of Upton Sinclair's *The Wet Parade* (Farrar & Rinehart, 1931), decides to live up to his principles by joining the Prohibition Bureau, he is partnered with veteran Agent Abe Shilling, a fun-loving Fed rather clearly modeled on Izzy Einstein. In the film version of Sinclair's novel (MGM, 1932), Abe is played by Jimmy Durante. In a particularly Izzy-like (and fact-based) scene, Durante, disguising himself as a Bulgarian diplomat with a not altogether convincing phony beard, takes a sip of a cocktail at a swanky nightclub, rips off his beard, and announces that, "In plain Bulgarian, dis jernt is knocked over." Abe's partner, the rigorously WASP-ish Kip, played by Robert Young, is certainly *not* modeled on Moe.

The only other fictional treatment of the pair's adventures with which I'm familiar is *Izzy and Moe*, a 1986 TV-movie starring Jackie Gleason as Izzy and Art Carney as Moe. Though the "Dry Guys" were hardly spring chickens, neither were they quite as superannuated as Gleason and Carney, who were both well into their 60s when the film was shot. This is to say nothing of the fact that the legendary comedy team, with faces as Irish as shamrocks, looked no more convincing portraying immigrant Jews than Jackie Chan would look portraying Henry VIII. Still, the two old pros, working together for what would prove to be the last time, played their parts with relish and gusto. The film, having only the most vestigial relation to historical fact, is highly recommended for its entertainment value.

When one stops to consider it, that's not altogether inappropriate. Ultimately, entertainment value may have been the longest-lasting legacy of the real-life Izzy and Moe.

THE CIGAR GIRL
AND THE STORYTELLER

The Short Mystery Story

On Wednesday, July 28th, 1841, the lifeless body of a young woman named Mary Cecilia Rogers was discovered floating on the Hudson River a little north of Hoboken. Before her remains were disposed of, she had apparently been the victim of a severe beating, multiple rapes, and, finally, strangulation.

The case soon captured the imagination of newspaper readers throughout the New York metropolitan area and beyond. Exactly why it should have done so is a bit puzzling. New York's waterfronts were wild areas even then and sudden, violent death was not at all uncommon. Neither was Miss Rogers a prominent public figure whose death would have been of interest to the general public (though she had, as we will see, been the subject of another series of newspaper articles some two years earlier).

By most contemporary accounts, Miss Rogers was an extremely attractive young woman and newspapers were just starting to learn the effectiveness of those twin bogies, sex and violence, as circulation boosters, but the main reason that *her* murder became such a *cause célèbre* was probably the simple fact that she was personally acquainted with so many of the city's newspapermen. From roughly the beginning of 1837 to the middle of 1839, Miss Rogers had been employed as a sales clerk at a tobacco store owned by one John Anderson. Anderson's store was frequented by many of the city's journalists and the "Beautiful Cigar Girl," as Miss Rogers became known, was the store's prime attraction. After leaving Anderson's employ, Miss Rogers moved with her mother into a boarding house on Nassau Street, the same street on which the offices of some 20 newspapers and magazines were located. To many of the journalists working in New York, the murder of Mary Rogers must have seemed like the murder of the quintessential "Girl Next Door." Whatever the reason, New Yorkers were treated to almost daily accounts of the investigation's progress for several weeks.

Few details of Miss Rogers's short life are known today. She was born in or around New York, probably about 1820. Her father died in a steamboat explosion on the Mississippi River a few years later. A nationwide financial crisis forced her at the age of 16 or 17 to seek paid employment, which she eventually found in Anderson's Broadway smoke shop. When a business venture of her brother's proved successful, he used part of his profits to buy Mary and her mother the boarding house, making it unnecessary for her to continue at Anderson's store.

There was one incident, occurring in the autumn of 1838, which attached some short-lived and unwanted notoriety to her name. On Thursday, October 5th, four New York dailies carried articles reporting that Mary's mother and aunt had awakened the day before to find her missing, the only clue to her whereabouts being a note left behind declaring her intention to end her life. At least three of the articles speculated that Mary's decision sprang from a love affair that had ended unhappily. By the next day, however, one of the four papers, the *Times and Commercial Intelligencer*, reported that Mary had only been visiting a friend and that the suicide note had been sent to her mother as a particularly cruel practical joke.

The "disappearance" was forgotten until 32 months later when Mary's corpse floated up to the surface of the Hudson. Then a number of papers recalled the incident and recounted it, speculating that it was somehow connected to the ensuing crime. The *Weekly Herald* added several details that had gone unreported in 1838, stating that the length of the disappearance had been two full weeks rather than one night as previously reported, and that during that time she had been seduced by a US Naval officer. The *Commercial Advertiser*, on the other hand, suggested that the abduction had occurred at the behest of Mary's employer, John Anderson, as a publicity stunt to improve sales in the cigar store.

Two other papers, the *Sunday News* and the weekly *Brother Jonathan*, flatly asserted that neither seduction nor publicity was at the bottom of the story, that the elopement had never occurred at all, and the whole thing was a hoax dreamed up by newspaper reporters as a practical joke. Unlikely as this may sound, it is actually perhaps the most probable explanation. Such deliberate hoaxes were very common in the rough-and-tumble world of early 19th century journalism. They were generally acknowledged within a few days of having been published, often with a tone of superior glee at having "put one over" on the readers. It's worth noting that the *Times and Commercial Intelligencer*, which had first published the retraction of the disappearance story on October 6th, 1838, reported the story the day before in a flippant, cavalier tone which suggested that they didn't regard the story in a very serious light to begin with. Although neither the *News* nor *Brother Jonathan* specifically named the paper responsible for the hoax, the *T&C*'s attitude, and the fact that it was the first to report the story as untrue, lends some credence to the assertion that the whole "disappearance and suicide" story was a hoax promulgated by the newspapers themselves. Such flights of fancy did little for the credibility of the Press, and newspaper readers regarded printed accounts of news items to be notoriously unreliable. Still, as we'll see, at least one of the people who undertook to investigate Mary's murder accepted the disappearance story on its face.

Whatever happened or didn't happen in 1838, Mary's activities in late July 1841 are well-established. On Sunday the 25th, Mary arose about 10 a.m., left her room on the second floor, stopped at the door of one of her mother's boarders, Daniel Payne, and advised him that she was heading Uptown to attend church services with some relatives. Payne, who was also Mary's fiancé, agreed to meet her at her Broadway Coach stop when she returned that evening. Payne was at the appointed spot at seven p.m., but a violent thunderstorm suddenly broke. After waiting some time, Payne decided that Mary had elected not to attempt a return in such weather, and was spending the night with her Uptown relations.

By noon on Monday the 26th, Mary had not returned. Payne went to the Jane Street home of Mrs. Downing, the aunt Mary had said she would be visiting, but found that Mrs. Downing had been away all day Sunday and had no information about Mary. Checks with Mary's relatives and friends elsewhere in Manhattan, as well as Brooklyn and Staten Island, yielded no data. On Tuesday, the 27th, Payne traveled to the Jersey side of the Hudson, which was then something of a resort area for New Yorkers, again with no results. Frantic, he returned to the city where he placed an ad in the *New York Sun* describing Mary and asking for information.

Alfred Crommeline, a former boarder of Mrs. Rogers and a former suitor of Mary's, read the ad on Wednesday the 28th. He and Archibald Padley, another former Rogers boarder, undertook a search for Mary themselves. Taking the ferry to Hoboken, they asked questions at the landing and began a northerly trek along the shoreline to the Elysian Fields. At Castle Point their search came to an end. A crowd of people was gathered at the riverbank around the body of a young girl lying in the sand. It had been found floating in the river by two boatmen roughly a half hour earlier. Realizing that it was a human body, they had attached a rope to it and pulled it ashore. Though the violence done to the body, and particularly the face, made it difficult to recognize, Crommeline was able to identify the body as Mary's from her clothing and from other physical characteristics with which he was familiar.

At a coroner's inquest held in Hoboken, Dr. Richard Cook declared the cause of death to be strangulation, adding that this had followed a repeated series of rapes by at least three men. This led to what would become the prevailing theory of the case, that Mary had been abducted, violated, and murdered by one of the roving gangs of rowdies that frequented the Hoboken area on weekends. This theory was strengthened by several eyewitness accounts of Hoboken residents describing a girl or several girls seen in the company of such gangs on the day in question. While these accounts led to several arrests, all suspects were able to clear themselves and were released.

Dr. Cook also noted that the knots found on Mary's bonnet and on a strip of skirt or petticoat tied about her waist indicated the culpability of a seaman. William Kiekuk, an enlisted sailor in the US Navy who boarded at the Rogers' when he wasn't on sea duty, was also questioned but also was able to clear himself. However, when the *Weekly Herald*, dredging up the long-forgotten story of Mary's 1838 "disappearance," asserted that Mary had eloped with a naval officer at that time, the sailors' knots seemed, to some, to take on a special significance.

Though it took several days for the murder to gain force in the papers, by August 1 virtually every New York journal was carrying a story of the Rogers case as a leading item. New Yorkers were treated to stories on Mary's death almost every day for six weeks. Every dead-end lead was examined. Every detail was described and re-described and re-redescribed as the case dragged on without solution. Sometime in late August, a brand new clue finally arose.

Mrs. Frederica Loss, the proprietress of the Nick Moore House, a roadside inn at Weehawken, near Hoboken, notified the police that her sons had found some articles of women's clothing in a thicket near the inn. The items found included a parasol, a handkerchief monogrammed with the initials "MR" (or possibly, depending on which account you read, with the full name "Mary Rogers"), a pair of gloves, a silk scarf, and a white petticoat. Two small strips of cloth were found clinging to one of the briars in the thicket. Mrs. Loss remembered that a girl who had been at the Inn on Sunday, the 25th of July, the night of Mary's disappearance, had worn that same scarf.

Mrs. Loss said that the young woman had arrived at the inn at approximately four p.m. in the company of a "dark-complexioned man." They refreshed themselves with some lemonade and left at about 4:30. Sometime after sunset, roughly nine p.m., Mrs. Loss stated that she heard what sounded like a young girl screaming something that sounded like "Oh, God!" in agonized tones. Believing the cry might have come from one of her sons whom she had sent out earlier to drive a bull off the property, she rushed out, fearing that her boy had been gored. Calling out her son's name, she heard no reply but did hear a rustling sound in the distance, as though a struggle was taking place, then something that sounded like a stifled scream. Frantic, she ran to a neighboring farm in search of her son. Finding him safe, she dismissed the screams she had heard as having been the result of a fight or some other unsavory activity arising from the infestation of "fire-rowdies, butcher-boys, soaplocks, and . . . riotous miscreants" who plagued the area every weekend. When, nearly a month after these events, Mrs. Loss's boys found the clothes in the thicket, she made the connection between the young girl who'd stopped at the roadhouse and the murder victim who'd been found a short distance away the following Wednesday, and informed the authorities.

The enclosed thicket was now presumed to be the scene of the outrage and, energized by the infusion of new information, the papers began a new round of speculation. Some stuck to the theory that one of the roving packs of hoodlums in the area that day had done for Mary, referring for support to Dr. Cook's post-mortem report at the inquest and to interviews of Mrs. Loss conducted by several New York reporters in which she specifically recalled a gang of some 15 or so ruffians who'd invaded a shanty next to the inn. Assuming it was a gang, it now seemed as though Mary's unidentified companion might also have been a victim.

Other papers suggested that this mysterious, "dark-complexioned" escort might himself be the offender, dragging her to the thicket, taking indecent liberties, throttling her and disposing of her body in the river to keep his crime concealed.

In the end, the promising discovery came to nothing. After examining the clothing and the thicket, questioning Mrs. Loss and her sons, and investigating anyone else who might have been at Weehawken on the night in question, the police were no closer to a solution. With no new details to keep the case alive, the murder of Mary Rogers lost its hold on the public and, except for occasional references, was no longer being mentioned in any of the New York papers. Mary Rogers was sliding back into the pool of anonymity from which her death or, more correctly, the manner of it had temporarily raised her.

And there she probably would have stayed if it hadn't have been for one particular person who'd been avidly following the case. His name was Edgar Allan Poe. In April 1841, just six months before Mary's death, a short story of his called "The Murders in the Rue Morgue" had been published in *Graham's*, the first example of a brand new literary genre that would become known as detective fiction. Poe decided that his master sleuth, the Chevalier C. Auguste Dupin, who'd found the Rue Morgue matter such child's play, was just the fellow to clear up the Rogers case.

Probably around March or April 1842, after careful, exacting study of the newspaper accounts available, Poe wrote "The Mystery of Marie Roget," in which Dupin investigates the murder of a young Parisian damsel whose death occurs in circumstances almost exactly paralleling the real-life case. Names and locations were changed, of course, along with a few unimportant details (e.g. Marie worked in a parfumerie rather than at a tobacconist's), but on the main points he stuck to the known facts. He had already created a brand new type of fiction. Now he was going to utilize it to do something that had never been done before. He was going to use the methods of "ratiocination" he had described in "Rue Morgue" on a genuine problem rather than an imagined one. He was going to use crime fiction to solve a real-life crime.

Dupin is called into the case by his old friend, Prefect G— of the Paris Police. Using the nameless narrator with whom he shares living quarters for legwork in the field, Dupin remains in his room. Once presented with the information gleaned from his companion's investigations, Dupin spends a week carefully perusing newspaper accounts of the crime before emerging from his solitude to explain his conclusions to his friend. Quoting particularly from six separate articles which, in Dupin's estimation, contain the most salient points, he explains that the prevailing theory that Marie was attacked by a gang is incorrect, that all evidence points to a single offender, and that the most likely candidate is the military officer with whom Marie had eloped during her first mysterious absence. The reader is then informed that, acting on Dupin's advice, the police apprehended a "single assassin," who subsequently confessed, vindicating Dupin's theory.

Poe had theorized (and, through the medium of his fictional master detective, argued) that it was logical to conclude that Mary's earlier disappearance in 1838 and the later one which led to her death were related. Presuming the vague reference to a "naval officer" in some accounts of that first absence to be reliable, he suggested that the "dark-complexioned" escort with whom Mary was seen in the Nick Moore House was that same officer.

There were serious flaws in Poe's reasoning, not the least of which was the fact that Mary's first disappearance did not in all likelihood occur at all. If there was no first elopement, there was no dashing military officer to elope with. And if there was no officer, the young man seen with Mary at the Moore House had to be someone else. Moreover, even if the earlier elopement did occur, there's really no reason to conclude that the two disappearances are related. Poe's reasons for concluding that the second elopement was with the same alleged naval officer are unconvincing when closely examined.

First he has Dupin say, "The chances are ten thousand to one, that he who had once eloped with Marie would again propose an elopement, rather than that she to whom proposals of elopement had been made by one individual, should have them made to her by another." Oh, really? Exactly why is that? Since the departure of this ephemeral sailor, at least two serious suitors had courted Marie's real-life counterpart. Are the odds really so high that there wasn't a third?

Second, he has Dupin point out that the elapsed time between the two disappearances is "precisely the general period of the cruises of our men-of-war." He never explains exactly how a period of time can simultaneously be both "precise" and "general." The fact is that military vessels, then as now, have no set periods either general or precise for cruising. It depends on the type of ship, the specific mission, and a host of other factors. Moreover, the reasoning assumes that the supposed naval officer (and, remember, the existence of this officer is doubtful) is on sea duty, when in fact he could have been assigned to any one of dozens of other tasks.

Finally, Dupin informs his friend that, according to Prefect G—, the official police investigation hasn't examined the possibility of the naval officer's involvement whatsoever. Well, maybe the Paris police didn't check out the possibility but the New York police did. The questioning of Kiekuk, the Rogers boarder who served in the Navy, indicates that the police were taking the suggestion of the murderer being a sailor very seriously. And the article in the *Weekly Herald* in which the possibility of a naval officer was first publicly broached had been printed specifically for the purpose of pressuring the police to investigate that possibility. They looked for a naval officer. They'd have found him if he'd been there to find.

Poe disregarded these points. As far as he was concerned, Mary did have a secret lover in the Navy and that secret lover was the man Mrs. Loss had seen with her on the night she vanished. That was, quite literally, Poe's story, and he was sticking to it. Or at least he would have, if real life had not overtaken him.

By June of 1842, Poe had completed "Marie Roget" and was submitting it to potential publishers, placing it eventually in the *Ladies' Companion*. At roughly 20,000 words, it was quite the longest piece of fiction Poe had ever written, and on account of its length, William Snowden, the editor of the *Companion*, decided to publish it in installments. It was scheduled for the November and December, 1842, and January, 1843, issues. The decision to serialize "Marie Roget" allowed events to catch up to Poe.

On either the first or second of November, 1842, Mrs. Frederica Loss, the proprietress of the road house where Mary Rogers was last seen alive, sustained a gunshot wound accidentally inflicted by one of her sons. While on her deathbed, she made statements to the local magistrate, Justice Gilbert Merritt, indicating that the young man with Mary on the night of her death was a physician and that Mrs. Loss had been engaged to provide them with a out-of-the-way place where the unnamed medico could perform an abortion on Mary. When Mary died unexpectedly in the course of the procedure, it was decided to dispose of her body by dumping it in the river, while her loose clothes were weighted down and thrown in a pond. Later, in the belief that they were not safe there, they were removed from the pond and scattered in the thicket where they were later "discovered." There was no elopement with a mysterious military officer, no violation and strangulation by a gang of ruffians.

On November 12th Mrs. Loss finally died of her wounds. A hearing was held in which her three sons were questioned, but they admitted nothing, and, given the delirium Mrs. Loss was suffering from when she made her statements to Justice Merritt, little legal weight could be attached to them. The hearing was, consequently, inconclusive. Still, once the story became public on November 18th, the general consensus was that the case was solved, though the responsible parties would likely escape justice.

By this time the first two installments of "Marie Roget" had been printed and were on the stands. The third was set to go to press in just a few days. Exactly what Poe did about this setback is unknown. It seems likely, however, that Poe hurriedly revised the last third of the story in order to make his fiction conform to the newly-discovered facts. Poe's original manuscript for "Marie Roget" no longer exists, so what revisions he might have made, or even whether or not there were any such revisions, is difficult to determine with absolute certainty.

However, we do know that the third installment did not appear in the January issue of the *Companion* as originally scheduled. Another prose piece, precisely the same number of columns, was substituted, without explanation. The last chapter of "Marie Roget" was instead published in the February issue. The timing of the delay, occurring almost immediately after the events at Weehawken, makes it very nearly impossible to avoid the conclusion that Poe requested and was granted a period of grace from Snowden in order to make the changes necessitated by the Loss revelations.

In the absence of the original manuscript, Poe's revisions, if any, must remain obscured. However, a careful reading of the last third as it appeared in the *Companion* makes it seem likely that the section in which Dupin presents all the arguments against the crime scene being the thicket, then asserting that, in spite of these arguments, he believes it was the thicket (a conclusion for which he offers no counter-arguments to the points he's already made against its being the thicket) is a revision. From his assertion that the murder did occur in the thicket, he goes on to reason that the murderer must be a single offender rather than a gang. The two lines of reasoning are directly opposed, giving the sequence a lack of clarity untypical for Poe. Further, Poe's theory of a single offender is not necessarily contingent on the thicket's being the scene of the offense, anyway. This indicates hasty rewriting rather than careful reasoning.

The final two paragraphs, in which Dupin's friend, the anonymous narrator, cautions against drawing parallels between the solution of Marie Roget's murder and a possible solution to the murder of her New York counterpart, Mary Rogers, because "the most trifling variation in the facts of the two cases might give rise to the most important miscalculations," seem like an obvious addition. First of all, the sentence which ends the paragraph immediately preceding the final two, "With God all is Now," seems like such a definite conclusion to the story. Secondly, in the first installment, the narrator deliberately invites readers to make the comparison. These two paragraphs, in all likelihood add-ons, were probably Poe's way of giving himself an alibi.

Other changes are more difficult to discern. In the first two installments, Dupin seemed to be moving inexorably toward the conclusion that Marie/Mary was killed by her mysterious paramour, the unnamed naval officer. In the final installment, the officer's role is downplayed and the reader is never actually told who Prefect G— finally arrested; only that the arrest and subsequent confession came about as the result of the clues unearthed by Dupin. A paragraph, supposedly inserted by the magazine's editors but actually written by Poe, stated that the murderer was caught without actually naming the culprit. In sharp contrast, the solutions to the other two Dupin stories are spelled out in clear, well-defined detail. Again, Poe seemed to be hedging his bets.

Almost exactly two years later, "The Raven," his most famous poem, was published to national acclaim. In the wake of the poem's success, Poe was able to place two books with a New York publisher, one a collection of poems, including "The Raven," and the other a collection of short stories, including the Dupin trilogy. This gave Poe the opportunity to do a more thorough job of revision.

The version of "The Mystery of Marie Roget" that appears in *Tales of Mystery and Imagination* (Wiley and Putnam, 1845) is different in several respects from the version that appeared in the *Ladies' Companion*. First of all, he made three significant deletions: a) Dupin's assertion that the thicket is the original scene of the crime despite the arguments against it; b) his description of the crime as it must have occurred in that thicket; c) the "editorial" statement that "an individual assassin" was arrested, confessed, and was convicted of the murder, leaving only the assertion that Dupin's investigations brought about the "desired result."

Secondly, he made 12 additions, all designed to allow for Marie/Mary having died as the result of a botched criminal abortion. I won't detail all of them, but two are especially pertinent.

In the section in which Dupin discusses the arguments regarding the thicket, he says, "There might have been a wrong here, or, more possibly, an accident at Madame Deluc's." Madame Deluc was the fictional counterpart of Mrs. Loss in Poe's story. Before preserving "Marie Roget" between hard covers, Poe wanted it to appear that Dupin (and, by extension, Poe himself) had figured the crime to have occurred in the road house all along.

Second, while ridiculing the conclusions of the doctor who examined Marie/Mary, Dupin states that the injuries sustained by the corpse give no grounds for presuming that the victim was raped and strangled by a gang, then asks a significant question that did not appear in the magazine version of the story. "[If] there was no ground for the inference—*was there not much for another?*" (Italics mine.) In other words, Poe lays the groundwork for Dupin to conclude that the injuries were caused by that illegal abortion rather than a sexual assault, as had been presumed.

There are 10 more additions also designed to cause the reader to draw the inference that Marie/Mary died accidentally in the road house rather than in a criminal attack in the thicket.

By these artful deletions and insertions that Poe incorporated into the *Tales* version of the story, "The Mystery of Marie Roget" was taken in a entirely new direction.

Third, to make it appear that he was right all along, he adds a footnoted introduction to the story (which has appeared in every subsequent reprinting of "Marie Roget"), in which he briefly describes the real-life crime, then asserts that the confessions of "two persons (one of them the Madame Deluc of the narrative), made... long subsequent to the publication, confirmed, in full..." Poe's theory on the case.

As we know, Mrs. Loss's confession was made in the midst of the original publication, not "long subsequent," and both the presumed alterations in the *Companion* version, and the provable alterations made in the *Tales* version indicate that this confession did everything but confirm Poe's solution. There is no record of a *second* confession ever being made. This may be more smoke thrown up by Poe.

Finally, Poe added a series of 23 footnotes to the story, mostly identifying either the New York area counterparts of the story's Parisian locales, the real-life figures on whom Poe based his characters, or the newspapers and magazines from which he paraphrased the articles quoted in the story. While this doesn't significantly alter the plot as the other changes did, it does add to the overall sense of verisimilitude and contributes to the illusion that Poe had correctly figured out the solution.

In the end, Poe had it at least partly his way. He didn't actually solve Mary Rogers's murder as he had hoped to do, but he was credited with having done so,and maybe, from his point of view, that was almost as good.

If "The Mystery of Marie Roget" didn't make any significant contributions to real-life criminal justice, it did make significant contributions to crime fiction. First, just by virtue of having written a second detective story, Poe took a major step toward crystallizing this type of fiction, which he himself had created in "The Murders in the Rue Morgue," into the separate, distinct literary genre to which we are all devoted.

Second, since "Marie Roget" is a sequel to "Rue Morgue" and features the same protagonist, Poe introduced to detective fiction the series character which, in later years, would become the genre's mainstay and bulwark.

Third, Dupin's efforts to solve the case without leaving his rooms, based on nothing but second-hand information provided either by his anonymous roommate or newspaper accounts, make "Marie Roget" the first example of genuine armchair detection, prefiguring characters like Baroness Orczy's Old Man in the Corner or Rex Stout's Nero Wolfe.

Finally, by basing his fictional plot on a real-life case, he started a tradition that mystery writers have continued ever since. From Marie Belloc Lowndes's *The Lodger* (Scribner's, 1913), fictionalizing the Jack the Ripper case, to Max Allan Collins's series of novels about Chicago P.I. Nate Heller, who has investigated such major real-life crimes as the Lindbergh kidnapping and the assassination of Chicago mayor Anton Cermak, mystery novelists have regularly derived their plots from real life (and, like Dupin, occasionally offered solutions at odds with the prevailing opinions). Perhaps the most famous example is Jack Webb's pioneering radio/television police series *Dragnet*, each episode of which, we were solemnly informed, was true with only "the names... changed to protect the innocent."

If Poe's attempts at amateur detective work weren't exactly a triumph, mystery writers who would try their hand at real-life criminal investigation in later years would find greater success. Sir Arthur Conan Doyle, using the methods of Sherlock Holmes, is credited with saving George Edlaji, an East Indian wrongfully convicted of vicious nocturnal attacks on animals, from unjust punishment. Perry Mason's creator, Erle Stanley Gardner, started the Court of Last Resort, a nonprofit organization made up of experts from various criminal investigative specialties, to look into questionable cases in which the organized forces of criminal justice may have snared the wrong quarry. Many unjustly convicted defendants were freed by the Court's efforts. John Ball, the creator of black Southern California super-cop Virgil Tibbs, found the police work he researched for his fiction so fascinating that he decided to become a cop himself, and wound up working as a deputy in the reserve branch of the LA County Sheriff's Office.

Would any of them have gone from crime writer to crime fighter had not Poe made the first attempt? Probably. But whether they would have or not, there is no denying that Poe blazed the trail. And, if he failed to actually solve the murder, he was brave in the attempt.

FURTHER READING

Most of the non-fiction literature on the Rogers case is contemporary to that case and difficult to track down. More recent magazine articles such as Winthrop D. Lane's "The Mystery of Mary Rogers" (*Collier's*, 8 March 1930), William K. Wimsatt's "Poe and the Mystery of Mary Rogers" (*Publications of the Modern Language Association*, Volume LVI, March 1941), or Samuel Worthen's "Poe and the Beautiful Cigar Girl" (*American Literature*, Volume XX, November, 1948), are a little more accessible.

Perhaps the best single work on the Rogers murder and Poe's attempts to solve it is *Poe the Detective* (Rutgers University, 1968) by John Evangelist Walsh. His scholarly examination of the relevant newspaper articles, the version of "Marie Roget" in the *Ladies' Companion*, the version of the story that eventually appeared in *Tales*, along with his rigorous interpretation of the timelines of the real-life events and the fiction that derived from them, give a satisfyingly complete picture of both the likely solution to the real case and of Poe's attempts to conceal his failure to arrive at that conclusion. Walsh won the Edgar award in the true-crime category for this work. A more recent Walsh book, *Midnight Dreary – The Mysterious Death of Edgar Allan Poe* (Rutgers University, 1998) attempts to shed some light on the questions still surrounding Poe's final days. *Midnight Dreary* was an Edgar nominee in the Critical/Biographical category. Both are highly recommended.

Two years after this article was first published, Holmesian scholar Daniel Stashower wrote *The Beautiful Cigar Girl – Mary Rogers, Edgar Allan Poe, and the Invention of Murder* (Dutton, 2006), another book-length study of the case. An avid researcher into the life and works of Poe's successor, Sir Arthur Conan Doyle, Stashower had seven years earlier won one Edgar in the Critical/Biographical category for *Teller of Tales – The Life of Arthur Conan Doyle* (Holt, 1999), and would one year later win a second for *Arthur Conan Doyle – A Life in Letters* (Penguin, 2007) in the same category. For *Cigar Girl* he was nominated for an Edgar in the true crime category. In addition to the Edgar nomination, he was also a finalist for the Macavity given by Mystery Readers International, the Anthony given by Bouchercon, the World Mystery Convention, and an Agatha given by the Malice Domestic Convention. Since it did not appear until after this article was completed, I was not able to use it as a research source, but I can recommend Stashower's books generally and this book, particularly.

UNSUNG FOR SIXTY YEARS

Senior Sleuths

Whether or not a police officer becomes famous to the general public often has more to do with chance and caprice than with whether or not he's done anything to earn that fame.

Wyatt Earp, for example, is celebrated in song and story as the lawman who tamed the Wild West country and "made law and order prevail." Yet an objective analysis of his relatively short career in law enforcement makes it clear that his record doesn't even begin to compare to those compiled by such frontier peace officers as Bill Tilghman, Heck Thomas, Bass Reeves, or Joe LeFors, none of whom enjoy a fraction of Earp's notoriety. Earp, however, had the good luck to survive well into the 20th century and to retire to Hollywood, where he met film-makers like Tom Mix, William S. Hart, and John Ford who all contributed to the overblown legend with which we are so familiar.

Eliot Ness's contributions to the efforts to bring Al Capone to justice were not inconsiderable but neither were they a solo campaign (as the real-life Ness always admitted). Ness's autobiography, however, was sold to television and when the series deriving from his book was broadcast, Ness's real name was used. Treasury Agent Frank Wilson, on the other hand, who actually put together the tax case that led to Capone's conviction, sold his autobiography to the movies, and the resulting film, *The Undercover Man*, used fictionalized names. Ness, in consequence, is known as "the man who got Capone," while Wilson is comparatively obscure.

Two NYPD officers of surpassing integrity, Officer Frank Serpico and Sergeant David Durk, developed a close friendship when they discovered their mutual distaste for the systemic corruption plaguing the Big Apple's police force. After years of getting the bureaucratic shuffle every time they tried to do something about it within the system, they decided to publicly expose the dirt by giving their story to the *New York Times*. In the wave of publicity that followed, Serpico met a writer named Peter Maas, who wrote a book about him which, in turn, became a classic movie and a short-lived (but well-made) TV series. In the film, Durk was represented by a fictionalized (and not particularly sympathetic) character and in the TV series was nowhere to be seen. Serpico

51

became the archetypal honest cop; Durk faded into anonymity.

The subject of this column, Carmine J. Motto, has had a law enforcement career that can only be described as phenomenal. He's arrested murderers, counterfeiters, and would-be presidential assassins. He's investigated Nazi spies, political terrorists, and Mafia figures. Because of his familiarity with organized crime, he was one of the first law enforcement officials to interview Joe Valachi after Valachi decided to go public with revelations about La Cosa Nostra. He's been played in the movies by Burt Lancaster, though under a fictional name. He wrote a book about the techniques of undercover work that's regarded as the standard text on the subject. And he was so well-respected within the police community that in the course of his career he retired four separate times and each time was immediately called back into service. In fact, he was recalled to duty so often that by the time he finally retired for good, he'd spent over six decades in the profession. Yet, much as he's respected by his brother and sister officers, he's relatively unknown to the general public. Like Tilghman, Wilson, Durk, and the others, he's an unsung hero.

Though Motto had been fascinated by police work from an early age, his decision to make the field his career was motivated as much by economics as interest. Growing up in New York City during the '30s, Motto, like millions of other big-city kids in that era, had experienced the ravages of the Great Depression first-hand and longed for the security of a civil service position. The NYPD was not accepting applications, however, and Motto had to be content with a position as a "junior executive" in Macy's receiving department at the princely salary of $27 a week.

On a vacation to upstate New York, Motto wound up staying at a hotel that was allegedly owned by the famous Manhattan mobster Jack "Legs" Diamond and which, in consequence, was under constant surveillance by officers of the state's patrol service. Impressed by the sharp appearance of the uniformed troopers, Motto decided that the New York State Police was the agency for him and put in an application shortly afterwards.

Ironically, Motto, who was 5 feet 9 7/8 inches tall, was almost disqualified. The job description called for applicants who were at least 5 feet 10 inches. Motto's distinguished career almost ended before it started on the basis of an eighth of an inch. Motto appealed the decision, however, and in 1936 was finally accepted into the force. His heavy interest in the field can be gauged by the fact that he fought so hard to win a position that only paid $15 a week. In taking on the job of a state policeman, Motto was voluntarily accepting a 45% pay cut. And this with the Depression on.

As a New York State Trooper, Motto performed a broad spectrum of police duties. Traffic enforcement, patrol of rural areas and, because of his "executive" experience at Macy's, a great deal of clerical work. The grisliest job he ever had was being ordered to serve as an "official witness" to the executions at Sing-Sing state prison of three convicted murderers in a single evening. The most unexpected and unusual duty he ever performed, however, occurred one autumn night when he and his brother troopers prepared to fight off a military invasion mounted by a predatory, extra-terrestrial race.

Motto and his partner were on mobile patrol. It was Sunday and the weekend traffic from the upstate rural resort areas back into the city was expected to be heavy. Since it was Halloween, the usual quota of adolescent pranks was also expected. State police cars were not equipped with any radio communication equipment at this time and, since troopers worked in primarily rural areas, there was no network of call boxes like those used by their municipal brethren. It was necessary to make periodic stops at their detachment's headquarters to get updates and be given assignments.

The trooper on duty in the teletype room when Motto and his partner checked in had the radio on and was listening to music. He told Motto and his partner that the regular program was being interrupted every few minutes to inform listeners about some sort of disturbance in the adjacent state. Just as he mentioned this, the music was interrupted again with an update. It had now been determined that what was formerly believed to have been a meteor landing in a wooded area of New Jersey was now definitely confirmed to be a spacecraft of alien origin. Scientists from Princeton were en route to make an examination. Moments later the on-scene announcer informed listeners that the aliens' intent was definitely hostile. They were armed with some kind of weapon that instantly vaporized its victims. The teletype operator informed the corporal in charge of the watch. The corporal called the lieutenant in charge of the detachment at his home. The lieutenant immediately barked a few orders and started for the barracks.

By this time the radio announcer was describing entire villages that were being systematically destroyed as the invaders laid waste to the surrounding area. Troopers still on the road called in to report a complete breakdown of compliance with traffic laws on the state highways. What was even more puzzling was that the traffic reversed the normal "end-of-the-weekend" pattern by being away from the city rather than towards it. They were informed that traffic conditions were the result of the panic caused by the Martian attack and ordered back to headquarters where they were issued rifles, shotguns, machine guns, and ammo.

While defensive positions were being set up, one of the troopers called down to his colleagues from the second floor. "The whole thing is a phony," he said. "It's only a radio show by some guy named Orson Welles." Much embarrassed, Motto and the rest of the troopers returned to normal duty.

Another duty Motto performed pretty frequently was providing security at President Franklin Roosevelt's vacation home in Hyde Park. During these details, Motto worked closely with the US Secret Service. One of the agents Motto worked with informed him that with war already raging in Asia and Europe and likely to eventually involve the States, the Service was planning to expand. He recommended that Motto apply. Motto took the advice and by 1941 was accepted as a Special Agent, a job he would hold (except for a short stint of military duty) for the next 33 years.

In addition to being the agency in charge of Presidential security, the Secret Service was at this time also the main criminal investigative arm of the US Treasury Department and, as such, responsible for safeguarding the integrity of the nation's currency. Motto spent most of the next three decades tracking down such threats to the monetary system as counterfeiters, check forgers, and currency thieves. Counterfeiting, however, is a crime that touches almost every other segment of the underworld so, in investigating his own particular specialty, Motto bumped heads with every type of criminal, from armed robbers to narcotics traffickers, from organized crime figures to enemy spies.

One of Motto's cases is a good example of how an investigation into one kind of crime can lead to the investigator getting involved in another type of case entirely. Motto had arrested a street hood named Corby for passing counterfeit bills. Corby, whose wife was in the late stages of pregnancy, was anxious to make a deal. It took very little persuading to convince him to give up and eventually set up his source, a low-level Mafioso named Adrian. Working undercover, Motto purchased some counterfeit from Adrian but was informed by Adrian that this was a one-time only deal. Having disposed of his supply of counterfeit, Adrian did not want to continue in that business. Perhaps, Motto suggested, Adrian could direct him to *his* source.

Motto was referred to another low-ranking organized crime figure out in the Midwest named Butch. A few days later Motto had made an appointment with Butch and was knocking on his front door. The door was opened by a man who identified himself as "Rocky." Finding out that Motto was from New York, he asked Motto what was going on back in the Five Boroughs. They spent a pleasant hour or so talking about familiar places and people around New York until Butch arrived.

Butch informed Motto that he was also out of the counterfeiting business. However, in the course of his conversation with the undercover agent, he admitted enough about his deal with Adrian that Motto was able to include him in a criminal conspiracy charge. Though he was not able to make any large seizures of counterfeit currency, he was able to obtain convictions against two organized crime members.

A few months later, Motto was working a case in another state. While stopping over at a state police barracks to confer with officers there, Motto noticed a "wanted" poster on the wall that looked familiar. The poster was for a man named Jimmy Deale who was wanted for a particularly vicious murder. Motto thought Deale looked familiar but couldn't quite place him. Studying the poster intently, it eventually dawned on him. Jimmy Deale was the man he knew as "Rocky," the man who'd been staying with Butch when Motto tried to make his counterfeit buy.

Contacting the homicide detectives in the city where the murder had taken place, Motto learned that Jimmy Deale was Adrian's brother-in-law and that it was believed that Adrian and his father, a much higher-ranking mobster, had spirited Deale out of the area when police started to suspect his culpability in the kidnapping, rape, and strangulation of a young single mother.

Meanwhile, Adrian, who'd already been on probation for burglary at the time of his counterfeiting arrest, was looking at eight years of federal time on the counterfeit conspiracy followed by another eight years of state time for breaking that probation. Since Motto already had a rapport with Adrian, the homicide detectives prevailed upon him to see if Adrian would be willing to trade Deale's whereabouts for a shorter sentence.

The code of *Omerta* exerted a strong influence on Adrian, particularly in light of the fact that Deale was his own sister's husband. But his resolve started to weaken when he was told that Deale was wanted for viciously attacking and killing a defenseless young woman and leaving her daughter orphaned. Deale had told Adrian that the cops wanted him for murdering another hood who had cheated Deale in a game. The irony of Adrian's doing 16 years while never committing an act of violence while his brother-in-law was walking around free after atrociously murdering a young woman (to say nothing of stepping out on Adrian's sister) was not lost on him. Still, Adrian was reluctant to break the code.

Eventually he was persuaded to give up the information in exchange for the state probation charges being vacated. Deale was located, arrested, and convicted. A comparatively small-time counterfeiting case had led to Motto's inadvertently becoming, in effect, the lead investigator on a major murder case that had nothing to with counterfeiting and, indeed, nothing to do with the federal government.

Perhaps the most important case Motto was ever involved in during his tenure as a Secret Service agent was his investigation of a terrorist group that had mounted an assassination attempt on President Truman. Since the White House was undergoing renovations, Truman and his family were staying across the street at Blair House, where temporary security posts had been set up by the Secret Service and their uniformed branch, the White House Police Force. Oscar Collazo and Gresilio Torresola, two members of a militant separatist group called the Puerto Rican Nationalist Party, decided to take advantage of the temporary change in security measures, forging a plot to rush Blair House with blazing guns and murder the President. They never got anywhere near Truman and, in fact, never even made it to the front door of Blair House, but one Secret Service employee, White House Police Officer Leslie Coffelt, was killed preventing their attempt.

Collazo and Torresola both lived in the Bronx. Motto, still working out of the NYC Field Office, was assigned to gather information about their party and see if he could uncover any other conspirators in the plot. Motto was able to identify, interview, photograph, and fingerprint every single member of the party in the NYC metropolitan area. Since Collazo and Torresola had been caught in the act, the evidence Motto gathered was not absolutely crucial in convicting them but it was valuable. In more than three decades as a Treasury Agent, Motto investigated and arrested many would-be assassins. This was the most significant such case he was ever associated with.

Much less important to the security of the nation, but providing a high level of human interest, was the case numbered "880" in the annals of the Secret Service. No other counterfeiting case in the history of the Service went unsolved for so long and none seemed quite as trivial. For 16 years, from 1932 until 1948, phony one dollar bills of extremely poor quality were passed in NYC's Upper West Side. No more than five or 10 such bills were passed each week but they were passed consistently until the War Years. It was assumed that whoever had been passing the poor quality counterfeits had passed away. Suddenly, when the war ended, the "880" bills started turning up again.

Investigators finally settled on a kindly old gentleman who made his living as a junk scavenger. His needs were meager, but fixing up junked items and reselling them did not produce an income sufficient to meet those needs. He'd been a printer and inventor in his youth so, to supplement his income, he fashioned a hand printer which he used to make up a few one dollar bills whenever the wolf needed to be chased from the door. When the Secret Service finally caught up to him, the elderly junk man noted that, had he gone on welfare, he'd have received far more money than he did by producing his counterfeits so by printing a few phony bills in times of extreme need he was actually saving the government money. He'd stopped passing the notes between 1941 and 1945, he explained, because he didn't want to tie up federal investigators on a trifling case while the country was at war.

Hollywood became interested in the story and Edmund Gwenn, who'd won an Oscar playing Santa Claus in *Miracle on 34th Street* (20th/Fox, 1947), was tagged to portray the elderly forger. The leading man in the film was Burt Lancaster, who played a fictionalized amalgam of the many agents, including Motto, who'd worked the case. *Mr. 880* (20th/Fox, 1950) won Gwenn another Oscar nomination and the script received an Edgar nomination from the Mystery Writers of America.

In 1970, "sky-jacking" had become epidemic and there was no single agency responsible for preventing the crime. President Nixon ordered that every federal police agency, including the various enforcement arms of the Treasury, should provide personnel for an *ad hoc* Sky Marshal program. Each commercial flight (or as many as possible) taking off from the United States would be protected by an armed federal agent. Tasked with coordinating the program for the Secret Service, Motto put the detail in motion within 48 hours of Nixon's issuing the order. He takes great pride in the fact that no plane with a Sky Marshal on it was ever hijacked and that the President's orders were fulfilled so quickly.

In 1974 Motto decided the time had come to retire. His Secret Service colleagues gave him the usual excellent dinner. Motto looked back on nearly 40 years of police service and prepared to enter his "Golden Years." But the Treasury Department was not through with him. Almost immediately after his retirement from the Service, Motto was offered the position of Deputy Director of Law Enforcement for the entire Treasury. This put him in charge of not only the Secret Service but the Customs Bureau, the Criminal Investigations Division of the IRS, and the Bureau of Alcohol, Tobacco, and Firearms. He held this job for four years.

The State of New York then called him out of retirement to serve as an investigative consultant to a commission investigating the riot at Attica State Prison. Upon completing this assignment, Motto was simultaneously offered two separate police positions. Former federal prosecutor Robert Morgenthau had been elected District Attorney of New York County and wanted Motto as his Chief Investigator, while retired Federal Narcotics Agent John M. Dolce had been appointed Commissioner of Public Safety in suburban White Plains, New York, and wanted Motto as his deputy. Motto chose the latter position, was sworn in on Feb. 1, 1976, and remained there for 16 years.

Motto was in his late 70s when he retired from the White Plains force but was still not quite finished with his police career. Harrison, New York, Mayor Phil Marricini wanted to hire Motto as his town's Police Commissioner. Since he was a resident of Harrison, Motto accepted. Happy to be finally running his own shop after nearly 60 years in the profession, he nonetheless found working as a suburban police chief to be less satisfying than he'd hoped. The political factors of running a small town force were annoying and, over time, he began to find the position less of an exciting challenge and more of an ordinary job. After three years at the head of Harrison's police department,

Motto, now well past 80, finally pulled the plug for good and left active law enforcement behind him.

Still, Motto says, "I don't think I can ever totally retire. I remain interested in modern policing techniques, as that 'cop bug' that bit me in 1932 is still under my skin." Since leaving the Harrison force, Motto has prepared a revised edition of *Undercover* (CRC, 1999), the classic text on clandestine law enforcement operations. His autobiographical memoirs, *In Crime's Way* (CRC, 2000), appeared a few months later.

"Hero" is an overused term, but Carmine J. Motto, quietly and professionally doing high quality police work for more than 60 years, truly deserves it. Thanks to the caprices of chance and time, however, he is like so many others who devote their lives to the Job, an unsung hero.

AFTERWORD

Carmine Motto passed away in 2002, shortly after this article first appeared in *Mystery Readers Journal*. He was 88. Few of us can look back on a career as fulfilling and productive as Motto's. He was truly a "cop's cop" and a "top cop."

Since the original edition of this book appeared, Motto has been used fictionally at least one other time.

The War of the Worlds Murders (Berkley, 2005) by Max Allan Collins is the sixth and, so far, final entry in his "Disaster Mystery" series, in which real-life famous mystery writers attempt to solve murders committed in the midst of major real-life disasters, such as the sinking of the *Titanic*, the attack on Pearl Harbor, or the fire that engulfed the *Hindenburg*. *The WotW Murders* describes the investigation into a murder committed in the radio studio from which Orson Welles's adaptation of H.G. Welles's novel is being broadcast. While, outside the studio, thousands are panicking in the belief that the interplanetary invasion is real, Welles and Walter Gibson, the creator of the masked super-sleuth known as "The Shadow" (whom Welles had portrayed on another radio show), collaborate on the investigation even as the live broadcast is going over the air.

As the novel progresses, Collins cuts from the radio studio to scenes in the outside world, where ordinary people, convinced that the end is at hand, react to what they believe are newsflashes about the Martian invasion. One of the characters representing such ordinary people is a New York State Trooper named Carmine who, in the course of the novel, goes from wondering why traffic patterns are so odd, to preparing to fend off the invaders, to feeling sheepish about having been taken in.

Mr. Collins kindly credited Mr. Motto's autobiography, *In Crime's Way*, as well as the first edition of *Just the Facts*, for inspiring those scenes.

THE "RAGGED STRANGER" MURDERS

Partners in Crime – Writing Partnerships

"Flash" Casey, crime photographer. Carl Kolchak, the night stalker. I.M. "Fletch" Fletcher. Cat Marsala. The annals of mystery fiction literally teem with crime-solving journalists. But the most famous of them, the granddaddy of all sleuthing newsmen, is Hildy Johnson, the fast-talking hero of *The Front Page*.

In his single appearance, Hildy makes his way through three acts worth of crooked, incompetent cops, crookeder politicians, golden-hearted whores, prison escapes, and suicide attempts, and manages to come out on top with a headline story. But what really gave this famous stage play (and the five movies that eventually were made from it) its savor was the fact that the playwrights, Ben Hecht and Charles Mac-Arthur, knew whereof they wrote. Before writing their play they, like Hildy, had been hard-charging Chicago newspapermen. In fact, like the many fictional heroes their classic stage play inspired, they even solved crimes.

Though they worked for rival papers, in at least one famous criminal case they actually collaborated on the investigation, pooling their efforts to uncover the truth behind a complicated murder plot. It involved a revered war hero, his wife, and a mysterious figure who became known as "The Ragged Stranger."

Carl Wanderer, the Chicago-born-and-bred son of German immigrants, gave in to a burst of patriotic fervor in 1916, leaving his home town to enlist in the Army. During the campaign against Pancho Villa, he displayed leadership qualities sufficient to earn him a lieutenant's commission when the US entered the war in Europe a year later. In France, he participated in every major battle involving US troops and, with a chestful of medals to prove his courage, returned to a hero's welcome in Chicago.

The following fall, he met and married Ruth Johnson and moved into the small apartment she shared with her parents. Within months Ruth had become pregnant.

Wanderer did not seem pleased by the news. As Ruth's pregnancy advanced, he became moody and temperamental, arguing with his wife and her folks at the slightest provocation and flying into a rage whenever the impending blessed event was mentioned. Over time, however, Wanderer's mood improved and, on June 21, 1920, he suggested to Ruth that the two of them enjoy a night on the town.

Later, as the Wanderers entered the vestibule of their apartment building after enjoying dinner and a movie, the night was ripped apart by the sound of gunfire. Ruth's mother rushed out of their apartment to find her daughter bleeding to death on the floor, the victim of multiple gunshots, while her son-in-law was bent over a shabbily dressed man, also lying on the floor and also bleeding from several bullet wounds. Wanderer was beating the dying man over the head with an empty pistol.

"You've killed my wife, you bastard!" he screamed. "You've killed my wife."

Ruth was still alive, but just barely. "My baby is dead," she told her mother. She died a few minutes later on her way to Ravenswood Hospital. Her apparent killer lived long enough to make it to the same hospital but, comatose, died a few hours later. There was no identification found on him and within days his newspaper sobriquet, "The Ragged Stranger," had become virtually a proper name.

Wanderer told police that he and his wife returned from their evening out to find the vestibule of their building in darkness. As Ruth tried to find the switch, they heard a voice order them to leave the light off. Wanderer reached for the .45 semi-automatic pistol he habitually carried. As he drew his weapon, he heard the voice shout obscene threats, then saw gun flashes as the voice's owner opened fire. Wanderer shot back, emptying his clip. When the gunfire ended, a total of 14 shots had been fired, and both Ruth and The Ragged Stranger had been hit. Though he'd failed to prevent his wife's murder, Wanderer was again celebrated as a hero for his brave attempt to defend hearth and home and for his defeat of the criminal who attacked them.

The gun that the Wanderers' assailant had been using was also a Colt .45 semi-automatic pistol, the standard military sidearm in the United States since 1913. Several Chicago papers ran a photo on their front page, showing the two identical weapons, one the hero's, the other the villain's, side by side.

The coincidence of the two opponents using the same pistol didn't sit well with Ben Hecht, the top crime reporter for the Chicago *Daily News*. Why would a guy so obviously down and out hold on to a gun, using it in a random robbery attempt that might've yielded nothing when he could pawn it for fifteen or twenty dollars? Of course, there were a lot of .45s floating around since the end of the Great War and it was not at all unusual for ex-soldiers to pack in peacetime the pistols they had carried in war. Perhaps The Ragged Stranger was a military veteran who, like so many other former servicemen, still carried his service weapon. Still, it was a puzzle.

Discussing the case with his buddy, Charles MacArthur, Hecht's opposite number at the Chicago *Herald-Examiner*, he found that his friendly rival had similar misgivings about the coincidence. They decided to follow it up.

MacArthur contacted the Colt firearms company and found that The Ragged Stranger's .45 had first been sold not to the War Department but to a sporting goods store right there in Chicago. The store in turn had sold it to a phone company repairman named Peter Hoffman. Hoffman told MacArthur that he had sold it to a mailman acquaintance some years earlier. The well-armed postal carrier was named Fred Wanderer who, it turned out, was a cousin of Carl's.

Fred Wanderer admitted that he had loaned his pistol to his cousin. In fact, it was his understanding that it had been Fred's pistol that Carl had used in the gunfight with The Ragged Stranger. Informed that it had been the Stranger who'd been armed with the postman's weapon, Fred Wanderer actually fainted.

This was more than just a coincidence but it still could be a misunderstanding. Perhaps the police had mixed the two pistols up, misidentifying The Ragged Stranger's gun as Carl Wanderer's and vice versa. Additional checking foreclosed this possibility. The second pistol at the scene had been issued to Carl Wanderer during his military service. This erased any doubt from the two journalists' minds. They reported their suspicions to the police, who brought Wanderer in for questioning.

Wanderer stuck to his story. He and his wife were attacked by The Ragged Stranger. He insisted The Stranger's gun had most likely been part of a large shipment of weapons sent to military training camps during the war and could not possibly have belonged to his cousin Fred. He had never borrowed Fred's pistol. The best efforts of Detective Lieutenant Mike Loftus could not shake Wanderer.

While Wanderer was in custody, Hecht had been following up other leads. A check at Ruth's bank disclosed that Wanderer had withdrawn $1,500 from her savings account on the day she had been killed. Hecht personally searched Wanderer's apartment and found the cash hidden behind a chest. He also found a number of love letters written by Wanderer, but never sent.

The letters were written to a man.

Hecht reported his findings to Loftus, who decided to let the reporter have a crack at questioning the suspect. Hecht told Wanderer that he'd found the letters he'd written to a man named "James." He added that he'd been in contact with James, who was on his way to the police station.

Confronted with the evidence of his double sexual life, Wanderer confessed. He'd married Ruth for her money. He'd grown to hate her, to hate all women, and the thought that she was going to bear his child was intolerable. Further, he feared that a child would come between him and his lover, James. He resolved to murder his wife and make it look like as though she'd been killed in an exchange of gunfire.

Cruising through skid row bars for several nights, Wanderer had struck up an acquaintance with an out-of-work Canadian named Al Watson.

Wanderer offered Watson a job. He told Watson that, despite his war record, his wife doubted his manliness. Wanderer would be willing to pay him to fake a robbery attempt, which Wanderer would then foil, thus shoring up his heroic image in his wife's eyes. Watson agreed, not dreaming that he was being set up as the fall guy in Wanderer's scheme to murder his wife.

That night, when Watson confronted them at the entrance to their building, Wanderer drew both pistols, emptying one into Ruth and the other into Watson, then arranging the crime scene so it would look as though they'd both died in a shootout.

Wanderer was tried separately for the two murders. Convicted of both crimes, he was sentenced to be hanged. Wanderer was visited several times by Hecht and MacArthur in the interim between his sentencing and his execution, developing an odd friendship with the two men who'd wrecked his murder scheme and, in effect, put him in Death Row.

Shortly before the date of his execution, Hecht loaned Wanderer a small amount of money. Excessively grateful for the small favor, Wanderer asked Hecht if there was anything he could do to repay them. Hecht replied that he and MacArthur would like to write Wanderer's last words. Wanderer agreed.

On March 19, 1921, just before Wanderer was marched to the gallows, Hecht handed him a slip of paper. On it was written a speech castigating the editors of the *Daily News* and the *Herald-Examiner*, Hecht's and MacArthur's bosses. Unfortunately, Wanderer never got a chance to recite it. His hands were tied, and he was not able to read the speech the two newshawks had so enjoyed putting down on paper. Instead he began singing a popular song of the day, "Dear Old Pal of Mine" as a tribute to his two reporter friends. He continued singing until the moment his neck was snapped by the noose.

MacArthur's impromptu epitaph was typical of the hard-boiled cynicism for which he was so well-known. He turned to Hecht and said, "The son of a bitch should've been a song-plugger!"

HOBBIES: PHOTOGRAPHY

The Southern California Mystery

Lorraine Vigil was a bit nervous. Not scared, mind you. Just a bit nervous. It was, after all, her very first assignment since signing on with the Diane Modeling Studio a few days earlier, and she was anxious to do a good job. She had no prior experience as a model, and her anxiety about performing well was understandable. If the customer was pleased, she'd get more and better assignments, and her potential income as a model would be much greater than what she'd been able to earn as a secretary, even if she catered to no one but amateur shutterbugs willing to pay high prices for the opportunity to snap their own private cheese-cake shots. But aside from her anxiety about doing well, there was the cryptic warning her boss had given her when she'd called about the job.

"Listen, Lorraine," she'd said, "about this guy…."

"What's wrong, Diane?"

"Well, he's sort of creepy. Definitely not a pro photographer, you know? Just watch yourself."

When the customer, who identified himself as "Frank Johnson," arrived at Lorraine's address on West Sixth Street, Los Angeles, she saw what Diane meant. Short, homely, and jug-eared, wearing a pair of goggle-lensed eyeglasses that evoked Wally Cox's old TV character "Mr. Peepers," Johnson wore unkempt clothing, and his nerdy demeanor was off-putting. Moreover, he gave off an obnoxious odor, as if he hadn't bathed in days. "Creepy" he certainly was.

But, reasoned Lorraine, "creepy" isn't the same as dangerous, and surely Diane wouldn't have assigned her to work with anyone who was truly unsafe. Inexperienced as she was in the business, she was savvy enough to know that the best assignments went to the most experienced models, and the only way to get experience was the take the less pleasant scut work when it was offered. Posing for this guy clearly wasn't going to put her on the cover of *Vogue*, but it might move her incrementally closer to that kind of lucrative assignment. As with any other job, she was going to have to pay her dues.

Recalling Diane's warning to "watch yourself," she asked to see Johnson's ID. He said he'd left it at home. She asked for payment in advance (the agreed-upon rate was $15 an hour). He said he only had $10 on him. If she'd been just a bit more experienced, she might have passed on the gig at that point. Not having the money on him gave her a reasonable out. But it *was* her first assignment with the agency, and she didn't want to get a reputation as a *prima donna* when she was just starting out. She took the 10-spot as earnest money and followed Johnson to his car.

Once she was inside, Johnson informed her that there'd been a change in plans. Instead of shooting at Diane's studio, as she'd been informed, they'd be going to his private studio in Anaheim.

"She's got some other people coming over," Johnson explained. "My studio's not too far. We'll be there in 30 or 40 minutes."

Lorraine was suddenly a lot more nervous but still not quite scared. She should have been. In slightly less than a year, the mousy little guy who called himself "Johnson" had managed to kidnap, rape, and murder three other girls without law enforcement even being aware of his existence. And he'd just selected Lorraine to be his fourth victim.

* * *

Johnson's real name was Harvey Glatman. He was born in New York City on December 10, 1927, to Albert and Ophelia Glatman. According to some sources, he displayed bizarre psychosexual behavior at a surprisingly early age. His mother reported that she once caught him at the age of only 3 naked from the waist down. He had, she said, tied a string tightly around his penis, shut the loose end in a drawer, then leaned back against the string.

Genital play is not unusual in tots, but this seemed to go a bit beyond the pale. Rather than seek professional guidance, however, Mrs. Glatman decided to pass it off. It was the earliest indication of Harvey Glatman's future obsession with ropes and knots.

When Harvey was 11, the family moved from New York to Denver, Colorado. Now approaching puberty, Harvey resumed the kinky activities that he had already shown a penchant for as a toddler. By the age of 12, Harvey had developed a taste for autoerotic asphyxia, tying one end of a rope around a rafter in the attic and the other around his neck, then deliberately choking himself while he masturbated.

By 1942, Harvey was a freshman at East Denver High School. Standardized tests indicated that he had superior academic aptitude. He managed to achieve an "A-B" average in his coursework, and was described as "well-liked by everybody." A notation in one school record lists, among his hobbies and interests, "photography." At the time it seemed a perfectly normal, innocent notation. Sixteen years later it would, in retrospect, be seen to have sinister connotations.

Whatever perverse urges were driving Harvey, they started to boil over during his high school years. By December 1944, in addition to his private rope games he began "cat prowling" apartments occupied by women who lived alone. Avoiding contact with the occupants, he rarely took anything, though on one occasion he stole a revolver and on another an automatic pistol.

Now that he was armed, he stepped up his activities. In addition to housebreaking, he started accosting women on the street, threatening them with one of the guns, tying them up to phone poles or nearby trees, molesting them once they were helplessly bound, and then making off with their purses. Once he actually forced one of his victims to take him to her apartment, where he tied her up, partially disrobed her and, after fondling her, took some of her clothes as a souvenir.

Harvey's string of muggings and burglaries, with their sinister psychosexual overtones, were sufficiently troubling to Denver Police that finding him became a high priority. Fortunately, Harvey's physical description was uncommon enough that, despite having no idea who he was, their chances of finding him were actually fairly high.

On May 18, 1945, two Denver police officers arrested Harvey after spotting him at a bus stop a few minutes after an attempted burglary had been reported a short distance away. After a night in jail, his steely resolve to remain silent evaporated and he made a complete confession of all his crimes to that point. He was formally charged on May 21.

His parents posted bond, which meant that Harvey was out of jail in time to attend his graduation ceremony in June. Despite the time his extra-curricular hobbies were taking, his grades were high enough to put him in his class's upper seventh.

By July, he was ratcheting up his activities. Since he was known in Denver, he took a trip to Boulder, where he confronted a young girl named Norene Laurel, threatened her with a gun and forced her into her car, where he tied her up and gagged her. He drove her to a secluded area and spent the next several hours molesting her, though apparently he stopped short of rape. At 1 a.m. he released her and even provided her with taxi fare.

Though he'd changed his base of operations to Boulder, Glatman was identified and arrested almost immediately and his bond on the earlier charges revoked. Ultimately, he was never charged with the abduction in Boulder. Precisely why is unknown. Perhaps the victim was reluctant to press the case. Or perhaps it was some sort of plea bargain, since, the following December on the advice of counsel, Glatman pled guilty to charges of first-degree robbery and was sentenced to Cañon City Penitentiary.

After completing eight months of a year-long sentence, Glatman was paroled and moved back to New York with his mother. Soon, Glatman was back to his old activities. He bought a pocketknife and a realistic-looking toy gun and began stalking prey.

In Yonkers he approached a young couple, Thomas Staro and Doris Thorn, threatened them with the gun, led them to a secluded alley, tied them both up and, after relieving Staro of some $30, began sexually molesting Miss Thorn. Staro freed himself while Glatman was distracted with the young woman and rushed to her defense. Glatman drew his knife, slashed at Staro, wounding him twice, and escaped.

Relocating to Albany, he'd learned to avoid couples. In New York's capital city, he targeted lone female victims, first stealing their money then attempting to tie them up and molest them. He became known as the "Phantom Bandit."

Albany Police set up a series of rolling stakeouts throughout the city. Plainclothes officers would place any vulnerable-looking potential victims under surveillance in the hope of catching the "Phantom" in the act. On August 25, 1946, just two days shy of a month since his release from Cañon City, Glatman was spotted by Detectives James Hall and Anthony Manning as he was about to close in on another victim, unconscious of her danger until the cops moved in and placed Glatman in cuffs.

Facing multiple robbery charges, Glatman agreed to plead guilty to a reduced charge of first-degree grand larceny, and received a five-to-10-year sentence. Barely 18 years old, Glatman was already a two-time loser.

Glatman, like many psychopaths, became a master at playing the system, at showing those in authority precisely the persona they wanted to see. He became known as a model inmate at Sing Sing and was paroled in April of 1951. Charges from the Yonkers case were still pending but these were dismissed on the basis of the Constitution's "speedy trial" requirement and, within days, Glatman was on his way back to Colorado.

For the next five years Glatman lived under the comparatively tight supervision of Denver parole officers. He visited a psychiatrist once, but no effort to put him into a regular program of therapy was ever initiated. He worked sporadically as a butcher and a grocery clerk but was unemployed most of the time. In September 1956, his parole completed, Glatman, now nearly 30 years old, became a totally free man for the first time in his adult life.

Turning his sights west, he headed off to the City of the Angels, that fabled land of beautiful movie stars and gorgeous models.

Obtaining occasional work as a TV repairman, Glatman once more took up his high school hobby of photography. And his favorite subject was beautiful women. This, in itself, didn't make him that different from a lot of other amateur camera enthusiasts. In conjunction with his criminal record, though, it was a bit unsettling.

One thing Los Angeles has always had plenty of is pretty girls. But after all, pretty girls are one thing that there is always plenty of demand for. That a woman was good-looking was, of course, no guarantee of a successful career in show business and the better modeling gigs, the magazine covers or fashion shows, had more hopefuls competing for positions than positions to fill. But if a pretty girl was willing to set her sights a bit lower, she could always make a living.

There were lots of amateurs who were willing to pay "professional models" to pose for them. An attractive woman who was willing to dress (or undress) according to their specifications, to pose according to their instructions, and to let it all be recorded on film for their eventual private use and enjoyment could always find work. And available models were as close as the ads they placed in the Yellow Pages or local papers.

As for the models, $10 to $20 an hour for honest, legal, not particularly difficult work was more than a woman was likely to make in any of the other jobs readily open to her in the late '50s. Occasionally better assignments came along; newspaper ads, catalogs, or similar work. In the meantime, if some of the "private" clients were unattractive or even a bit odd, well, after all, a frog's money was as good as a prince's.

Glatman was one of the frogs. And he was beginning to find that women who existed for him only as photographic images just weren't satisfying. He wanted the real thing. Since he couldn't persuade a pretty girl to give him the real thing, he was going to have to take it. But, as a two-time loser, he was going to have to go at it carefully. He was going to have to exert total control. He obtained a pistol. And rope. Lots of rope.

Posing as a small-time commercial photographer named Johnny Glynn, Glatman had made the acquaintance of a model named Lynne Lykels. He decided that she'd be the subject of his first "special project."

Late in July 1957, Glatman showed up unannounced at Miss Lykels's West Hollywood apartment which she shared with two other girls, both of them pin-up models like Lynne. Glatman was greeted by one of Lynne's roommates, Betty Ruth Carver, who told him that Lynne was out. Glatman asked if he could see Lynne's portfolio, as long as he was there. While Betty was getting it, Glatman noticed a photograph of a singularly beautiful blonde on the living room wall. He was told that was Judy Dull, who shared the apartment with Betty and Lynne. Immediately forgetting about Lynne, Glatman said that Judy was exactly the type he was looking for and asked if her portfolio was also available.

For no better reason than that her roommate's picture had been hung on the living room wall, the noose that had, unbeknownst to her, been tightening around Lynne Lykels's neck, had suddenly been removed and placed around Judy Dull's. For the moment, that noose was still metaphorical, but it would become literal soon enough.

Two days later, on Thursday, August 1, Glatman called Judy and made arrangements to hire her for what he said was "a rush job" for a magazine. Judy, who'd already heard about this weird "Johnny Glynn" character from Betty, wasn't exactly passionate about the assignment, but the 19-year-old model was headed for a bitter battle with her estranged husband over custody of their daughter and she needed every cent she could scrape up for legal fees. They made arrangements for "Johnny" to come to her apartment at 2:00 p.m..

Glatman arrived a bit early. After introducing himself, he drove her to his apartment, less than 10 minutes away, telling her it was a "friend's studio." When they entered the sparsely furnished living room of the "studio," he told Judy that he was shooting photos for a "true detective" magazine, the kind that often featured bound and gagged women on the covers. Judy was undoubtedly aware of the kind of shots used for such magazines, though there's no record that she'd ever posed for that type of photo before. She *had* posed in lingerie and in the nude (in fact, this had been the cause of the rift between her and her husband), so while the prospect of getting tied up might have made her uncomfortable, actually wearing clothes might still have seemed like an improvement from her more typical assignments. In any case, $20 an hour was money she couldn't afford to discard. She sucked it up and got ready for the shoot and, while "Johnny" went into a another room to get some rope, changed into the skirt and sweater ensemble "Johnny" had asked her to wear to get a "girl next door" look.

When she was ready Glatman tied her wrists together behind her back, then tied her ankles and knees together. A small length of rope encircled her head to simulate a gag. He pushed up her skirt to expose a bit of thigh and began shooting.

After snapping off a number of shots of her seated and some more of her lying on the floor, he put the camera down and approached her. She probably thought he was going to untie her. He quickly disabused her of that notion.

Instead of releasing her, Glatman told Judy that he was going to leave her tied up while he "had some fun." He showed her the gun he'd been carrying concealed until that moment and told her he'd done time and would kill to keep from going back to prison.

After fondling her for several minutes, he untied her. Then, keeping her covered with the pistol, he forced her to strip. He retrieved his camera and took some more pictures of her nude. Then he raped her.

When he was done, he allowed her to dress then forced her to sit down with him on the couch while he watched television for several hours. At 10:30, he told Judy they were going to drive out to a remote rural area far from town where he'd release her. He tied her hands behind her once more and walked her down to the car. They headed east, into Riverside County. A hundred miles or so outside of Los Angeles he turned off, proceeded for another mile and stopped. He said that he wanted her to service him one more time before he set her free. For the sake of privacy, they'd leave the car and walk into the desert. Removing a blanket and some more rope from the trunk, he walked Judy away from the car and into the wilderness. When the car was no longer visible, he stopped, spread the blanket on the ground, and helped Judy to a supine position. Then he took a length of the rope and tied her ankles together.

Suddenly, he flipped her facedown, looped one end of another length of rope around her already-tied ankles, and looped the other end around her neck. In that position, with her neck and feet naturally pulling away from each other, she probably would have slowly choked to death, but Glatman didn't want to wait. He gripped the rope with both hands and pulled back with everything he had, simultaneously jamming his knee against the small of her back to hold her down. For what may have been as long as five or 10 minutes, they struggled like that. When he was sure she was dead, he removed the ropes, dug a shallow grave and rolled her body into it. Just before covering it up with loose sand, he removed her shoes, tossing one aside and taking the other with him. When he was sure the body was sufficiently well-hidden, he gathered up the ropes and the blanket and drove back to L.A.

Judy's roommates filed a missing persons report the next day. The investigating officer, Detective Sergeant David Ostroff, working out of the LA County Sheriff's West Hollywood Station, followed every available lead but could find no trace of the mysterious "Johnny Glynn."

On December 29, Judy's skeleton was discovered by a man walking his dog in the area. Although the remains yielded no indication of what had caused her death, police were proceeding on the presumption that it was a homicide. As Riverside County Sheriff's Captain Sam Hoffman put it, "She didn't bury herself." The main problem was identifying her. Glatman knew it was Judy's remains that had been found but no one else did, and precious little remained that could be used to determine her identity. Police hoped she might be identified by a ring she wore on her left hand.

Sgt. Ostroff, hearing about the remains buried in the desert, obtained a photo of the ring and showed it to Judy's husband and to her two roommates. None of them were able to identify it. Officially Judy Dull became "Jane Doe."

Glatman's itch, in the meantime, was starting to require scratching. It had been seven months since his "date" with Judy, two months since her still-unidentified remains had been found in the desert. He was pretty sure he was in the clear. The cops hadn't even made a connection between Judy and the Riverside County skeleton. They'd even *tried* to establish a connection and were unable to. He'd gotten away with it. He was sure he could get away with it again. But he decided to change his MO. Instead of making a pretense of hiring a model for a photo session, he'd make an actual date. A blind date.

He registered with a singles club operated by Patty Sullivan, using the name George Williams, was given some phone numbers and began making dates. The first woman or two he met through the Sullivan Club hadn't appealed to him. Judy Dull, after all, had been a knockout. But he was sure he'd connect with just the right girl if he persevered. And he'd know her the instant he saw her.

Shirley Ann Bridgeford, a 24-year-old single mother, was just the right girl. Divorced three years earlier, she supported herself and her two sons as a factory worker but still hoped to meet the right guy. Despite being a singularly attractive young woman, the demands of parenting two young boys by herself while simultaneously working full-time made meeting guys difficult. At the suggestion of a co-worker, she enrolled in Patty Sullivan's Lonely Hearts Club at around the same time Glatman did.

The first call she received was from a guy who introduced himself as George Williams. They made a date for Saturday, March 8. Shirley had never been a on a blind date before, so she arranged to have George greeted by a reception committee made up of her two sons, her mom, Alice Joliffe, her two sisters, Ruth and Mary, and Ruth's husband, Hubert Boggs. Just a way of letting Mr. Williams know there were a lot of people looking out for her.

If meeting Shirley's family gave Glatman any second thoughts, he quickly dismissed them. Shirley *was* just the right girl, and that was just too bad for her. But he had all the time in the world.

The couple drove down to Oceanside and got acquainted over dinner. At least *he* got acquainted with *Shirley*. Shirley, on the other hand, got acquainted with the totally fictional George Williams, successful Pasadena plumber. After dinner they returned to the car and, according to Glatman, necked for awhile until Shirley said that it was time they started back home. Glatman agreed but instead of heading back to LA, he drove southeast into San Diego County, finally parking along the shoulder of a remote mountain road. He produced his gun and demanded sex. She submitted. When he was finished he allowed her to dress, tied her up, and drove out of the mountains and into Anza-Borrego Desert State Park.

Finding a suitably deserted spot, he parked again and ordered her out of the car. Carrying the same blanket and extra rope he'd used on Judy and the same trusty camera, he forced Shirley to walk some two miles, spread out the blanket, and ordered Shirley to sit. It was perhaps 10 or 11 o'clock by this time. He informed her that he wanted to take some pictures. But he decided not to take a chance on ruining the shots with flashbulbs. There was no real hurry. She wasn't going anywhere, and he didn't have to be anyplace special. Why not enjoy this lovely woman's company for another few hours, and let her experience one more sunrise?

He tied her legs together at the ankles and knees, and gagged her with a handkerchief. They sat like that for the rest of the night. At 6:30 the next morning, Glatman shot a half a roll of film, posing Shirley in positions that emphasized her complete helplessness and vulnerability. When he decided he'd snapped enough shots, he posed her one more time, facedown. Then, instead of picking up the camera, he picked up the loose piece of rope, looped one end around Shirley's ankles and the other around her throat and slowly strangled her in the same way he'd strangled Judy.

This time he didn't even bother to bury her. Just rolled her underneath a cactus. He ripped off the buttons of her dress, fearing that they might hold fingerprints, and took her panties with him as a souvenir. This, along with Judy's shoe and the "special photos," would be placed in a plain metal toolbox that Glatman kept hidden in his home. Then he gathered up the rope, blanket, and photography equipment, returned to the car, and drove home.

Mrs. Joliffe, Shirley's panic-stricken mother, made a missing persons report to the LAPD early the next morning. Investigating officers got a good description of George Williams from Patty Sullivan, the proprietor of the dating service, from the first girl George had dated through the service, and from Shirley's family. Over at the LA County Sheriff's Office, Sergeant Ostroff, examining the description of Shirley's date, thought there was more than just a coincidental resemblance between this "George Williams" character LAPD was seeking, and "Johnny Glynn," the supposed commercial photographer he'd been looking for since August. And, for that matter, more than a few parallels in the way both women had simply dropped out of sight.

But a good physical description hadn't gotten LASO very far seven months earlier, and it didn't seem likely to move LAPD that much farther now. Two young women were missing, were in all probability dead, and it seemed pretty clear that Glynn/Williams would continue to cause beautiful young women to "disappear" until he was stopped. But neither the city police nor the sheriff's office had a clue who he really was.

For his part, Glatman was on top of the world. He'd committed two murders and had managed to stay completely off the cops' radar. Confident in his ability to kill without detection, he only waited four months to set up another "special date." The lonely hearts avenue was closed off for the moment. Perhaps it was time to hire another model.

Ruth Mercado, a 24-year-old Air Force veteran from upstate New York, had lived in Los Angeles for several years, hoping for the big break that would get her into show business. Billing herself as "Angela Rojas," she earned her keep as a nightclub stripper and pinup model. Instead of signing with an agency, she operated independently, working out of her small apartment on West Pico Boulevard, advertising her services in the daily papers.

Harvey responded to her ad on July 22, identifying himself as a magazine photographer named Frank. They made arrangements for him to come by and take some shots that evening. When he arrived, however, she told him she had to beg off, due to a sudden illness.

"I would've called you but I didn't have your number," she explained. Harvey said he'd take a rain check. She said that would be fine and asked again for his number.

"I'll call you," he said.

He returned the next evening.

"Frank, right?" she said when she opened the door to his knock.

He nodded. "Are you feeling better?"

She said that she was. He asked if she was free. Gently scolding him for not calling ahead, she invited him in.

Ruth had a pet dog, who took an instant dislike to Glatman. She apologized, scooped up the dog and put him in the bathroom. She failed to notice that Glatman didn't have a camera with him. He'd had to park some distance from Ruth's apartment building and thought carrying around camera equipment on a city street might make him stand out in some witness's memory, so he'd left his gear in the car. He'd brought his pistol, though, and when she returned, he threatened her with it.

Forcing her into the bedroom, he ordered her to undress, laid her on the bed, and repeatedly raped her for the next two hours.

When he was sated, he turned to her and told her they were going on a picnic. He ordered her to dress, tied her wrists together behind her back and draped a coat over her shoulders to hide her being tied up. With his hand on the pistol hidden in his pocket, he walked her out of the building to the car two blocks away.

Again, Glatman drove south towards Oceanside then east towards the desert. They were on the road for the rest of the night. Some time past dawn, they finally stopped at a secluded place that he felt would be private. For the rest of the day, Glatman alternated between raping her and taking pictures of her in a succession of bondage poses. That afternoon, with the desert sun beating down, Glatman moved them to a cooler spot. When the sun set, they moved once more.

Glatman ordered Ruth out of the car again, told her to take off her dress but leave her slip on. Once again he tied her up, gagged her, and posed her on the blanket. He took several more shots, using his flash equipment for the first time. Finally, he took out the same loose piece of rope he'd used on Judy Dull and Shirley Bridgeford, and tied it around Ruth's ankle and throat the same way. When he'd finally choked the life out of her, he stripped her, covered her with some loose brush, gathered up his equipment, and headed back to LA. Three murders in less than a year and the cops were no closer to him than when he'd started.

Ruth lived alone. She wasn't missed until Sunday, July 27. Her apartment manager, noticing the mail piling up in Ruth's box, knocked on her door. She got no answer but heard the dog whining piteously. Using her passkey, she found the dog and Ruth's two parakeets nearly dead from hunger and thirst.

Rather than report the odd circumstance to the police, the apartment manager wrote to Ruth's mother in Plattsburg, New York. Mrs. Mercado notified the Plattsburgh PD who in turn contacted Detective Lieutenant Marvin Jones at LAPD's Wilshire Division. He assigned Detective Sergeant Paul Light to investigate.

Light followed several leads but all of them dead-ended. A musician Ruth dated pretty regularly had an out of town gig and, consequently, an iron-clad alibi. A guy who'd harassed Ruth with a series of obscene phone calls and notes at her last apartment was also able to account for his time from Wednesday night through Thursday. No other likely suspects turned up.

Jones noticed the striking similarities between Ruth's disappearance and two other still-open missing persons cases, Judy Dull and Shirley Bridgeford. But, whereas "Johnny Glynn" and "George Williams" had very similar descriptions, Jones and Light had no suspect description at all in Ruth's case. There was no sign of a struggle at her apartment and, as unlikely as it might seem, it was possible she'd just decided to pack up and leave. In the end, all they could do was put out a bulletin to other jurisdictions. No one answered.

* * *

Now it was late in October and less than three months after Ruth's murder, Harvey was heading south again with victim number four, Lorraine Vigil, seated docilely at his side, having absolutely no idea what his plans for her were.

For awhile, he chatted amiably with Lorraine, until he hit the Santa Ana Freeway. The he became grimly silent, totally intent on the road ahead. Lorraine was no longer just a bit nervous. She was genuinely alarmed. And when they passed the last off-ramp to Anaheim she became downright frightened. Something was definitely wrong. Suddenly, he pulled off the freeway into the off-ramp leading to Tustin Ranch Road, just outside of Tustin in Orange County.

"I think we've got a flat," he said as they merged onto the road. He pulled over to the shoulder.

Lorraine started to protest but suddenly Glatman pulled out his gun and covered her with it. He told her he was an ex-con with nothing to lose. With his free hand, he pulled a length of rope from his pocket and ordered her to put her hands behind her back. Lorraine was petrified at what would happen to her if she was tied up, completely at his mercy. She begged him not to bind her wrists, but he was unrelenting.

She suddenly realized that he was using both hands to tie her up, and if he was using both hands, he couldn't be holding the gun. She pulled away from him and tried to exit the car. He grabbed her by the neck and again picked up the gun, but Lorraine wasn't going to be taken without a fight. She made a grab for the weapon and for the next few moments they struggled for it. Suddenly it went off, creasing her thigh.

The shot was as surprising to Glatman as it was to Lorraine. As he sat dazed for a moment, Lorraine decided this was her best chance to escape. She threw herself against the door and ran out onto the shoulder of the road expecting to be shot any second.

Glatman was right behind her. Shooting her wasn't the point. Making her his helpless captive was. And he needed her alive for that. He'd kill her later, at a time and place of his choosing. Now he needed to get her back into the car.

But she wasn't making it easy. He caught up to her, and managed to wrestle her down to the ground. She kicked, scratched, bit, and tried to get the gun away from him. Suddenly it was in her hand. She pointed it at him. But she had no idea how a semiautomatic pistol worked.

"If I had known how to fire it," she said later, "I believe I could have killed him."

Given time, Glatman would in all likelihood have been able to overpower her, retrieve the weapon, and regain control of the situation. But his time was about to run out.

Motorcycle Officer Thomas Mulligan of the California Highway Patrol was coming to the end of his shift and he was headed to the station to sign off duty. When he saw the couple scuffling on the shoulder of Tustin Ranch Road, he pulled over to investigate.

To Lorraine, the sight of a uniformed policeman appearing at that moment must have seemed like the embodiment of an answered prayer. She ran up to Mulligan, handed him the gun and screamed, "He's trying to kill me! Help me! He's crazy! Here's his gun! I got it away from him!"

Mulligan ordered Glatman to stand still and keep his hands visible.

"He had a lunatic stare," he said later during a press interview. "I'll never forget that wild look he had in his eyes."

Mulligan requested some backup and, within minutes, was joined by a unit from Tustin PD, two more CHP officers, and a couple of deputies from the Orange County Sheriff's Office, which held primary jurisdiction since the incident had occurred in an unincorporated part of the county. Mulligan turned Glatman over to the custody of the two deputy sheriffs.

Once Glatman was identified and booked, an APB went out to neighboring agencies, including LASO and LAPD, requesting any information they might have on similar cases involving photography models. The bulletin reached the desk of Lieutenant Jones at Wilshire Division, who immediately thought of Ruth Mercado. Noting that Glatman also fit the "Johnny Glynn" and "George Williams" descriptions from the Dull and Bridgeford disappearances and that Glatman's LA address was close to the Wilshire station, he decided to drive out there and have a look. The wall of Glatman's living room was covered with pinups, some showing women in bondage. That was enough to convince Jones.

He sent two men from the Wilshire homicide detail, Sergeants Pierce Brooks and Elmer Jackson, down to Santa Ana to see if anything connected Glatman to the Bridgeford or Mercado cases. Meanwhile, Captain Jim Bruton and Sergeant Jack Lawton of LASO's Homicide Bureau were already on their way to determine if Glatman had anything to do with Judy Dull's disappearance.

The detectives decided to question Glatman in shifts. Lawton would handle the interrogation on Judy Dull, Brooks on Shirley Bridgeford, and Jackson on Ruth Mercado. For the next two days they grilled him continuously. Finally he broke.

"You must've found my toolbox," he said. "You're just playing with me now."

Captain Hertel, commander of the LAPD's citywide Central Homicide Division, was notified of Glatman's reference to a toolbox. While the three detectives kept at Glatman in Orange County, Hertel obtained a search warrant and sent a team to Glatman's home. In addition to the pinups seen by Lieutenant Jones when he gave the place a brief once-over, they found over a thousand dollars worth of pornographic material; hundreds of photos of women, nude or in black lingerie, being bound and tortured.

They found dozens of personal snapshots Glatman had taken of his television screen. He'd apparently sat by the television with his camera at the ready and snapped a shot every time an actress was shown bound and gagged. In the garage they found the toolbox, containing the damning evidence of Glatman's string of murders.

They had Glatman absolutely nailed for three murders. The next step was to determine if he was good for any others. For a brief time, he was considered a viable suspect in virtually every unsolved LA-area homicide involving a young female victim, including the murder of Geneva "Jean" Ellroy, a divorced nurse, whose now-orphaned 10-year-old son, Lee Earle, would someday change his given name to "James" and, in an effort to purge the demons instilled by her death, grow up to write slickly hard-edged cop novels set in '50s-era Los Angeles. Lawton, who'd also caught the Ellroy homicide, questioned Glatman at length about the case. Glatman steadfastly denied involvement in any other murders except the ones he'd already confessed to.

"Aren't three enough?" he asked. "They can only give me one shot of gas."

Once they had the details of the three murders down on paper, they signed Glatman out of the Orange County Jail and took him to San Diego County, where he showed them the dump sites for Shirley Bridgeford and Ruth Mercado. Their remains were gathered up and processed. Three days later they took him to Riverside County where he showed them the approximate spot that he'd buried Judy Dull. A name could finally be attached to the skeleton that had remained unidentified for so many months.

The murderer had been caught and the evidence that was certain to secure his conviction had been gathered. So far the investigation had been a model of interdepartmental cooperation. Now the problem was deciding who had primary jurisdiction. Seven different police agencies either had been or would be involved in some key aspect of the investigation and four different district attorneys' offices had a claim on prosecuting him. All four victims, including Lorraine Vigil, had been abducted from LA County. Lorraine had been shot and wounded in Orange County. Shirley and Ruth had been murdered in San Diego County, Judy in Riverside County. The Glatman case had all the makings of a jurisdictional quagmire. Ultimately it was agreed that the murders were clearly more important than the non-lethal crimes that had occurred in Los Angeles and Orange, and that San Diego's two murders trumped Riverside's one. San Diego would prosecute the Bridgeford and Mercado homicides. Riverside would hold the Dull prosecution in reserve in case San Diego failed to secure a death penalty.

Glatman, for his part, was doing everything he could to make things easier. After being turned over to the custody of the San Diego County Sheriff's Office, he repeated his detailed confessions to Lieutenant Tom Isbell and Sergeant Robert Majors. Curiously, though he made no effort to duck responsibility for his crimes, he did go to some lengths to make them seem less depraved. It's anybody's guess whether he was trying to convince the detectives or himself of his relative normalcy.

He claimed, for example, that his victims "seemed to enjoy" having sex with him. Never mind that he was threatening them with death if they resisted. He seemed to *need* to believe that Judy, Shirley, and Ruth considered him a skillful lover.

As for the murders, he insisted that he never wanted to kill anyone. He just wanted to have sex. He only killed the girls to prevent them from testifying against him. He was already a two-time loser, after all. A third felony conviction could put him away for life. It wasn't as if killing those women brought him any *enjoyment*.

In retrospect, those justifications ring hollow and false. In the first place, Judy's two roommates and Shirley's entire family had gotten as good a look at him as his victims, so the assertion that he killed only to eliminate witnesses has no logical basis. Aside from that, he was armed with a gun and if the murders were really intended as coldly clinical acts to keep his victims from testifying, he could have quickly and mercifully shot them. Instead he slowly strangled them in a particularly cruel and vicious manner, using the rope that was simultaneously his instrument of captivity, of pleasure, and finally, of murder. Killing those women brought him nothing *but* enjoyment. Still, if he wasn't admitting to the perverted motives that induced him to commit the murders, he *was* freely admitting the murders themselves, and that was the important thing.

His spirit of cooperation continued once the case came to court on November 21. Against the advice of his attorney, Willard Whittinghill, he pled guilty to two counts of first degree murder. The trial, in consequence, was dispensed with and the state was able to proceed directly to the penalty hearing. This was held on December 15, 1958, in San Diego Superior Court, Department 4, presided over by Judge John Hewicker. After hearing the evidence, Hewicker sentenced Glatman to the gas chamber.

"There are some crimes," he said in pronouncing judgment, "that are so revolting that, in my opinion, there is only one penalty that can be imposed. And that is the death penalty."

Glatman contested neither the conviction nor the sentence but, according to California law, all death penalty cases were automatically appealed to the State Supreme Court as a fail-safe against this ultimate penalty being visited on an innocent defendant. In the absence of any new evidence calling Glatman's guilt into question, Whitinghill's only alternative was to allege that Judge Hewicker had made a reversible procedural error when he considered, during his deliberation on the sentence, evidence of the murder of Judy Dull and the abduction and assault of Lorraine Vigil, since neither of those offenses were part of the charge. The Court rejected this argument and, in a unanimous decision, affirmed the sentence on June 5th, 1959.

At 10:01 a.m. on Friday, September 18, 1959, Glatman was strapped into the chair in San Quentin's lethal gas chamber. He had only one comment about his impending execution.

"It's better this way."

At 10:03, the cyanide gas was released. By 10:12, he was pronounced dead.

One of the official witnesses to the execution was Detective Sergeant Pierce Brooks, there as LAPD's designated representative. Of the many police officers involved in some aspect of the Glatman investigation, Brooks was the one who would become most identified with the case, less because of his particular contribution to the investigation itself, considerable though that was, than because he alone was able to see the long-term ramifications of the type of crimes Glatman had committed.

Despite the inability of law enforcement to connect Glatman to any cases except the ones he confessed to, Brooks had always remained un-convinced. Glatman obviously enjoyed capturing and killing beautiful women and he'd perfected a technique for acquiring victims that heightened his pleasure. Given the prolificacy of other multiple murderers of the era, like Stephen Nash (who admitted to 11 murders, calling himself the "King of the Killers") or Wisconsin's Ed Gein (who was convicted of two murders, and strongly suspected of four more), it struck Brooks as unlikely that Glatman had been responsible for only three. But there was no informational system that Brooks could use to check his theory. In the absence of such a system, Brooks was reduced to the painstaking and unscientific method of checking articles on similar cases from the central library's out-of-town newspaper files. He was never able to connect Glatman to another murder but the labor-intensive methods he used to investigate that possibility convinced him that there had to be a better way, some sort of centralized database where the kind of information he'd been looking for could be collected, collated, and analyzed.

Over the next few years, as Brooks was transferred to the elite Central Homicide Division, rising through the ranks to eventually become a Detective Captain commanding that division, he became legendary in law enforcement circles as one of the best homicide detectives in the country, and one of the foremost experts on a particular kind of murderer, a type that would eventually come to be referred to as a "serial killer." After his retirement from LAPD, his appointments to police chief positions first in Springfield, Oregon, and then in Lakewood, Colorado, added the extra luster of being one of the country's most forward-thinking law enforcement administrators to his already glowing reputation as one of the country's best criminal investigators. All of this gave him the clout to bring his concept of a central informational "clearing house" to fruition.

In 1982 Brooks testified before the US Senate in an effort to persuade them to appropriate funds for a computerized program that would collate and analyze data on unsolved crimes from all over the country. This would help to determine, as early as possible, whether there were patterns indicating that a serial killer was operating. Convinced by his presentation, Congress voted to provide funding for a Violent Criminal Apprehension Program (ViCAP for short). On May 29, 1985, more than a quarter of a century after Glatman's murder spree planted the seed for the idea in his mind, Pierce Brooks was present at the FBI's Behavioral Science Unit in Quantico, Virginia, to watch the ViCAP computers go into operation for the first time. It was, in many ways, the crowning moment of his career.

But that was all in the future. On that particular September morning in 1959, his mind wasn't on the long-range effects of the case. He was focused on Glatman himself, on Glatman's victims, and particularly on Shirley Bridgeford, whom he'd personally represented in the interrogation room. This was a case he *had* to see all the way to its final conclusion. His thoughts about the impending execution most likely echoed Glatman's.

"It's better this way."

In a long and distinguished law enforcement career, Brooks would eventually put, or help to put, 10 different killers on Death Row, but Glatman was the first and, ultimately, he'd be the only one whose execution Brooks would personally witness. The sight of the condemned man gasping and choking as the cyanide gas took effect would haunt Brooks for the rest of his life.

When asked later what his thoughts about the death penalty were, now that he'd actually seen it administered, he said, "I'm still not against capital punishment. But I've got to be *real* sure of my cases from now on. *Way* past reasonable doubt."

If nothing else, witnessing the execution of the pathetic, jug-eared nebbish whom the press had dubbed "The Lonely Hearts Killer" turned Pierce Brooks, already an investigator with a reputation for single-minded diligence, into the most rigorously thorough homicide detective in Los Angeles.

FURTHER READING

By far, the most detailed account of the Glatman case is Michael Newton's *Rope* (Pocket, 1998). Prolific as both a true-crime journalist and as a novelist, Newton is something of an authority on serial killers and is also the author of such general reference works on the subject as *Hunting Humans* (Breakdown Productions, 1991) and *The Encyclopedia of Serial Killers* (Facts on File, 2000).

Joseph Geringer's e-book, *Harvey Murray Glatman: First of the Signature Killers* (Dark Horse Multi-Media, 2000) is, as far as I've been able to determine, the only other book length treatment of the case. An accurate, highly readable account, it's available free of charge on the Crime Library website www.crimelibrary.com.

James Ellroy's *My Dark Places* (Knopf, 1996) is a non-fiction memoir describing the traumatic effects of growing up the son of a murder victim whose murderer was never caught. Because Glatman was briefly a suspect in his mother's death, Ellroy talks about the "Lonely Hearts Killer" at some length.

Joseph Wambaugh's *The Onion Field* (Delacorte, 1973) tells the story of another infamous kidnap-murder investigated by Pierce Brooks and goes into some detail about Brooks's reactions to witnessing Glatman's execution.

Among the many books that either mention or give short accounts of the Glatman case are *The Serial Killers* (W.H. Allen, 1990) by Colin Wilson and Donald Seaman; *Killers Among Us, Book II: Sex, Madness, and Mass Murder* (Warner, 1997) by Colin Wilson and Damon Wilson; *Signature Killers* (Pocket, 1997) by Robert D. Keppel with William J. Birnes; *The Evil That Men Do* (St. Martin's, 1998) by Steven G. Michaud with Roy Hazelwood; *Whoever Fights Monsters* (St. Martin's, 1992) by Robert K. Ressler and Thomas Schactman; *Fallen Angels* (Facts on File, 1986) by Marvin Wolf and Katherine Mader; *My Name's Friday* (Cumberland, 2001) by Michael J. Hayde; *The Encyclopedia of American Crime* (Facts on File, 1982) by Carl Sifakis; and *The Encyclopedia of World Crime* (CrimeBooks, 1990) by Jay Robert Nash .

THE "LONELY HEARTS KILLER" IN FICTION

In 1965, a half-dozen years after Glatman's execution, Jack Webb was contacted by executives at Universal Studios, whose parent organization, Music Corporation of America, had bought the rights to *Dragnet* more than 10 years earlier, and asked if he'd be interested in directing and starring in a two-hour *Dragnet* movie for broadcast on his old network, NBC. A multi-millionaire several times over thanks to that MCA sale, Webb nevertheless lived for his work and he hadn't worked in two years. He jumped at the chance. He immediately got in touch with Chief William Parker at LAPD to see what cases might be ripe for fictionalization. Parker turned him over to Pierce Brooks, now a Captain of Detectives and the commander of the Homicide Division. Brooks dug out the Glatman file and suggested it might make a hell of a *Dragnet* story. Webb agreed, and got in touch with one of his closest friends, Oscar-winning screenwriter Richard Breen, about turning it into a script. Brooks became the film's police technical advisor.

The film, completed and ready for airing in 1966, so impressed network and studio honchos that it led to the revival of the series from 1967 to 1970. For reasons both complicated and trivial, the film was not actually broadcast until 1969, during the third season of that revived series. But when it finally did make it onto the screen it was a ratings blockbuster.

The show's famous introductory phrase notwithstanding, Webb and Breen changed a bit more than just the names. The crimes of the fictionalized Glatman figure (called "Negler" in the film) all take place within the municipal limits of Los Angeles, rather than the whole length and breadth of Southern California so that LAPD, in the person of Joe Friday, could be depicted as the only involved agency. A completely unrelated crime, the murder of a man who closely resembles the suspect Joe and his partner are pursuing (but who they don't find out is someone else until after they've solved his murder), is worked into the plot. And the real-life rescue of the fourth victim by a passing CHP motorcycle cop is blown up into a full-scale hostage situation played out against a driving rainstorm. Despite all the fictionalized details, the movie was easily recognizable as deriving from the Glatman case.

It's also one of the best things Webb ever did on film; suspenseful, well-acted, well-written, with touches of tragic irony, and Webb's signature visual style in full vigor. And for all of Webb's reputation for seeing the world in unnuanced shades of black and white, it's worth noting that Negler (ably portrayed by Vic Perrin) is, despite his awful crimes, made to seem oddly sympathetic. This *Dragnet* telefeature, the first fictional treatment of the "Lonely Hearts Killer" case, is also far and away the best.

Best-selling suspense novelist Mary Higgins Clark first heard of the Glatman case when she attended a lecture on serial killers given by FBI Agent Robert Ressler, one of the Bureau's top criminal profilers. Intrigued by the idea of a serial killer who used newspaper ads to troll for victims, she incorporated some elements of the Glatman case into her novel *Loves Music, Loves to Dance* (Simon and Schuster, 1991). In an interview that appeared in the paperback reprint edition of the book, she described the effect hearing about the case had on her.

Set in New York rather than Los Angeles, the novel's villain kills far more victims over a far longer period of time than Glatman. And, in sharp contrast to the real-life "Lonely Hearts Killer," Clark's fictional counterpart is a handsome, successful professional who's highly attractive to women. Neither does he display the bondage fetishes that marked Glatman's crimes. Where Glatman responded to an ad placed by one of his victims, Clark's villain places the ads himself and kills women who respond to them. Like Glatman, he does photograph his crimes, though he takes videos rather than still shots. And he does steal one of his victim's shoes in each case, mirroring Glatman's theft of one of Judy Dull's shoes.

Ressler acted as Clark's technical advisor while the novel was being written and served as the model for heroic federal cop Vince D'Ambrosio who conducts the official investigation of the case while the spunky heroine conducts an unofficial one. A TV-movie version aired on the Pax Network in 2001 failed to do justice to the novel.

Ads for the long-running TV series *Law & Order* described the plots of its episodes as being "ripped from the headlines." Often the cases that provided fodder for *L&O* scripts were so recent that the fictionalized court cases are disposed of on TV long before similar closure occurs in real life. However, in "Vengeance," an episode from the second season, the writers (Michael Chernuchin, Rene Balcer, and Peter Greenberg) go all the way back to 1958 to find some headlines from which to "rip" their plotline. The story involves a mild-mannered ex-con who becomes a suspect in the murder of a beautiful young girl whose body has been found with rope burns on the wrists and ankles. As the cops investigate, it becomes evident that their suspect is a serial killer, and this is confirmed when a search turns up a box containing photographs of all his victims in various stages of bondage. To this point, the story is recognizably derived from the Glatman case but once the cops turn the plot over to the prosecutors it begins to diverge.

First of all, the search is declared illegal, so the photographs and other evidence arising from it are suppressed. Second, there's a subplot involving the victim's mother, who claims that her daughter was in Connecticut when she received the call that led to her abduction and eventual murder. If she's telling the truth, it means that the State of Connecticut can claim jurisdiction. The Connecticut DA is certain that the photos will be admitted in a Connecticut court. Moreover, Connecticut has a death penalty while New York does not. If the Manhattan DA's Office will not oppose extradition, a conviction in Connecticut is a deadbang certainty. Assistant DA Ben Stone (Michael Moriarty) is opposed to the death penalty, however, and, since he's sure the victim's mother is lying, feels ethically bound to prosecute the case in New York, even if the chances for conviction are much slimmer. In other words, the inter-jurisdictional cooperation, the careful gathering of evidence so its legality was unquestioned, and the ease with which a conviction was obtained, all of which marked the real-life case, are all turned on their head in *L&O*'s fictionalized depiction. Ably directed by Daniel Sackheim, "Vengeance" is a very interesting look at what *might* have happened in the Glatman case had things been different.

THE WINDIEST COP IN THE WINDY CITY

Chicago Mysteries

The problem with writing a true crime article for which a Chicago setting is the only limitation, is that in Chicago there's so much true crime to choose from. Al Capone alone can provide fodder for dozens of such articles. The St. Valentine's Day massacre. The murder of Chicago *Tribune* reporter Jake Lingle. The Pineapple Primary. The Chicago connection to the Lindbergh kidnapping. Capone was at the root of all of these stories and many more besides.

And while he was arguably the most famous, Scarface wasn't the only colorful mobster Chicago ever produced. His predecessor Johnny Torrio, his rivals Dion O'Bannion and "Bugs" Moran, his successors Frank "The Enforcer" Nitti, Paul "The Waiter" Ricca, Sam Giancanna, and Tony "Joe Batters" Accardo all did their part to make Chicago and the Outfit synonymous.

Nor have such urban, corporate-style gangsters held a monopoly on Chicago crime. The more traditional, more rural desperadoes like Alvin Karpis, the Barker brothers, "Baby-Face" Nelson, and "Pretty Boy" Floyd, whose ill-gotten gains were earned by old-fashioned banditry rather than new-fangled racketeering, tended to range throughout the Midwest in their lawless pursuits but generally used Chicago as a sort of unofficial base. The most famous of them, John Dillinger, died in a shootout with federal officers in front of a Chicago movie theatre.

And that's just the professional league. Chicago's had its share of celebrated amateur criminals. Thrill-killers like Leopold and Loeb, or Richard Speck. Serial murderers like William "The Lipstick Killer" Heirens or John Wayne Gacy. They've left their mark on Chicago, too.

And, despite its unsavory reputation, Chicago's even managed to produce a few good guys. A young Scottish immigrant named Allan Pinkerton, for example, began his crime-fighting career in Chicago, first as an official policeman then as America's first private eye in a small two-room office.

US Justice Department Operative Eliot Ness and US Treasury Agent Frank Wilson earned roughly equal claims to the title of the "Man Who

Got Capone." Caught between the hammer of Ness's flying squad, now known throughout the world as the "Untouchables," and the anvil of Wilson's staff of financial investigators, the Big Fellow suffered a pounding that didn't end until he entered his prison cell at Alcatraz.

Federal officers who followed, such as Melvin Purvis and Bill Roemer, would also forge enviable, even legendary records as gang-busters; while local cops like Chief of Detectives John Stege, Robbery Lieutenant Frank Pape, South Side Detective Sylvester "Two-Gun Pete" Washington, DA's Investigator Pat Roche, and Sheriff's Lieutenant Jack Reed would be heralded as tough, honest, conscientious officers in a time and place where one had to be *extra*-tough to be the least bit honest and conscientious.

Without a doubt, however, the most colorful, the most bombastic, the most flamboyant, and the most fun-loving of all Windy City lawmen was Detective Clifton R. Wooldridge.

Wooldridge, who served in the Chicago Police Department from 1888 until 1910, was never one to hide his light under a bushel. He referred to himself as "the world's greatest detective, the incorruptible Sherlock Holmes of America," adding that "no braver, more honest, or efficient police officer ever wore a star or carried a club."

But if he seemed boastful, he had plenty to boast about. In his two decades on the job, he made nearly 20,000 arrests, roughly a third of them felony arrests. This averages out to three a day for every day he carried a badge. That would be impressive enough, but when you consider that he achieved a 65% conviction rate to go along with that arrest record, his feat becomes truly amazing. He didn't just do quantity police work; he did quality police work.

A veteran of nearly 50 gun battles, he was wounded 23 times. Though an expert shot, he never once tried to kill an opponent, rendering himself especially vulnerable in shootouts. "A policeman's duty is to preserve order," he once said, "not to kill." He lived, and often nearly died, following that credo.

In his 22 years of service, he turned down hundreds of bribe offers ranging from $500 to $20,000. He recovered hundreds of thousands of dollars in stolen cash and property, raided and closed over a hundred brothels (in the process rescuing hundreds of under-aged girls, kidnapped or enticed under false pretenses, from white slavery), broke up over a hundred fraudulent matrimonial agencies, shut down some 75 opium dens, seized and destroyed 60 wagonloads of pornography, closed down 300 illegal gambling concerns, and still found time to write several books about his career before finally retiring.

Born on February 25, 1854, in Franklin County, Kentucky, Wooldridge was in his 30's before deciding to make a career in law enforcement. Before joining the Chicago force, he worked as an office clerk in St. Louis, an employee of the US Signal Bureau in Washington, a prospector and miner in Colorado, a railroader in the Dakotas, Colorado, and Arkansas, and a newspaperman in Denver. In 1886 he arrived in Chicago and started a paper geared for professional railroad men called *The Switchmen's Journal*, but a fire put him out of business. He returned briefly to railroading until a prolonged strike left him unemployed once again. He finally applied to the police department, not out of any sense of mission, but for the most prosaic of all reasons. He needed to make a living. The sense of mission would come later.

While still a uniformed officer, Wooldridge was assigned to look into complaints of a "disorderly" house in his precinct. Other officers detailed to the case had been unable to secure the evidence needed to shut the house down. After studying the exterior of the house from all sides, Wooldridge had an idea. In those days, buildings were often fitted with rope/pulley contraptions outside the windows for lowering and raising buckets, making it easier to empty garbage and ashes from the upper floors to the alley. There was such an apparatus alongside the suspect dwelling. Wooldridge tied the rope to a large vinegar barrel in which a couple of peepholes had been drilled, had two partners raise him up to the windows and personally witnessed enough criminal activity to put the place out of business. This imaginative piece of surveillance helped earn him a position in the detective bureau.

As a plainclothes investigator, Wooldridge's main stock-in-trade was his penchant for bold (and often zany) acts of derring-do which made him the darling of Chicago's daily papers. The most famous example of this was his courageous, yet comical, arrest of a stick-up man named Eugene Buchanan. Buchanan, wanted for a particularly vicious robbery during which he kicked out one of his victim's eyes, bragged that he "ate cops for breakfast." He was particularly contemptuous of Wooldridge, who, though wiry and athletic, was small of stature and easily underestimated.

When Wooldridge encountered the burly thug in an alley near the Levee District (the roaring downtown area that was later, after the arrival of public transit, dubbed the Loop), he was met with violent resistance as Buchanan, kicked, bit, head-butted, and clubbed the determined little detective in an effort to peel him off. In the course of the battle, Buchanan ran his head between Wooldridge's legs in an attempt to lift and throw him. Instead, Wooldridge clamped down on Buchanan's neck with both legs, pulled his gun, screwed it behind Buchanan's ear and ordered him to march to the Harrison Street Police Station while carrying the diminutive sleuth on his shoulders. Being publicly forced to give Wooldridge a seven-block-long piggy-back ride lowered Buchanan's status in Chicago's criminal community considerably.

Another time, during a rooftop foot pursuit of two suspects, Wooldridge witnessed his quarries leap from the roof to a soft pile of refuse below. Unhesitatingly, Wooldridge plunged after them, landing headfirst with such force that it took the combined efforts of two other officers arriving a few minutes later to pull him loose. Though stuck fast in the pile of garbage, Wooldridge managed to successfully accomplish the arrests, grabbing hold of both of his suspects, one in each hand, before they made their escape.

Wooldridge had his share of spectacular shootouts, too. Once, a killer named Henry Foster barricaded himself in a bar, keeping police at bay with sporadic gunfire. Wooldridge arrived on the scene, assessed the situation and, picking up a wooden plank as a makeshift shield, charged the saloon, revolver in hand, screaming at the top of his lungs. Foster was in the middle of taking a drink when Wooldridge burst in. Dropping his bottle, he picked up his gun but, rattled by Wooldridge's sudden appearance, panicked and wound up shooting himself. He survived his self-inflicted wound to be hanged a few months later.

Another time, Wooldridge came upon a burglary in progress in a residence on Michigan Avenue, a few miles south of what is now known as "The Magnificent Mile." The trio of burglars opened fire on Wooldridge as he attempted to take them into custody. One shot blew off his hat, grazed his skull, and cut off a lock of hair. Another hit him just below the belly, but was deflected by his belt buckle, in all probability saving his life. Crack shot Wooldridge returned fire and was able to take all three of the thieves alive.

Wooldridge solved more than his share of interesting homicide cases. Some were bizarre, like the murder of the wealthy socialite who was shot in his library while his family in the next room heard nothing. The slug, unlike any Wooldridge had ever seen, was a triangular missile that seemed to suggest a dart more than a bullet. No other clue presenting itself, Wooldridge took to carrying the mysterious slug around with him. The case was finally solved some months later in a weird twist that was equally suggestive of both Edgar Allan Poe and television shows such as *Lassie* or *Flipper*.

While walking in the neighborhood where the murder took place, Wooldridge noticed a black cat following him. Not particularly superstitious, Wooldridge nevertheless had no great fondness for cats and the sight of a black one following him made him uneasy. Catching up to the detective, the cat started to tug on his trousers as if he wanted Wooldridge to follow him. Curious, Wooldridge obliged. The cat led him to an alley where he began digging in the ground. Wooldridge looked closer at the object the cat was digging at and found it to be an oddly shaped air-gun, the barrel of which fit the slug from the murder perfectly. Wooldridge traced the gun to its inventor and, eventually, the man who purchased it. The murderer turned out to be the victim's prospective son-in-law. Wooldridge nailed him one day before he was scheduled to marry his victim's daughter.

Some of his homicide investigations had their humorous side, like the case of a barkeep named Reilly who murdered the husband of a woman he coveted and, with her help, tried to pass it off as having occurred in the course of a robbery. Wooldridge managed to break the widow's story when he revealed to her that Reilly was often known to spend the night at the home of a certain Mrs. O'Brien. In a jealous rage, the widow recanted on the alibi she'd given Reilly, unaware (because Wooldridge had somehow neglected to tell her) that the Mrs. O'Brien with whom Reilly spent his nights was Reilly's mother.

Wooldridge was particularly zealous in his campaigns against vice and prostitution. One of his most famous cases involved the breaking up of a white slavery ring run by Mary Hastings, the most notorious madam in the Levee. Hastings habitually traveled around the Midwest, enticing young ladies looking for work to accompany her to Chicago. She had no trouble finding naive and trusting girls to join her. Upon arriving at her establishment, Hastings, her lover Tom Gaynor, and other henchmen, physically overpowered the hapless girls, stripped them of their clothing, and imprisoned them in locked rooms. Eventually, they would either submit to the attentions of Hastings's clients or have those attentions forced on them.

On September 26, 1895, four of the prisoners escaped, found the nearest police station and reported their captivity. Wooldridge arrived at

Hasting's establishment shortly after receiving the report, rescued five more victims and placed the procuress under arrest.

A series of delaying tactics, efforts at intimidating the witnesses, and attempts to bribe or discredit Wooldridge all followed. The tactics were ultimately successful. Hastings was able to finally avoid prosecution when, worn down by the endless delays, the witnesses against her scattered. But the victory was Pyrrhic. Hastings had spent the bulk of her fortune in fines, forfeited bonds, bribes, and legal fees. Bereft of property, she left Chicago after her case was dismissed in May of 1897.

Wooldridge was able to handle another Levee madam, Big Susan Winslow, with more of his characteristic high-spiritedness. Big Susan weighed some 450 pounds and her sheer girth made her proof against any attempt to take her into custody. Named in more than a score of arrest warrants, no officer could figure a way to serve her because no door or window of her house was big enough for her to fit through. How she managed to get into the house in the first place was a mystery that would have baffled John Dickson Carr.

Wooldridge drove up to the back door of Big Susan's dive in a horse-drawn patrol wagon, removed the door from its hinges and sawed an opening around the doorframe large enough for Big Susan to pass through. Then he unhitched one of the horses, tied one end of a rope around its neck, tied the other end around Big Susan and simply had the horse pull her out of the house.

In failing health, Wooldridge finally retired from the Chicago Police in 1910. He died five years later. One of the Chicago papers for which Wooldridge had provided such rich material noted that it was "sad to see the end of such a source of levity in the grim business of crime battling."

FURTHER READING

For those interested in further information on the man the Chicago underworld dubbed "that damned little flycop," the available material is sparse. There are good, though brief, entries on Wooldridge in Carl Sifakis's *Encyclopedia of American Crime* (Facts on File, 1982) and Jay Robert Nash's *Encyclopedia of World Crime* (CrimeBooks, Inc., 1990).

Wooldridge himself is credited with writing *Hands Up! In the World of Crime* (Stanton & Van Vliet, 1901), though in the text Wooldridge is referred to in the third person and it's very possible he utilized a ghost. *Hands Up!* is a collection of accounts of his various cases arranged in no particular order. A follow-up, *Twenty Years a Detective* (self-published, 1906), also contains a bit of biographical information as well as accounts of some more cases, but is mostly a "how-to" book explaining how to be alert for con games. Both books deal almost exclusively with Wooldridge's professional life, and nothing I've been able to turn up in researching this article indicates whether or not he was ever married, whether he had children, what his childhood was like, nor any other details of his personal life.

Like so many fictional detectives, Clifton Wooldridge seems to have had no life apart from his job.

CENTS-LESS KILLING

Murder in Transit

In the 1880s and '90s, train robbery, particularly out West, was regarded as the most potentially lucrative of criminal enterprises. It was risky, true, but many outlaws were willing to take their chances for the treasures that were routinely shipped on express cars.

But as the 19th century gave way to the 20th, train robbery suddenly declined. By 1907 William Pinkerton, long-time guardian of the railroads, declared the train robber "almost extinct," and by 1909 train robbery was so infrequent that it wasn't even included on the agenda of a national convention of railroad police held that year.

There were a number of reasons for this decline. Better, more strategically advantageous deployment of railroad police and other law enforcement personnel, for one. Congress declaring train robbery a federal offense, for another. And the simple fact that, as the population of the western states and territories continued its rapid growth, with that growing population more and more interconnected through an ever-widening network of telegraph and telephone lines, the wide-open frontier that had spawned the type of outlaw most inclined to rob trains was disappearing.

Perhaps the main reason for the decline in train robberies, however, was the introduction of a parcel service by the US Post Office. Shipping packages through the mail was far less expensive than shipping them through a private express company and as express companies became less likely to be carrying items worth stealing, express cars, in turn, were less likely to become the targets of bandits. Mail cars, on the other hand, though they were now actually carrying the valuable items that outlaws coveted, were a lot more difficult to rob, since they were also carrying lots of stuff that wouldn't do the outlaws any good at all. There wasn't time go through dozens of mail sacks to find the good stuff. And the sacks were too big and bulky to steal them all and then sort through them at their leisure. The game was no longer worth the candle.

In the 1920s, however, railroads suddenly and inexplicably experienced an alarming upsurge in train robbery. The increase was so severe that postal clerks were all issued firearms to defend against hold-ups. When, despite this, train robberies continued to increase, a thousand US

Marines were seconded to the Post Office as guards and given the order that if a successful mail robbery occurred "there must be a Marine dead at the post of duty."

Authorities puzzled over the reason for the increase but just as the decline at the turn of the century probably was, ultimately, the consequence of a change in postal procedures, so, in all likelihood, was the sudden upturn following World War I. The valuable stuff, the negotiable Treasury bonds, the gold and silver, the jewelry and precious stones, were now almost always being sent by *registered* mail. And since registered mail was segregated from the rest, robbers no longer had to sort through dozens of sacks to find the loot. Further, the regularity and predictability of mail made it relatively easy to find out about important shipments. Train robbery, for the first time in nearly two decades, was once again potentially lucrative.

It was this lure of sudden riches that tempted three brothers to commit the most brutal train robbery of the 20th century, the so-called "Siskiyou Outrage."

Twin brothers Ray and Roy D'Autremont and their younger half-brother, Hugh, had grown up in Oregon, thrilling to the exploits of legendary sibling outlaws like the Jameses, the Daltons, and the Youngers. Aside from this early childhood identification with famous criminals, Ray, who had been a member of the Industrial Workers of the World and who'd spent a year in jail for his IWW activities, was developing a deep and abiding contempt for big-time capitalists.

"Hatred ate away at my compassion," he would say later, "as I saw how the people in power cheated and stole from the masses. Thousands of men and women were starving and dying. Thousands more, honest working men, were receiving less than half of what they should."

Following Ray's release from prison, he and Roy made their way to Chicago, where they hoped to fulfill their childhood dreams of big-time crime by joining one of the Prohibition gangs then so active in the Windy City. Mob bosses were apparently unimpressed with their résumés, however, and the twins were unable to find entry-level work in urban organized crime.

It's a bit difficult to reconcile Ray's loudly voiced political views with a career in the rackets. He can't have seriously believed that working for someone like Al Capone or Bugs Moran would advance the Revolution and, in any case, his later activities indicated that he was less concerned with the redistribution of wealth, Robin Hood style, than with bettering his own lot.

He wanted to rob from the rich.

And keep it.

Since he and Roy were receiving no encouragement in Chicago, they returned to the Pacific Northwest where Roy, who was already showing signs of the crippling mental illness that would plague him later in life, found work as a lumberjack.

As the twins pondered what direction their criminal enterprise should take, a man named Roy Gardiner was making headlines in California with a series of raids on trains and mail trucks. Gardiner eventually netted more than $350,000 before being captured.

Roy and Ray were inspired. Look how much Gardiner had gotten away with! His problem, they reasoned, was that he ran his string out too long. If the twins simply made one really good strike then quit, they could be set for life.

Recruiting younger brother Hugh, the twins began closely monitoring the movements of Southern Pacific's Train 13, the *Gold Special,* a passenger express from Portland to San Francisco, so named because it once carried—and occasionally still did carry—large quantities of gold. They noted that at Tunnel 13 (a half-mile bore a few miles south of Siskiyou, Oregon, and a few miles north of the California state line) the train, coming to a fairly steep downhill grade on the other side of the tunnel, had to slow down in order to test its brakes per railroad regulations.

Keeping their ears open, the D'Autremonts heard that on October 11, 1923 the mail car of the *Gold Special* would be carrying more than a half-million dollars in gold and currency, and began planning the job with meticulous care. After gathering the equipment they'd need to carry out their plan, they camped out in the woods near the tunnel and waited for the fateful day.

Shortly before noon on October 11, Train 13 slowly entered Tunnel 13. Roy and Ray jumped on the train as it slowly passed and worked their way over the engine tender as the train slowly made its way through the tunnel. When the engine emerged from the tunnel, the twins, both wearing overalls, their faces covered with makeshift masks, jumped into the steam engine, covered the engineer, Sidney Bates, and his fireman, Marvin Seng, with shotguns, and ordered them to stop the train. Bates immediately complied. Both the engine and the tender had completed the exit from the tunnel. The mail car was half in and half out. The rest of the train, passenger cars, dining car, baggage cars, and sleepers, were still in the bore.

Hugh was waiting at the south end of the tunnel with a home-made bomb. Roy and Ray ordered the two trainmen off of the engine. While Ray continued to cover them, Roy and Hugh set up the bomb on the doorsill of the mail car, apparently reasoning that if they set off an explosion while the mail car was still in the tunnel, it would muffle the sound of the blast.

They detonated the bomb but, far from muffling the explosion, the blast was heard all the way to Siskiyou, several miles to the north, and all the way to Hilt, California, several miles to the south. Enclosed in the confines of the tunnel, the blast couldn't expand outward. Rather than simply blowing the door off, the entire car immediately caught fire. Mail Clerk Elvyn Dougherty was instantly killed.

With the fire raging in an enclosed space, the D'Autremonts couldn't get in. The gold was as closed off as if the door was still in place and the currency was burning along with the car.

Hugh pulled out a handgun and ordered Engineer Bates to move the train forward a bit. Bates pulled the throttle, but was able to get no forward movement. He explained that the sudden stop had probably caused the old engine's interior mechanism to break down.

At that point a third crew member, Brakeman Charles Johnson, came up to the engine to see what was causing the delay. Hugh pointed his gun at Johnson and ordered him to uncouple the mail car from the rest of the train so that the engine would have less weight to pull. Johnson grappled with the coupling, but couldn't move it. Hugh, enraged at the valuable loot going up in smoke and not being able to do anything about it, shot him on the spot.

Seng and Bates were the next to die, shot down seconds after Johnson, perhaps in anger at the botched robbery, perhaps to eliminate witnesses. At that point, in their panicked, frustrated state, it's doubtful even the D'Autremonts could say for sure. Thirteen, coincidentally the number of both the train and the tunnel, had indeed been bad luck for everyone involved. Four innocent men were dead and the robbers hadn't gotten a cent.

Within minutes local police were on the robbers' trail. Within the hour, word of the crime had passed to Chief Special Agent Daniel J. O'Connell, head of the Southern Pacific Railroad Police. With three of his top men, he immediately headed north to take personal charge of the case.

A tough, tall, taciturn lawman, known as "Hardrock" to the nearly 1,000 patrolmen and detectives under his command, O'Connell had joined Southern Pacific's law enforcement arm shortly after emigrating from County Kerry, Ireland, at the turn of the century. He'd been the head of the force for about four years at the time of the Tunnel 13 robbery.

O'Connell was somewhat unusual among cops of that era in his approach to crime scene investigation. He was among the first in the American police service to insist on careful, methodical inspection of crimes scenes, and on properly preserving and noting items of evidence that were gleaned from such searches. He wasn't a "scientific detective" himself but he was among the first old-fashioned street cops to recognize the value of science in criminal investigation.

That being the case, he was probably dismayed when he and his men arrived at the murder site to find it overrun with officers from various jurisdictions, swarming off in various directions with little coordination. Local Sheriff's deputies, railroad police, and federal agents (including US Postal Inspectors) were combing the area in an effort to find either the killers or any evidence they might have left behind.

They were joined by soldiers from the Oregon National Guard, both infantrymen who assisted with the ground search and pilots who scanned the surrounding area from planes. The Siskiyou case may have been the first American crime, and was certainly the first train robbery, in which aircraft were used to aid in the investigation.

A detonation device had been found just outside the north end of the tunnel. Close to the detonator was a worn pair of blue denim overalls, apparently abandoned by one of the killers. Nearby searching officers had also found a pair of gunny-sack shoe covers, creosote-soaked in order to thwart scent dogs. The revolver used by Hugh D'Autremont had also been discovered, apparently thrown away in a panic.

O'Connell asked if the overalls had been thoroughly searched. Officers had carefully gone through the pockets, he was assured, but to no avail.

The search continued for the next 12 days. A garage mechanic in nearby Ashland was picked up by a pair of county deputies based on the fact that the garage sold the sort of batteries used in the detonator and the overalls seemed to fit the mechanic, but nothing else seemed to connect him to the crime. Aside from this arrest, no progress had been made.

At this point, O'Connell announced that he was calling in Professor Heinrich from the University of California at Berkeley.

Edward Oscar Heinrich, known variously as "The American Sherlock Holmes" and "The Edison of Crime Detection," was a pioneer in forensic criminal investigation. Knowledgeable in geology, biochemistry, physics, botany, an expert handwriting analyst, an acknowledged authority on ballistics and explosives, Heinrich was one of the foremost scientific detectives of his day. It was said that the finest defense lawyers in the country routinely gave up in despair whenever they saw Heinrich's name on a list of prosecution witnesses.

Heinrich operated a private crime lab in Berkeley, California, where he'd earned a professorship in criminology at the university and made himself available to police agencies across the country. The overalls and gun were both sent to Heinrich's laboratory.

Several days later O'Connell received a preliminary report. He was told he should look for "a left-handed lumberjack who's worked around fir trees." The suspect, Heinrich said, was white, roughly 21 to 25 years old, no more than 5 feet 10 inches in height, in the neighborhood of 165 pounds, with light brown hair. He was fair-complected and had small hands and feet, was somewhat finicky, and he lived and worked in the Pacific Northwest.

When asked how he'd arrived at such a precise description from a pair of overalls, Heinrich explained that bits of dust, determined to be fragments of fir leaves, and wood chips found in the pockets indicated the suspect's occupation. The particular fir from which the leaf fragments and wood chips came could only be found in the Pacific Northwest, and they were found in the right-hand pocket, strongly suggesting that he sawed left-handed. The size and weight of the suspect was, of course, suggested by the size of the garment. A hair strand lodged on one of the buttons provided conclusive clues to the race, hair color, and complexion of the suspect. Nail cuttings in another pocket indicated the size of the owner's hands and feet, and also indicated a person fastidious in his personal habits.

He stressed, however, that this was only a preliminary report and he might be able to give them further data once he'd examined the garment more minutely.

In another few days, he gave O'Connell the most important clue of all.

Heinrich went through the pockets of the overalls one more time with particularly exacting care. Wadded up in the narrow pencil pocket of the garment, he found a piece of paper, which proved to be a receipt for a postal money order. O'Connell turned the document over to investigators from the Postal Inspection Service, who found that it had been sent by Roy D'Autremont to a relative in New Mexico. Upon investigation, Roy was found to meet the description suggested by Heinrich's forensic examination of the overalls in every respect. From Roy, police were naturally led to Ray and Hugh. Soon wanted posters on all three brothers were being displayed from coast to coast. A reward of more than $5,000 was offered for each of the brothers. Now that they had their men identified and had a mountain of evidence to use against them in court, all they had to do was find them.

Finding them, however, proved to be the sandbar against which the investigation would be lodged for nearly four years. The manner in which the D'Autremonts carried out the robbery may have made them appear to be incompetent amateurs, but when it came to hiding out, they acted like the most experienced pros.

The first trace of the D'Autremonts came in March of 1927, when US Army Sergeant Thomas Reynolds, temporarily stationed in San Francisco after a long tour of duty in the Philippines, saw a wanted poster for Hugh on the wall of the base post office. He immediately recognized him as a private soldier named Brice, with whom Reynolds had served in the Islands. Seeing that a reward was offered, he reported his discovery to the Southern Pacific Railroad Police. In a short time, Hugh D'Autremont was apprehended in Manila and transported back to the United States. He admitted his true identity, but insisted that he'd had nothing to do with the Tunnel 13 robbery. When he was formally charged in Jackson, Oregon, he pleaded "Not guilty."

As preparations were made to try Hugh's case, the reawakened public interest was causing the noose to tighten around Ray and Roy. Newspapers and magazines across the country ran pictures of the twins. Radio stations broadcast descriptions of the pair on a regular basis. 75,000 new wanted posters, with additional information, were circulated across the county by the Postal Inspection Service.

In Steubenville, Ohio, a steel worker named Albert Cullingworth was reading the magazine supplement to his Sunday newspaper which included an article about the Siskiyou outrage complete with pictures of the three suspects. Looking closely at the photos of Ray and Roy, he recognized them as the "Goodwin brothers," fellow employees at the mill. Cullingworth reported his suspicions to the authorities and shortly afterwards the twins were arrested by federal agents, only days before Hugh's trial was set to begin. It was decided that the arrest of Roy and Ray wouldn't be publicized immediately, so that Hugh would remain ignorant of his brothers' capture.

When Hugh's trial began in Jackson, Professor Heinrich appeared as the main prosecution witness, weaving a web of convincing forensic evidence from which the youngest D'Autremont brother was finding it impossible to shake free. Ray and Roy arrived in Jackson just as the prosecuting attorney was completing his final summation to the jury. The jury took only a few minutes to return a verdict of "guilty."

Upon hearing of the verdict, the twins decided to confess, hoping that making a clean breast of things would save them from the gallows. Hugh also made a full confession before sentence was passed, also in hopes of avoiding the death penalty.

In consideration of their full confessions, all three brothers received life sentences and were sent to the Oregon State Penitentiary in Salem, Oregon.

Roy's mental state continued to deteriorate. He suffered a nervous breakdown in 1949 and was transferred to a state mental hospital, where he was given a frontal lobotomy. In March 1984, he was transferred to a nursing home where he died three months later.

Hugh, whom prison authorities called "a testament to reform," was paroled in November 1958, but died of cancer a few months later.

Ray's sentence was commuted to time served in 1972. He moved to Eugene, where he became a custodian at the University of Oregon and filled out the rest of his time writing and painting. He died in 1984.

The D'Autremonts spent a cumulative total of more than 130 years behind bars for a vicious crime that resulted in four needless deaths. Certainly a stiff penalty for a crime that yielded not a single penny of profit, but to the survivors of their victims, still an inadequate one.

FURTHER READING

At least three books devoted exclusively to the D'Autremont case were published in the 1970's. The first of these three to appear was *Oregon's Great Train Hold-Up* (Ye Galleon, 1974) by Bert Webber. A slender book, less than 100 pages long, it was bulked up somewhat in a revised edition published by Webb Research in 1988, on which Bert Webber collaborated with Margie Webber.

All for Nothing (BLS, 1976) by Larry Sturholm and John Howard, was written with some cooperation from Ray D'Autremont, who was befriended by Howard in 1960.

Tunnel 13 (Pine Cone, 1977) by Art Chipman rounds out the trio of D'Autremont books, all put out by local Oregon publishers, possibly to take advantage of growing interest in the case arising from the 50th anniversary of the crime.

Eugene R. Block, a former police reporter for both the San Francisco *Post* and the San Francisco *Call-Bulletin*, has perhaps made the most frequent use of the case in his true crime publications. His first book, *The Wizard of Berkeley* (Coward-McCann, 1958) was a biography of Edward Oscar Heinrich, the pioneering scientific investigator whose forensic examination of Roy D'Autremont's overalls eventually led to the identification of the Tunnel 13 bandits. Block's next book, the Edgar-nominated *Great Train Robberies of the West* (Coward-McCann, 1959), includes a detailed chapter on the Siskiyou robbery, stressing the contributions to the case made by both Daniel "Hardrock" O'Connell and Edward "The Edison of Crime Detection" Heinrich. *Famous Detectives* (Doubleday, 1967) is a collection of 13 chapter-length biographies of well-known investigators, including one each on Heinrich and O'Connell; it also includes information on the D'Autremont case. *Science vs. Crime* (Cragmont, 1979), a history of forensic criminal investigation, also discusses Heinrich and his part in solving the Siskiyou robbery.

Other books that contain accounts of the case include *Bandits and the Southern Pacific* (Stokes, 1929) by C.G. Glasscock; *Southern Pacific – The Roaring Story of Fighting Railroad* (McGraw-Hill, 1952) by Neill C. Wilson and Frank J. Taylor; *The Railroad Police* (Thomas, 1955) by H.S. Dewhurst; *Train Robbery* by Richard Patterson (Johnson, 1981); and those two closest friends of the true-crime researcher, *The Encyclopedia of American Crime* (Facts on File, 1982) by Carl Sifakis and *The Encyclopedia of World Crime* (CrimeBooks, 1990) by Jay Robert Nash.

Shorter articles on the case include "The Great Siskiyou Train Robbery" by Fred E. Green, found in the Summer 1994 issue of *The Dogtown Territorial Quarterly*; "The Last Great Train Robbery" by Paul Fattig, first published in the October 11, 1998, issue of the Medford, Oregon, *Mail-Tribune*, and since reproduced on several different Internet sites; and "The Siskiyou Outrage" by J.D. Chandler, found on his internet site, www.jdchandler.com. "Murder on the Gold Special" is a particularly interesting article by M. Constance Guardino III , who knew Ray D'Autremont when they both worked as part-time custodians at the University of Oregon and was flabbergasted to find that this apparently gentle soul was "the most infamous man on campus." The article can be found on a website Guardino operates with her companion, Rev. Marilyn A. Reidel, at users.wi.net/~maracon/, and includes a poem about the case by Guardino and Reidel.

THE D'AUTREMONT MANHUNT IN FICTION

The earliest fictional treatment of the D'Autremont case I've been able to find was a two-part episode of the long-running cops-and-robbers radio drama *Gangbusters*. Chapter One of "The Capture of the D'Autremont Brothers" was first broadcast on CBS on April 22, 1936, and the conclusion a week later on April 29.

Milton M. Raison's *Tunnel 13* (Murray & Gee, 1948), not to be confused with Art Chipman's non-fiction account, is described as a "powerful suspense novel," clearly based on the D'Autremont case, in which the number of brothers involved in the crime is lowered to two, and the number of murder victims increased to seven. Raison is better known for a series of lighter-hearted mysteries featuring a crime-solving New York drama critic named Tony Woolrich.

A year later, a film version of Raison's novel was released. *Special Agent* (Paramount, 1949), directed by William C. Thomas from a screenplay by Whitman Chamber and Lewis R. Foster, was made in the semi-documentary style popularized in such post-war police films as *The House on 92nd Street* (20th/Fox, 1945), *T-Men* (Eagle-Lion. 1947), and *The Naked City* (Universal, 1948). It starred William Eythe as Railroad Detective Johnny Douglas, hot on the trail of the two "Deveraux" brothers, one of whom is played by George Reeves, who in two years would achieve his greatest (and arguably, most tragic) success as TV's Superman. Filmed on a limited budget (which perhaps accounts for the fact that most of the actual train robbery takes place off-screen), it is nonetheless a solid, entertaining movie bouquet to cinder cops. Interestingly, in the film and the novel from which it derives, the two brothers actually get away with their loot, though they never get to actually spend it.

That same year, *White Heat* (Warner Brothers, 1949), perhaps the greatest of all American gangster films, was released. James Cagney, in one of his most powerful performances, starred as mother-fixated criminal mastermind Cody Jarrett. The film opens with the hold-up of a Southern Pacific train. In almost all respects, this robbery parallels the D'Autremont crime. The trainmen are forced at gunpoint to stop the train just as it's emerging from a tunnel, so that the engine, tender, and part of the mail car have exited, but most of the train is still in the tunnel. The tunnel is seen to be just a bit north of the California border. The State of Oregon is not specifically mentioned but we are told that the robbery occurred roughly 300 miles north of Lake Tahoe which, as the crow flies, is just about where Siskiyou is. The mail clerk, the engineer, the fireman, and another trainman are all ruthlessly murdered, obviously replicating the murders committed during the Tunnel 13 robbery. And the robbers are identified by the analysis of forensic clues, deliberately reminiscent of the analysis provided by Heinrich in real life. There are also some parallels between Cody Jarrett, who is depicted as a mentally deteriorating psychotic who has a nervous breakdown in prison, and Roy D'Autremont, who was transferred from prison to a mental hospital after a real-life nervous breakdown just a year prior to the film's release. The major difference between the actual train robbery and the film version, and it's *quite* a major difference, is that in *White Heat* (as in the novel *Tunnel 13* and its film version, *Special Agent*), the bad guys get away with a substantial haul.

As far as I've been able to determine, no one else has ever made a connection between the Siskiyou robbery and the opening scene of *White Heat*. Perhaps that's because once the train robbery is completed, there are no further parallels (aside from Jarrett's mental illness) between the D'Autremont case and the plot of the film. I don't know whether the idea for basing the movie's beginning on the D'Autremont crime originated with Virginia Kellogg who wrote the original, Oscar-nominated screen treatment; with Ivan Goff and Ben Roberts, who developed that treatment into a full-fledged script; or with Raoul Walsh, the two-fisted filmmaker who directed the film with his usual nuts-and-bolts expertise; but I'm certain the similarities are not just coincidental. Whoever came up with the idea, the sequence, like the rest of the film, is pure gold.

Elsewhere in this book, I suggest that the famous British forensics investigator Sir Bernard Spilsbury might have been the prototype for

R. Austin Freeman's pioneering scientific sleuth, Dr. John Thorndyke. In this chapter, I'm tempted to speculate that Professor Heinrich might have been the inspiration for Thorndyke's American counterpart, Professor Craig Kennedy. Little-remembered by contemporary readers, Kennedy, the creation of journalist Arthur B. Reeve, was once the most popular fictional detective in the country. Reeve first conceived the character, who debuted in the short story collection *The Silent Bullet* (Dodd, Mead, 1912), after writing a series of articles about "scientific crime detection." It seems likely that Reeve would at least have heard of Heinrich while preparing those articles. Certainly there are a number of parallels. Both were professors at major universities (the real-life Heinrich at UC Berkeley and the fictional Kennedy at Columbia), both were masters of a variety of scientific disciplines useful in criminal investigations, and both operated private crime labs which they put at the disposal of official law enforcement. Interestingly, both were known by the same sobriquet, "The American Sherlock Holmes." As I say, this is all speculation and whether or not those parallels are deliberate or coincidental we'll probably never know for sure.

WILL THE REAL CHARLIE CHAN PLEASE STAND UP?

Ethnic Detectives

By 1924, Earl Derr Biggers was already one of the most popular mystery writers in the United States, largely due to the success of his first novel, *Seven Keys to Baldpate* (Bobbs-Merill, 1913), and the equally successful Broadway play that legendary showman George M. Cohan had made out of it. But, though he didn't know it at the time, the character that would make him an iconic figure in the annals of crime fiction was still in his future. And he probably would never have been inspired to create that character if he hadn't hung onto a stack of Hawaiian newspapers he'd bought during a 1919 vacation to the Island Territory.

Biggers wanted to set his next mystery in Honolulu and, to jog his memory of the city, he dug up those old newspapers he'd saved from his trip and began paging through them. One article about a dangerous arrest made by a Chinese-American detective on the Honolulu police force caught his eye.

A Chinese policeman?

Biggers was suddenly struck by the concept of an Asian who solved crimes instead of committing them and, in an era when the best-known Chinese character in detective fiction was Sax Rohmer's archetypal master criminal Dr. Fu Manchu, it really was an original idea.

"Sinister and wicked Chinese were old stuff in mystery stories," Biggers said in an interview years later, "but an amiable Chinese acting on the side of law and order had never been used up to that time." So he decided to create one. Detective Sergeant Charlie Chan, Honolulu PD, became the protagonist of that Oahu-set mystery novel, *The House Without a Key*. In 1925 it began to appear serially in the *Saturday Evening Post*, causing an immediate sensation.

As popular as the serial was on the Mainland, it was followed almost fanatically in Hawaii, where readers speculated on which prominent Island figures might be the real-life models for Biggers's characters. Of course, they had no doubt who the prototype for the detective was. Chan was described as the most famous officer on the force, and no Honolulu cop was more famous than Chang Apana.

111

While it was in fact Chang Apana that Biggers had been reading about when the notion of an Oriental sleuth first struck him, the real-life cop had (aside from his being a Chinese-American and a Honolulu police detective) little in common with his fictional counterpart.

When Charlie Chan makes his very first appearance in *The House Without a Key*, he is described as "very fat indeed." Chang Apana was pencil-thin, carrying barely 145 muscular pounds on his five-foot three-inch frame. Chan was a very literate fellow, whose English, though clearly a second language, was always spoken with a stylish refinement. Chang Apana was fluent in Cantonese and Hawaiian, but spoke only pidgin English, and read and wrote only Hawaiian. Chan resorted to physical force only in very rare instances, relying like most Golden Age sleuths on his brains to outwit criminals. Chang Apana, on the other hand, was described by one of his colleagues, Detective John Jardine, as "rough and ready—rough with suspects and ready with a blacksnake whip for loiterers, toughs, and hoodlums on the street wherever he might meet them."

This last point is perhaps where real life and fiction diverge most sharply. Though he carries a badge, Charlie Chan is really a gentleman sleuth, specializing in high-society murders, who figures out the identity of the culprit with brilliant deductive logic, courteously and sagely explaining his reasoning process with a ready supply of elegantly phrased pseudo-Confucian aphorisms. Chang Apana was a hard-nosed street cop, who spent his 30-odd years in law enforcement working Honolulu's waterfront and Chinatown's mean ghetto streets, going toe-to-toe with dope smugglers, pimps, panderers, peddlers, punks, grifters, gamblers, gangsters, muggers, and other assorted low-lifes. He had scars all over his body from a lifetime of violent encounters with professional crooks. In surviving photographs, an ugly knife scar across his right eye clearly visible, Chang looks not merely tough, but almost sinister.

Chang Apana was born on Oahu somewhere between 1865 and 1871 (different sources give conflicting information). At the age of three, he moved to China with his immigrant parents but returned to Oahu with his uncle when he was seven. When his uncle died, he was raised by another family where he learned how to tend horses. Reaching adulthood, he used the skills he'd honed in his foster home to find work as a horse wrangler around Oahu. In the early 1890s he moved to the Big Island of Hawaii, where he became a *paniolo* (cowboy) on the cattle ranches of rural Waimea. It was during this period that he became adept in the use of a blacksnake whip. A few years later, he returned to Oahu where his experience with animals earned him a position as the Hawaiian Humane Society's first enforcement officer.

In 1898 Chang was appointed as an officer in the Honolulu Police Department. According to some sources, his official title was probably "constable," a possible holdover from the British influence that permeated the Islands during the time that Hawaii had been a monarchy. Eventually, the title probably changed to "police officer" or "patrolman."

The head of the Honolulu Police Department at this time (and indeed during Chang Apana's entire tenure with the force) was an elected sheriff rather than an appointed municipal police chief, reflecting the fact that HPD had, as it still has, county-wide (which is to say island-wide) jurisdiction.

Early on, Chang's value as a plainclothes undercover officer was recognized and before long he was assigned to infiltrate opium smuggling rings and gambling outfits to bring them down from the inside. On one occasion in 1904, he single-handedly conducted a raid on a hidden casino, arresting 40 gamblers, his personal best for the most arrests in a single day.

Wiry and athletic, Chang liked to surprise his prey by climbing up multi-story buildings in downtown Honolulu and crashing through windows to nail his suspects in the act. On one such second-story foray, the criminal he was after resisted arrest by throwing him back out the window. Chang not only survived the fall but successfully completed the apprehension.

In fact, his penchant for derring-do and acting alone caused him to sustain numerous injuries throughout his career. In addition to being thrown from a building, he was stabbed six times, run over with a horse and buggy, and beaten with an ax handle. And it wasn't always criminals who caused the injuries. One of Chang Apana's most dangerous arrests wasn't for a crime at all, but for an illness.

At that time, one of the more distasteful police duties in the Territory of Hawaii was arresting lepers who, refusing to voluntarily accept medical evacuation and treatment, had to be forcibly removed to the Molokai leper colony. Early in Chang's detective career a married couple named Kokuma was diagnosed with the disease. They fled to the massive Oahu ranch of Honolulu businessman Walter F. Dillingham and successfully evaded the police for weeks. They were eventually located at a cabin on the ranch property high on up on the Kawaihapai slopes, where any approach could be seen by the couple well in advance. Reportedly armed to the teeth, the couple would be able to hold off the police indefinitely. Since they weren't really criminals, but victims of a dreaded disease, it was desirable that they be taken with a minimum of violence. The only way to approach the cabin unseen was through the brush adjacent to the cabin, which required that several miles of jungle be penetrated.

In company with four other officers, Chang made his way through the brush and was the first man to push through to the clearing where the cabin could be seen. Kokuma was sitting relaxed near the cabin's front door. The detective and the leper saw each other simultaneously. Kokuma made a dash for the front door to get a weapon while Chang sprinted toward him to head him off. Chang got to Kokuma before Kokuma got to the door and they began struggling. Kokuma managed to grasp a sickle that was hung on the wall of the cabin and began slashing at the detective. Despite being cut several times, Chang managed to overpower Kokuma without seriously hurting him.

Once Kokuma was cuffed up, Chang entered the house to find Mrs. Kokuma, who was just as determined to resist exile as her husband. He found her in the bedroom where she had been laying down. As he entered, she jumped up from her bed and made a lunge for a rifle that had been left leaning against the wall. Apana grabbed a handful of her hair and pulled her down but she fought back savagely. Bleeding from the cuts inflicted by her husband, Chang was starting to lose strength, but the other four officers broke in and subdued her before he passed out.

Despite the many injuries he received in the course of his duties, Chang rarely carried a gun himself. He had an extreme distaste for firearms and, left to his own devices, refused to use one. His weapon of choice was the blacksnake whip he'd developed such skill with during his cowboy days. A departmental edict was eventually issued stating that Apana was the only Honolulu officer permitted to use a blacksnake whip as a police weapon.

By the mid-1920s, Chang Apana was the senior man in HPD's Detective Division. Rarely sent out on live cases anymore, he was placed in charge of the prisoner-trusties assigned to perform janitorial duties around the police station. A conference table in the detective squadroom was decorated with an ornamental top made from mah jong pieces and dominoes Chang had confiscated in long-ago Chinatown gambling raids. Chang liked to spend his days sitting by that table, spinning yarns about his old cases to spellbound young detectives awed to be working alongside the legendary cop.

Though he rarely conducted investigations any more, the blacksnake whip that had once been the terror of street criminals had become the stuff of legend. Chang had been the only Honolulu policeman allowed to use the blacksnake whip, but in 1925 the Detective Division tried an experiment.

Street gangs had been terrorizing the downtown area, attacking servicemen on leave and unescorted women. To quell the violence, five young detectives were equipped with blacksnake whips and sent out to clean up the streets Chang Apana-style. For awhile it worked quite well. But when a pair of detectives aiming their whips at a hoodlum accidentally "flicked" an innocent bystander instead, the program became controversial and the same public that had been screaming for action only weeks earlier, was now complaining about the "extreme" measures. The experiment was discontinued and the blacksnake whip again became an item of police equipment approved only for Chang Apana's use.

In 1928, a few years after striking gold with the Chan novels, Earl Derr Biggers returned to Honolulu for a visit and finally met the man who had inspired the creation of his iconic character face to face. By this time, local papers routinely cited Chang Apana as the model for Chan and Chang's colleagues jokingly nicknamed him "Charlie." Chang, pleased with the attention his connection to the character drew, even signed autographs as "Charlie Chan."

Biggers and Chang became friends and stayed in touch for several years, but the author denied that the detective was the specific model for his character.

"I'm sorry to disillusion anyone," he said, "but that 'real persons' notion is a myth."

Exaggeration perhaps, but not a myth. While Charlie Chan was a undoubtedly a creature of Biggers's imagination, Chang Apana was just as undoubtedly the spark that fired that imagination.

In 1931 Apana met his screen counterpart, Warner Oland, the actor who was playing Chan in an extremely successful series of films for 20th Century Fox. *The Black Camel*, the only entry in the series to be filmed in Hawaii, was shooting scenes in Waikiki, and Chang was asked to pose with Oland for some publicity shots. Photos of the portly actor, in make-up as Chan, standing next to the slender veteran cop, are visual evidence of the differences between the fictional sleuth and his real-life prototype.

That same year, Chang, who'd accumulated more time on the job than any other Honolulu police officer, was offered a pension in consideration of his more than three decades of continuous service. He declined.

"What would I do if I weren't a policeman?" he said. "I'm only 67. Chinese live a long time and some have been known to raise another family of nine at my age."

He actually had already raised eight children by this time, and had been presented with 10 grandchildren. Like his fictional doppelganger, Chang apparently believed in the "multitudinous blessings" that derived from having a large family.

The next year, however, events got the better of him. Chang was seriously injured in a traffic accident and just wasn't able to bounce back as quickly as in his younger days. Reluctantly, he retired from the Department in May of 1932, supplementing his pension with a private security job at the Hawaiian Trust Building. He never completely recovered from his injuries.

Biggers heard that Chang was having a tough time and made arrangements for him to appear in the next Chan film at a salary of $500 a week. In August of 1933, shortly after making that deal on Chang's behalf, Biggers unexpectedly died at the age of 48.

Chang intended to accept the movie offer that Biggers had pulled strings to get for him but had become increasingly infirm since the accident, making the long trip to California impossible. Early in November, he became seriously ill. On December 2, 1933, he was admitted to Queen's Hospital, where he died six days later.

When another veteran Chinese-American officer, Captain En You Kau of HPD's Patrol Division, learned of his friend's death, he said, "He was the greatest person I have ever known." His sentiments were echoed by HPD officers up and down the hierarchy.

Detective Chang Apana was buried with full police honors at the Manoa Chinese Cemetery. The Royal Hawaiian Band performed at his funeral service, an unusual honor signifying not only Chang's outstanding service to law enforcement over so many years, but also the legendary status he'd attained as the real-life inspiration for one of detective fiction's most popular figures.

FURTHER READING

Oddly, no book-length biography exists about this legendary Island lawman, but if there's anyone qualified to write one, it's retired HPD Officer Eddie Croom, who is the curator of the Honolulu Police Museum and an unabashed Chang Apana buff. For the moment, we have to be satisfied with a short article, "The Real Charlie Chan," that Croom has written for the Honolulu Police webpage. That article can be found at www.honolulupd.org/museum/apana.htm. I should also point out here that the Honolulu Police Museum, located on the ground floor of Police Headquarters at 801 South Beretania Street and open to the public weekdays free of charge, is one of the finest law enforcement museums in the United States. A Chang Apana exhibit, displaying photographs of Chang, arrest reports, news clippings, and the fabled blacksnake whip with which he kept the peace on the streets of Honolulu, is one of the museum's most popular attractions. But the entire museum, showing the history of Hawaiian law enforcement from the days of the monarchy through the territorial era and into statehood, is a must-see for any true-crime aficionado.

And if you're in Honolulu anyway, you might want to take in a meal at the Halekulani Hotel's alfresco restaurant, The House Without a Key. In Chang's and Biggers's day, this popular Waikiki eatery was known as Gray's-by-the-Sea. Since Biggers stayed at the Halekulani during that 1919 vacation that led to his first hearing about Chang Apana, the restaurant changed its name in memory its famous guest, the character he created, and the real-life policeman who inspired him.

Three articles from the Honolulu *Star-Bulletin* were helpful. "Black Camel Kneels at Home of Chang Apana," an unsigned obituary first published on December 9, 1933, gives a short account of the detective's career, his part in inspiring the Chan character, and the reactions of his brother officers to his death. "The 'Real Life' Charlie Chan," another unsigned article appearing in the March 19, 1955, issue of *Hawaiian Life Weekend*, the *Star-Bulletin*'s weekend magazine insert, is a more comprehensive look at the policeman's life and career. More recently, Jaymes K. Song's "'Charlie Chan' Isle's Toughest Crime Fighter," was published on October 2, 1999, as part of a series the paper was running on the "100 Most Influential Persons in the Modern Era of Hawaii."

Two more recent articles, "Charlie Chan and the Case of the Cop Who Inspired Him" by Patrick Williams, and "Number-One Detective: Hunting Down the Real Charlie Chan" by Deborah Gushman, also provided helpful details. Williams's particularly comprehensive article first appeared on April 25, 2000, on a professional police website called APBnews.com. It has since dropped off, but can now be found on www. charliechanfamily.com, a website developed for fans of the Charlie Chan books and movies. Gushman's piece appears in the August-September 2003 issue of *Hana Hou!*, the in-flight magazine of Hawaiian Airlines.

In his autobiography *Detective Jardine – Crimes in Honolulu* (University of Hawaii, 1984) John Jardine, one of Chang's HPD colleagues, devotes several effusive pages to his legendary co-worker. The book, written in collaboration with journalists Edward Rohrbough and Bob Krauss, also gives a particularly good account of Chang's harrowing arrest of the Kokumas. Jardine, Honolulu's "Dean of Detectives," served in the HPD from 1923 through 1968, becoming almost as great a legend as Chang. As a rookie detective, Jardine was one of the officers chosen for the "Blacksnake Whip Squad," the ill-fated attempt to emulate Chang's preferred method of crime-fighting.

Hawaiian writer Glen Grant is a student of the state's crime history, and he conducts walking tours of Honolulu, pointing out sites where some of the city's most notorious crimes occurred. He has also written a series of historical private eye short stories featuring a Depression-era gumshoe named Arthur McDougal, former HPD Chief of Detectives and current top operative of the International Detective Agency. McDougal is rather obviously modeled on real-life HPD Chief of Detectives Arthur McDuffie, who left the department under a cloud in 1923 to join the Honolulu International Detective Agency. In a collection of McDougal stories, *McDougal's Honolulu Mysteries* (Mutual, 1995), Grant includes a long introduction, "When Merchant Street Wasn't for Sissies," describing McDuffie at length as well as many other famous HPD officers of the era, including Jardine and Chang. It also contains an account of the Kokuma case.

CHANG APANA IN FICTION

Shortly after its initial serial publication in the *Post*, the first Chan novel, *The House Without a Key* (1925) appeared in book form. It was followed by *The Chinese Parrot* (1926), *Behind That Curtain* (1928), *The Black Camel* (1929), *Charlie Chan Carries On* (1930), and *The Keeper of the Keys* (1932; all Bobbs-Merrill). The novels became so popular that they spawned a miniature Chan industry. Over the next half-century or so, Chan appeared in nearly 50 movies, four radio series, a live-action television series, a made-for-TV movie, an animated Saturday morning TV series, four different comic book series, a syndicated newspaper strip, and at least one stage play.

Keye Luke, who gained fame playing Chan's oldest son in the Warner Oland movies, provided the voice for the detective in the TV cartoon, becoming the first Asian actor in the sound era and the first Chinese actor in any era or medium to portray the character. The title of this chapter, by the way, is borrowed from the title of an episode of this Hanna-Barbera series, *The Amazing Chan and the Chan Clan*.

Of course, as has already been pointed out, the gentle Chan of fiction had little to do with the hard-nosed Chang of Honolulu's real-life mean streets. Chang appears under his own name in Max Allan Collins's *Damned in Paradise* (Dutton, 1996), in which Collins's popular series private eye, Nate Heller, travels to Hawaii to investigate the notorious Massie rape/murder case and meets the famous Chinese-American policeman. Though there is no record that Chang actually worked on any aspect of the Massie case, Collins couldn't resist bringing Heller face to face with the "real Charlie Chan." Chang's facility with the blacksnake whip is displayed in the novel as well as his delight in being the inspiration for the popular sleuth of fiction. One compromise with real life that Collins made in his depiction of Chang was allowing the detective to speak with the elegant phrasing of his fictional counterpart rather than the pidgin he spoke in real life, feeling that having him speak in a broken English "would get in the way of the characterization." Another liberty he took was having Chang drop the same kind of Confucianlike proverbs that Chan used. In fact, at one point, after using such an aphorism to illustrate a point, Chang is asked if he is quoting Confucius. "No," he replies, "Earl Derr Biggers."

Given the fact that Chang took a great deal of pride in being Chan's model, this divergence from real life seemed a permissible method of merging the real-life figure with the popular public image created by Biggers's character.

So far, Collins's use of Chang as a supporting character is the only comparatively authentic fictional depiction of the tough Honolulu street cop. There was talk some years ago of an upcoming feature film, tentatively entitled *The Adventures of Charlie Chan*, to be written and directed by Pulitzer Prize-winning playwright and screenwriter David

Mamet. Public announcements about the project suggested that it would be set in the 1920's on Honolulu's violent waterfront and Chinatown areas. Given the crime screenplays and teleplays Mamet had written to that point (*The Untouchables, Homicide,* and an episode of *Hill Street Blues*, among others), it seems likely that his depiction of the title character, had it ever come to fruition, would have been closer to Chang than to Chan, but the project never worked its way out of "development hell" so we'll never get to find out.

THE INNOVATIVE TRADITIONALIST

Pacific Northwest Mysteries

Occasionally, certain regions of the country tend to be identified with certain types of criminal activity. Chicago, for example, always suggests organized crime. New York City, where the stench of Tammany Hall can still be smelled a century later, brings political corruption to mind. The Deep South, for better or for worse, is associated with racial terrorism. The Midwest heartland seems the natural home of flamboyant bandits like John Dillinger and "Pretty Boy" Floyd. Florida is synonymous with the drug trade.

For some reason the Pacific Northwest seems to have spawned more than its share of serial killers. Jerome "The Lust Killer" Brudos. Randall "The I-5 Killer" Woodfield. Harvey "The Want-Ad Killer" Carignan. They've all stalked their victims in states like Oregon, Washington, Alaska, and the far northern regions of California.

There may be all sorts of reasons why the Northwest seems to be such a fertile ground for the growing of mass murderers. Perhaps it's the weather. Perhaps (applying the famous advertising tagline of a popular Pacific Northwest beer) it's the water. Perhaps it's simply the juxtaposition of some of the fastest growing metropolitan regions in the country with some of the widest-ranging, most lush rural areas, providing both fertile fields for the acquisition of victims and thousands of acres of convenient places in which to dispose of them.

Whatever the reason, serial killers seem to like operating in the Pacific Northwest. So a homicide detective working there probably thinks a lot about just what it takes to catch such a criminal.

If we are to believe movies, novels, and television, serial killers are caught by the nearly psychic efforts of gifted criminal profilers. The facts, however, don't always bear this out. David "The Son of Sam" Berkowitz was identified by the meticulous examination of parking tickets issued near the murder scenes. Wayne "The Atlanta Child Killer" Williams was caught by a well-planned and superbly executed series of stakeouts on the likely dump sites. William "The Lipstick Killer" Heirens was brought down by an alert and observant beat cop who caught him in the act of committing an apparent burglary.

Profiling can be a valuable tool in tracking down unknown subjects,

121

but in the end it's usually good, solid, basic police work that brings them in. Dr. Robert Keppel, one of the most experienced investigators of serial killer cases in the world, illustrates this point beautifully. Throughout his law enforcement career, though he's used profiles and even on occasion developed, or helped to develop, profiles, he's been a staunch advocate and a faithful practitioner of the doctrine of basic police work. At the same time, he's earned a well-deserved reputation as one of the most innovative homicide detectives in the country.

Shortly after his graduation from Washington State University where he'd majored in police science, Keppel became a deputy in the King County Sheriff's Office. He quickly won a promotion to detective and, while still in his mid-20s, was assigned to the department's Major Crimes Unit, which was responsible for, among other things, murder investigations.

His very first case as a homicide cop took him to Ecumclaw, a small village southeast of Seattle near the Pearce County line. Rookie King County detectives were usually assigned the cases originating in such remote areas. In this instance, the dead body belonged to a local business owner named Robert Stergion, the victim of an apparent burglary gone wrong.

Stergion lived and worked in the same building. He had been awakened the night before by the sound of someone opening his cash register. He got up to investigate. It was the last thing he ever did. He was discovered in his bathtub, dead from over 20 stab wounds.

Keppel and his partner, Roger Dunn, discovered that a homeless young drifter had arrived in Ecumclaw the day before. He'd been given some money for food by sawmill workers who'd taken pity on him and Stergion had given him permission to sleep in his truck. Keppel and Dunn were able to identify the teen-aged drifter as James Slade. Since Slade seemed a likely suspect, Keppel put out a bulletin. A beat cop picked up Slade a short time later.

In short order, Keppel was able to easily coax a confession out of Slade and close the file. The case was a comparatively simple one but this in no way diminishes Keppel's performance. Despite his lack of experience, he'd managed the case with the sure-handedness of an old pro. It had taken him less than a day to assemble the necessary physical evidence, identify a likely suspect, and persuade that suspect to give a full confession, all of which would ultimately lead to a conviction. He'd have very little time to rest on his laurels, however. He was assigned to his next homicide case just three days later. And he'd find this one a lot more complicated than the Stergion murder.

A few months earlier, Keppel and Dunn had been assigned to investigate the disappearances of Janice Ott and Denise Naslund, who vanished from Lake Sammamish State Park on July 14, 1974, the latest in a series of mysterious disappearances in and around Seattle. All of the missing persons were attractive, long-haired, college-aged girls. Janice and Denise had last been seen speaking to a man who identified himself as "Ted," described as young and boyishly good-looking, driving a Volkswagen bug.

On September 7, less than 72 hours after jailing Slade, Keppel and Dunn were directed to the small town of Issaquah, where a pair of hunters had discovered some human skeletal remains. The bones were found to have belonged to Janice Ott and Denise Naslund. Keppel's missing persons case had just become a homicide.

On March 2, 1975, a second burial site was found at Taylor Mountain. Forestry students at nearby Green River Community College had discovered a human skull.

Keppel, who in the months following the discovery of the dump site at Issaquah, had been familiarizing himself with missing persons cases from Washington, Oregon, and British Columbia, recognized the dental work on the skull as that of Brenda Ball. She'd last been seen at the Flame Tavern, five miles south of Seattle, dancing with a man who fit the description of the "Ted" suspect from Lake Sam. An intensive search of the Taylor Mountain area uncovered the remains of three more victims.

Law enforcement bureaucracies are reluctant to accept the possibility that a serial killer is operating in their area and there was an entrenched belief (or perhaps, more correctly, a hope) that the disappearances of young women throughout the Pacific Northwest had been unrelated. The discovery of the Taylor Mountain dump site forced the brass to recognize that the paradigm had shifted. A special joint task force made up of personnel from both the Seattle Police and the King County Sheriff's Office was set up and Keppel and Dunn were assigned. Now they'd be hunting Ted full-time.

Early on the newly-formed task force asked a psychiatrist and a psychologist to work up a psychological description of the murderer. This "profile," one of the first ever put together for a serial murder case, turned out to be correct in virtually every detail. But until the detectives had a suspect to compare to the profile, it did them little good. To track down that suspect they'd have to fall back on basic investigative work, first developing leads and then following them up.

The problem, however, wasn't developing leads. It was an embarrassment of riches. At times the task force was getting up to 500 tips a day. Keppel realized that the basic police work would have to be carried out in an innovative manner. Some method had to be devised for prioritizing the leads that they were developing.

One of the first things Keppel and his colleagues did was design a "tip sheet." This allowed information that the task force received in the form of individual tips to be reported in a systematic manner. The form was simple. Blocks indicated which aspect of the investigation the tip was about. There was also a section for the name, address, and phone number of the tipster and a "free text" block allowing the detective to summarize the information provided. This "tip sheet," simple and elegant in concept but never before conceived, allowed task force members to gauge the importance and likely usefulness of each piece of evidence. It has since become the model for such investigations. At the same time, Bob Shmitz, the detective sergeant assigned by King County to help supervise the "Ted" unit, developed a cross-referencing system whereby suspects and tipsters could be checked with earlier tips as new ones came in.

Even so, the volume of information the task force was receiving was staggering. By June 1975, 30 separate lists containing a total of nearly *300,000* names of possible "Ted" suspects had been compiled. Keppel felt sure that one of those names was the "Ted" he and his colleagues were hunting but there was no way to adequately investigate every name on those lists. Somehow they would have to be winnowed down to a manageable number.

The first method for bringing the number of suspects to a manageable size was to concentrate strictly on the 3500 names gathered from the tip sheets. These were sorted by such criteria as the physical description of the suspect named, the cars available to that suspect, how closely a suspect seemed to match the psychological profile that had been developed, etc. In this way, the list of 3500 was reduced to 100. These files were assembled in alphabetical order and each suspect in each file was scheduled to be investigated in depth. The seventh file down was for a suspect named Theodore Robert Bundy.

But there were still the names on the other lists to consider. Keppel suggested that King County's payroll computer be utilized to collate all the names on the 30 lists. Over the course of a month, the 3500 names from the task force's tip sheets, the 41,000 names of registered VW owners, the names of 1500 transfer students from all Pacific Northwest universities, the names of 600 participants of a company picnic held at Lake Sam the day of the Ott and Naslund disappearances, and thousands of additional names from over two dozen other lists, were entered into the computer. This required making punch cards for every entry, and feeding those cards into a gigantic mainframe nearly 100 feet long by 50 feet wide. Keppel's hypothesis was that the most viable suspects would appear on several different lists. The suspects whose names appeared on the most lists would be designated the prime "Ted" candidates.

The program identified 25 men who were on four or more lists. One of these was Theodore Robert Bundy, who'd already been identified as one of the task force's top 100 "Ted" prospects. Not only was Bundy on four lists, he was mentioned a total of eight times. Three separate tip sheets had been made out on him. He was the registered owner of a Volkswagen. He had been a classmate of Linda Healy, one of the first "Ted" victims; in fact, he'd been in three of Linda's classes and consequently turned up three different times on that list. Finally, he was on a list of people identified as having been seen driving a VW in areas near where two of the victims had last been seen.

One week after the computer program was run, the task force received a call from Detective Ben Forbes of the Salt Lake County Sheriff's Office regarding Bundy. Utah and the adjacent state of Colorado had been experiencing a series of missing persons cases, all of college age women, strikingly similar to the Washington/Oregon cases that Keppel and his partners were investigating. The disappearances had begun shortly after Bundy had moved from Washington to Utah to attend law school. At just about the same time Bundy moved, the Pacific Northwest series of murders seemed to have ended. One of the Colorado disappearances had later been confirmed as a homicide.

There also appeared to have been one failed attempt on the part of the Utah/Colorado murderer. In November of 1974, Carol DaRonch had been approached by a man claiming to be a police officer and coaxed into his car, a VW bug, on the pretext of helping with an investigation. Once they had driven a short distance, the man, described as young and boyishly handsome, attempted to secure Carol with a pair of handcuffs. In the ensuing struggle, she managed to escape.

On August 16, 1975, as Sergeant Bob Hayward of the Utah Highway Patrol neared the end of his shift, he spotted a VW bug driving without headlights. Following, he soon saw the car run two stop signs. Despite the fact that he was due to go off-duty shortly, Trooper Hayward decided that he was going to have to investigate. The driver, one Theodore Robert Bundy, gave evasive answers to Sergeant Hayward's questions. A search of the VW uncovered a ski mask, a pantyhose with eye slits cut into it, and an ice pick.

While Keppel was proving the efficacy of meticulous detective work in Washington, Hayward had just proved the importance of alert beat patrol in Utah. Basic police work.

Clearly Sergeant Hayward had more than a mere traffic violator on his hands. He notified the Salt Lake County Sheriff's Office where his older brother, Captain Pete Hayward, commanded the homicide detail, and requested that a detective be dispatched to his location. Night Watch Detective Pete Ondrak arrived a short time later. Conducting a more thorough search, he found a pair of handcuffs in the trunk of the vehicle. Bundy was placed under arrest.

The next day, Detective Forbes recalled that the name Bundy had been passed on to him months earlier by King County Detective Randy Hergesheimer. Hergesheimer had received a tip from a girl friend of Bundy's whose suspicions were raised by the fact that the Northwest disappearances had ended and the Utah disappearances had begun at just about the time that Bundy had moved from Washington to Utah. This was one of the tips that had made Bundy one of the 3500, then one of the top 100, and ultimately one of the select 25. Forbes was now calling King County to follow-up.

Over the next few months, as Keppel and his colleagues worked on connecting Bundy to their murder cases and as Aspen detectives tried to connect him to the murder of Caryn Campbell, Salt Lake detectives were putting together a case of aggravated kidnapping based on Carol DaRonch's complaint.

Bundy was convicted of kidnapping in 1976 then immediately extradited to Colorado to stand trial for the Campbell murder. During his trial, Bundy managed to escape from the Pitkin County Courthouse but was apprehended a week later. He broke jail a second time six months later, this time staying at large long enough to make it to Florida, where he committed three more murders before finally being arrested in Pensacola, tried, and sentenced to die in Florida's electric chair. Bundy's career as a serial killer was finally ended.

Keppel's career as a hunter of serial killers was just beginning.

In 1977, Keppel was still assigned as the lead investigator on the Bundy case, though, with Bundy identified as Washington's "Ted" killer, convicted of kidnapping in Utah, and facing murder charges in Colorado, the urgency of the investigation was no longer as pressing. On August 9 the body of an unidentified woman was found at the South Park Marina, a block outside of Seattle's city limits, putting the case in the jurisdiction of the Sheriff's Department. Keppel was called from the "Bundy Room" to participate in the investigation.

The body, an attractive white female apparently in her 20's, had been positioned in a supine position with her legs spread apart. She had been viciously beaten to death (a later autopsy disclosed that she had sustained 81 separate injuries) and raped with some sort of blunt object. A fingerprint check identified the victim as Rosemary Stuart, who'd been arrested numerous times for prostitution by the Seattle PD.

Keppel called his counterparts at the Seattle Police to thank them for their assistance in the identification of the victim, and was informed that, coincidentally, the city detectives were investigating a similar case.

Less than two weeks before Rosemary Stuart's murder, the body of Iantha Buchanan, a 27-year-old black woman also with a record for prostitution, had been found at a construction site just five miles from the South Park Marina. Like Rosemary Stuart, she'd been savagely beaten, raped with a foreign object, and arranged in a humiliating post-mortem pose. Still, the Seattle detectives said, it couldn't be the same killer, because the MO was so strikingly different. Rosemary Stuart had been white. Iantha Buchanan had been black. And the conventional wisdom was that serial killers, particularly prostitute killers, never crossed racial lines. The similarities must have been coincidental.

Keppel wasn't convinced. He theorized that while MOs might change in some particulars, a criminal's particular *style*, what Keppel would eventually come to call the criminal's "signature," would still be discernible. And, in Keppel's opinion, both of these murders had the same signature.

Keppel convinced his colleagues that they were looking for a single killer, a killer who would strike again soon if he wasn't caught. Witness statements indicated that the killer was probably driving a 1969 Dodge Charger. Keppel put out an APB throughout the Seattle metropolitan area which yielded results on August 15, when a plainclothes Seattle

PD unit pulled over a car matching the description of the suspect vehicle. Examining the car the officers found bloodstains and other physical evidence indicating that this was the very Dodge Charger they were looking for. The driver, Morris Frampton, was immediately taken into custody. The Charger and a second vehicle owned by Frampton, a pickup truck, were both impounded and thoroughly processed by crime lab technicians. Both vehicles teemed with trace evidence indicating that Frampton was their man. After long, frustrating years of trying unsuccessfully to solve the "Ted" murders, Keppel found it particularly satisfying to be able to close the Stuart/Buchanan case in just a few days.

Keppel's next serial killer case took him out of the Pacific Northwest and into the Deep South. In 1981, Lee Brown, Atlanta's police chief, requested that he come to Georgia as a consultant in the hunt for the Atlanta Child Killer. Keppel would be one of several highly regarded homicide detectives from throughout the country who'd been in charge of some of the most infamous, high-profile murder cases ever recorded. This was the second such group of "supercops" assembled by Commissioner Brown. In the opinion of the Atlanta PD brass, the efforts of the first group, dubbed the "Seven Samurai" by the press, had been compromised by the media attention paid to them. It was Brown's intention to keep the efforts, even the existence, of this second group of serial killer experts secret.

The prevailing theory was that the victims, all of whom were black, were being preyed upon by a white racist who intended the murders to be a political statement. The consultant group's profile of the killer was directly at odds with that theory. Leaving aside the fact that it was unlikely that a white man could troll for victims in black neighborhoods and not stand out, none of the murders suggested either implicitly or explicitly any specifically racist attitudes. They were sex murders with no racial agenda.

Brown would later call the consultants' contribution the most valuable part of the investigation. However, the fact of the matter is that even before the arrival of the second group of "supercops," Atlanta PD had already put a plan for apprehending the killer in place. They had set up a series of well-planned, well-manned surveillances of the likeliest dump sites based on where the previous bodies had been found. It was on one of these stakeouts that, on May 22, 1981, Wayne Williams was observed and identified. Although not taken into custody at the time, his identification ultimately led to his arrest and conviction for several of the Atlanta Child murders. The murders stopped after Williams' confinement.

* * *

In March of 1982, Keppel left the King County Sheriff's Office to accept a newly created position with the State of Washington, Chief Criminal Investigator for the State Attorney General. That title was actually a bit misleading, at least at first. Although Keppel's unit would eventually grow to a staff of 17 investigators, in the beginning it consisted only of Keppel. He was Steve McGarrett without the Five-O.

As one of the leading experts on serial murder, one of Keppel's first duties in his new job was to assist in the creation of a national clearing house of information on violent offenders. The idea for such a center was first proposed by Pierce Brooks, the legendary LAPD detective who'd helped break some of Southern California's biggest murder cases. It was during his investigation of Harvey "The Lonely Hearts Club Killer" Glatman that Brooks began to see the value of such a centralized information storehouse. Glatman, like Bundy and many other serial killers, had ranged through several different jurisdictions. The Balkanized nature of police jurisdictional responsibilities in the United States often kept investigators from recognizing the fact that they were dealing with a serial killer, and even if they suspected that this was the case, they had no way of systematically checking other jurisdictions to see if similar cases were occurring elsewhere. The resulting system, the Violent Criminal Apprehension Program (ViCAP), administered by the FBI, fell short of what Brooks and Keppel had hoped for, but was a step in the right direction. Years later, Keppel would develop a similar regional program for the Pacific Northwest, called the Homicide Investigation and Tracking System (HITS). The primitive computer program he'd run years earlier to sift through the thousands of "Ted" suspects turned out to be the prototype for what is now a standard investigative technique.

On July 15, 1982, a few months after Keppel assumed his new duties at the AG's office, the body of 16-year-old Wendy Coffield, a white female with a history of prostitution arrests, was found in the Green River, running south of Seattle. Three more bodies were found floating in the river the following month: Deborah Lynn Bonner, a 23-year-old white female, 31-year-old Marcia Faye Chapman and 17-year-old Cynthia Jean Hinds, both black females. All three, like Wendy Coffield, had prostitution records. These were the first four victims whose deaths would be attributed to the Green River Killer.

In September, a fourth body, belonging to Giselle Lovorn, white female, 16, with a record for prostitution, was found near the Sea-Tac Airport's southern runway. At first, her death appeared unconnected to the Green River series since she was not a floater like the first four victims. But she hooked in the same red-light district, the Sea-Tac strip area near the intersection of 216th and Pacific Highway South and she was killed in the same way, ligature strangulation.

The following February, Keppel was approached by King County's lead investigator on the Green River case, Detective Dave Reichert. Reichert was making no headway and he hoped that Keppel's looking at the case with fresh eyes might provide some insight. Reichert's request for an informal look at the case was followed by an official request from the King County Sheriff's Office for a formal review. On the basis of Keppel's recommendations a full-time Task Force was formed and, at the personal request of Sheriff Vern Thomas, Keppel was assigned to the unit full-time.

More than a year later, the Task Force had made no headway and the bodies were continuing to pile up. In October of 1984, Keppel received a letter from an acknowledged expert in the field of serial murder offering to consult on the case. The letter came from Florida's Death Row. It was signed by Ted Bundy.

Why did Bundy make the offer? Perhaps he was anxious to participate in serial murders once more, if only vicariously. Perhaps he thought that if he made a genuinely valuable contribution to the investigation it might delay or even prevent his impending execution. Perhaps he'd read the scene in Thomas Harris's novel *Red Dragon* (Putnam, 1981), in which FBI Agent Will Graham, on the trail of an elusive murderer, consults with the imprisoned Dr. Hannibal Lector, a notorious serial killer he himself once pursued and helped jail, and was intrigued by the idea of acting out that fictional situation in real life. Perhaps he sincerely wanted to atone in some way for the crimes he'd committed. In any case, whatever his reasons, the offer was genuine.

Keppel and Reichert thought that it was possible Bundy would be able to help. At the very least they might be able to gain insights that would be helpful in serial murder cases generally, if not the Green River case specifically. And if Bundy was not able to help on the Green River case, in the course of trying to help he might reveal things about his own case that were still a mystery to the authorities.

Over the next five years, Keppel interviewed Bundy three times. In 1984, Bundy gave Keppel and Reichert his specific impressions about the Green River case. In 1988, Keppel and Bundy talked at length about other serial killers Bundy had either read about or met in prison, using the insights he had gained in his studies of other killers to advise Keppel on the best, most effective ways to interrogate serial killer suspects. Bundy spoke with Keppel one last time just days before his execution in 1989, finally giving up heretofore unknown details about his own crimes.

In 1987, a suspect who closely fit the profile given by Bundy was developed by Task Force Detective Matt Haney. The suspect, named Gary Ridgway, had come to the attention of law enforcement twice during the Green River investigation. The first time was in 1982, when Ridgway was stopped by police while in his truck. His passenger, Keli McGinness, would later turn up as one of the Green River victims. In 1983, police spoke to Ridgway again when a witness who had seen another Green River victim, Marie Malvar, enter a truck on the night she disappeared, thought he recognized Ridgway's truck, which he saw parked in Ridgway's driveway some weeks later.

Haney decided that Ridgway bore closer examination. Conducting an intensive background check, he learned from one of Ridgway's ex-wives that his suspect often frequented areas that were later used as dump sites by the Green River Killer. A number of prostitutes who routinely worked the Sea-Tac strip reported that a man closely resembling Ridgway was frequently seen cruising the area. Haney also discovered that Ridgway was either absent from work or taking a regular day off on days that coincided with the disappearances of every single one of the Green River victims.

Ridgway was arrested and his home searched. He was also required to give up "bodily samples" to see if they could be matched to semen samples left in several of the victims. Though both the evidence uncovered by the search and the forensic examination of the physical samples corroborated Ridgway's guilt, they did not prove it conclusively. Ridgway was released.

By 1991, leads had petered out and the Task Force had been reduced to one single investigator. Despite the thousands of man hours, despite the millions of dollars spent, despite Bundy's contributions, the Green River Killer was still at large by the time Keppel retired from active law enforcement in 1999.

But, in the meantime, there were other serial killers who were captured and convicted thanks to Keppel's efforts.

George "The Bellevue Yuppie Murderer" Russell, for example, killed three young woman in 1990, two in the upper-middle-class Washington town of Bellevue and a third in nearby Kirkland. Because the MO in each case was slightly different, detectives at first proceeded on the assumption that there was more than one killer. Keppel was able to show through his HITS computer program that a single offender was responsible for all three murders. When Russell was arrested by alert patrolmen, police were able to tie him to the first murder conclusively on the basis of DNA evidence but physical evidence was skimpy on the second and third deaths. Keppel's testimony convinced jurors that, based on his theory of a criminal "signature" separate and distinct from a criminal MO, all three deaths were related. Russell was convicted of all three murders.

In 1997, Dave Reichert, who had been the lead detective on the Green River case so many years earlier, became Sheriff of King County. This put him in a position to take the long-unsolved case off the back burner and make it a top priority again. In 2001 he formed a brand new Task Force, staffed by forensics experts and, particularly, DNA experts, as well as field investigators. Using new technology that had been unavailable in1987, the semen samples procured from three victims (Opal Mills, Marcia Chapman, and Carol Christensen) were compared to bodily samples from those suspects Reichert and Keppel had regarded as the strongest candidates. The semen samples were all found to be a perfect match with the DNA of Gary Ridgway. Ridgway was charged with the murders of Mills, Chapman, and Christensen, as well as a fourth, Cynthia Hinds, who was tied to Ridgway by a strong circumstantial case. King County Prosecutor Norm Maleng originally intended to ask for the death penalty, which would have meant years of long, drawn-out appeals, forestalling emotional closure for the victims' loved ones, and for the investigators who put so much effort into the case. In a surprise move, however, Maleng agreed to accept Ridgway's guilty plea on 48 separate murders. Ridgway's plea included 42 of the 49 murders attributed to the Green River Killer and an additional six that law enforcement had not connected to the case prior to Ridgway's confession. In exchange for Ridgway's plea, which was entered on November 5, 2003, Maleng did not seek the death penalty. Instead Ridgway was sentenced to 48 separate life sentences without the possibility of parole. Maleng was induced to accept the plea bargain partly to get questions about Ridgway's many victim answered and possibly to save the county the cost of a long, drawn-out, expensive trial.

Maleng's decision angered many people, including some of the victims' family members, and has even called the whole concept of capital punishment in the State of Washington into question. If a man can admit to 48 separate murders and still not get the death penalty, who can?

Moreover, the plea will not bring the closure Maleng apparently hopes for. There are many details about Ridgway's plea still left unexplained and a number of "Green River" murders still officially unsolved. As Keppel put it in an interview after Ridgway's plea, "It ain't over. I don't think the book is going to close at all. The process won't end until the detectives quit." Of Ridgway he said, "It's hard for me to believe this guy has said all he could say about all these murders."

Further, the plea was specifically limited to murders committed in King County. At least one victim attributed to the Green River Killer, 15-year-old Colleen Brockman, was found in adjacent Pierce County. And a number of Green River victims were found over the state line in Oregon, which also has a death penalty. Despite the admitted killer's plea bargain, a move that Keppel believes to be unprecedented in the annals of serial killer investigation, Ridgway is still not assured of escaping the ultimate penalty.

As of this writing, however, there has been no move on the part of law enforcement officials in Pierce County nor in the State of Oregon to pursue additional charges against Ridgway.

So the bottom line is that the prime suspect in the Green River murders was convicted of the bulk of those murders which, despite Keppel's comments, does give one a sense that the book has, for all practical purposes, been closed.

After leaving the AG's office, Keppel, who'd earned a Ph.D. from the University of Washington, decided to devote more time to teaching and other activities. At the time of his retirement, he'd participated in more than 2,000 homicide investigations, including some 50 serial murder cases. He continued to serve as the President of the Institute for Forensics in Seattle, to write, and occasionally to consult on cases. He moved to Texas and became an Associate Professor of Criminal Justice at Sam Houston University.

Ann Rule, perhaps the country's most respected true-crime writer, calls Keppel "a superlative detective" and "one of the most gifted and intelligent investigators I have met." It's hard to argue with her assessment. Throughout his career, Keppel has managed to combine the virtues of traditional police work with innovative techniques that old-timers disdained. He knows the value of solid investigative procedure, top-flight interrogation skills, expert surveillance, etc. In fact, he's as good at "basic, old-fashioned detective work" as any cop you'll find. But he's not afraid to combine those traditional skills with tools that have never been used or even conceived of as law enforcement resources, like specialized computer programming. Nor has his mastery of the traditional approach kept him from being able to sense paradigm shifts, to think "outside the box." His open-mindedness has helped him to see the similarities between crimes and link them to a single perpetrator where others saw only the differences and ineffectually went off in different directions looking for different offenders.

He's something unique in criminal investigation. He's an innovative traditionalist.

FURTHER READING

"Washington's Strange Case of Murder Without Rhyme or Reason," an article about Keppel's first homicide case, the Ecumclaw murder of Robert Stergion, was published in the July 1975 issue of *Master Detective*, under the by-line "Andy Stack," the pseudonym of a former police officer and aspiring true-crime writer named Ann Rule.

A few years later, after discovering to her shock that she was personally acquainted with the man who turned out to be the notorious "Ted Killer," Rule wrote *The Stranger Beside Me* (Norton, 1980), regarded by many as the definitive Bundy book. She released updated editions of the book in 1989, the year Bundy was executed, and 2000, the twentieth anniversary of the book's original publication. Another Seattle area journalist who turned out to be personally acquainted with Bundy, Richard W. Larsen, wrote his own book on the case, *Bundy: The Deliberate Stranger* (Prentice-Hall, 1980) which appeared the same year as Rule's book. Both Larsen and Rule mention Keppel prominently.

An early book about the Green River case, *The Search for the Green River Killer* (Penguin, 1991) by Carlton Smith and Tomas Guillen, was perhaps the first full-length examination of the Seattle area's (and indeed the country's) longest-running serial murder investigation. At the time of its publication the killer was still unidentified and the investigation, for all practical purposes, had ground to a halt and would not power up again until several years later when Dave Reichert assumed the post of Sheriff, but it's rightly regarded as a good source of information on the case to that point. Rachael Bell's *Green River Killer: River of Death* (Court TV, 2003), an e-book currently available free of charge on the Crime Library website (www.crimelibrary.com), is a more up-to-date look at the case, containing information on Ridgway's early development as a suspect by Detective Haney and the re-examination of the physical evidence that conclusively linked him to several of the murders. A chapter added after its initial appearance on the Web describes Ridgway's plea agreement and the possible ramifications.

Ann Rule had expected to hold off for several more years before writing her own book about the Ridgway case but with Ridgway's unexpected confession and guilty plea was able to get it completed much sooner than expected. *Green River, Running Red* (Free Press, 2004) came out the year following Ridgway's guilty plea. Before starting that book, while the case was still being investigated, she found herself referring to the victims as numbers, simply because there were so many of them.

"I was horrified when that dawned on me," she later said. "I never wanted to do that again."

In consequence, her book devotes more space to each of the individual victims than other accounts of the case.

The best book that gives a cop's-eye view of both the Bundy and Green River cases currently is Keppel's own autobiographical account, *The Riverman* (Pocket, 1995). Written in collaboration with William J. Birnes, it describes in detail both the pursuit of Bundy and Bundy's consultations on the Green River case. A few years later Keppel and Birnes wrote *Signature Killers* (Pocket, 1997), in which Keppel takes several serial killer cases he's investigated, as well as others he's studied, and uses them to illustrate his theory of criminal "signatures." Both books are highly recommended.

Another cop's-eye view of the Ridgway murders is former Sheriff Dave Reichert's autobiographical narrative of the Green River investigation, *Chasing the Devil – My Twenty-Year Quest to Capture the Green River Killer* (Little, Brown, 2004). An absorbing account of the case from the inside, it provides a good deal of insight into the close relationship between Reichert and Keppel. The office of sheriff in King County,

Washington, as in most US counties, is an elected position. Apparently, serving as King County's top cop awakened Reichert's political ambitions. No longer in law enforcement, he was elected to the US House of Representatives the same year his book came out and is, as this is being written, serving his fifth term as the Congressman from Washington State's District 8.

In 2000, Australian policeman turned crime journalist Patrick Bellamy conducted a book-length interview of Dr. Keppel which, like Bell's report, appears as an e-book on the TruTV (formerly Crime Library) website. It provides profoundly interesting insights into the personality and views of this dedicated, gifted cop.

THE FICTIONAL KEPPEL

Keppel hasn't yet passed into popular culture as a real-life figure who's better remembered for his fictionalized depictions than his real life, but he has been fictionalized several times.

Frederic Forrest (who actually resembles Keppel to a degree) was the first to portray him in *The Deliberate Stranger* (NBC, 1986), a TV-movie that dramatized Richard Larsen's book. Unlike some of the other cop-figures in the film, the character based on Keppel actually uses Keppel's name. Mark Harmon's chilling performance as Bundy earned him a Golden Globe nomination.

Years later, Ann Rule's book was turned into a well-done made-for-TV film, *The Stranger Beside Me* (USA Network, 2003), featuring Barbara Hershey as Rule and Bill Campbell as Bundy. Matthew Bennett appears as "Detective Payton," who is depicted as a close friend of Mrs. Rule's. Payton is, apparently, intended as a composite figure representing all the Seattle area investigators who worked on the case.

Roderick Thorp's book *River* (Fawcett-Columbine, 1995) is described as a "novel about the Green River Killer," but the hero is a Seattle vice cop not a state investigator, and, presumably, is not modeled on Dr. Keppel.

Canadian actor Bruce Greenwood portrayed Keppel in *The Riverman* (A&E, 2004), a TV-movie version of Keppel's book which also featured Sam Jaeger as Reichert, Cary Elwes as Bundy, and David Brown as Ridgway. The sequences in which Keppel and Reichert interview Bundy are inevitably reminiscent of similar scenes in *Manhunter* (De Laurentis, 1986) and *The Silence of the Lambs* (Orion, 1991), in which investigators interview Hannibal Lector. It makes one wonder if that might not have been what Bundy had in mind all along.

While Dave Reichert was a major character in the film version of Keppel's book, Keppel is nowhere to be found in *The Capture of the Green River Killer* (Lifetime, 2008), the TV-movie adaptation of Reichert's *Chasing the Devil*. And for that matter Bundy, as played by James Marsters, has a surprisingly small role. Tom Cavanugh as Reichert is appropriately dedicated and purposeful, but he looks very little like Reichert, and Reichert is enough of a public figure that it would have seemed advisable to cast someone who more closely resembled him. Told in two parts, I found the film somewhat slow-moving. A subplot involves the story of a fictional teen-aged runaway, played by Amy Davidson, who becomes a prostitute in the Sea-Tac area to escape an abusive home life, and, ultimately, one of the girls Ridgway (John Pielmeier) murders. It would not have been possible to personalize all of Ridgway's victims in a dramatized account like this and the film deserves credit for trying to honor them all by giving them a personal, if composite, face. What it does not deserve credit for is excluding Keppel from an investigation in which he was so intimately involved, particularly when Reichert did no such thing in his book.

CHOCOLATE-COVERED MURDER WEAPONS

Culinary Crime, First Course

Major Herbert Rowse Armstrong was not a professional military officer. In fact, he was a small-town lawyer and his small stature and shy demeanor combined to make the profession of arms the calling one would be least likely to associate with him. But, like many who'd served their country as citizen-soldiers during the Great War, he insisted on being addressed by his Army rank once he'd returned to civilian life.

Despite the exaggerated pride Armstrong took in his wartime service, one place he did not command was in his own home. Mrs. Katherine Mary Armstrong was, to put it mildly, a nag who, when she wasn't ridiculing her husband, belittling his military accomplishments, and otherwise making his life miserable, was constantly complaining about her health. The couple and their three children lived in the tiny Welsh village of Hay-on-Wye, where Armstrong conducted a moderately successful practice as a solicitor. He was also an avid gardener and was particularly relentless in his efforts to rid his property of unwanted weeds, purchasing large amounts of arsenic to use as plant-killer.

In July of 1920, some weeks after making out a will in which she bequeathed all her property to her husband, Mrs. Armstrong was committed to a mental hospital after experiencing several delusional and hallucinatory episodes. Free from his wife's henpecking, Armstrong began to take short holidays to London and spent more time at his gardening hobby while at home.

Later in the year, Mrs. Armstrong seemed to have recovered and was allowed to return home in time for the New Year. Within weeks of her return, however, she became ill once again and passed away on February 22, 1921. A combination of heart failure and gastritis was listed as the cause of death.

Armstrong apparently bore his loss with what might charitably be described as great fortitude. Indeed, he seemed to blossom. Previously mild-mannered, his personality became more effusive and ebullient. His law practice began to flourish as he actively pursued new clients. His vacations to London became more frequent. Facing life without his "beloved" spouse, he developed a never-before-experienced *joie de vivre*.

Solicitor Oswald Martin was Major Armstrong's main competitor in Hay-on-Wye, but from all appearances it was a friendly competition. After all, as another small-town attorney, Abraham Lincoln, once noted, "One lawyer in town starves. Two get fat." However, there would soon be reason to suspect that the appearance of friendliness was misleading.

Shortly after Armstrong's personality transformation, Martin received a box of chocolates. The gift was sent anonymously and Martin concluded that the package had been sent by a grateful client. Shortly after receiving the candy, he served some as dessert to a dinner guest who immediately became violently ill. A toxicologist who later examined the chocolates determined that they had been injected with arsenic. Since whoever sent the candy had no way of knowing that they would be served to a dinner guest, it appeared that the target of the poisoner had been Martin himself, but he was at a loss to name anyone who held such a lethal grudge against him.

In October of 1921, Martin arrived at Major Armstrong's home in response to an invitation to tea. In the course of the meal, the major reached for a buttered scone from a serving plate and passed it to his guest with the comment, "Excuse my fingers." This was hardly proper serving etiquette but Martin, passing the social *faux pas* off as the result of the middle-aged widower's recent bereavement, ate the scone. Some time later he, like his guest of a few weeks earlier, became violently ill.

Dr. Thomas Hincks treated Martin. Believing that the solicitor's erratic pulse was atypical for a stomach disease, he sent a sample of Martin's urine for lab analysis and was informed that a significant amount of arsenic was present. Hincks had also been the physician who attended Mrs. Armstrong during her final illness and, while he had signed off on heart disease and gastritis as the cause of death, he'd never been entirely comfortable with that conclusion. Finding that Martin had been given a dose of poison roughly coincident with his having shared a meal with the husband of the late Mrs. Armstrong, Hincks became suspicious and notified the local police. Major Armstrong was arrested on December 31, 1921, and charged with Martin's attempted murder. At his arrest, the major was found to be in possession of a small packet of arsenic which he attempted to hide from the officers.

Shortly after taking Major Armstrong into custody, the police obtained an exhumation order for Mrs. Armstrong's body. One of the most famous criminal investigators in Great Britain, Dr. Bernard Spilsbury, the so-called "Scalpel of Scotland Yard," was brought in to conduct the autopsy.

Dr. Spilsbury, a graduate of Magdalen College in Oxford, attended medical school at St. Mary's Hospital in Paddington, where he was mentored by three pioneers in the field of forensic pathology; Arthur Pearson Luff, Augustus Joseph Pepper, and William Willcox. By 1905 he'd been appointed an assistant demonstrator at St. Mary's, where he first developed the skill at public speaking and lecturing that would stand him in great stead as a professional witness in the coming years. He also became president of the Medico-Legal Society.

Highly respected within the field, Spilsbury first came to public prominence during the trial of Dr. H. Harvey Crippen in 1910, when he was able to demonstrate through scientific analysis that the defendant had poisoned his wife. As a result of his masterful testimony during the Crippen trial, Spilsbury was named junior honorary pathologist to the Home Office.

Over the next three and a half decades, Spilsbury, who, wherever he went, was always in possession of his "murder bag" containing all the necessary implements of a medical detective, dominated the field of forensic pathology. He investigated dozens of celebrated murder cases in which there was no apparent clue to be found and never failed to uncover the crucial scientific evidence that led to the identification and conviction of the killers. In 1925, his efforts on behalf of British law enforcement culminated in a knighthood. British barrister, true-crime writer, and mystery novelist Edgar Lustgarten summed up the esteem in which Spilsbury was held by the general public when he said, "To the man in the street he stood for pathology as Hobbs stood for cricket or Dempsey for boxing or Capablanca for chess. His pronouncements were invested with the force of dogma and it was blasphemy to hint that he might conceivably be wrong."

The post-mortem examination of Mrs. Armstrong was relative child's play for Spilsbury. He had no trouble detecting large traces of arsenic in her remains.

It was now up to the Crown to prove that Major Armstrong had administered that arsenic. His trial on the charge of murdering his wife began on April 3, 1922. Attorney General Sir Ernest Pollock was prosecuting. Sir Henry Curtis-Bennett was retained as defense counsel. Lord Justice Charles J. Darling presided.

Sir Henry advanced the argument that Mrs. Armstrong had committed suicide while in an unbalanced state. This contention was ably refuted by the prosecution which produced one of the nurses who had attended Mrs. Armstrong. She testified that her patient had said, "I have everything to live for—my husband and my children." This was hardly something a woman intent on taking her own life would say.

The most damning evidence was the packet of arsenic found by the police when they placed Major Armstrong under arrest. A later search uncovered 20 more separately wrapped packets of poison. Armstrong claimed that these were nothing more than packages of homemade weed-killer he had compounded to get rid of the dandelions in his garden. When asked why he had taken the trouble to painstakingly wrap a score of separate packages, Armstrong replied, "I really do not know. At the time it seemed the most convenient way of doing it."

This indecisive response, coupled with the fact that only 19 dandelions were counted in Armstrong's garden while 20 separate packets had been prepared, made it appear that the extra packet was intended for Martin.

The clincher came when a doctor who had examined Armstrong on behalf of the prosecution testified that the diminutive solicitor, who had been depicting himself as a moral paragon who would never stoop to anything as base as murder, was suffering from an advanced case of venereal disease. Killing your wife and attempting to kill your business rival was one thing, but picking up a dose of the clap? That was downright disgusting.

Armstrong was found guilty, sentenced to hang, and executed on May 22, 1922.

FURTHER READING

I have been able to find no book dealing exclusively with the Armstrong case. However, biographies of many of the principal characters include information about the crime and its subsequent investigation. Those interested in reading more about the timid small-town lawyer and his ill-fated wife might want to hunt up books like *The Scalpel of Scotland Yard* (Dutton, 1952) by Douglas G. Browne and E.W. Tullett, *The Famous Cases of Sir Bernard Spilsbury* (Nicholson, 1936) by Leslie Randall, *Lord Darling and His Famous Trials* (Hutchinson, 1929) by Evelyn Graham, or *Great Cases of Sir Henry Curtis-Bennett, K.C.* (Holmes Beach, 1996) by Edward Grice. Popular books of famous criminal cases such as Colin Wilson's *Encyclopedia of Murder* (Putnam, 1963) or Jay Robert Nash's *Encyclopedia of World Crime* (CrimeBooks, 1990) also contain accounts of the case.

THE FICTIONAL ARMSTRONG

"The Giaconda Smile," a short story by Aldous Huxley included in his collection *Mortal Coils* (Chatto, 1922) is obviously based, at least in part, on the Armstrong case. In 1948 Huxley adapted the story into a stage play. Catherine Meadows found enough material in the story of the Armstrongs to make a full-length novel, *Friday Market* (Macmillan, 1938). A few years prior to the Armstrong murder, another Welsh solicitor, Harold Greenwood, was also charged with the murder of his wife in similar circumstances. Unlike Armstrong, Greenwood was acquitted. It's been speculated that the Crown's inability to convict Greenwood may have been what inspired Armstrong to resort to murder himself. The possibility that Greenwood proved difficult to convict because he may actually have been innocent seems not to have occurred to him. In any case, it's likely that both "The Giaconda Smile" and *Friday Market* combine elements of both the Greenwood and Armstrong cases.

Anthony Berkeley's short story, "The Avenging Chance," which was later expanded into *The Poisoned Chocolates Case* (Doubleday, 1929), a perennial entry on dozens of "Best Mystery Novel" lists, was actually inspired by a real-life case wholly separate and distinct from the Armstrong murder. However, it seems possible, even likely, that Berkeley may have borrowed the murder method used in the book, the injection of chocolates with poison, from that used by Armstrong in his unsuccessful attempt to rid himself of his business competitor, Oswald Martin.

If Berkeley probably used Armstrong's murder method for *The Poisoned Chocolates Case,* he certainly used the entire Armstrong case for *Malice Aforethought* (Harper, 1931), which he wrote as "Francis Iles," the pseudonym he reserved for his more "serious" crime fiction. Though the small-town lawyer of real life became a small-town physician in the novel, the plot was, nevertheless, clearly derived from Armstrong's murder of his wife. Today *Malice Aforethought* is remembered as one of the first crime novels to be told from the point of view of the killer. A well-received television drama based on the novel was broadcast to British audiences in 1979 and was later shown in the United States as a presentation of PBS's *Mystery!*

It's tempting to suppose that the famous fictional medico-legal detective Dr. John Thorndyke may have been based on Sir Bernard Spilsbury. Certainly there are many striking parallels, including their shared habit of carrying their portable "crime-lab-in-a-bag" with them wherever they went. However, R. Austin Freeman's first Thorndyke novel, *The Red Thumb Mark* (Hodder, 1907), appeared several years before Spilsbury became a public figure in the wake of the Crippen case, and the first short story to feature the crime-solving physician, "31, New Inn," was published even earlier. On the other hand, it's possible that Freeman, a medical practitioner himself, knew of Spilsbury and his accomplishments before the general public did and, displaying remarkable prescience, might have used him as the model for Thorndyke. It's also possible that Spilsbury, as he rose in fame and prominence, may have been aware that he was playing in real life the role that Thorndyke played in fiction and, in a case of life imitating art rather than the reverse, may have used Thorndyke as the model for his own public persona. Since their public careers ran along roughly parallel tracks, Thorndyke in fiction from 1907 through 1942, and Spilsbury in real life from 1910 through 1947, perhaps the likeliest possibility is that they started out independently but were each influenced by the other as they progressed.

I'm not the first to speculate that there might be a connection between Thorndyke and Spilsbury. Raymond Chandler, who was, surprisingly enough, something of a Freeman fan, also made the link in a letter he wrote to Sherlockian scholar James Keddie in 1950.

Whether or not Spilsbury was the model for Thorndyke, it is generally acknowledged that he *was* the model for Sir James Lubbock, the "famed Home Office analyst" who plays a supporting role in many of Dorothy L. Sayers's novels.

THE CASE OF THE TERRIFIED TENOR

Music and Mysteries: Overture

When one speaks of the "Melting Pot" one is generally assumed to be referring to the entire United States in all its multi-ethnic glory. However, when the term first was coined it was meant to describe not the whole country, but only its greatest city, New York.

In the early 1900s, it was often said that New York City had more Irish than Dublin, more Jews than Jerusalem, more Poles than Warsaw, and more Russians than Moscow.

I'll leave verification of these statistical claims to others. The fact that such claims could be credibly made, whether or not they were accurate, is enough indication of how much a city of immigrants New York had become in the closing years of the 19th century and the opening years of the Twentieth.

Whatever the actual numbers of Irish, Jews, Poles, and Russians living there at that time, it *is* a statistical fact that, with the sole exception of Naples, more Italians lived in New York than in any other city on Earth. 500,000 of the city's residents, more than a quarter of its population, were either Italian immigrants or Americans of Italian descent. Most of New York's Italians, finding it difficult to assimilate because of their language and customs, to say nothing of the hostility their language and customs generated among "respectable" Americans, crowded together in a teeming ghetto in the Lower East Side that became known as "Little Italy," where they lived lives of grinding poverty. But there were a few who were able to rise to positions of prominence through the old-fashioned recipe of hard work, good luck, and talent.

That third ingredient, talent, was certainly the major factor behind the success of the man who was undoubtedly the *most* prominent of New York's Italian residents, the Metropolitan Opera's star attraction, Enrico Caruso. Indeed, Caruso, already acknowledged as the greatest operatic tenor of his generation, perhaps of *any* generation, was, with the possible exception of Pope Pius X, the most prominent Italian on the face of the planet. His fame and popularity prefigured the kind of cult worship that would be paid, in later years, to performers like Frank Sinatra and Elvis Presley, which is only fitting, since Caruso was the music industry's very first recording superstar.

Businesses like the Victor Talking Machine Company were marketing a new-fangled gadget called the Gramophone. In fact, they were marketing it so successfully that it was taking the country, indeed the world, by storm, and every household that included one of these instruments was certain to have a few of Caruso's records to play on it. His recording income made him so wealthy that he could actually afford to turn down a long-term contract with the Chicago Opera that would have paid him $5000 a performance, preferring to stay with the Met, which paid him only half of that. Wealth, talent, and fame had kept Caruso out of the slums to which most of his countrymen were condemned, but it failed to immunize him from one of the most pernicious torments then plaguing New York's Italian community.

It was known as the Black Hand.

Today, the term "Black Hand" is understood to mean the Mob in its embryonic stage and this isn't entirely incorrect. But at the turn of the century, "Black Hand" didn't refer so much to an organization as it did to a method, an absurdly simple and prosaic method, of extortion. It consisted of nothing more than a letter demanding money with instructions on how to pay, signed with the figure of a hand in black ink. The alternative was usually death, although threats to kidnap the victim's children or sabotage his livelihood were also common. Virtually any Italian who'd managed to reach a certain level of prosperity was targeted. And the threats were real. Those who refused the demands were killed, or their children were kidnapped, or their homes or businesses were bombed.

That's all there was to it.

It was a far cry from the sophisticated, corporate style of law-breaking that became the hallmark of the Mob in later years. In fact, though many Black Handers had been Sicilian *mafiosi* or Neapolitan *camorriste* prior to coming to the United States, it's unlikely that there was a single, monolithic "Black Hand" society. At that point it was merely a number of loosely-knit gangs that used the same method to terrorize the immigrant population. Nevertheless, they were the seed from which the Five Families of New York and, ultimately, the entire nationwide syndicate of crime would grow.

As the most famous, most prosperous Italian resident of New York, it was inevitable that Caruso would be victimized. Early in his career at the Met he began to receive "Black Hand" notes ordering him to turn 10% of his performance fee over to the extortionists on penalty of death, the kidnapping of his children, or the destruction of his livelihood.

In Caruso's case, his livelihood was his voice and many of the notes graphically threatened that if he failed to pay as demanded his tormentors would see to it that chemical agents that would ruin his larynx and end his fabled career would be secreted in his food and drink.

Faced, like so many of his countrymen, with the choice of "pay or die," Caruso paid. After every Met performance he dutifully followed the extortionists' instructions and did so for several years.

When a note came demanding not merely 10% of his performance fee but a large lump sum payment (according to some accounts, the amount demanded was $5000; others place it as high as $15,000), one of Caruso's aides took it upon himself to seek help from the authorities. Specifically, from Caruso's fellow Neapolitan, Detective Lieutenant Giuseppe Petrosino.

If Enrico Caruso was New York's most famous Italian resident, Joe Petrosino had a firm hold on second place. The highest-ranking Italian-American in the NYPD, he commanded an elite detail of specially selected Italian-American officers organized specifically to combat the Black Hand. Over the course of more than two decades on the Force, he'd become one of the best-known policemen in the country.

Petrosino was born in Salerno in 1860, emigrated with his family to the United States at the age of 13, and became a naturalized American citizen at 17. A year later he obtained a position with the City of New York, not as a policeman, but as a street cleaner. It happened, however, that at that time in New York, street cleaning came under the jurisdiction of the NYPD. Thus the teen-aged Petrosino found himself embarking upon a career in law enforcement, though as a civilian employee rather than as a sworn officer.

Promoted to foreman a year after being hired, his direct supervisor became Inspector Aleck "Clubber" Williams, the legendary "Tsar of the Tenderloin."

When Petrosino first arrived in the States, there were only a few thousand Italians living there. Petrosino and his family were part of a small trickle. By the 1880s, that trickle had become a tidal wave, swelling New York's Italian population to unprecedented levels. The largely Irish police force found itself overwhelmed by a flood of new residents who spoke no English.

Inspector Williams, finding that one of the "whitewings" under his supervision was a bright, literate young Italian, fluent in English as well as virtually every Italian dialect, felt that he would be of far greater use to the city helping to clear the streets of criminals rather than litter, and recruited him as an unofficial undercover agent. For the next few years Petrosino worked essentially as an informer, passing to Williams data on any criminal activity he heard about in Italian neighborhoods.

With Inspector Williams's sponsorship, Petrosino eventually won an official appointment as a New York City police officer and was sworn in on October 19, 1883. Seven years later, he was promoted to detective. Given a roving assignment to suppress criminal activity in Italian neighborhoods, he began his long war with the "Black Hand." Joe Petrosino's greatest handicap was getting cooperation from law-abiding Italians. There was a strong tradition of suspicion of the authorities among the newly-arrived immigrants, to say nothing of fear of retaliation from the gangsters, so the most common response of Italian crime victims was silent forbearance.

Undeterred, Petrosino adopted disguises and subterfuge, scamming the evidence he couldn't obtain by more orthodox police methods. Petrosino, against all odds, was managing to arrest a lot of criminals, and he had a reputation for being rough with them. It was rare for him to bring in a collar unmarked by bruises or scrapes. "So you'll remember Petrosino," he'd say.

As tough as he could be on thugs, he could be just as tender with victims. And whatever lengths he'd go to in bringing down the guilty, he'd go even farther to save the innocent. On one occasion, when a young man named Angelo Carboni was sentenced to die for a murder that he insisted he hadn't committed, Petrosino was persuaded to take a second look at the case. Convinced after examining the evidence that Carboni had been wrongfully convicted, he launched a single-minded search for the real killer. As the date of Carboni's execution drew closer, Petrosino developed another suspect named Salvatore Ceramello and began a chase that took him over a good portion of the Atlantic Seaboard. Ceramello's trail led the detective south to Jersey City, New Jersey, then to Philadelphia, Pennsylvania. From there Petrosino was led north to Canada, barely missing his quarry in Montreal and Nova Scotia. Returning to New York, new clues led him to Baltimore, Maryland, where he finally caught up with the fugitive, made his arrest, and obtained a confession, saving Carboni from the electric chair just days before his scheduled execution.

As stories like this began to circulate in Little Italy, trust began to slowly build between the implacable cop and the immigrant community he was single-handedly trying to protect. Little by little, Petrosino was finding that people were more willing to come to him for help or to pass along information.

In 1895 Petrosino was promoted to sergeant and he began to lobby for both the recruitment of more Italian-American policemen and the establishment of a special squad of Italian detectives. "In this city," Petrosino would say, "which has a half-million Italians, the number of policemen who can speak Italian is exactly 11. And one of them is really French and Irish."

The department was reluctant to take Petrosino's recommendations. Italians on the police force? Didn't really seem to be quite the thing. Petrosino had worked out well, of course, but he was the exception that proved the rule.

But with new Italian immigrants arriving every day and crime rising in Little Italy as the number of potential victims for the underworld predators rose, they eventually had to give his ideas a closer look. In 1905, Sergeant Petrosino was put in charge of a small Italian Branch made up of five picked officers. Within months they started to make major headway against crime in the Italian quarter, and the squad was expanded to 25. By 1906, with Petrosino now a lieutenant, the Italian Branch had become the Italian Legion, with a 10-officer detachment in Brooklyn (annexed by New York City in 1898) supplementing the main force in Manhattan. Hundreds of Italian criminals were being placed under arrest, with thousands of heretofore unreported crimes coming to light, as law-abiding immigrants, now convinced that the police force was on their side, began to testify against the gangsters. Newspapers, finding the colorful Petrosino to be great copy, reported that Black Hand ranks had been cut in half as a result of the efforts of the lieutenant and his men, and if that item was perhaps statistically dubious, it reflected the obvious fact that the unit was getting unprecedented results.

Petrosino was a driven man, totally consumed by his vocation, leaving little time to devote to personal pursuits. But one of the few diversions he did allow himself was music. Like his fictional counterpart, Sherlock Holmes, Petrosino was a violinist, a surprisingly accomplished violinist according to those few who were privileged to hear him play. He was also a devoted opera aficionado and a great admirer of Caruso, so it was not surprising that he took personal charge of the case.

Caruso, likewise, had a high regard for Petrosino. Nonetheless, it was not his choice to have the police involved with the case and now that they had been informed, he was still inclined to simply pay the extortionists' demands.

Petrosino strongly advised the singer against taking this course. Paying now, he insisted, would only make him vulnerable to even greater demands in the future.

"Let me handle this in my own way," he told Caruso. "You'll have no cause for worry."

Leaving a detail of detectives to act as bodyguards, Petrosino put his plan for catching the Black Handers into effect.

If the Black Hand extortion racket was ridiculously simple, it also had a ridiculously simple weakness. Extortion, after all, is a cash business, and the only way a criminal can profit from it is to actually show himself at some point in order to physically take possession of that cash. All Petrosino had to do was stake out the designated payoff location and trap the Black Handers in the act of making the pickup.

Selecting a man from his squad who bore a resemblance to Caruso, Petrosino instructed him to make the money delivery to the tenement house corridor specified in the extortion note. Meanwhile, Petrosino and a half-dozen other detectives in various disguises posted themselves at strategic observation points near that location.

Shortly after the delivery was made, three Black Handers arrived to make the pickup. Petrosino's surveillance team immediately took two of them into custody but a third escaped.

This third culprit was soon tracked down personally by Petrosino, who commenced to beat the living hell out of him. After reducing the extortionist to an acceptable level of docility, the detective, ignoring formal deportation proceedings, marched him onto a ship bound for Italy, pulled his revolver, screwed it up against the gangster's head and said, "If you ever come to this country again, I'll blow your brains out. If you ever bother Mr. Caruso again, I'll blow your brains out."

The two extortionists captured at the drop site, were tried, convicted, and sentenced to serve a severe 10-year sentence.

Newspaper editorials complimented the successful investigation and prosecution of Caruso's tormentors and singled out Petrosino for particular praise.

"When murder and blackmail are in the air, [read a New York *Times* editorial] and the men folk are white-faced but swearing and the women folk are saying litanies to the Blessed Mother that their dark-haired cherub children may be saved from Black Hand kidnappers, a telephone call comes to Police Headquarters in Mulberry Street for Petrosino, and all Little Italy looks to the Italian detective for protection."

Following the successful conclusion of the Caruso case, Petrosino continued his crusade against the Black Hand. In 1909, at the orders of Theodore Bingham, New York's police chief, he traveled to Italy to confer with law enforcement officials there. His plan was to examine Italian police records and match them to records of Italian criminals in New York so that they could be deported or extradited.

Petrosino, traveling under an assumed name to preserve the secrecy of his mission, was able to match many of the criminals on his list to penal records in Rome, Naples, and Palermo, sending the documentation back to Commissioner Bingham for action. But his investigation was never completed. Wanting to capitalize on the publicity value of Petrosino's mission, Bingham leaked news of his undercover assignment to the papers, which proceeded to publish detailed accounts of Petrosino's supposedly confidential itinerary, alerting the very gangsters he was gathering evidence against.

On March 12, while walking the streets of Palermo, Sicily, the detective stopped to admire the statue of Garibaldi in the Piazza Marina. Two men approached him from behind, drew pistols and opened fire. Petrosino fell, fatally wounded, but managed to hang on long enough to draw his own revolver and return fire before succumbing. He was the first Italian-American police officer to die in the line of duty, and the first American police officer of any ethnic group to die while on duty on foreign shores.

On March 18, a Requiem Mass was offered in the small church attached to the hostel in which Petrosino had been staying. From there, the martyred policeman's coffin was escorted through the streets of Palermo in a procession that was attended by an honor guard of 80 Palermo city policemen, a detail of *Carabinieri* in full dress uniform, and representatives of the Night Watch, the Port Police, and other Italian law enforcement organizations. The procession continued throughout the city for more than three hours until the coffin was finally loaded into the British steamer *Slavonia*, bound for New York City.

When his body arrived home, the process was repeated in Manhattan. On April 12, a second Requiem Mass in St. Patrick's Cathedral was followed by a second ceremonial procession as pallbearers, all drawn from Petrosino's Italian Squad, escorted the coffin through the city's streets, and the Police Band played "Nearer My God to Thee" and Verdi's *Requiem*. They were followed by 1,000 NYPD officers, on horseback and on foot, uniformed representatives from more than 60 Italian-American fraternal organizations, 2,000 schoolchildren, and a crowd of about 200,000 mourners. The procession wound through Manhattan, finally arriving at Calvary Cemetery where the legendary gangbuster was laid to rest.

Less than a year after Petrosino's death, a petition requesting an early release of the convicted Caruso extortionists was circulated. Curiously, one of the first signatures on the petition was none other than Enrico Caruso's.

Or maybe it wasn't all that curious. Maybe he simply decided that, with Petrosino dead, and the protection he'd once been able to offer no longer available, signing the petition was the prudent thing to do.

FURTHER READING

This article is considerably more speculative than usual—certainly more so than is entirely appropriate for anything entitled *Just the Facts*. In my defense, I can only point to the conflicting accounts of the case given in the available research material as a mitigating factor that made such speculation necessary.

To illustrate, most biographies of Caruso contain at least a brief mention of the Black Hand's attempts to extort tribute from the fabled tenor. For example, *Caruso: An Illustrated Life* (Trafalgar Square, 1991), by Howard S. Greenfeld (the author of several books about Caruso) devotes its entire twelfth chapter, "An Encounter with the Black Hand," to the case. However, nowhere in the chapter is Petrosino mentioned. Moreover, although just a bit vague about dates, Greenfeld seem to indicate that the extortion attempt took place in the early months of 1909, when Petrosino would have been in Italy conducting his tragically well-publicized "undercover" investigation.

Even more surprising, since the Caruso investigation is generally regarded as one of Petrosino's most famous cases, there is no mention of it anywhere in the book generally considered to be the most comprehensive biography of the legendary sleuth, Arrigo Petacco's *Joe Petrosino* (Macmillan, 1974). Despite this puzzling omission, Petacco's well-researched account of the legendary cop's life is mandatory reading for anyone interested in finding out more about this great American hero.

JIM DOHERTY

Eugene B. Block's *Famous Detectives* (Doubleday, 1967), a collection of short biographies of well-known criminal investigators, includes a chapter on Petrosino, which gives one of the most detailed accounts of the Caruso case I've been able to find. Block states that there was a single extortionist whom Petrosino and his men arrested at the drop site. *NYPD – A City and Its Police* (Holt, 2000) by James Lardner and Thomas Reppetto, an extraordinarily well-written and meticulously researched history of America's largest law enforcement agency, devotes considerable space to Petrosino and includes a report on the Caruso case essentially conforming to Block's version and, like Block, they attribute the crime to a single offender. By contrast, in the aforementioned Caruso biography, Greenfeld states that police who were staked out at the drop site observed the arrival of three gangsters to claim the money, two of whom were captured and convicted, while the third successfully made his escape. Both *Famous Detectives* and *NYPD* assert that the sole culprit was brought to trial and convicted.

Jay Robert Nash's massive, multi-volume *Encyclopedia of World Crime* (CrimeBooks, Inc., 1990) has an entry on the Black Hand which includes the story of Petrosino marching Caruso's lone victimizer onto a ship bound for Italy after beating him half to death and threatening to complete the job if he was ever seen again. *To Serve and Protect* (Turner, 1995) by Glenn Gamber and Connie Clark, an illustrated history of both the American police service and the National Law Enforcement Officers Memorial (proceeds from the sale of *To Serve and Protect* go to support the Memorial), has a short article on Petrosino which confirms this account.

Carl Sifakis's *The Mafia Encyclopedia* (Facts on File, 1987), which contains separate entries on both Caruso and Petrosino, is particularly confusing on this point. The Caruso article states that two extortionists were captured and convicted, while the Petrosino article asserts that the detective tracked down a single offender whose fate is not specified.

Some sources say that Caruso personally sought Petrosino's help. Others say it was an aide who called in the police without Caruso's knowledge. Some say that Caruso had been paying off the Black Handers for years, while others indicate that he went to the authorities the first time he received a Black Hand letter. Even more annoying, no source I consulted gave a definite date of the incident, and none actually named the criminal (or criminals) arrested in the case.

I felt that writing a comparatively speculative piece was the only way I could reconcile so many differing, conflicting, contradictory, or just plain missing details.

THE CARUSO CASE IN FICTION

With one single exception, fictional depictions of both Joe Petrosino and Enrico Caruso tend to run along parallel lines without ever actually intersecting.

The main character in the 1950 MGM film *The Black Hand*, directed by Richard Thorpe and written by Luther Davis and Leo Townsend, is a young Italian-American lawyer named Johnny Columbo (played by Irish-American hoofer Gene Kelly) out to extract vengeance from the ruthless gangsters who murdered his father in turn-of-the- century New York. However, the second lead is Lieutenant Louis Lorelli (played by another Irishman, the great character actor J. Carroll Naish), a tough, straight Italian- American cop obviously based on Petrosino. While the film dramatizes a number of incidents from Petrosino's life, including his murder while on assignment in Italy, the Caruso case is never referred to.

A year later, MGM released *The Great Caruso*. Also helmed by Thorpe, from a script by Sonia Leview and William Ludwig, it starred another legendary tenor, Mario Lanza, as the title character. But, just as *The Black Hand* had made no reference to the opera star, *The Great Caruso* made no reference to the star detective.

The British suspense writer Frederick Nolan wrote two novels based on the life and career of Petrosino. The first, *No Place To Be a Cop* (Barker, 1974), is set at the very beginning of Petrosino's career and shows the 20-something rookie detective just starting to get an inkling of the widespread criminal conspiracy afoot in Little Italy. The sequel, *Kill Petrosino!* (Barker, 1975), is set decades later and fictionalizes the veteran lieutenant's ill-fated mission to his homeland. Neither book depicts the Caruso case and, curiously, neither has ever been published in the United States.

A few years after Nolan used Petrosino's life as grist for his fictional mill, American mystery writer Barbara Paul wrote *A Cadenza for Caruso* (St. Martin's, 1984), the first in a series of novels featuring the legendary singer as an amateur detective. However, all of Paul's Caruso books are set in 1910 or later, long after the Black Hand incident and, while the extortion attempt and Petrosino's role in it are occasionally referred to, they are not part of any of the plots.

The only fictional depiction of the Caruso extortion case I'm aware of comes about half-way through a very fine Allied Artists film entitled *Pay or Die*. Directed by Richard Wilson, written by Richard Collins and Bertram Milhauser, and released in 1960, the modestly budgeted sleeper features Ernest Borgnine in his best performance aside from his Oscar-winning turn in *Marty* as Petrosino. The film, which dramatizes several of Petrosino's cases, devotes a good portion of its running time to a sequence in which Petrosino and his men are assigned to act as Caruso's bodyguards after the Met star receives some Black Hand letters. This storyline opens with a rather nice scene in which Petrosino, seated at his desk, gets a call from Caruso reporting the extortion and asking for the detective's help. When the shrewd cop seems unconvinced that he's actually speaking with the world-famous tenor, Caruso responds by singing an aria into the phone as proof of his identity.

It probably didn't happen that way, but it should've.

THE FORGOTTEN MAN

Mysteries in the Southwest

On November 22, 1963, Officer J.D. Tibbit, 39, an 11-year veteran of the Dallas Police Department, pulled his patrol car over to the curb of the 400 block of East 10th Street and stepped into history.

Tibbit was a devoted family man, who took his lunch break at home every day. He was a solid, if not spectacular cop, who'd received a citation for bravery eight years earlier. He supplemented his salary of $490 a month by moonlighting at a restaurant on Friday and Saturday nights and at a movie theatre on Sundays.

On this particular day, Tibbit went home for lunch as usual. When he cleared from his meal break at approximately 11:30 a.m., he resumed patrolling his assigned beat in the South Oak Cliff area of town. Soon after returning to service, a radio call went out that a sniper had fired on a car passing through the downtown area, wounding at least two of the occupants, one of them fatally. Tibbit was instructed to move closer to downtown and keep an eye out for the suspect, described as being a white male in his mid-20s with close-cropped hair and a ruddy complexion.

At roughly 1 p.m., Tibbit spotted a man fitting the description of the suspect walking along East Tenth Street. He parked his car and apparently called the suspect over. The suspect leaned into the car for a moment, then stepped away. Tibbit exited the car, stepped onto the sidewalk, and began to approach the suspect.

Without warning, the suspect drew a concealed .38, fired at Tibbit four times and fled. Tibbit was still alive when the ambulance reached him, but he died en route to the hospital.

The cop-killer, in the meantime, bought a ticket at the Texas Theatre at 231 West Jefferson Boulevard, and calmly went in to see the movie, *War is Hell*. It was there that he was finally apprehended.

At Dallas Police Headquarters, the suspect was booked for the murder of Officer Tibbit. It wasn't until later that a connection was made between Tibbit's killer and the downtown sniper.

The suspect's name was Lee Harvey Oswald. The fatal victim of the downtown sniping incident was John F. Kennedy, the President of the United States.

A lot of books have been published casting doubt on Oswald's culpability in the Kennedy murder. It's not within the scope of this chapter to examine or comment on the evidence in that case. But there's no doubt that Oswald shot Officer Tibbit, a dependable honest, honorable lawman who, like so many cops who go down in the line of duty, had the bad luck to be in the wrong place at the wrong time.

One of the most visited sites in the Washington, DC, area is President Kennedy's grave at Arlington National Cemetery. It is a fitting monument to a martyred head of state who died while engaged in the service of his country.

A far less well-visited site in the nation's capital city is located in Judiciary Square. It is the National Law Enforcement Officers Memorial, dedicated to American police officers who have been killed in the line of duty. The name of every American law enforcement officer known to have died on the Job, beginning with Sheriff Cornelius Hogeboom of Columbia County, New York, who was murdered in 1791, and continuing down to the present day, is chiseled onto the walls of this monument. On panel 63E, line 9, Officer J.D. Tibbit's name is inscribed, coincidentally next to the name "John Kennedy," a New York City police officer who was killed in the 1920s. That's the only remembrance to be found in the Federal City to a brave man who died trying to apprehend his president's killer.

Only four US presidents have been murdered in office. When you consider that there have only been about 40 in the history of the republic, that seems like a high percentage. Still, it doesn't happen all that often. In the 20th century, it only happened twice. When it does happen, it's a gut-wrenching experience for the entire country. By contrast, an American police officer is killed roughly every two days. Most are forgotten by the general public soon after they're put in their graves. And, perhaps because it happens so often, it doesn't cause anywhere near the angst that the death of a president does.

And, after all, cops choose their professions, knowing that it might put them in harm's way. Nobody twists their arm. Nobody forces them to pin on a badge.

But anyone who willingly sacrifices his life to keep us safe deserves to have that sacrifice marked. Since it was first dedicated on October 15, 1991, the National Law Enforcement Officers Memorial has been doing just that.

If you're ever in Washington, DC, and you happen to visit President

Kennedy's grave, give a thought to stopping at Judiciary Square and paying your respects to the second man to be murdered in Dallas that day.

Officer J.D. Tibbit, the forgotten man.

BLOOD FOR OIL

The Southwestern Mystery Revisited

In 1803, the Osage, a tribe of Sioux-speaking Plains Indians, was the dominant group of North American natives south of the Missouri River, controlling an area that included seven-eighths of what is now the State of Missouri, the northern half of what is now Arkansas, and millions of additional acres in what is now Oklahoma. That same year, this Osage homeland was annexed by the United States when President Jefferson closed the deal on the Louisiana Purchase. By 1825, after a series of bad real estate transactions, the Osage had been relocated to a large reservation in Kansas, ceding title to their traditional land holdings. In exchange for this they received, in addition to the Kansas reservation, a lump sum cash settlement, a cash annuity, and a quantity of livestock and agricultural equipment. They lived in relative peace for the next few decades, until the South tried to secede from the rest of the Union.

One of the consequences of the Civil War was the stimulation of white migration to the West. As more and more white settlers entered Kansas (in the words of one Osage elder, "They just kept coming like ants"), the valuable, fertile Osage property began to be more and more encroached upon. Rather than protect the Osage's property rights, the response of the US Government was to renegotiate their treaty with the Osage in 1868, persuading them to move out of Kansas and into the adjacent Indian Territory.

The Osage had always been known as shrewd traders and their experience with the white man had caused them to become shrewder still. At the same time, President Grant had removed the responsibility for administering Indian affairs from the Army and assigned it to civilians, many of them Quakers, who were determined to deal with Indians fairly, at least according to their lights. The consequence of this coincidence of growing Indian shrewdness with Quaker ethics was that the Osage were paid nearly $8,500,000 in 1870 for their Kansas holdings, making them the wealthiest Indian tribe in the country.

The government then brokered a deal wherein the Osage would buy an area of Indian Territory just below the Kansas state line from the Cherokee tribe. The Cherokees were not really enthusiastic about the arrangement but having cast their lot with the Confederacy during the

161

Civil War (indeed, the great Cherokee war chief, Stand Watie, was the last general officer in the Confederate Army to surrender, more than two months after Lee and Grant had met at Appomattox), they didn't have a lot of clout. The Osage got the land that became their new reservation (ironically an area that had once been part of their ancestral homeland, which they now had to buy back) at a price, 74 cents an acre for 1.47 million acres, that still left the tribe with the bulk of the money they had received from the sale of their Kansas land, now drawing interest in the US Treasury.

The land they'd bought was hilly, rocky, and difficult to farm, but some elders took that as a plus. If the land was of negligible value, at least that would keep the covetous whites away. As one tribal leader, Wah-ti-an-kah, put it, "The white man does not like country where there are hills, and he will not come." True enough, perhaps, in the short run, but in the long run Wah-ti-an-kah's prediction proved tragically inaccurate.

In 1887, the Dawes Act, also known as the "General Allotment Act" or (with no sense of irony) the "Indian Emancipation Act," was passed. This provided that all of the reservations in the western part of Indian Territory, each of them commonly owned by all members of each tribe, would be disbanded as autonomous administrative entities. Instead, each individual member of each tribe would be allotted 160 acres of land, free and clear. Any reservation land left over after each Indian had received his 160 acres would be opened for settlement by non-Indians. The western part of Indian Territory would be renamed Oklahoma Territory, which was established officially in 1889.

Years later, when Oklahomans began to campaign for statehood, it was decided that the Twin Territories should be reunited and enter the Union as a single state. This required, however, that the Allotment Act be extended to the Eastern tribes. However, simply repealing the parts of the Dawes Act that had exempted the tribes in the now-shrunken Indian Territory wouldn't work with the Osage because they had acquired their land by purchasing it outright, rather than by Federal grant.

Still, the Osage tribal leaders could see the writing on the wall. The term "Indian giver" had, after all, been coined to describe the US Government, with its persistent policy of giving land or other concessions to Indians, then taking the gift back once white people decided they wanted it. A bellicose Congress was already threatening to impose allotments on the Osage in spite of their having bought the property.

In 1906, to avoid having allotments forced on them under disadvantageous terms, the Osage struck a compromise bargain. The Osage reservation was disbanded as a geographic entity and became Osage County, then as now the largest county in Oklahoma.

Each individual member of the tribe received the federally mandated 160 acres. However, the remaining tribal property was not opened up to non-Indian settlement. Instead, once the initial 160 acre parcels had been granted, the remainder was also divided equally among the individual members. In this way, each of the 2229 Osages then listed on the tribal rolls received a total of 657 acres apiece and all Osage property remained in Osage hands.

The final kicker had to do with mineral rights. Under the Osage proposal, individual ownership applied only to the surface land. Mineral rights continued to be held in common by the tribe. If gold or silver, for example, was discovered on one tribal member's property, any mining profits generated by that discovery would be divided up equally among all tribal members rather than held by the original property owner.

Each of the 2229 tribal members was issued a mineral "headright" which entitled that member to 1/2229th of all mineral profits derived from Osage land. This would be a perpetual right, no matter who the land might be sold to in the future. The number of headrights would remain constant no matter how much tribal membership might increase or decrease in the future. A headright could be bequeathed to the owner's heirs, even if the heirs were neither Osage nor any other kind of Indian. And an Osage who already owned a headright could theoretically be bequeathed additional headrights and thus become the owner of several headrights simultaneously.

For example, a family consisting of a full-blooded Osage father, a full-blooded Osage mother, and a single male child, would each be awarded one headright apiece. If the father and the mother both died, their headrights would pass to their son, making him the sole beneficiary of three headrights.

What made all this more than simply theoretical was that oil had been discovered on Osage land in 1897. Oil was destined to fuel unimagined technological changes over the next few decades, and the profits earned from its production would be enormous. Now, thanks to the savvy bargaining of their tribal leaders, each of the 2229 officially registered members of the Osage tribe would be reaping the benefits of those profits.

In a few short years, this deal would make the Osage the single wealthiest population group in the world. It should have been a blessing, but historically, whenever Indians were in possession of something that white men wanted, Indians wound up holding the dirty end of the stick.

And history was about to repeat itself.

In 1920, a single headright generated $8090 of income. Adjusting very roughly for inflation, this would be approximately equivalent to $650,000 in early 21st century purchasing power. And this was in addition to individual land holdings and interest on each tribal member's share in the money paid for the sale of the Kansas reservation. Stories began to appear about the childish manner in which Osage people handled their unaccustomed wealth. Having no concept of economy or thrift, some Osage squandered their money. A number were persuaded to buy grand pianos, which they left outdoors during all seasons because there was no room for them in the one- or two-room houses many Osage still lived in despite their wealth. Osage Indians who bought expensive cars (it was said that there were more Pierce-Arrows, the most costly automobile of the era, in Osage County than any other county in the US), but who had no experience in their operation, might wreck the vehicle or get it stuck in mud or just run it into the ground through improper maintenance. When that happened they simply left the car where it was and went off to buy a new one. One Osage woman was reported to have spent more than $40,000 in one afternoon, buying, among other things, a diamond ring, a new car, a houseful of new furniture, and, sight unseen, a plot of Florida real estate. There were dozens of other such stories.

Much of this was to be expected. It was the predictable behavior of a group of relatively unsophisticated people who were the sudden recipients of great wealth. And, of course, the many Osage who handled their financial affairs sensibly never made it into the news.

The response of non-Osage was equally predictable. Regarding the oil-rich Indians as pigeons ripe for the plucking, a plague of parasites descended on Osage County, eager to do the Osage out of as much of their oil money as they could. Some opened stores that charged Osage customers as much as five times more for any given item than they charged white customers. Others married pretty young Osage women to gain control of their fortunes. Still others loaned Indians money, when they were between oil checks, charging usurious interest rates.

In an effort to keep the Osage from being victimized by such bloodsucking predators, the Government instituted a "guardian" system. Osage Indians who were judged capable of handling their own finances were issued certificates of competency. All others were assigned financial guardians by Oklahoma courts. This was, no doubt, a well-intentioned measure but, judged from a present-day perspective, it was insultingly condescending, to say nothing of racist. If a hypothetical group of equally unsophisticated white people, hill dwellers in Appalachia, for example, were the sudden recipients of similarly great wealth and reacted in a similarly irresponsible manner, it's hard to imagine that the Government would even consider taking it upon themselves to decide which white people were or were not "competent" to handle their own money.

More to the point, the program did little or nothing to protect the Osage from being victimized. On the contrary, the more common outcome of the guardian system was to give the practice of swindling Indians an official imprimatur as unscrupulous men sought, and received, appointments as financial caretakers to Osage "clients."

But far more immediately frightening to the Osage than simply being cheated of their money was the sudden increase in violent or mysterious deaths among their people between 1919 and 1924.

A few examples:

- Charles Whitehorn, a young Osage, found in the woods just outside the town of Pawhuska, shot in the head.
- Kenneth Rogers, shot by an unseen assailant while sitting by the window of his home reading.
- Nina Smith, a young Osage woman married to a white man, found poisoned to death.
- Champion Osage cowboy Bill Stetson, a hard-drinking Army veteran, found dead of whiskey poisoning in 1922.
- Mrs. Kelsie Morrison (formerly Mrs. Bill Stetson), found dead of unknown causes, a few months after her first (Osage) husband's death, and a few weeks after marrying her second (white) husband.

How many Osage were murdered during that five year period? Nobody's really sure. It's certain that there were literally dozens. One official law enforcement tally puts the number of confirmed Osage murders at 24. Other estimates put it as high as 45 to 60. One frustrated investigator, in a report on the high number of homicides among the Osage, writes about there being "hundreds and hundreds" of murders, though it's unclear whether this is an honest estimate or hyperbole employed to express his horror and anger. In any event, the death rate among Osage was much higher than the national rate and given the presumed higher standard of living that came with the oil wealth, it should have been much lower. Many of these deaths were unexplained. Many of those that were explained remain suspicious despite the official verdicts. The number of confirmed murders is so high that it's almost impossible to believe that, among those Osage deaths that were either unexplained or suspicious, there weren't additional murders.

Even presuming that the most conservative number, 24, is accurate, this averages out to roughly five murders every year during the operative five year period among a population group barely numbering 2,000. Washington, DC, the most murder-plagued big city in the United States, recently reported an annual murder rate of 69.3 per 100,000, or less than 1 murder per 1,000. The annual murder rate among the Osage came to roughly 2.5 per 1,000, more than triple the murder rate of the most dangerous metropolis in the nation 80 years later.

The Osage had achieved the dubious distinction of simultaneously being the single wealthiest population group on the face of the planet and the single most murdered population group on the face of the planet. Small wonder this period was known as "The Reign of Terror."

Little progress was made in the investigation of these murders. Local police tended to be unsympathetic and even hostile to Indians. For example, a well-known Osage who made regular weekly trips to the town of Pawhuska to shop for food, always accompanied by his beloved pack of pet dogs, happened to enter during a rabies scare. He was accosted by a local officer who, without even examining the dogs, began precipitately shooting them to death one by one in front of their owner, who begged and pleaded to be allowed to take them home. On another occasion, an Osage who was stopped for drunken driving by Pawhuska's police chief, exited his car after signing the ticket and began walking home. The police chief ordered him to stop as he was crossing the street, then fired two shots into the Indian's back when he kept going. Loading the Osage into a car, the chief took him to a local mortuary, dumped him on the front steps, and left him there to die. A special investigator appointed by the governor to look into the rising crime wave in Osage County, wound up getting himself arrested and convicted for bribery.

In light of such incidents, the Osage Tribal Council felt that they could expect no satisfaction from local or state law enforcement, so, early in 1923, the Council passed a resolution requesting "the services of the Department of Justice in capturing and prosecuting the murderers of the members of the Osage Tribe." The request was passed along to Attorney General Harry Daugherty, who turned it over to FBI Director William Burns.

(Note: At that time the criminal investigative and enforcement arm of the Justice Department was called simply the Bureau of Investigation. In 1933, after the passage of the New Deal's Omnibus Crime Act, it changed its name to the Division of Investigation. In 1935, it changed back to the Bureau of Investigation but now with the somewhat redundant prefix "Federal" officially added, making it possible to refer to the agency by what would soon become the most famous set of initials in American law enforcement. For the sake of clarity, I am in this chapter referring to the agency by its best-known name.)

Burns, a former US Treasury Agent famous for the private security and detective agency he'd founded, was a close friend of Attorney General Daugherty, which is what had led to his appointment to the FBI's top post. He sent a few agents to Oklahoma to look into things but, since none of the crimes appeared to be federal offenses, the most his men would be able to do would be to gather data which would then have to be turned over to local authorities anyway, so the investigation was not being pursued with much vigor. In any case, Daugherty and Burns were both caught up in the Teapot Dome Scandal, which divided their attention somewhat. The Osage file was closed after a few months of unenthusiastic investigation failed to produce any leads, despite the fact that the year 1923 had been perhaps the bloodiest of the five-year Reign of Terror.

When Daugherty and Burns were both forced to leave federal service in the wake of the scandal, J. Edgar Hoover, then a 29-year-old Justice Department attorney, was appointed the Bureau's Acting Director. One of his first official acts was to reopen the Osage case.

The Osage murders were starting to draw national, even world attention. Politicians like Senator Charles Curtis of Kansas (himself a member of the Kaw Indian tribe and a future Vice-President of the United States) were showing an intense interest in the case. Hoover himself was personally horrified by the scope of the crimes. And leaving aside his personal feelings, he desperately wanted to be permanently appointed to the Director's job. If the Bureau under Hoover could solve a high-profile crime, one that had stumped both local law enforcement and his own predecessor, this permanent appointment would be assured.

Hoover, though a gifted administrator, was not an experienced investigator. To track down the murderers, he'd need a career cop, not a career bureaucrat. The agent he chose to be his point man on the case was Inspector Tom White.

Then 46 years old, the 6-foot-4-inch, 250-pound Texan brought more than two decades of law enforcement experience to the Osage case. He'd started his career as a Texas Ranger just after the turn of the century, leaving state service in 1909 to become a railroad detective, first with the Santa Fe and then with the Southern Pacific. He joined the FBI in 1917, rising rapidly to simultaneously become the Special Agent in Charge of the Bureau's Houston Field Office, and Inspector for the Southern and Western States, making him responsible for keeping every Field Office from Oregon to Georgia shipshape and up to standard. White was the first FBI agent to hold the title of "Inspector."

White was transferred from Houston to Oklahoma City where, in addition to being the lead investigator on the Osage case, he'd continue to be responsible for supervising all Bureau activities within the purview of his Field Office.

White reasoned that the earlier investigation had failed to bear fruit because no one in Osage County, Indian, white, or otherwise, was anxious to be seen talking to a government man, particularly a government man who was obviously from the urban East. In order to overcome this obstacle, he assigned a number of agents to assume undercover roles in and around Osage County. Each of the agents chosen for this assignment was a Southwesterner, each with extensive local or state law enforcement experience, and each having a good general knowledge of the customs and traditions of the Plains Indians.

Alex Street, who had been Sheriff of Quay County, New Mexico, prior to joining the Bureau, was the supervisor of the undercover detail. He was posing as a cattle buyer from Fort Worth, which would put him in contact with the many ranchers and cowhands in the area.

Gene Parker was, like White, a former Texas Ranger. And, like Street, he had assumed the role of a cattle buyer from the Lone Star State. He'd first entered federal law enforcement as a US Customs officer patrolling the Texas/Mexico border, where he'd become fluent in Spanish. Parker's friendly, nonchalant manner made it easy for strangers to warm up to him, an invaluable asset in a job where the whole point was getting strangers to talk about matters they didn't really want to talk about.

Charlie Davis, in his late 40s, was the oldest of the undercover agents. Aside from his police background, Davis's résumé included several years of experience as an insurance agent in his native Texas. After moving into Osage County, he set up an insurance office in downtown Fairfax, which put him in an excellent position to mix with townspeople and pick up valuable pieces of gossip and information.

Special Agent John Wren was part Ute Indian and part Mexican. As an investigator, Wren's greatest asset was a phenomenal memory for details and an ability to connect, and draw conclusions from random, seemingly unrelated bits of information. Wren's role was that of a roving Indian medicine man. Though he was not Osage, his ethnic background would be helpful in breaking down communication barriers between the Bureau and the Indians they were trying to protect.

Other undercover men posed as drifters, hoboes, cowboys, or oil prospectors. While Inspector White and his chief assistant, Special Agent Frank Smith, conducted a public investigation, the undercover detail quietly gathered information behind the scenes.

Early on, the agents were faced with the same jurisdictional problem that the earlier FBI team had encountered. Murder is not a federal offense, so the most they could hope to do was gather enough evidence to make a case in state court and then turn that evidence over to local authorities. They were, in effect, acting as private investigators for the Osage Tribal Council. In fact, the Osage Tribe was underwriting the investigation.

It was for this reason that the murder of Henry Roan, which had occurred early in 1923, drew their particular interest. The body of Roan, who had been missing for more than 10 days, was found in car parked in a canyon 200 yards off the main road. He'd been shot behind the right ear. The area where the body had been found was within the original federal homestead allotment of Rose Little Star. Although the Osage Reservation had ceased to exist as an administrative entity, homestead allotments were still under what is called Special Maritime or Territorial Jurisdiction, which meant that the Federal Government, not the State of Oklahoma, had primary authority over criminal matters. In other words, the murder of Henry Roan was the FBI's case.

One person who profited from Roan's death was a local rancher/

businessman named William Hale, who was listed as the beneficiary of a $25,000 life insurance policy on Roan. Hale claimed that the insurance policy had been purchased as security against a cattle deal he and Roan were entering into.

Hale was not the only person with a motive to kill Roan. Roan's wife, Mary, had been involved in a love affair with Roy Bunch, a white storekeeper, for some time. Roan and Bunch had had a number of violent encounters. Shortly after Roan's death, Mary and Bunch got married. Bunch appeared to be truly in love with Mary Roan, but leaving that aside, Mary now controlled two headrights, her own and her late husband's. By marrying her, Bunch benefited financially as well as romantically. Love and money are the two most common motives for murder. Hale only had one of those motives. Roy Bunch had both of them.

On the other hand, the agents were learning that Hale profited not only from the death of Henry Roan, but from the death of nearly every other Osage murder victim. Hale wielded a lot of influence in Osage County. He'd been instrumental, for example, in getting many friends of his appointments as Osage financial guardians. Consequently, whenever an Osage who was a financial ward of one of Hale's cronies wound up on the death list, and that happened quite often, Hale routinely showed up with some sort of claim against the victim's estate, which was just as routinely paid, no questions asked.

Even Osage Indians who had certificates of financial competency were not immune from the grasp of Hale. For example, when Joe Grayhorse, an Osage deemed competent to handle his own affairs, was found mysteriously dead, Hale was able to produce a deed showing that ownership in several valuable tracts of real estate had been transferred by Grayhorse to Hale. Grayhorse's relatives fought it, but the deed was upheld in court.

Other murdered Indians were often buried through the Big Hill Undertakers, a mortuary in which Hale owned a controlling interest. As with any other good or service available in Osage County, Indians were routinely overcharged for funerals. If Hale could profit by an Osage murder in no other way, he could at least make some money by selling cheap caskets at expensive prices.

Bunch had benefited from the death of Roan. Hale had profited from the deaths of many different Indians, Roan among the rest. The federal agents weren't ruling Bunch out, but they were coming to regard Hale more and more as their prime suspect.

Four other obvious murders and one mysterious death that might be a murder, all of them peripherally related to the Roan case, also seemed to lead back to Hale.

Late in May 1921, about seven months before Roan's death, the badly decomposed body of Anna Brown, Roan's cousin, was found near a hunting trail, shot through the back of the head. At the inquest, it was revealed that Bryan Burkhart, Hale's nephew, had been the last person to see her alive.

Two months later, Anna's mother, Lizzie Que Kile, died mysteriously. Kile was old enough that her death might have been ascribed to natural causes had it not been for the many calamities being visited on the Osage tribe generally and her own family specifically. Under the circumstances, many people strongly suspected that she'd been poisoned but no autopsy was ever performed and no proof of murder ever surfaced. Kile, also known as Lizzie Q, had been married to Jimmie Kahesey, who'd died several years earlier. Kahesey was a widower at the time he married Lizzie Q and had inherited his first wife's headrights upon her death. Thus, Lizzie Q inherited both of her husband's headrights when he died. When her daughter Alice had passed away of natural causes in 1918, Lizzie Q also inherited her headright. With Anna's murder, Lizzie Q inherited a fifth headright. Upon Lizzie Q's death, the entire estate passed to her daughter, Mollie Burkhart. Molly's husband, Ernest Burkhart, was the brother of Bryan Burkhart and the nephew of William Hale.

Lizzie Q had one more daughter, Rita Smith, whose white husband, William Smith, had been vocal in his suspicions that William Hale had been involved in the deaths of his various in-laws. Moreover, he and Hale had become involved in a financial dispute over an unpaid loan Smith had made to Hale. On March 9, 1923, the Fairfax home of Bill and Rita Smith exploded into splinters. Subsequent investigation disclosed that a bomb had been planted underneath the house. Rita Smith and their 17-year-old live-in servant, Nettie Brookshire, were both immediately killed. By some quirk of fate, Bill Smith, though fatally injured, did not die right away. At the hospital to which he was brought, he hung on for four days before finally succumbing. Had he died in the blast with his wife, her estate would have passed to her sister Mollie. As it was, since Bill survived Rita, though only by a few days, the estate passed to him and, with his death, to Bill's adult daughter by a prior marriage. And since Bill's daughter was both white and a resident of Arkansas, she was safe from the violence plaguing her Osage step-relatives.

No one could have predicted that Bill Smith would live through the bomb blast, and it seemed clear that the intent was to kill all the residents of the home simultaneously. Had that intention been realized, Mollie Burkhart would have become the beneficiary of seven separate headrights. As it was, she had six. In the year of Bill and Rita's death, a single headright generated $12,440 in annual income. Adjusting for inflation, the 1923 payments from six headrights would be equivalent to slightly less than $6,000,000 in contemporary spending power. For just one year. With the absolute certainty of more to come in every future year for as long as oil continued to flow.

And Mollie, the last surviving Kahesey daughter, was the niece, by marriage, of William Hale.

Hale had moved to Osage County from Greenville, Texas, roughly a quarter of a century earlier. In a short time he established himself as a cattle rancher, owning 5000 acres of Osage County grazing land outright and controlling the grazing lease rights on another 45,000. In addition to the already mentioned mortuary, Hale also owned controlling interests in a local store, the Big Hill Trading Company, and the town bank of Fairfax. He also controlled much of Osage County's underworld and had been manipulating criminal activity for some years, escaping official notice because of the political influence he wielded. One way or another, Hale seemed to find a way to get at least a portion of every dollar, legitimate or crooked, made in Osage County. He was often referred to as the "King of the Osage Hills."

All of this information about Hale was picked up bit by bit through the efforts of the undercover squad. But gossip wasn't evidence.

One of Hale's criminal associates was a man named Henry Grammer, who'd operated Osage County's bootlegging business under Hale's auspices. Grammer, a champion rodeo cowboy in his younger days, employed John Ramsey as a strong-arm man. The undercover agents had been hearing whispers of a man named "John" whom Grammer had mentioned as being the one who performed "that Indian job." And White and his staff learned that John Ramsey had been seen with Henry Roan immediately before Roan disappeared, later turning up dead.

As the agents continued their investigation and it became evident that, this time, they were going to go the whole distance, previously intimidated witnesses began stepping forward and giving information. Hale and his associates, confident that no Oklahoma court would ever try white men for the murder of Indians and that everyone in Osage County was so thoroughly cowed that nothing they said would ever be repeated, had been foolishly loose-tongued, freely admitting their culpability in the murders. As the FBI men doggedly kept at the investigation, witnesses who'd heard these admissions began offering statements, detailing the things they'd heard Hale and the others say.

The agents were getting a picture of what had happened. As they moved closer to having a case they could take to court, Hale's co-conspirators started dying in sinister circumstances. Henry Grammer was killed in a suspicious auto accident. Asa "Ace" Kirby, whom agents believed to be the man who had actually planted the bomb under the Smith house, was killed during an attempted robbery of a country store. The store owner reported that William Hale had warned him of the possibility of a hold-up and advised him to be ready with a shotgun. It was strongly suspected that Hale had suggested the robbery to Kirby specifically to set him up for the kill.

The sudden deaths of Hale's associates were meant to have the dual effect of silencing them and intimidating the remaining accomplices. But when conspiracies fall apart, it usually becomes easier to flip the members of that conspiracy.

The first domino to fall was Ernest Burkhart, the nephew of Hale and the husband of Mollie Burkhart, the last surviving heir to the Kahesey family fortune. Burkhart admitted to recruiting John Ramsey to murder Henry Roan and Ace Kirby to murder Bill and Rita Smith, and to conspiring with his brother Bryan and Kelsie Morrison to murder Anna Brown. The long-range plot, as everyone suspected, was to concentrate all of the Kahesey headrights in Mollie, bringing them under Hale's control.

John Ramsey became the next domino, confessing to murdering Henry Roan at the behest of Hale.

Kelsie Morrison confessed to shooting Anna Brown while Bryan Burkhart was distracting her. It also became known that he'd killed his wife, the widow of Bill Stetson, for her headrights.

On the basis of the confessions, the statements by witnesses, and the evidence painstakingly gathered in an investigation that had gone on for years, William Hale, the Burkhart brothers, Morrison, and Ramsey were all arrested and indicted in state court for the murders of Anna Brown, and Bill and Rita Smith. Additionally, Hale and Ramsey were indicted in Federal District Court for the murder of Henry Roan.

For the next three years, prosecutors fought a series of bitter court battles with Hale and his attorneys. Efforts to keep the Roan case out of federal court, to suborn perjury, to bribe or intimidate witnesses and jurors, were all attempted, but, in the end, to no avail. On January 16, 1929, Hale was convicted in federal court of Henry Roan's murder. He was sentenced to serve a life term at Leavenworth Federal Penitentiary. Ironically, when he arrived to begin his sentence the newly appointed warden who greeted him was Tom White, who'd transferred from the FBI to the Bureau of Prisons while the trial was in progress.

On November 20, 1929, in a separate federal trial, John Ramsey was also convicted of his part in Roan's murder, and also sentenced to life in Leavenworth.

By this time, Kelsie Morrison and Ernest Burkhart had already been convicted in state court and were also serving life sentences, Burkhart at McAlester State Prison and Morrison at the Federal Penitentiary in Atlanta (to keep him separate from the other conspirators).

Bryan Burkhart, Ernest's brother, turned state's evidence in the Anna Brown case, and was never tried for his part in the Osage murders. He was arrested several years later for passing counterfeit money and received a short sentence.

Though convictions had been secured and the murders stopped, it can't really be said that justice was served. All those convicted in the Osage murder case were eventually paroled. Some of the Osage murderers were later convicted of other crimes they committee while on parole and one, Kelsie Morrison, was actually killed in a shootout with police. But none of them paid the ultimate price for viciously cold-blooded multiple murders committed for no other reason except simple, unabashed greed.

Moreover, there were still murders that were never cleared. In all likelihood, there were murders that never even came to light. Though the conviction of Hale and the others served notice that it was no longer open season on Osage Indians, it's possible, even probable, that dozens of killers were never identified and punished for the crimes that had already occurred.

Still, the Osage murder case, the first really high-profile crime ever investigated by the FBI, was one in which J. Edgar Hoover and his agents took a great deal of justifiable pride. Hoover, of course, did receive the permanent appointment to the Director's post, serving in that capacity until his death in 1972.

Inspector (now Warden) Tom White remained in corrections until his retirement from federal service in 1951. He was immediately offered a position on the Texas Board of Parole and Probation. As he'd later put it, "I began by catching criminals and sending them to prison. Then I spent 25 years taking care of them while they were serving their time. Finally, I spent the last six years of my career deciding when they should be released. I had come full circle." He spent 14 years in prosperous, happy retirement before quietly passing away in 1971.

In 1933, Special Agent Frank Smith, White's second-in-command, would be one of the lawmen attacked by gangsters during a prisoner exchange outside of the Union Station in Kansas City, Missouri. This event, in which four policemen (including FBI Agent Raymond Caffrey) were killed and another two seriously wounded, became famous as "The Kansas City Massacre." Smith, who was the only law officer present to escape injury, thus participated in one of the most famous incidents in the Bureau's history, one which led to the passage of the Omnibus Crime Bill and the broadening of the FBI's powers during the Depression. In 1939, he left the Bureau to accept a position as Oklahoma City's Chief of Police, a post he held until 1943 when he returned to the FBI for wartime service as an instructor. He retired in 1948 and died of a stroke in 1953.

I've been able to find no information on the later careers of the other 30-odd FBI agents who worked the case, but all of them received special commendations from the Osage Tribal Council and Agent John Wren, the Ute Indian who'd posed as a roving medicine man, was adopted as an Osage blood brother.

Additional commendations came from the Bureau of Indian Affairs and the Justice Department. But, as a wave of relief swept over Osage County with the imprisonment of the Reign of Terror's mastermind, perhaps the most heartfelt commendation came from one individual citizen who, initially fearful of offering information to investigators, was eventually persuaded to testify in court.

He became willing to appear as a witness because, he said, thanks to the FBI, "the day is past when a man will be shot down for doing right."

FURTHER READING

If you're willing to slog through hundreds and hundreds of pages of dull official reports, and don't mind reading them on a computer screen, many of the FBI's declassified files have been reproduced on CD-ROM and are commercially available. The twelfth volume in a series of CD-ROM's entitled *20th Century FBI Files* (Progressive Management, 2001) includes documents from the Osage murder case. A number of those documents have also been reproduced on the Internet.

If, like me, you prefer books, the most complete account of the FBI's investigation of the case is Lawrence J. Hogan's *The Osage Indian Murders* (Amlex, 1998). Hogan, a former FBI agent, was, in the mid-'50s, assigned the task of going through all of the Bureau's files on the case and preparing a summary that could then be used for a proposed movie about the case. That movie was never made, but Hogan expanded that summary into this book many years later. The complex case is laid out in an easy-to-follow form, but Hogan's writing style is pretty dry, and his insistence on not naming any of the FBI agents involved in the case (they are referred to by phrases like "the agent in charge," "the assistant to the agent in charge," "the agent who was posing as an Indian medicine man," "the agent who was posing as an insurance agent," etc.) becomes tiresome very quickly.

A biography of the lead investigator on the case, Vernon R. Adams's *Tom White – The Life of a Lawman* (Texas Western, 1972), devotes three of its 12 chapters to the Osage case. The rest of the book details White's career with the Rangers, the Railroad Police, the US Bureau of Prisons, and the Texas Parole Board.

Journalist Dennis McAuliffe, informed as a child that his Osage grandmother had died of natural causes, and later informed that she'd committed suicide, became convinced as an adult that she was actually one of the last victims of the Reign of Terror. That, in fact, it was his own grandfather who had murdered her. His book, *The Deaths of Sybil Bolton* (Time Books, 1994), is the story of his investigation into his grandmother's death. A detailed record of the larger Osage murder case is included as background. One of the best-written accounts of the case, it should be noted that McAuliffe has a preexisting agenda that's evident on almost every page. Critical of the FBI investigation, he presumes, for example, that accusations of third-degree interrogation techniques made by Hale and the others during their trials are absolutely true, despite having no evidence for their veracity other than the word of men who were eventually convicted of the murders. Indeed, he can't seem to find a kind word to say about *any* white person who ever came in contact with an Indian. Thomas Jefferson, the Quaker church, white members of his own family, even famed "Little House" author Laura Ingalls Wilder, are all treated to heaping doses of his withering criticism. If you can overlook the ax he spends so much time grinding, the book is a very valuable source of information about the case. Paperback reprints appear under the title *Bloodland*.

"Murder by Proxy," the ninth chapter of Don Whitehead's Hoover-approved history of the Bureau, *The FBI Story* (Random, 1956), is a short account of the Osage case, glossing over the more complicated details but providing a pretty accurate portrait of the mastermind behind many of the murders, William "King" Hale.

One of the first book-length accounts of the case is the hard-to-find *Tragedies of Osage Hills* (Osage Printery, 1935) by Arthur Lamb.

THE REIGN OF TERROR IN FICTION

The earliest example of a fictional depiction of the Reign of Terror that I've been able to uncover is a half-hour radio drama entitled "The Osage Indian Murders," which was broadcast on August 8, 1935, the third episode in a popular but short-lived series entitled *G-Men*. *G-Men* only lasted 13 episodes, from July through October 1935, and no recordings of any of those shows are known to exist. The show was canceled, not because of ratings, but because the show's producer and creator, Phillips H. Lord, and the head of the FBI, J. Edgar Hoover, couldn't agree on the approach the show should take. Lord, knowing he had a solid concept with *G-Men*, decided to tinker with the format. If he couldn't secure the cooperation of the FBI specifically, he'd try to secure the cooperation of American law enforcement generally and dramatize cases from local and state agencies as well as federal ones. The retooled program, now entitled *Gangbusters*, debuted in January 1936. *Gangbusters*, of course, went on to set broadcasting history, lasting more than 20 years.

A film version of Don Whitehead's non-fictional history of the Bureau, *The FBI Story* (Warners, 1959), directed by Mervyn Leroy and written by Richard L. Breen and John Twist, dramatized a number of the cases described by Whitehead in his book. To provide a consistent viewpoint, the scriptwriters created a fictional FBI agent, Chip Hardesty (James Stewart), who happens to be conveniently on hand every time the Bureau is investigating one of its most famous cases. Dramatizing six or seven different cases, the film devotes roughly a half-hour to the

Osage Indian murders, casting the fictional Hardesty in the role of one of the undercover men investigating the crimes. Given the tight time frame, the Osage sequence of the film is extremely compressed, but the picture of a rough and tumble oil-boom town, and the depiction of the fictionalized Hale figure are both compelling.

The Reign of Terror has always exerted a strong influence on western novelist Fred Grove. Osage on his mother's side, Grove was only 10 years old when, during a visit with relatives, he was awakened by the explosion that blew apart the residence of Bill and Rita Smith in 1923. Since that time the Osage case has always haunted him. Years later, as a young journalist, he collaborated with one of the FBI agents assigned to the case on a non-fiction book about the Osage investigation. That book never sold, but, years later, he put that research to work when he became an award-winning writer of fiction.

His very first novel, *Flame of the Osage* (Pyramid, 1957), is the story of a passionate affair between a trained killer and a half-breed woman, with the Reign of Terror as a backdrop. Years later he would return to the case with *Warrior Road* (Doubleday, 1974), which tells the story of the murders from the point of view of a young Osage, returning to Oklahoma after a long absence, who takes it upon himself to investigate the crimes. *Drums Without Warriors* (Doubleday, 1976) tells a similar story, but from the viewpoint of one of the undercover FBI agents assigned to the case. *Flame of the Osage*, *Warrior Road*, and *Drums Without Warriors* fictionalize names and compress events for dramatic effect, but Grove's last fictional treatment of the case (and the last novel he wrote), *The Years of Fear* (Five Star, 2002), uses the real names of all the characters from the actual case, and, with minimal embroidery, follows the events, from the bombing of the Smith residence to the final sentencing of Hale, as faithfully as possible. In fact, *The Years of Fear* reads less like a novel than a non-fiction account, and one wonders if, possibly, Grove simply resurrected that long-unpublished true-crime manuscript, added dialog and other imagined scenes to make it read more like fiction, then marketed it to publishers as a novel.

Another Spur-winning, Oklahoma-born western novelist, Matt Braun, whose fictionalization of Bill Tilghman's career as a frontier lawman was one of the inspirations for this book, used the Osage case as the basis for *Black Gold* (St. Martin's, 2003), the second of two novels featuring Prohibition-era FBI Agent Frank Gordon. Assigned to investigate the mysterious deaths of the oil-rich Osage, Gordon is partnered with a legendary frontier-era peace officer who, to a degree, evokes Tilghman, Deputy U.S. Marshal Will Procter. Together, they uncover the conspiracy behind the murders, and bring the case to an action-filled conclusion.

The most honored fictional treatment of the case is surely *Mean Spirit* (Atheneum, 1990), by famed Chickasaw poet Linda Hogan, which won the Oklahoma Book Award and was a finalist for the Pulitzer Prize. The main law enforcement figure in the book, Lakota Sioux FBI Agent Stace Red Hawk, fills the role that John Wren played in real life, but Hogan is less concerned with the criminal investigation than with the effect the murders have on the Indian community and, in particular, on one specific family. Where Grove, in *The Years of Fear*, follows the events with journalistic faithfulness, Hogan uses the case as a jumping off point for observations she wants to make about the way Indians have been treated. For her, the Osage murders are a metaphor for the injustice Native Americans have routinely suffered throughout this country's history.

A Pipe for February (University of Oklahoma, 2002), the first novel of another Osage writer, Charles H. Red Corn, tells the story of a young Osage artist, a cousin to the Kahesey sisters, who investigates the murders as a matter of family obligation. Apart from providing a suspenseful depiction of the murder case, Red Corn uses the medium of fiction to demonstrate the effect oil wealth had on different generations of Osage, suggesting that, even had there never been the swindling and violence that came with the Reign of Terror, the community might have been better off had the oil never been discovered, and the Indians never tainted by the easy prosperity it brought.

SOMETHING HE ATE

Culinary Crime: Second Seating

Some years ago, a McDonald's ad bragged about the fact that the first job of nearly 50% of the American workforce was under their Golden Arches. I don't know if that statistic is true, but it's the kind of popular factoid that sounds as if it *should* be true, even if it's not.

Whether or not McDonald's statistical claims are true, there's no denying that the fast food industry is absolutely dependent on teen-agers for their staffing needs and that teen-agers are almost as dependent on the fast food industry for steady employment. Older, more experienced workers would demand higher wages and benefits, cutting into the ability to charge low prices for the meals served and, consequently, into profits. It's not a job a person can support a family on and it's not particularly pleasant work, though neither is it particularly unpleasant. But it is a chance to get work experience and some extra spending money, which is exactly what a part-time, entry-level job is supposed to be.

What it's *not* supposed to be is dangerous.

But all too often it is. Going in harm's way isn't part of the job description when you sign up to cook burgers and ring up sales, but the fast-food business is a cash business and cash attracts crime, often violent crime, and all too often violent death.

Bob's Big Boy in Los Angeles, California, 1980. McDonald's in San Ysidro, California, 1984. Luby's Cafeteria in Killeen, Texas, 1991. Lee's Famous Recipe Chicken in Tulsa, Oklahoma, 1992. All of these restaurants have been the sites of multiple murders. And a disproportionate number of the victims have been kids who worked there.

On January 8, 1993, seven employees of Brown's Chicken and Pasta in the Chicago suburb of Palatine were found murdered, beginning a years-long investigation into one of the worst, and one of the most notorious, fast-food massacres.

Like most suburbs in most metropolitan areas, Palatine had experienced a tremendous boom in the post-war years, doubling from a population of roughly 2,000 in 1945 to more than 4,000 in 1950. By 1970, it had ballooned to 16,000.

Brown's Chicken and Pasta was a major fast-food presence in the Chicago area, not altogether surprising since that's where the corporate headquarters was located. Roughly half of the 115 Brown's Chicken outlets in Chicagoland, including Palatine's, were franchises owned by independent operators.

The owners, Richard Ehlenfeldt, 50, and his wife Lynn, 49, had bought the restaurant just a few months earlier when Richard lost his job as a cable TV executive during a corporate merger. They were regarded as uncommonly considerate employers and were known in Palatine as community activists still steeped in the idealistic values of the '60s. Inexperienced at the business of running a restaurant, they both put in long hours as they slowly learned their way around.

The first intimation of trouble came at 11:45 p.m., when the family of one of the employees called the Palatine Police, informing them that, though the restaurant had closed some time earlier, their son hadn't arrived home yet. A beat officer drove by, saw nothing amiss, and didn't investigate further.

At 1:30 a.m., the police received a second call from another family. The officer who responded to this call found the rear door unlocked and investigated. He found the bodies of the Ehlenfeldts, along with five of their employees, in one of the walk-in refrigerators, six of them shot to death, the seventh, Mrs. Ehlenfeldt, dead of a slashed throat.

The other victims were Guadalupe Maldonado, 46, Thomas Mennes, 32, Marcus Nelson, 31, Michael C. Castro, 16, and Rico L. Solis, 17.

The Palatine Police had a reputation as a progressive, forward-thinking department. Only a few years earlier, in another homicide case, they had been one of the first Chicago-area law enforcement agencies to use the then-embryonic method of DNA profiling to solve a case. But this kind of mass murder was beyond the experience of the most veteran Palatine officer. Even seasoned homicide detectives working the most violent inner-city jurisdictions might go their whole careers without encountering so horrific a crime scene. The Palatine Police immediately requested assistance from more experienced investigators in the Cook County Sheriff's Office and the Illinois State Police. A multi-agency task force was formed before the case was more than a few hours old.

Since the crime scene was closed off, the forensics specialists had the luxury of being particularly meticulous in processing it. Anything that was conceivably valuable as evidence was collected. Significantly, and presciently, items were gathered that, given the analytical technology available in 1993, were of no evidentiary value at the time. They were collected anyway against the time when technology might advance to the point where they *could* be analyzed. One such piece of evidence was a partially eaten chicken dinner. Preserving this meal would prove to be the single most valuable action taken during the early hours of the investigation.

Over the next few weeks, dozens of officers worked the case full-time. Every employee and former employee of the restaurant was intensively interviewed, but no usable leads developed. Suspects came to light, but there was never sufficient evidence to bring charges.

Weeks turned into months. Months turned into years. The case remained unsolved. The Palatine Police were the targets of increasingly strident criticism about their handling of the investigation. By 1999, five years after the original crime, the number of officers assigned to the case, once roughly a hundred, had been reduced to four full-time detectives and one part-time computer analyst from the FBI.

In April of 2000, the first real break in the case was announced. New advances in DNA technology had enabled crime lab technicians at the Illinois State Police to analyze saliva from the unfinished chicken dinner. The DNA proved to be from none of the victims, nor from any of the suspects that had been developed to that point. Crime scene investigators who'd insisted on saving the partially eaten meal had been vindicated. The police now had a solid piece of physical evidence to work with.

But it wouldn't do them any good until they had a suspect with whom to compare that evidence, and they had no suspects. Nor would they for almost another year.

The information that would break the case came from a 26-year-old college student named Anne Lockett. In 1993, Lockett, then a student at Fremd High School in Palatine, had been the girlfriend of another Fremd student, Jim Degorski. Degorski, in turn, was a close friend of Juan Luna, another Fremd student and a former employee of Brown's Chicken before the Ehlenfeldts bought it.

A few days after the murders were discovered, Degorski and Luna asked Anne Lockett if she was interested in hearing what had actually gone down at the restaurant. Naturally, she said yes.

Luna and Degorski admitted to Lockett that they had been responsible for the murders and, for the better part of an hour, proceeded to give a detailed account of their crime.

Degorski told Lockett how he and his partner had acquired a .38 caliber revolver; how, during the crime, they would exchange it back and forth in the course of the robbery; how Luna fired initial shots into the victims and Degorski would fire additional shots into those who weren't immediately killed. Then Luna demonstrated how he had held Lynn Ehlenfeldt around her neck while cutting her throat.

Luna and Degorski capped off their story with a threat to kill Lockett if she ever revealed their crime to anyone. Then, possibly in an attempt to increase her culpability, Degorski made Lockett accompany Luna when he went down to Palatine's police station to be questioned along with other former Brown's employees. She never doubted the sincerity of the threat, and said nothing while she waited for Luna at the station. Though the relationship with Degorski ended shortly afterwards, she continued to remain silent for nearly nine years.

In the fall of 2001, she finally shared her knowledge with her new boyfriend. Although they took steps to protect themselves, applying for Firearms Owner Identification cards so that they could legally purchase weapons, they did not go to the police.

In March of 2002, another friend of Lockett's heard her discussing the case with her boyfriend. This friend informed the Palatine Police that Lockett might have valuable information about the Brown's Chicken case, then tried to persuade Lockett that telling the authorities what she knew was the right thing to do.

On March 25, when police finally contacted Anne Lockett, she told them everything Degorski and Luna had told her.

From Anne Lockett, police were led to a second woman in whom Luna and Degorski had confided (and from whom they had even obtained a false alibi for Luna). This second woman (at this writing her name has still not been published) also admitted that the pair had described the crime in detail. She said they paid her $50 out of the nearly $2,000 stolen in the robbery for providing the alibi and helping to clean out the car they'd used that night.

In mid-April, with the information now available to them, police were able to compel Degorski and Luna to provide them with samples of their DNA. On May 9 they matched the DNA from the partially eaten chicken dinner to the sample provided by Luna.

On May 16, Degorski and Luna were arrested.

On May 18, they appeared in court and were formally charged with seven separate counts of capital murder.

By January 2004, when this chapter was revised for the original edition of this book, attorneys for both sides were still presenting pre-trial motions. No trial date had then been set. Luna and Degorski both managed to postpone their days in court for more than three years.

On May 10, 2007, Luna was convicted of seven counts of murder and sentenced to life without the possibility of parole. The prosecution had pushed for the death penalty, but the final vote of the jury during the penalty phase was 11 to 1 in favor of the execution, and the vote had to be unanimous.

On September 29, 2009, Degorski, in a separate trial, was also convicted of all seven counts. By 2009, Illinois's death penalty had been suspended, and the harshest available sentence was life without parole, which was imposed.

It's poetically resonant, given that the crime occurred in a restaurant, to consider that Luna's conviction, which led inevitably to his partner being taken down with him, was the result of something he ate.

FINAL APPEAL

Mysteries South of the Mason-Dixon Line

Catholic theology, the theology with which I'm most familiar after eight years with Franciscan nuns and four with the Jesuit priests, holds that a genuine miracle is an extraordinary event perceptible to the physical senses of manifestly supernatural origin. When a terminal cancer patient bathes in the waters of Lourdes and experiences a complete cure, it's a miracle. When a cancer patient, undergoing surgery, chemotherapy, or some other standard medical regimen, later experiences a full and complete recovery, however remarkable that recovery may be and however fervently the patient and others may have prayed for it, it's *not* a miracle because the return to health is not attributable solely to divine intervention.

Church investigations into assertions of miraculous events are long, drawn-out affairs, usually taking years. And even then, the Church stops short of declaring absolutely that a miracle has occurred. It merely says that an apparent miracle is "worthy of belief."

The vast majority of potential miracles investigated by the Church don't even get that carefully worded semi-endorsement but are positively declared to be *non*-miraculous.

On the other hand, the Church never says that God has nothing to do with those non-miraculous events. That an extraordinary event turns out to have had natural rather than supernatural origins doesn't mean that the Almighty didn't take a hand in things. Consider the case of Will Purvis, who, in 1893, was a 21-year-old farmer in Marion County, Mississippi.

The Ku Klux Klan, which arose during the post-Civil War era ostensibly to curb Northern injustices during the years of occupation—and which almost immediately degraded into an organization of racial terrorists—had, with Reconstruction's end, gone into a period of decline. It would not recover until well into the 20th century, when the publication of Thomas Dixon's novel *The Clansman* (Doubleday, 1905) and the release of D.W. Griffith's 1915 film version, *Birth of a Nation* (Epoch Producing, 1915) would spark a regeneration.

In the meantime, the Southern tradition of racial terrorism was carried on by a similar group known as the White Caps who, like the Klan, rode out at night dressed in flowing white sheets and masks to intimidate blacks, poor whites, and anyone else they considered deviant.

One such "deviant" was a black farm worker who had had the audacity to resign from the employ of a Marion County widow in order to accept a better-paying job with a farmer named Will Buckley. Some White Caps, taking offense at the idea of a black working man's efforts to better himself, visited Buckley's property, captured his new employee, and horsewhipped him. Buckley was not a man to be intimidated. Enraged at his worker's treatment, he took the case to law. His testimony resulted in Grand Jury indictments of three White Cap leaders. This was certain to arouse the ire of the organization. According to some accounts, Will Buckley was a member of the group himself, which would have made his testimony not merely defiant but traitorous in the eyes of the masked night riders. In either case, retribution would be swift and merciless.

Immediately after the Grand Jury hearing, Buckley, his brother Jim and the black farm worker rode home. As they crossed a small stream, they were fired upon by two ambushers hiding in some nearby brush. Will Buckley fell dead. His brother and employee managed to escape unharmed

Jim Buckley was absolutely certain that one of the murderers was Will Purvis. Within hours, local law officers acting upon the sworn testimony of Jim Buckley arrested Purvis for the crime. The identification was given credence by the widely-held belief that Purvis was a White Cap.

At his trial, Purvis insisted that he was at home with his family at the time of the murder. Numerous friends and relatives supported this alibi. It was also shown that Purvis's shotgun had not been fired and, therefore, couldn't have been the weapon used in the murder. But Jim Buckley's testimony couldn't be shaken, and in the end, he was the one the jury believed. Purvis was convicted and sentenced to die.

While his conviction was being appealed, Purvis drew solace from the regular visits of Reverend J. G. Sibley of the Columbia Methodist Church, who had become his spiritual advisor during his confinement. Sibley had become convinced that Purvis's conviction was a miscarriage of justice. Every Wednesday he conducted prayer services at his church devoted solely to gaining a reprieve for Purvis. Hundreds of local residents had, like Sibley, come to believe in Purvis's innocence and became regular attendees of those Wednesday night services.

Despite the prayers, Purvis's appeals were unsuccessful and on February 7, 1894, he was led to a scaffold erected in Columbia's courthouse square for the execution of sentence. Five thousand people, the vast majority of them unsympathetic, had gathered in the square to watch his execution. Public executions took on a circus atmosphere in those days. Picnic lunches, children's games, peddlers and food vendors, and spontaneous revival meetings were all part of the picture.

Purvis looked out at the crowd, hoping to see a relative or friend. "I can't hardly see a friendly face," he told his executioner.

Some of the crowd began to urge the hangman to proceed and get the thing over with. One woman yelled up at Purvis to confess before he died "for the sake of your immortal soul." In seconds, the woman's call for an admission from Purvis had become a chant that the whole crowd seemed to take up. "Confess! Confess! Confess!"

Just before the hangman placed the noose over his neck, Purvis responded to the crowd's demand for a final confession. In a voice surprisingly calm he said, "You are taking the life of an innocent man. There are people here who know who *did* commit the crime and, if they will come forward and confess, I will go free. I didn't do it. I am innocent."

Most of the crowd remained unsympathetic when no one else came forward to claim responsibility for the murder. Still there were some in the crowd who believed in Purvis's innocence, including Reverend Sibley and his congregation. On the eve of the execution, Sibley and his parishioners had met by the gallows in the courthouse square and prayed that somehow the execution would be prevented. Now, with only seconds to go before Purvis made the final drop, they prayed more fervently than ever.

As the noose was placed over Purvis's neck, the hood over his head, and his ankles were tied, Sibley stood at the foot of the gallows and prayed in a loud, deep voice, "Almighty God, if it be Thy will, stay the hand of the executioner."

The sheriff, supervising the execution, placed his hand on Purvis's shoulder in a friendly manner and said, "God help you, Will Purvis." Then the stay rope holding the trap door closed was chopped loose.

The trap door opened.

Purvis dropped through.

* * *

The noose began to tighten around his neck. In less time than it takes to snap one's fingers, the rope would reach its full length and the weight of Purvis's body would cause the knot to break his neck cleanly, killing him instantly.

But, incredibly, the rope did not check Purvis's fall. Instead of cleanly breaking his neck, the knot mysteriously came undone. The rope slipped away, causing a burn but otherwise leaving him unharmed. Purvis landed on the ground, unconscious, but very much alive.

As Purvis put it later, "I heard the door creak. My body lunged down and all went black. When I regained consciousness I heard someone say, 'Well, Bill, we've got to do it all over again.'"

What had happened? Had the hangman's noose been incorrectly tied? No, only minutes before the execution, a committee had examined the scaffold, the rope, and the knot and found everything in order.

Purvis got to his feet. The hood fell off his head. He turned to one of the deputy sheriffs who had reached him and said, "Let's get this over with."

As far as a lot of the spectators were concerned, it already *was* over with. Purvis's survival was a sign of his innocence and they weren't about to let him be hanged again. An almost equal number of spectators were just as convinced that Purvis's survival had been an accident and nothing more.

One of the officials leaned over the railing of the gallows and shouted down to a member of the crowd, Dr. W. Ford, to toss the rope back up. Ford, a vocal critic of the White Caps, who had been convinced of Purvis's guilt, and who had publicly spoken against him during the trial, replied, "I won't do any such damned thing! That boy's been hung once too many times now!"

As the crowd started to divide into pro-Purvis and anti-Purvis factions, and deputies assisted the hapless young farmer back up the scaffold, Sibley rushed past them to the top of the gallows and, standing on top of the trap door himself so Purvis couldn't be positioned on it, addressed the crowd.

Sibley was on all occasions a powerful preacher, and this time the Spirit was really on him. Every ounce of his oratorical talent was brought to bear.

"People of Marion County," his voice boomed, "The Hand of Providence has slipped the noose! Heaven has heard our prayers! All those who want to see this boy hang a second time hold up their hands!"

Not a single hand was raised.

Reverend Sibley continued, "All those who are opposed to hanging Will Purvis a second time hold up your hands!"

Every spectator's hand shot up. One witness later remarked later that it appeared as if each hand had been "magically raised by a universal lever." The force of Reverend Sibley's heartfelt eloquence had persuaded the entire crowd.

"What are we going to do, Sheriff?" said one of the deputies to his boss.

The Sheriff was not an irreligious man but he had a sworn duty to carry out the court's sentence, and that sentence was "hung by the neck until dead." Purvis may have fulfilled the first part of the sentence but the second part remained uncompleted.

To be sure of his legal ground, the Sheriff consulted with a lawyer who'd pushed his way to the front of the crowd. Purvis and Sibley stood to the side, their heads bent in silent prayer. Dr. Ford remained at the foot of the scaffold.

The attorney insisted that the letter of the law demanded that Purvis be executed. The Sheriff nodded reluctantly and began to mount the scaffold to supervise a second attempt to carry out the sentence. At this point Dr. Ford, standing at the base of the scaffold turned to the young attorney.

"I don't agree with you," he said. Then to the Sheriff, he shouted, "If I go up on that scaffold and ask three hundred men to stand by me and prevent the hanging, what are you going to do about it?" As he spoke scores of men gathered around him, ready to back up the doctor's threat.

Slowly they started up the stairs, Dr. Ford in the lead. "I'm ready to do it, too," he told the Sheriff as he approached.

The Sheriff was a dutiful man, but standing against the doctor, the preacher, the crowd and, it appeared, the Creator Himself was more than he was prepared to do for the sake of duty. He walked over to Purvis and cut him loose from the ropes that were binding him.

"I ain't one to go against five thousand folks and God, too," he said later.

Purvis was escorted back to his jail cell until his fate could be decided in a less heated venue. In the meantime an investigating commission attempted to find out exactly what had caused the noose to fail in the first place.

One of the staff executioners, Henry Banks, suggested that the problem was with the rope itself. "[It] was too thick," he said. "It was made of new grass and very springy. After the first man tied the noose he let the free end hang out. It was this way when the tests were made, but when it came to placing this knot around Purvis's neck it looked untidy. The hangman didn't want to be accredited with this kind of a job, so he cut the loose end off so that the rope was flush with the noose knot. It looked neater, but when the weight of Purvis's body was thrown against it, the rope slipped and the knot became untied."

Banks's published statement was very likely the correct explanation, but the investigating commission didn't give it an official endorsement, and adjourned without coming to any conclusion. Not that it mattered to the average Marion County resident. They knew exactly why Purvis had been spared.

He'd been spared because God had spared him.

Over the next two years, a new round of legal briefs were filed on Purvis's behalf, but the governor refused to commute the sentence and the State Supreme Court denied two separate appeals. Purvis's execution was rescheduled for December 12, 1895.

Public opinion in Marion County, on the other hand, was nearly 100% in favor of Purvis. The Sheriff, as has already been pointed out, was a dutiful man. But he was also an elected official.

A few weeks before his execution, Purvis was moved from the secure facility at the county seat to a small, dilapidated jail structure closer to his home town where, the sheriff said, "he could be near relatives and friends in the last few weeks of his life."

During Purvis's stay in the run-down structure, a few of those relatives and friends came to visit. When they left, they took Purvis with them. Reportedly, very little resistance was put up by members of the Sheriff's Office.

Over the next few years, Purvis lived in hiding. In 1897, Jim Buckley, who had been so certain of his identification at Purvis's trial, recanted. He was no longer sure that he had named the correct man.

A new governor, who had been elected partly on a campaign promise that he would commute Purvis's sentence if he won the office, was as good as his word. Soon after his inauguration he announced that, if Purvis turned himself in, his sentence would be reduced to life imprisonment. Purvis presented himself to the Sheriff in Columbia as soon as he heard the news.

Almost as soon as Purvis began serving his sentence in the state penitentiary, a campaign to free him began. A petition signed by thousands was presented to the governor begging for the young farmer's release. One of the signatures on the petition was that of the District Attorney who had prosecuted Purvis. On December 19, 1898, just two months short of five years since the botched execution, Purvis was granted a full pardon and walked out of prison a free man.

That still left the question of who shot Will Buckley unanswered. Was it actually Purvis? Had the young farmer been saved from just punishment because a chain of coincidence had generated a wave of public sympathy? Or had his assertion of innocence been the simple truth?

The answer finally came nearly two decades later. In the spring of 1918 an elderly reprobate named Joe Beard staggered into a midnight church service. At first he sat silent in one of the back pews. Then he arose, walked up to the pulpit, and began the most startling confession any of the congregants had ever heard. It was Beard, acting in concert with another White Capper named Louis Thornhill, long since dead and gone, who'd ambushed Will Buckley back in 1893. In his youth Beard had closely resembled Will Purvis and, when the mistaken identification was made by the victim's brother, he'd just taken it as a stroke of amazing good luck.

After completing his story, Beard collapsed. He was carried to a sickbed where he repeated the confession in front of official stenographers and a group of witnesses before passing quietly away. Supplying details that could be known only by one of the actual perpetrators, his final act cleared Purvis's name from any hint of suspicion.

In the wake of that final confession, the Mississippi State Legislature made Purvis's innocence official, awarding him $5,000 as compensation for his years of wrongful imprisonment and passing a resolution "removing all stain and dishonor" from his name.

In the years between his pardon and Beard's deathbed statement, Purvis had lived a remarkably happy life, falling in love with and marrying a clergyman's daughter with whom he would eventually raise 11 children. He lived for another 25 years after the legislature's endorsement of his innocence. Just before his 1943 death, at the age of 71, Purvis, who still bore the scar of the rope burn around his neck, spoke one last time about his brush with the hangman back in 1894, when every legal appeal had been exhausted and there was only one Judge left to hear his plea.

"God heard our prayers," he said simply. "He saved my life because I was an innocent man."

The story of the failure of the hanging rope has never been examined by the Vatican and if at some future date it ever was, it's almost certain that it would never pass muster as a genuine miracle.

But miracles aren't the only way God has of answering prayers.

FURTHER READING

As far as I've been able to determine, there's never been a book devoted solely to the Purvis case. However, many books dealing generally with the pros and cons of capital punishment, or the history of the practice, refer to the case, often at length.

Accounts of the failed execution of Will Purvis and its aftermath can be found in Edwin Borchard's *Convicting the Innocent* (Yale University, 1932), August Mencken's *By the Neck* (Hastings, 1942), Justin Atholl's *Shadow of the Gallows* (Long, 1954), George V. Bishop's *Executions* (Sherbourne, 1965), and Frederick Drimmer's *Until You Are Dead* (Citadel, 1990).

"THE FUGITIVE" CONNECTION?

I know of no novel, story, or drama specifically fictionalizing the Purvis case, so what follows is pure speculation.

When Roy Huggins created the television series *The Fugitive* in 1964, most people assumed that the central situation of a Midwestern physician accused of murdering his wife derived from the famous Dr. Sam Sheppard case in Ohio. The additional conflict between the hero and the relentless police officer obsessed with recapturing him, Huggins admitted, had been lifted from Victor Hugo's *Les Miserables*.

But the whole notion of a falsely accused man unable to prove his innocence legally facing execution until a twist of fate saves him then remaining on the run for several years suggests that Huggins might have had more than a passing familiarity with the Purvis case. Of course, a train wreck was substituted for a badly tied hangman's noose and, while Purvis was technically a fugitive for several years, it doesn't appear as though any members of official law enforcement were trying all that hard to track him down during the years he spent in hiding. Still, the parallels between the fictional predicament of Dr. Richard Kimble and the real-life one of Will Purvis seem almost deliberately resonant.

Maybe it was a coincidence. Or maybe Huggins, in addition to relying on Dr. Sheppard's trial and Victor Hugo's novel for source material, took some inspiration from the Purvis case as well.

EYE FOR AN EYE,
TOOTH FOR A TOOTH

New England Mysteries

In one of Ed McBain's 87th Precinct novels, I don't recall just which one, there's a scene in which Steve Carella is reading a private eye novel or maybe looking at a private eye show on TV. Annoyed at the way the fictional hero detects rings around official law enforcement, Carella testily remarks that the last time he ever heard of a private detective cracking an actual murder case was never.

Well, it's quite true that, in real life, it's unusual for PI's to investigate homicides. Still, never's a long time and there are, after all, murder cases in which the official cops stumble, at least at the beginning. In one such case, the murderer would have certainly gotten away with it were it not for the dedicated efforts of a private eye.

In 1986 Keith Mayo, the first, indeed the only private detective in New Milford, Connecticut, had been in business for about six years. In many ways, he fit Raymond Chandler's paradigm of the ideal private eye. Like Philip Marlowe (and maybe 95% of all fictional PI's who followed), Mayo was a 30ish ex-cop having served in both the New Fairfield Constabulary and the New Milford Police Department. Like Marlowe and his descendants, he'd left official law enforcement and gone private because of his inability to get along with his superiors. Like Marlowe, he was the owner and operator of a one-man show (or more correctly, one-and-a-half, since he did on occasion employ Sue Schneider as a part-time assistant investigator). And like Marlowe, though his reputation as a detective was excellent, he had a tendency to be sarcastic, overbearing, quick to take offense, and impatient to the point of alienating others. To top it off, the native New Englander even shared a name with a popular fictional New England sleuth (though Phoebe Atwood Taylor's Asey Mayo was from an entirely different school of detection than Marlowe).

In other respects, however, Mayo did not fit the Marlowe model. For one thing, he was a family man with a wife and a couple of kids. For another, New Milford was hardly a major metropolis like Los Angeles or New York or Chicago (though, being an hour's drive from Manhattan, it could be regarded as being in NYC's metropolitan area). Finally, unlike Marlowe, Mayo was willing to do divorce work. In fact it was a divorce assignment that led to his involvement in what would become one of Connecticut's most infamous murder cases.

On September 4, 1986, Pan Am stewardess Helle Crafts, acting through her lawyer, hired Mayo to mount a surveillance on her husband Richard Crafts, a pilot for Eastern Airlines and a part-time police officer in the Southbury (Connecticut) Constabulary. A native of Denmark, Helle lived with her husband and their three children in Newtown, Connecticut. Although Connecticut was a no-fault divorce state, proof of adultery could be used when deciding matters like child custody. After 10 unhappy years with a husband she knew was cheating, Helle had decided to file for divorce. To insure the best settlement possible, she wanted Mayo to develop evidence that her husband was seeing other women.

By October 2, Mayo was able to provide photographic proof that Crafts was regularly visiting a woman in Middleton, New Jersey, named Nancy Dodd. Helle had been wavering on the question of divorce for many years but the photos provided by Mayo stiffened her resolve and she filed. Over the next few weeks, however, her husband was able to avoid the process servers sent by the sheriff to officially notify him of the action.

On November 18, after a long European flight, Helle was dropped off at her Newtown home by two of her co-workers. It was the last time they saw her. Over the next few days, whenever anyone asked about her, Richard claimed that she was in Denmark taking care of her mother who had suddenly taken ill. But she hadn't called her supervisors at Pan Am to ask for emergency leave, which was totally unlike her. Further, if she missed three consecutive flights without asking for leave and Pan Am was unable to contact her she could be summarily dismissed, presumably the last thing she'd want if she was heading for a divorce that would tighten her finances.

Her friends contacted Helle's mother, Lis Nielsen, in Copenhagen and found that, not only was Mrs. Nielsen not sick, but that Helle wasn't there and wasn't expected. They contacted Helle's cousin in California but he could shed no light on her disappearance, either. Discussing Helle's mysterious disappearance, her friends discovered that she had made the same cryptic statement to several of them.

"If anything happens to me, don't think it was an accident."

In late November, Helle's divorce layer, Dianne Andersen, tried without success to reach her. In Andersen's experience, it was unusual for a lawyer to hear so little from a client during the early stages of a divorce action. On December 1, three of Helle's friends contacted Andersen and informed her of the disappearance. Learning that no one had seen or heard of Helle since November 18, she recalled that, in her initial consultation, Helle had made the same ominous statement to her that she now learned had been made to her friends.

"If anything happens to me, don't think it was an accident."

Immediately after hearing from Helle's friends, Andersen called Keith Mayo and informed him of the disappearance. She wasn't hiring him, just asking advice. But Mayo became deeply concerned. Mrs. Crafts had struck him as a devoted mother and he couldn't conceive of her voluntarily leaving her kids without a word to anyone. That her husband had lied about her whereabouts and now couldn't be pinned down to a straight story was also worrisome. Mayo strongly suspected foul play and decided to investigate.

His first step was to notify the Newtown Police Department. Police Chief Lou Marchese seemed less than enthusiastic about his overworked department having to take a missing persons case but instructed Mayo to call back later and make a full report to Lieutenant Mike DeJoseph, the head of Newtown's four-man detective bureau.

The Craftses' live-in baby-sitter, Marie Thomas, was still living at the Craftses' home, alone and unprotected, a dangerous situation if Crafts was indeed a killer. Impatient to get official attention on the case as early as possible, Mayo didn't wait around until DeJoseph was available. Instead he contacted a friend of his in the local prosecutor's office, Robert Brunetti, in an effort to light a fire under the Newtown Police, then went out to contact Thomas on his own.

Marie told Mayo that she had gotten home from her part-time job at the local McDonald's at roughly 2:00 a.m., so she wasn't there when Helle returned from her flight. At 6:00 a.m. she was awakened by Richard Crafts, who informed her that the power in the house was out and he was driving her and the three kids over to his sister's in Westport before the house got too cold. When Marie asked where Helle was, Crafts replied that she had already left and would meet them at his sister's. Not only wasn't she there but Crafts' explanation totally contradicted what he had told Helle's co-workers. He also learned from her that, in the days following the disappearance, Crafts had suddenly removed the wall-to-wall carpet in his and Helle's bedroom and replaced it. Marie could see a large brownish stain on the carpet which Crafts said was the reason he was replacing it. Asked what had caused the stain, he replied that it was kerosene.

Mayo was soon joined by Patrolman Henry Stormer and Detective Harry Noroian of the Newtown PD, who took over the interview, thus beginning the official investigation into Helle's disappearance. However, at least in those early stages, they were treating it as a voluntary flight. Mayo was more and more convinced it was a murder and he decided to continue looking into things on his own.

This was a standard plot in any one of a dozen private eye novels. A former client of the hero is the victim of foul play, possibly arising out of the very investigation he has conducted for her. Despite having no client and, consequently, no income, he decides out of a sense of obligation to investigate anyway. Now Keith Mayo, in real life, was living that clichéd situation.

From December 1 through December 5, Mayo worked the case full-time, trying to find some trace of Helle. He found her car in a parking lot at JFK Airport but was able to find no record that she had flown to Europe from there. He'd learned that Crafts disliked driving his wife's car, which suggested that if Crafts' print could be found in the car, it would be a strong indication that he, and not Helle, had driven the car to JFK which, in turn, would indicate that her disappearance was not voluntary, and that Crafts was trying to cover his tracks. To his chagrin, airport officials would not let him search the car without Crafts' permission and the Newtown Police failed to seize it to search for evidence.

In fairness to the Newtown Police it should be noted that, after nine murder-free years, two separate homicides had suddenly occurred in the small New England town just before Helle's disappearance. The department's four detectives were all diligently working cases they *knew* were murders and were understandably disinclined to put a lot of effort into a case that was, in all statistical likelihood, nothing more than a wife running off from her husband.

Indeed that was the latest story offered by Crafts. Helle, he said, had run off to be with her long-time boyfriend. However, he could not give the boyfriend's name or any background about him other than his being an Asian who lived in Westchester County, New York. To bolster his story, Crafts offered to take a polygraph exam.

On December 4, the polygraph exam was administered to Crafts at the Connecticut State Police headquarters in Meriden by Sergeant William Dyki. Dyki was able to find no evidence of deception and reported this to the Newtown detectives. However, he found Crafts to be almost unnaturally calm. As a police officer, Crafts would have been familiar with polygraphs. He had already been tested when applying for his position in the Southbury force. And as a airline pilot, he was trained to be cool under pressure. Could he have fooled the lie box?

By this time, Mayo had put in all the time he could afford to on his own. Every hour he spent on Helle's case represented $35 he'd failed to earn. He was a businessman, after all, with a family to support. Maybe he could get some of Helle's friends and family to underwrite his investigation.

On December 8, Mayo met with Diane Andersen and five friends and co-workers of Helle at a meeting in Andersen's office. The Newtown PD was not going to press forward with the case, Mayo told the group. Since Crafts had passed the lie detector test, Chief Marchese and his men would treat Helle's disappearance as a routine missing persons case rather than a possible homicide. Mayo informed the group that during military duty in Southeast Asia in the early '60s Crafts had been a pilot in Air America, the air cargo company that fronted CIA operations in the area. As a CIA agent, as well as a pilot and a cop, it would not have been hard for Crafts to figure out ways to fool the box. Mayo was becoming more and more convinced that Helle had been murdered by her husband and if someone didn't press forward the murder would go unavenged. The group decided to hire Mayo. Andersen personally contributed the $1000 Helle had paid her as retainer.

Re-interviewing Marie Thomas, the Craftses' baby-sitter, Mayo learned that since they had last talked Marie had found Helle's flight bags. Helle always took her flight bags when she was traveling, yet they were still in the house. She also described the dark stain she had seen on the bedroom rug in greater detail. Mayo became convinced that the stain was blood. Helle's blood. He decided that finding the discarded carpet was his top priority.

Learning that garbage in the area was sent to a landfill in Canterbury, near the Rhode Island border, Mayo contacted the fill's owner and told him he was searching for evidence in a possible murder. With a pair of cop buddies and some local help, Mayo scoured the landfill. A small strip of the original carpet had been provided by Marie Thomas for comparison purposes. After several days of digging, the searchers found a section of carpet with a large stain. Preliminary tests indicated the stain might be blood.

This was enough, finally, for State's Attorney Walter Flanagan to decide that Newtown PD should no longer be the lead agency on the case. On December 18, he directed that the State Police Western District Major Crime Squad be placed in charge.

Ironically, it was later determined that the rug found at the landfill was not the one Crafts had removed from the bedroom and that the stain was not blood, but by that time it didn't matter. The police were finally pursuing the case with vigor. From that point, Mayo's involvement, for practical purposes, ended. Having finally convinced official law enforcement to take the matter seriously, he became superfluous once that purpose had been accomplished. Still, his contribution was crucial. "The state shamefully enough concedes," Prosecutor Flanagan would later say, "that without Mayo as catalyst the Crafts case might never have" been solved. There was no denying that Mayo had cracked the case, but it would be left to others to actually break it. From now on, the story of Helle Crafts' mysterious disappearance would more closely resemble a police procedural than a private eye novel.

Actually, even before the entry of the Connecticut State Police, the local cops under Newtown's chief of detectives, Mike DeJoseph, had begun to suspect that Crafts might have played a more sinister part in his wife's sudden departure than they'd been led to believe. But since the police chief, Lou Marchese, was still convinced it was a simple missing persons case, they'd had to tread lightly. Marchese had a reputation as a good, solid cop, but as a boss, he was something of a martinet who demanded absolute obedience from his subordinates. Neither Lieutenant DeJoseph nor any of his men were comfortable conducting a non-approved investigation behind Marchese's back.

Still, the polygraph results notwithstanding, DeJoseph grew more and more suspicious of the inconsistencies in Crafts' statements and on December 8, the same day Helle's friends retained Mayo, DeJoseph decided to move ahead with his own investigation. He and his staff spent the next few days checking the contents of Helle's safe deposit box, following up leads sent by outside police agencies through the FBI's National Crime Information Center, and checking Crafts' airline and police schedules during the relevant days. On December 11, DeJoseph asked Crafts to come to the Newtown police station for a follow-up interview. In the course of the interview, DeJoseph discerned three more possible lies. DeJoseph's strategy at this point was to play a waiting game, continuing to intermittently interview Crafts, catching him out in more lies until Crafts was caught up in a web of his own falsehoods.

Although according to jurisdictional agreements the State Police could not enter the case until a local invitation was forthcoming, Lieutenant James Hiltz, the commander of Western District Major Crimes, had been made aware of the case by Mayo. He contacted DeJoseph with an offer of help, but was rebuffed. There was no way DeJoseph was going to ask the troopers for assistance. Not as long as he was working for Chief Marchese.

Before taking over the Newtown PD, Marchese had spent 30 years as a Connecticut state policeman, rising to the number two spot in the force. He fully expected to be appointed to the top position when Commissioner Leo Mulcahy retired in 1971. Instead, the newly elected governor used the post to pay off a political IOU and one of the new commissioner's first acts was to demand the resignation of six top officers, including Marchese. Bitterly disappointed, he was able to find a new job almost immediately when Newtown hired him. But Marchese never forgot the slight and, under his leadership, relations between the Newtown PD and the Connecticut State Police would be forever strained.

By the time the State Police entered the case at Prosecutor Flanagan's invitation, Marchese himself was finally coming around to the idea that Helle's disappearance had sinister overtones and, despite his legendary parsimony, had authorized overtime for the case. He also ordered his men to share as little as possible with the troopers, hoping to beat them to a solution. After a few fruitless days of trying to work effectively with the locals, Hiltz became fed up and simply cut Newtown PD out of the case. From that point, the only local cops who would be actively involved in the investigation would be State's Attorney's Investigators Robert Blumequist and Anthony Dalessio.

The lack of cooperation between municipal and state law enforcement led to the loss of at least one important piece of physical evidence: Helle's car, still parked at the JFK lot. By the time it was agreed which arm of the investigation had the right to retrieve the vehicle, it had been removed from the airport.

On December 26, acting on a warrant, Hiltz and his men searched Crafts' home. During the search, Dr. Henry Lee, director of the state police crime lab, found blood droplets on the mattress of the Craftses' bed. Concluding from the shape of the droplets that they'd landed on the mattress with "medium velocity" as though from a blow rather than a gunshot or stabbing wound, Lee decided that if Helle had been murdered the murder had taken place in that room (though at that point he'd only go so far as to say that "something happened"). Lee had already shown that the rug Mayo found was not the right one. Now he'd developed evidence that an act of violence had occurred in the Craftses' bedroom. These were to be Lee's opening appearances in the drama of Helle Crafts. If Mayo had been the hero of the first act of that drama, Lee would soon develop into the hero of the second.

The blood droplets convinced the cops that they were on the right track but they were a long way from being able to justify an arrest, let alone insure a conviction. Hiltz set his men to doing legwork.

On little more than a fishing expedition, State Detective Sergeant Martin Ohradan dropped in at the Southbury Constabulary to interview some of Crafts' fellow officers. By chance, it came out that two Southbury officers had seen Crafts driving a U-Haul truck towing a large woodchipper on November 20, two days after Helle's disappearance. Later investigation disclosed that Crafts had been seen with the woodchipper that same night by the Housatonic River near a 3.6 acre lot the Craftses owned.

Ohradan recalled an animal cruelty case that had occurred the previous summer in which a man had put a dog through a woodchipper. The case had been widely publicized throughout Connecticut. Had it given Crafts ideas?

Further investigation uncovered the fact that Crafts had rented the woodchipper in Darien, despite the fact that there were dealers closer by and more convenient. He had also bought for cash, without giving his name or address, a new freezer unit, picking it up himself rather than having it delivered.

The pieces seemed to fall into place. Crafts had killed his wife in their bedroom, possibly by a blow to the head with a blunt instrument, froze her solid in the new freezer unit, and disposed of her body by running it through the woodchipper and dispersing the chips in the river. The woodchipper had been reserved prior to Helle's disappearance and Crafts had even paid for two extra days to insure that it would stay in his name when he was unable to pick it up at the appointed time. His crime had been premeditated.

Hiltz mounted a massive search of the culvert where the woodchipper had been seen. All they had at this point was speculation. They needed physical evidence that Helle Crafts had been put through that woodchipper. Ultimately, the usable pieces of physical evidence that the search uncovered could be held in the palm of the hand and weighed less than three ounces. They consisted of two fingernails, a piece of blue fabric, 60-odd bone splinters, some hair, and two teeth caps. They had to establish beyond any reasonable doubt that those items represented the remains of Helle Crafts.

The ball-carrier for the good guys was now Dr. Henry Lee, the Director of the State Police Forensics Lab. Finding proof sufficient to convince 12 jurors of Crafts' guilt would be his daunting responsibility, but he was up to the task. In the seven years he'd been running the troopers' crime lab, he'd quickly built a reputation as one of the top forensics investigators in the world.

Dr. Lee had been born in mainland China. Fleeing to Taiwan as a child to escape the Maoist takeover, he enrolled in the Taiwan Central Police College at the age of 18. After earning a bachelor's degree he was commissioned as a Taipei police officer, serving two years and rising to the rank of captain. He decided he didn't have the temperament for street-level law enforcement, however, and left the Force to work as a journalist for a few years before emigrating to the United States. Settling in New York with his wife, he entered the John Jay College of Criminal Justice where he earned a second bachelor's degree in 1967. Accepted into New York University for graduate work, he earned his Ph.D. in biochemistry in 1975. Joining the faculty of the University of New Haven, he established a forensics program and received tenure in a record three years.

When he was hired as head of the State Police crime lab in 1979 that facility consisted of one microscope in a refurbished washroom. Over the next few years, Lee lobbied successfully for an increased budget and staff and built the lab into one of the top forensics centers in the world.

It would be up to Lee and his staff to prove that the tiny remnants of human bone and tissue belonged to Helle Crafts. DNA testing was still embryonic in 1987, so they'd have to use more circuitous routes to reach their conclusions.

They were able to establish that most of the bone splinters were human. Step one in a long trip.

The hair was found to be from a blonde Northern European. The fact that the hair was tinted indicated that it had come from the head of a woman. Step Two. Still a long way to go.

The fingernails were colored with a combination of polishes that corresponded to Helle's two favorites and they were able to establish that she often combined these two polishes before applying them. Strongly indicative but not absolutely conclusive. Still not there.

The blue fabric matched exactly the fabric used to make a nightgown Helle habitually wore. Getting closer, but still not quite there.

Finally two forensic odontologists working under Lee, Dr. Gus Karazulas, who'd been a regular lab consultant to the State Police for 10 years, and Dr. Lowell Levine, an independent consultant retained by the State's Attorney's Office, compared the tooth crowns to oral x-rays provided by Helle's dentist. They concluded that the caps had come from Helle's mouth and no one else's. That put Lee and his team of lab cops over the goal line.

On January 13, 1987, Crafts was placed under arrest by Lieutenant Hiltz and Sergeant Ohradan. It was almost exactly two months since Helle was last seen. State's Attorney Flanagan personally prosecuted the case. Judge Barry Schaller presided. It would be the first time in Connecticut history that a defendant would be tried for murder without a body being produced. Jury selection began on March 14, 1987. This is always an important part of any court case, but, at the time, no one realized just how important it would be in *this* case.

The first witness called for the prosecution was Lis Nielsen, Helle's mother. During her testimony, her eyes briefly met Crafts', who was seated at the defense table. She smiled nervously. That single smile turned out to be more important than all of the testimony and evidence that would subsequently be offered.

One of the jurors, observing that nervous smile, immediately concluded that no mother could or would smile at the murderer of her daughter. He decided then and there, before any other evidence was presented by either side, that Crafts must be innocent. When the case was turned over to the jury on Thursday, June 23, this lone juror (identified in some accounts by the pseudonym "Bart Cummings" which I'll use from this point) voted to acquit. By July 11, he was still voting that way. The vote had remained at 11 to 1 for the better part of a month with no sign of the deadlock ever breaking. It would later come out that, in addition to making up his mind before the first witness had finished testifying, Cummings had encouraged his wife to attend each court session. He and his wife discussed that case at length every evening while the trial was going on. They avidly watched news coverage of the case.

All of this was in direct violation of the judge's instructions.

On Friday, July 15, when the jury reported that they were hopelessly deadlocked, Judge Schaller read what is known as a "'Chip' Smith Charge," essentially an instruction to those jurors in the minority (which, in this case, amounted to Cummings and nobody else) of a deadlocked jury to closely and objectively examine the reasoning behind the decision of the majority. The "Smith Charge" has been criticized occasionally for being overly coercive to minority jurors but it's a fairly well-established practice in Connecticut jurisprudence. In this case, however, it would have no effect. Not only didn't Cummings objectively examine the reasoning behind the votes of the other jurors, he refused to deliberate at all any more. When the jury broke for dinner he was nowhere to be found. He'd just skipped out. At this point Schaller had no choice but to declare a mistrial. Flanagan refiled.

A second trial began in March of 1989. Flanagan again personally prosecuted under presiding Judge Martin Negro. When it was completed the jury took exactly six working days to come to a "Guilty" verdict. Twenty-three out of 24 jurors who'd deliberated on the case concluded beyond a reasonable doubt that Crafts had murdered his wife. He was sentenced to 50 years.

Mayo continued to operate his business in New Milford for several years. Famous as the man who cracked the Crafts case, his success in the detective business was assured. Tragically, that success was short-lived because Mayo himself was destined to be short-lived. Some time after Crafts' conviction, Mayo's marriage broke up, and he moved to Florida where, in 2000, he was killed in a car accident at the age of 46.

Lee's success, on the other hand, is still continuing. His reputation as one of the nation's most eminent criminalists continued to soar and he was consulted on such highly publicized cases as the O.J. Simpson trial and the JonBenet Ramsey investigation. Ultimately, he was promoted to Commissioner of Public Safety, perhaps the first Asian-American ever to head up a state police force. He recently retired from the top job but, as of this writing, still holds the title of Chief Emeritus for Scientific Services. He operates a website, www.drhenrylee.com, on which his career is described in greater detail.

FURTHER READING

A more complete account of the Crafts case can be found in Arthur

Herzog's *The Woodchipper Murder* (Holt, 1989). Irritatingly, the hardcover edition, apparently rushed into print, ends with the adjournment of the inconclusive first trial. The 1990 paperback reprint published by Zebra contains additional material describing the second trial.

Dr. Lee devotes a chapter to the Crafts murder in his autobiographical account of five of his most famous investigations, *Cracking Cases* (Prometheus, 2002) written with Thomas W. O'Neil. Obviously stressing the forensics aspects of the case since that's his specialty, Dr. Lee doesn't stint on detailed descriptions of the regular detective work or the two court cases. It's an intensely interesting look at the "Woodchipper Murder" from the inside.

THE WOODCHIPPER MURDER IN FICTION

The Oscar-winning crime film *Fargo* (Gramercy, 1996), written by Ethan and Joel Coen, and directed by Joel, opens with the line "This story is true."

That's not quite the case. Elements of the plot apparently derived from several different real-life cases but there was no one, single crime that provided the filmmakers with inspiration, and the end credits, in direct contradiction of the opening credits, include the standard disclaimer "all persons fictitious."

Nevertheless, according to the "Special Features" interviews on the DVD release of *Fargo*, the method used to dispose of the body of the murder victim, running it through a woodchipper, was based on Crafts' method of disposing of the body of his wife, Helle.

Espionage Chic

"Oxbridge" Mysteries

Early in October 2001 in Los Angeles, Kathleen Soliah pled guilty to charges of having planted pipe bombs in the police cars of two randomly chosen LAPD officers in 1974, apparently in retaliation for the SLA shoot-out. On the run for more than a quarter century, she was finally apprehended in St. Paul, Minnesota, (where she'd been living as Sara Jane Olsen) and returned to California for trial. After six months of delaying tactics, she abruptly decided to end the legal proceedings by changing her plea to guilty but later stated publicly that she was innocent of all charges and that her plea was made, not because she actually was guilty, but because she believed that in the wake of the September 11 attacks it would be impossible for an accused terrorist to get a fair trial. There was some initial question about whether or not her guilty plea could be accepted in light of her public renunciation of it, but ultimately the plea was officially entered and the trial consequently avoided.

While the question of whether or not her plea was legitimate was still up in the air, political commentator George Will suggested in an issue of *Newsweek* that it might be useful for her trial to be allowed to proceed, if for no other reason than to reacquaint the public with the violent facts of the Marxist radicalism that was so pervasive on college campuses decades ago and that, nowadays, tends to be remembered with a kind of rosy, romanticized, and altogether inappropriate, nostalgia.

The '60s and '70s, however, were not the beginning of campus radicalism, as Will seems to think. It was just as pervasive in the '20s and '30s. The true believers of that era, however, didn't riot, plants bombs, assassinate school administrators, or kidnap newspaper heiresses. Instead, they quietly spied on their country and turned whatever secrets they uncovered over to the enemy.

Indeed, the members of the most famous ring of traitors ever assembled by the Soviets were all recruited during their undergraduate years at Trinity College in Cambridge. The four members of this ring, Kim Philby, Anthony Blunt, Guy Burgess, and David Maclean, not only did untold harm to Great Britain (and, by extension, to all the Western democracies) over a period of more than 20 years, but all of them managed to escape punishment.

The espionage career of a lesser-known Trinity graduate, Allan Nunn May, was of shorter duration but its consequences were probably further reaching. Like Philby and the rest, May attended Trinity during an era when the rise of European fascism and the effects of the world-wide Depression caused a great many students to lean left. Nunn May, like the others, was radicalized during his Cambridge years.

Unlike his colleagues, however, Nunn May did not pursue a career in any of Britain's security or intelligence services. His Ph.D. was in physics and it was as a physicist that he betrayed his country and served his Soviet masters.

After receiving his degree, Dr. Nunn May became a lecturer for King's College at the University of London. It was during this time that he joined Britain's Communist Party. When Britain entered World War II, Nunn May was invited back to Cambridge by Dr. James Chadwick to work on the University's nuclear research program. Later he and Chadwick became part of the Manhattan Project, assigned to Tube Alloy Research (a euphemism for atomic weapons research) at the university's Cavendish Laboratory. According to some sources, Nunn May's communist affiliations were known but were not thought to be a bar to his participation in the project since the Soviet Union was then an ally.

During this time, Nunn May was among the scientists who were informed of reported Nazi efforts to build a radioactive "dirty bomb." His Communist Party membership had lapsed by this time, but if no longer an official member of its British organ, he apparently was still a fervent believer in Marxism. In any case, he believed that the Soviets, then fighting a losing battle against the Nazis on the Russian Front, ought to be informed of the potential German threat, so he passed the information along through contacts he had made while a party member. The KGB marked Nunn May as a potential friendly asset at this time. (Note: The Soviet espionage agency went through more than a half-dozen name changes between the USSR's founding in 1917 and its final collapse in the early '90s. For the sake of brevity and clarity, I am referring to it here by its final, longest-lasting, and best-remembered set of initials).

In 1943, the laboratory sent Nunn May to Ottawa, Canada, where he continued his work on nuclear weapons. It was during this period that he was contacted by the KGB and ordered to set up a radio communications center for sending out information. He was reluctant to expose himself in this manner but he was told that it was "his duty." By the time he actually arrived in Canada, however, the Nazis had been defeated at

Stalingrad and the tide had turned on the Russian Front. Reluctant to set up a communications center when the Soviets were losing, he saw no reason to take such a risk now that they were winning. Nunn May would later claim that his refusal to obey the orders of the KGB made him, for practical purposes, "a defector."

His self-avowed defector status was more than invalidated, however, by what he did next. He became convinced that it was dangerous for the US to have a monopoly on the atomic bomb and that the USSR should have information about the weapon. Consequently, throughout his Canadian assignment Nunn May, using the cover name "Alek," was passing information and materiel to either his KGB control, Lieutenant Angelov, or to Angelov's supervisor, Colonel Nikolai Zabotin. Moving back and forth between Montreal and Chicago, he handed over samples of uranium 233 and 235, along with technical details of the "Little Boy" bomb that would eventually be used on Hiroshima.

For this he was reportedly paid $200 (which he said he burned) and a couple of bottles of whiskey.

In September of 1945, Igor Gouzenko, a cipher clerk in the Soviet Embassy to Canada, presented himself to officers of the Royal Canadian Mounted Police, announced that his comparatively unimportant embassy duties were merely a cover for his activities as an agent of Soviet military intelligence, turned over a massive amount of espionage data he had stolen, and requested that he and his family be put into protective custody by the Mounties. Gouzenko had just become the Cold War's first important defector to the West. Among the materials Gouzenko turned over the RCMP were several pages torn from the notebook of Colonel Zabotin, the head of the spy network of which Nunn May was a part.

Believing that he had been compromised, Nunn May decided to return to England, where he resumed his position at King's College as a physics lecturer. Prior to his departure from Canada, Nunn May was instructed by Zabotin to meet another KGB contact in front of the British Museum in London on October 17, 1945. Somehow, British Counter-Intelligence got wind of the meeting and placed the Museum under surveillance. Nunn May, however, was warned that the meeting place was staked out and failed to show.

He remained safe for the moment but Canadian authorities were in the process of running down the leads in the notes and materials given to them by Gouzenko and his time was running short. On February 15,

1946, it ran out. Leonard Burt, the head of the Special Branch, Scotland Yard's domestic counter-espionage unit, turned up at Nunn May's doorway to ask his assistance on some "routine inquiries."

In the course of the polite conversation that followed, Burt informed Nunn May that the police were aware of his missed appointment at the British Museum. He left the question of why he missed the rendezvous unasked but Nunn May answered it anyway.

"I decided to wash my hands of the whole business," he said. Then, before Burt could utter the words that would place Nunn May under formal arrest, he offered to make a complete confession. He wrote out a hasty statement, signed it, and handed it to the detective. The statement implicated no one except himself. He claimed that he had broken no laws, that he had done nothing but turn over material to a foreign power, which he did not name but which he stated was an ally of both Britain and the US, united with those nations in a common purpose during the recently ended conflict. From that point on he stuck to his story, refusing to name any names and giving no additional information other than what he'd already offered in his initial statement.

Nunn May demanded a jury trial then pled guilty before the prosecution could begin presenting its case, preventing the presentation of any further evidence beyond his written confession. That statement, carefully contrived to put himself in the best light, was the only documented evidence of his betrayal to be presented in court.

Though he named no names, Nunn May's arrest had a domino effect. British and American law enforcement, now alert to the reality of Soviet penetration into the Manhattan Project, were able to use their knowledge of KGB espionage codes to uncover Dr. Klaus Fuchs, another atomic scientist who'd passed secrets to the USSR. After his arrest in Britain, Fuchs implicated his courier, Harry Gold, who was apprehended in the US. From Gold, lawmen were led to David Greenglass, who'd spent his World War II army service as a machinist at Los Alamos. From Greenglass the trail led to his sister, Ethel Rosenberg, and her husband, Julius. The atomic spy ring had been broken but the horse had already escaped from the barn by the time security forces finally managed to get the door closed. The Soviet Union already had enough information, thanks to Nunn May and company, to develop its own nuclear arsenal. They successfully exploded an A-bomb in 1949, setting the decades-long Cold War arms race in motion.

The more renowned of the Trinity turncoats would continue to operate for several years after Nunn May's arrest. In 1951 Maclean and Burgess were exposed but managed to escape behind the Iron Curtain just before they were arrested. There they maintained that they were innocent of all charges and had defected to the East because of their disillusionment with the hypocritical West. They were given KGB commissions and lived in the USSR until their deaths.

Philby lasted until January 23, 1963, when he suddenly deserted his family and fled to Russia like Burgess and Maclean, barely a step ahead of the British security forces planning his arrest. According to some sources, Philby was commissioned as a KGB general upon his arrival in Moscow.

Blunt, the mysterious "Fourth Man" whose very existence was doubted by many, was finally uncovered in 1964. Rather than flee as Burgess, Maclean, and Philby had, Blunt simply cut a deal. For total immunity, he'd reveal everything he knew about Soviet espionage operations. The British reluctantly decided that Blunt's information was important enough to justify the bargain. Blunt escaped prosecution and, until 1979, when Prime Minister Margaret Thatcher responded to a direct question from the floor of Parliament with characteristic candor, he escaped public exposure as well. He died in disgrace, but in total freedom, in 1983.

Dr. Allan Nunn May, the first of the Cambridge spies and the first of the atomic spies, to be exposed, proved to be one of the most honorable, to the degree that a word like "honorable" can be applied to a traitor. When faced with exposure, he did not run as Burgess, Maclean, and Philby would do, but stood firm and took his punishment. Neither did he try to bargain his way out of the consequences of his act by implicating his colleagues as Blunt, Fuchs, Gold, and Greenglass would all do. To the end, he remained a "stand-up guy." Only the Rosenbergs, facing death rather than a term of imprisonment, were more resolute.

After his conviction, Nunn May was sentenced to a term in Yorkshire's Wakefield Prison. He was released in January of 1953, returning to Cambridge where he met and married Dr. Hilde Broda. With his record of espionage, however, he could find no work there.

In 1961, he and his family moved to Ghana at the invitation of President Kwame Nkrumah. His wife established a medical practice there while he carried out research on solid state physics and created a national science museum.

He returned to Cambridge in 1978. From then until his death, he insisted that he had only done what he did for the sake of world peace, that he believed then and still believed that a Western monopoly on atomic weapons was dangerous and had to be balanced by equivalent Soviet power.

"I felt," he said, "that this was a contribution I could make to the safety of mankind. I certainly did not do it for gain."

Even presuming that he was lying about burning the $200 (and there's no real reason to presume that), his claim that he was not motivated by greed is probably the truth. Given his radicalization at Cambridge and the example Nazi Germany had given of what could come of a country's possessing unopposed military power, his belief that American nuclear muscle had to be balanced is understandable.

In light of subsequent events, however, in light of the Soviet-backed invasion of South Korea by the North, the brutal occupation of Hungary, the erection of the Berlin Wall, the Cuban Missile Crisis, the invasion of Afghanistan; in light of the whole history of Soviet aggression *after* they obtained the West's atomic secrets and used them to develop their own nuclear arsenal, what is far less understandable is how he could continue to believe it.

FURTHER READING

Alan Moorehead's *The Traitors* (Scribner's, 1952) was probably the earliest book-length account of the cases of Nunn May, Fuchs, and the other atomic spies. H. Montgomery Hyde's *The Atomic Spies* (Atheneum, 1980) covers much of the same ground with the advantage of a greater sense of historical perspective. Igor Gouzenko's *The Iron Curtain* (Dutton, 1948) describes the events that led up to his defection which ultimately resulted in Nunn May's exposure. Leonard Burt's *Commander Burt of Scotland Yard* (Heineman, 1959) describes the atomic spy cases from the perspective of British law enforcement, while former FBI Agent Robert Lamphere's *The FBI-KGB War* (Random, 1986) does the same thing from the American point of view. Regrettably, Commander Burt's long out-of-print memoirs have, to the best of my knowledge, never been published in the US making them difficult, though not impossible, to find.

There is a good entry on Nunn May in Jay Robert Nash's massive encyclopedia on the history of espionage, *Spies* (M. Evans, 1997), but it states that Nunn May moved to the Soviet Union after his release from prison and was never heard from again, a major error that calls the rest of the information in the article into question. Other articles on Philby, Burgess, Fuchs, the Rosenbergs, etc., serve to place Nunn May into the broader context of Soviet espionage during this period.

ALLAN NUNN MAY IN FICTION

Nunn May, a rather shy, unprepossessing man, lacked the colorful dash and charm of Philby and the other Trinity spies, and while the material he passed to the Soviets was important, it wasn't as crucial as that provided by Fuchs. Further, Nunn May acted more or less independently, while Fuchs was part of a larger ring that included the Rosenbergs, tending to increase the scope for drama in the Fuchs case while decreasing it for Nunn May. His story tends to be something of a footnote in accounts of both the Cambridge Spies and the Atomic Spies. Consequently, there have been very few fictional depictions based directly on the Nunn May case.

The Iron Curtain (20th Century Fox, 1948), a film version of Gouzenko's book written by Milton Krims and directed by William A. Wellman, reunited *Laura* co-stars Dana Andrews and Gene Tierney. Andrews portrayed Gouzenko and Miss Tierney his wife in a dramatized depiction of Gouzenko's personal journey from loyal Soviet citizen to defector. "Dr. Harold Preston Norman," a supporting character in the film played by Nicholas Joy, is a British scientist involved in Soviet efforts to obtain information on the A-bomb, clearly a fictionalized version of Nunn May who even uses the real-life Nunn May's code name, "Alek." *The Iron Curtain* may have been Hollywood's very first "Cold War" film.

Other such movies soon followed. *Walk a Crooked Mile* (Columbia, 1948), written by George Bruce and directed by Gordon Douglas, teams an FBI agent played by Dennis O'Keefe with a Scotland Yard inspector played by Louis Hayward in a collaborative investigation into a Western nuclear physicist who's voluntarily passing secrets to the Soviets. Though not directly based on the Nunn May case (the turncoat is American rather than British and the setting is California), the notion of a treacherous scientist acting as a Soviet spy was almost certainly drawn from real-life events. Since to that point Nunn May was the only Western traitor who'd been publicly exposed, it's easy to conclude that the story was loosely inspired by the Nunn May case.

The most direct fictionalization of the Nunn May case is Clare George's first novel, *The Cloud Chamber* (Sceptre, 2003), which fortuitously hit the stands of British bookstores almost exactly one month after Nunn May's death early in January 2003. The main character is Walter Dunnachie, a physicist and clergyman (apparently modeled on the author's grandfather), whose pacifist principles put him outside the mainstream of the scientific community during World War II. When the war ends and his closest friend from his undergraduate days, the Marxist-leaning Allan Nunn May, returns to England after participating in the Manhattan Project, Dunnachie innocently comes under suspicion when a British security officer, keeping Nunn May under surveillance, observes the two old chums meeting. Not published in the United States (but readily available through various Internet sites), the novel has gotten good reviews in Britain.

THE MAD DOCTOR AND THE UNTOUCHABLE

Medical Mysteries

Thanks to sportswriter Oscar Fraley, TV producer Desi Arnaz, and actor Robert Stack, he became world-renowned as "the man who got Capone," arguably the most famous policeman of the 20th century. In fact, TV and movies so exaggerated his real-life accomplishments that many latter-day true-crime writers have been inclined to write him off as a media fabrication.

He was, of course, Eliot Ness, legendary as the sternly upright, implacable foe of Depression-era gangdom, who with a small, specially selected flying squad of incorruptible sleuths known throughout the world as the "Untouchables," dried up Chicago and drove the country's most notorious organized crime figure straight into a jail cell. And the most amazing thing about the story is that, dismissive naysayers notwithstanding, it's mostly the Lord's truth.

Among the lesser-known facts about Ness is that this most famous of real-life cops was the partial inspiration for the most famous of fictional cops, Dick Tracy. Tracy creator Chester Gould, during an interview in which he described his original concept of pitting "a modern-day Sherlock Holmes against the Mob," admitted without actually identifying Ness by name that "this young G-man they sent after Capone" fit perfectly with his notion of a latter-day Holmes. Coincidentally, Ness, like Gould, was a lifelong Conan Doyle fan, which may have been one of the factors leading him to a career in law enforcement. In any case, despite revisionists who've insisted that Ness's feet were clay, Gould chose his model well for, as Gould's successor on the *Tracy* comic strip, Max Allan Collins, would later put it, "Ness really was as close to Dick Tracy as any real lawman ever came."

Still, the single accomplishment for which Ness is best-remembered, jailing Capone, was one for which he had to share the credit. After all, Capone was finally convicted of tax evasion, not Volstead Act violations (though he *was* indicted on more than 5000 bootlegging charges on the basis of Ness's investigation, they were never brought to trial), and while some of the evidence used in the tax case was uncovered by Ness and his men, it wasn't Ness who put that case together. It was a criminal investigative team from the IRS headed by U.S. Treasury Agent Frank Wilson.

And when you come right down to it, what did putting Capone away really accomplish? Did organized crime in the Windy City shrivel up and blow away? On the contrary, it continued to thrive and it could be reasonably argued that the only thing jailing Scarface did was clear the way for subsequent mob kingpins like Frank Nitti, Paul Ricca, Sam Giancanna, or Tony Accardo, to each in their turn take the Big Fellow's place at the top of Chicago's crime pyramid.

I don't mean to seriously suggest that putting a powerful figure like Al Capone out of commission is insignificant. But I do believe that Ness's most impressive accomplishments in law enforcement, for all that they've received far less publicity, came after he'd moved out of Chicago and traded in his federal investigator's badge for that of a metropolitan police chief.

At the controls of the law enforcement apparatus of Cleveland, Ohio, America's seventh largest city, Ness broke the power of local Mob figures, either jailing them or driving them out of town altogether. He turned one of the dirtiest, most corrupt police departments in the nation into one of the cleanest. He significantly curbed labor racketeering. He cut overall crime by nearly 40%. And, in what he would later say was the achievement that of all his work as a policeman he was most proud, he initiated a program of traffic safety and enforcement that reduced fatal accidents by more than 50%, earning his town the title of "Safest City in the USA" from the National Safety Council.

There was, however, one goal he set for himself during this period that seemed to perpetually slip out of his reach: the identification and apprehension of a vicious serial killer whose five-year reign of terror roughly paralleled Ness's tenure at the head of Cleveland's police department. At least 13 victims, each discovered in varying states of dismemberment, were attributed to the unknown predator. Then, as suddenly as they started, the murders stopped. It remained the most galling failure of the legendary cop's career.

But was it a failure? At the height of the killer's fame, the media began reporting unsubstantiated rumors that Ness had identified some unnamed suspect. These rumors were never confirmed by Ness or any his staff but shortly after they began to circulate, the murders stopped. No one was ever brought to trial, however, and officially the case remained and still remains open. Though Ness never acknowledged that he had ever developed a viable candidate for the crimes, at least not while he remained in office, the story of "Ness's Secret Suspect" became part of the folklore surrounding the case.

Nearly two decades after the last murder, while putting the finishing touches on *The Untouchables* (Messner, 1957), his autobiographical account of the Capone investigation, Ness talked about the "Mad Butcher" case with Fraley, his collaborator, and finally confirmed the rumors. Fraley was told that Ness and his department had actually solved the case. Moreover, they'd managed after a fashion to put the killer (whom Ness referred to by the alias of "Gaylord Sundheim") behind bars. But, because of political and evidentiary considerations, the precise nature of which Ness only hinted at, they were forced to keep the killer's identity secret and to keep the file on the case officially marked "unsolved."

Was Ness just blowing smoke? Many of his detractors, and even a few of his admirers, thought so. A small, possibly excusable bit of prevarication, designed to shield his reputation from tarnish. But, in fact, Ness's stated belief that he had identified the killer was sincere and, if he was right, what has always been regarded as his most spectacular defeat must be counted as at least a partial triumph.

* * *

That Ness enjoyed *any* triumph in law enforcement after his departure from Chicago might have come as a surprise to many because his career post-Capone gave every appearance of being profoundly disappointing. At first, of course, things seemed quite promising, as Ness, his small detail of "Untouchables" disbanded, was promoted to Agent-in-Charge of the Prohibition Bureau's entire Chicago office. But, when the "Prohis" were absorbed into the FBI (or Division of Investigation, as it was then known), things began to take a definite downward spiral.

Actually, this highly-publicized reorganization, part of the Omnibus Crime Bill passed during the frenetic "First 100 Days" of the New Deal, for the most part occurred strictly on paper. The Prohibition Bureau did change its name to "Alcohol Beverage Unit," and at least officially became a subsidiary of the FBI but for practical purposes it remained a separate, autonomous agency. J. Edgar Hoover wanted nothing to do with liquor enforcement and he wanted his own hand-picked agents mixing with the corruption-tainted "dry cops" even less. The only significant change resulting from this "reorganization," aside from making it appear as though FDR's Department of Justice was getting tough on crime, was to put Hoover in charge. And that may have been the rub.

Hoover's extreme displeasure at agents under his command getting more publicity than he did and the vindictive measures he took against such agents is well-known and well-documented. He couldn't have been pleased that a firebrand whose taste for personal publicity had earned him the nickname "Eliot Press" was now part of his own agency, even if only on paper and only by bureaucratic caprice.

In any event, soon after the reorganization, Ness was transferred south to a district covering the mountainous regions of Ohio, Kentucky, and Tennessee, assigned to curb the activities of hillbilly moonshiners as a federal "revenooer." I'm aware of no evidence positively indicating that this assignment was Hoover's way of getting Ness out of the spotlight and, with Prohibition winding down (Congress had passed the 21st Amendment repealing the ban on alcoholic beverages in February of 1933 and it was quickly working its way through the state legislatures) a legitimate argument could be made that the rural moonshiners of the nascent "Dixie Mafia" really were the last major liquor violators left. Nonetheless, in retrospect, coming so quickly after the reorganization, this new assignment seems awfully suspicious.

Whether it was the result of agency needs, Hoover's petty jealousy, or some combination, Ness found himself facing an extraordinarily dangerous and thankless job. Urban bootleggers knew that there was a heavy price to be paid for firing on cops, particularly federal agents, so while gun battles were not unheard of neither were they everyday occurrences. Their rural counterparts, however, had no such compunctions. Interfere in their business and they'd come up shooting.

"Those mountain men and their squirrel rifles gave me almost as many chills as the Capone mob," Ness would later declare.

Faced with all the death and none of the glory, Ness was anxious for a change of scene, and shortly after Repeal was ratified he got it. Now that liquor was legal again the federal government's main interest became not its suppression but the collection of revenue from its sale and manufacture. Consequently, the FBI's Alcohol Beverage Unit was transferred *en masse* to the Treasury Department where it was reorganized, yet again, into the Alcohol Tax Unit (ATU), known today as the Bureau of Alcohol, Tobacco, Firearms, and Explosives (ATF). In August of 1934, Ness was transferred to Cleveland, as the agent-in-charge of the ATU's Northern Ohio office. From an obscure, but dangerous rural assignment, Ness was back in a major metropolitan area, about to find himself, as he had in Chicago in 1929, the right man, in the right place, at the right time.

Over the next 16 months, Ness and his men made substantial headway against Cleveland's still-flourishing, though much smaller, illegal liquor racket. While he was happy to be working again in an urban setting, he was getting little of the publicity he so savored. With Prohibition nothing but a memory, liquor enforcement was small potatoes. Still there were plenty of reporters who were aware of Ness and familiar with his Chicago reputation and this would soon prove useful to Cleveland's top Treasury Agent.

The Cleveland area at that time was one of the most crime-ridden regions in the country. Cuyahoga County, of which Cleveland was the seat, derived its name from an Indian word meaning "crooked," and in the early 1930's that seemed entirely appropriate. The local Mafia family controlling the city's illegal activities, known as the Mayfield Road Mob, held Cleveland and its elected officials in an iron grip. The police department was so corrupt that it made the notoriously dirty Chicago force look, in the words of one observer, "like a bunch of choir boys." Labor racketeers extorted money from local businesses with impunity while doing nothing for the rank-and-file members whose interests they were supposed to be protecting.

In November 1935, Cleveland's citizens finally responded to the situation by voting in a reform ticket headed by former Ohio State Representative Harold Burton. Burton's mayoral election could probably be attributed to one single man, Martin J. Lavelle, Cleveland's Director of Public Safety. As the man in charge of both the Police and Fire Departments, Lavelle's personal conduct and rank incompetence had so outraged the citizenry that he had been transformed into the living symbol of the lawlessness and corruption plaguing Cleveland; a symbol which ultimately became the rallying point that had swept Burton and his slate into office. Now the success of Burton's administration would hinge on his ability to keep one single promise: reduce crime in Cleveland. To make good that pledge, he'd need a strong hand at the tiller of municipal law enforcement and the appointment of a new Safety Director became his first order of business.

Mayor Burton was that rare thing in politics, an honest man. He fully intended to make good on his pledge but, personal integrity notwithstanding, he *was* a politician and he knew the value of publicity. Government agents were suddenly getting a very glamorous reputation with the voting public, so it's not surprising that all of the candidates he was considering for the job came from the ranks of federal law enforcement. Burton eventually narrowed his choices down to four. The name at the bottom of the list was "Eliot Ness."

Burton had never actually heard of Ness and had only placed him on his short list because of the strong recommendations the young G-man had received from business leaders, city officials, and, in particular, reporters. Though impressed by what he'd heard, Burton was still inclined to appoint someone more seasoned and experienced. But when his first choice, Joseph Keenan, a veteran prosecutor then serving as a top assistant to the U.S. Attorney General, turned him down and added his own recommendation of Ness, Burton reconsidered.

On December 11, 1935, Burton called Ness to his office and offered the position to him. Ness immediately accepted on the conditions that he'd have a free hand and that he'd be able to turn as much of the desk work and administrative details as possible over to subordinates, leaving him free to operate in the field. Burton agreed and, after appropriate announcements were made, his new Safety Director was sworn in. Ness, at the age of 32, had just become the youngest major city police chief in the United States.

He hit the ground running, quickly making headlines with the same kind of rip-snorting, fast-action police work that had served him so well (and had generated so much gratifying newspaper coverage) during the Capone years. At the request of County Prosecutor Frank Cullitan, he personally led a group of off-duty Cleveland policemen on an "Untouchables"-style raid of the Harvard Club, a notorious road house and casino operated by the Mayfield Road Mob just outside the city limits, then followed up with a series of gambling raids in downtown Cleveland, closing down nearly a dozen of the Syndicate's "sporting" locations.

At the same time he was personally conducting an investigation into police graft, a probe which ultimately led to the conviction and imprisonment of 11 high-ranking Cleveland police officers on corruption charges and the early retirement or resignation of dozens more.

* * *

Though Ness was enjoying singular success at putting mobsters and crooked cops behind bars, the criminal who would prove his most elusive quarry was, at this point, operating well below his radar. He was a different kind of lawbreaker, against whom the high-profile, kick-in-the-door style of law enforcement that had become Ness's specialty would prove frustratingly ineffective.

His first victim was found on September 5, 1934, when the torso of a human female was discovered washed up on the sand of a Lake Erie shoreline near Euclid Beach, barely a month after Ness's arrival in Cleveland to take over the local office of the Alcohol Tax Unit. The body's head, arms, and calves had all been removed. Additional body parts were discovered in adjacent Lake County and matched to the torso but no head was ever found. Dubbed by the press "The Lady of the Lake," the woman was never identified.

Over a year later, on September 25, 1935, nearly three months before Ness assumed his duties as Cleveland's Safety Director, a couple of kids playing on Jackass Hill in the industrial gully known as Kingsbury Run discovered another dismembered corpse. They immediately reported this to the Erie Railroad Police, who mounted a search of the area and discovered a second torso. The railroad cops were soon joined by Cleveland homicide detectives. Together the city and railroad officers continued the search, finding heads belonging to both bodies and additional body parts, including severed genitals matching both corpses. The first victim was identified as Edward Andrassy, a small-time criminal with a long record of petty offenses. The second victim was never identified. At the time, no connection was made between these bodies and that of the previous year's "Lady in the Lake."

On January 26, 1936, slightly more than two weeks after Ness's raid on the Harvard Club, a bushel basket covered by a burlap sack was found abandoned in an alley in the Cleveland PD's Third Precinct, the notorious "Roaring Third." The basket was found to contain a human arm, two thighs, and the lower half of a human torso. Cuyahoga County Coroner Arthur Pearse determined that the partial corpse was that of a female who had been murdered perhaps two days earlier. Police fingerprint expert George Koestle, after painstaking examination of 10,000 records, identified the victim as Florence Polillo, a known prostitute with an arrest record that stretched from Cleveland to Washington, DC. Though articles in the Cleveland *News* suggested a connection between Polillo's death and the earlier dismemberment murders, possibly the earliest intimation that a serial killer was operating in Cleveland, Detective Sergeant James Hogan, the commander of homicide, was unequivocal in his opinion that Polillo's death was unrelated to either "The Lady in the Lake" or to the two corpses found in Kingsbury Run. The Polillo murder, Hogan insisted, would be investigated as a totally separate case.

On June 5, 1936, as Cleveland prepared to host the Republican National Convention and as Ness continued his gambling raids and his investigation into police corruption, a discovery was made that forced the official line to change. In an eerie parallel to the events of the previous September, two young boys, deciding to get a jump on the upcoming summer vacation, cut school to spend the day fishing on the lake. Taking a shortcut through Kingsbury Run, they saw a pair of pants rolled up and partially hidden beneath a bush. "We think maybe there's money in the pockets," one of the boys said later, "so we take a fish pole and poke the bundle and out pops the head." The head that popped out was that of a blue-eyed, red-haired young man. Scared witless at the grisly discovery, they ran back to the house of the older boy, cowering there until the boy's mother arrived home, got their story out of them, and notified the authorities.

Police found the head exactly where the boys had left it, less than a mile from the spot where Edward Andrassy and his unidentified companion had been found nine months earlier. The next day the rest of the body was discovered elsewhere in the Run. Unlike the earlier corpses this body was, with the obvious exception of the decapitation, not dismembered. Six tattoos, including one on the left leg depicting the comic strip character Jiggs from *Bringing Up Father*, were found on various parts of the body, and the hands were both unmutilated. The police were confident that the victim would be quickly identified, but this proved not to be the case. The prints were not on file anywhere, and attempts to identify him by his tattoos all led to dead ends. The press dubbed the victim "The Tattooed Man". A "death's head" cast of the victim was placed on display at the Great Lakes Exposition in hopes some visitor might recognize him, but without result.

However, the discovery of this fifth corpse did lead both the media and official law enforcement to decide, reluctantly on the part of the police and gleefully on the part of the press, that a psychopathic multiple murderer was indeed on the loose in Cleveland. This changed the character of both the investigation and the news coverage. On June 6, the headline of the Cleveland *Press* read "Hunt Fiend in 4 Decapitations," and the *News* and the *Plain Dealer* joined in the media uproar. Curiously, "The Lady in the Lake" wasn't yet regarded by either cops or reporters as part of the killer's tally. Moreover, Sergeant Hogan, though now admitting that there was a single killer responsible for most of the deaths was, according to some sources, still disinclined to include Flo Polillo on the roster of victims. But however many victims were being attributed to him either officially or unofficially, the hunt for the murderer soon to be christened "The Mad Butcher of Kingsbury Run" was now on.

A little more than month after the discovery of "The Tattooed Man," the next corpse was found in the tiny suburban hamlet of Brooklyn Village in the western part of the county. Discovered in a state of well-advanced decomposition in a gully between the Big Creek and the B&O Railroad tracks, this body was headless but otherwise unmutilated. The victim's head was found roughly 10 feet away from the rest of his corpse. This was the first victim to be found outside of Cleveland's city limits. Local village constables were soon joined by detectives from the Cleveland Police and the Cuyahoga County Sheriff's Department as well as officers from various nearby suburban forces anxious to participate, if only peripherally, in a major homicide investigation.

There were intimations on the part of some of the police that the murderer may have been some sort of health care professional, such as a physician or a nurse. Dr. Pearce seemed to agree, noting the skillful manner in which the beheadings had been performed and hinting that it might indicate the possibility that the killer was a surgeon. This was the first time that a medical background for the killer had been suggested and the *News* ran with it, writing that the killer was "cool and calculating" and that he "decapitated his victims with the skill of a physician." The state of decomposition indicated that this most recently discovered victim might have met his death before "The Tattooed Man." The frequency of the murders seemed to be increasing.

The killer returned to Kingsbury Run to dump his next victim. On September 10, 1936, a rail-riding hobo attempting to hitch a lift on an eastbound freight tripped over the upper half of an armless, headless torso. He ran to a nearby oil tank station and reported his discovery to the clerk there who, in turn, called the police.

The first officers on the scene found the rest of the torso within minutes of their arrival. Despite an intensive search, during which the police were assisted per Safety Director Ness's direction by members of the

Fire Department, no other body parts were found. After examining the partial corpse, Coroner Pearce and his staff described the victim as a white male, roughly 25 to 30 years old, who'd been dead approximately two days.

The department's immediate response to the discovery of the latest body was to assign a new team of detectives to work the entire series of torso murders full-time and exclusively. Chief George Matowitz, who ran the police department's overall day-to-day operations, personally selected the senior member of the team, Detective Peter Merylo. Merylo was generally regarded as one of Cleveland PD's top investigators and the "go-to guy" whenever someone was needed for especially difficult assignments. On the day the two halves of Victim Seven were found, he was assigned to the midnight shift at the Third Precinct. That same day he was awakened from his daytime slumber and informed that he was being reassigned to Homicide where he and his new partner would be devoting their whole attention to tracking down the Butcher.

Merylo's partner on the new assignment was Detective Martin Zalewski, a veteran cop who'd spent three of his 20-plus years on the Job patrolling a beat near Jackass Hill, where the bodies of Edward Andrassy and his unnamed companion had been found. Like the Ukrainian-born Merylo, Zalewski was multi-lingual, a skill that would be invaluable working among the diverse immigrant communities that populated the area in and around Kingsbury Run.

Inspector Joseph Sweeny, the head of Cleveland PD's detective bureau, announced the assignment of Merylo and Zalewski to reporters but the press release did little to alleviate the wave of negative publicity that the latest torso victim engendered.

Mayor Burton was feeling the heat, particularly as his most formidable political foe, U.S. Representative Martin Sweeney (no relation to the police inspector) was doing everything he could to keep the fire stoked. Denouncing what he called "the Ness-Burton failure to solve the horrible Torso crimes," he suggested that if voters turned out Burton in the upcoming election, "we can send back to Washington the Prohibition Agent who is now Safety Director." Sweeney's protégé, Democrat mayoral candidate John McWilliams, echoed the criticism. What Cleveland needed to run its police force, he said, was not "a G-Man from Chicago," but a local figure applying local knowledge to crimes like the torso slayings.

With the election just two months away, Burton felt his job was on the line and he knew something more dramatic than assigning a couple of new detectives to the case was called for. On September 12, at the behest of Burton, Ness announced that he would be taking personal charge of the Torso case.

"I want this psycho caught," Ness told reporters. "I'm going to do all I can to aid in the investigation." Cleveland's top cop had publicly made the Butcher's capture his personal business.

* * *

At the request of Coroner Pearce, Ness took his first official action on the case, helping to organize a brainstorming session of "Torso experts" in an effort to assemble some picture of the killer's psychological make-up and personality. This meeting, possibly the first attempt to profile an unknown subject in a serial murder case, was held on September 15 in the police crime lab at Central Station. In addition to Ness and Pearce, over 30 law enforcement officials and medical experts attended, including Chief Matowitz, Chief of Detectives Sweeny, Sergeant Hogan and every detective who'd worked some aspect of the case (presumably including Merylo and Zalewski, though no press coverage of the meeting mentions them by name), Detective Lieutenant David Cowles (the head of the crime lab), County Prosecutor Cullitan, County Pathologist Reuben Strauss (who'd actually performed most of the torso autopsies), psychiatrists Royal Grossman and Guy Williams, and Western Reserve University Med School professors T. Wingate Todd and W.M. Krogman.

After several hours of discussion the members of what the press called the "Torso Clinic" agreed on a "synthetic portrait" of the murderer made up of seven general conclusions:

1. The killer worked alone and had killed all of the presumed victims except "The Lady in the Lake," whose death, despite startling similarities to the other murders, was regarded as having taken place too early to be counted as part of the series.
2. The killer displayed knowledge of anatomy and surgical techniques. However, despite the expertise exhibited by the dismemberment, all of the assembled medical personnel insisted that the killer was most likely not a physician but more probably a butcher or a hunter. However, they stopped short of absolutely

ruling out a physician.

3. The killer lived in the area of Kingsbury Run, which enabled him to become acquainted with potential victims and to quiet their suspicions over time before actually striking.

4. The killer committed his crimes in a workshop or lab where he could privately decapitate and dismember his victims without fear of discovery.

5. The killer was a demented psychopath, possibly even insane, but not in any obvious way. The murders probably satisfied some deep-seated sexual perversion.

6. The victims were chosen from transient, marginal members of the population, who would not be missed if they disappeared. Had the torsos not been discovered, it was extremely unlikely that the murders would have ever come to light.

7. Physically, the killer was big and strong.

Much of this was nothing more than the quantification of the obvious and the broadest consensus among the participants was probably their agreement with a comment made by Sergeant Hogan as the meeting commenced.

"Gentlemen," he said, "tonight we're right where we were the day the first body was found."

Ness's next official act, much less public than his participation in the "Torso Clinic," was a confidential meeting with Lieutenant Cowles. Though the largely self-taught criminalist now ran the crime lab, he had been a street cop of singular reputation years earlier and he still had contacts in Cleveland's criminal community. Cowles was informed the Cleveland *Press* was willing to finance a secret and unorthodox avenue of investigation. On the theory that Cleveland's street criminals might have access to information unavailable to the police, Ness suggested that this secret fund might be used to organize and pay for a network of informants chosen from among Cowles's underworld contacts and known only to him, along the lines of Sherlock Holmes' Baker Street Irregulars (Ness, as noted earlier, had been an avid Conan Doyle fan from his boyhood).

At the same time, Ness was turning his own team loose on the case. Shortly after his appointment, Ness had publicly organized a special detail of promising young policemen, dubbed by the press "Ness's Minute Men." They were attached directly to Ness's office and very publicly assigned to whatever crime problem he felt was in need of immediate attention, somewhat like a roving police commando unit. Behind the very public "Minute Men," however, was a very private, very elite squad of detectives, personally selected by Ness and assigned to sensitive investigations where discretion was needed. As his special detail in Chicago had been dubbed the "Untouchables," this Cleveland unit was referred to as the "Unknowns," because their names were never publicly revealed. Usually recruited from outside the department (one is said to have worked under Ness as an "Untouchable" during the Chicago years), they were issued Cleveland Police credentials and reported only to the Safety Director, conducting secret probes on any crimes in which he took a personal interest. Some time during this period, most likely after Dr. Pearce's Torso conference, Ness assigned his secret squad to the case. So in addition to the front-page investigation being conducted by Cleveland's homicide detail with Merylo and Zalewski taking the point (and a good deal of the public criticism), Ness had two separate, *sub rosa* units, one of them composed entirely of professional criminals working the case behind the scenes and under his personal supervision.

While Ness's public entry into the case apparently saved Mayor Burton's job (he won a close election a few weeks later), the lack of any solution lost Coroner Pearce his. In an upset victory, Dr. Samuel Gerber, a young Democratic Party activist whose campaign consisted largely of criticizing the way the Mad Butcher investigation was being conducted, was elected coroner over the incumbent. Shortly after taking office, Gerber was himself initiated into the fraternity of Mad Butcher investigators when the torso of a woman was found floating just off the Lake Erie shore on February 23, 1937.

The discovery of a partial female torso so close to the spot where the "Lady of the Lake" had been found in '35 forced law enforcement officials to re-examine their long-held belief that the Lady was not part of the Butcher's roster. Sergeant Hogan and Inspector Sweeny stuck to their guns, insisting that neither Torso Number 1 nor this latest victim were part of the series. Gerber, however, in a five-page report to Ness, concluded not only that this newly discovered corpse was the work of the Butcher but also that the surgical precision with which the dismemberments were performed indicated that the killer was "highly intelligent in recognizing the anatomical landmarks as they were approached." He went on to state flatly that the killer had some kind of medical background. He was probably a physician, medical student, or at least a nurse or orderly. Gerber was the first medical expert to insist that the Butcher was some sort of health care professional. Meanwhile, Gerber's assistant, County Pathologist Strauss, opined that not only was the latest corpse a Butcher victim but that Torso Number 1, the Lady of the Lake, was also the work of the Kingsbury Run killer.

Torso Number 8 was never identified.

The next body, found a little more than three months later, was discovered near the Cuyahoga River. On Saturday, June 6, 1937, a 14-year-old boy walking along the riverbank stopped to kick over a pile of carefully arranged rocks and was shocked to discover that they were concealing a human skull. Police who responded to the discovery found a burlap bag inside of which were a set of human ribs, hips, shoulder blades, a complete set of vertebrae, and a strip of decaying human skin approximately 12 inches long, all wrapped in a copy of the Cleveland *Plain Dealer* dated June 5, 1936, almost exactly a year earlier.

Coroner Gerber, working with Dr. Todd of Western Reserve University, concluded that the incomplete skeleton belonged to an African-American woman, who had been dead for at least a year, possibly as long as 15 months. Gerber confidently included the latest discovery in the Butcher's canon.

Detective Merylo tentatively identified her from the extensive dental work in the skull as Rose Wallace, a resident of the "Roaring Third," who'd been missing since August 21, 1936. She was the first victim since Flo Polillo, Torso Number 3, to whom the police were able to attach a name. This identification was never absolutely confirmed, however and Gerber, for one, flatly rejected it since reports that Wallace had been seen as late as August of the previous year conflicted with his conclusion that the body had been killed as early as March or April.

Though the dental evidence was indicative, it was not conclusive. Still, Rose Wallace fit the general description of the victim and had last been seen wearing clothes similar to those found near the body. Moreover, she fit the victim profile, being a resident of the Third Precinct with a record for prostitution and public intoxication. Most compelling of all, she was never seen again after her disappearance. If Rose Wallace was Torso Number 9, however, her tentative identification did not move the police any closer to a solution. Though several promising leads developed, including tips on a number of suspicious doctors developed by Ness's staff and followed up by Merylo and Zalewski, none of them came to anything.

One month to the day after the discovery of Rose Wallace's presumed remains, the Butcher's next victim turned up. Talks between the CIO and Cleveland's steel companies had broken down in May and the legendary "Little Steel Strike" had been in full swing for several weeks. Governor Martin Davey had activated soldiers from the Ohio National Guard and sent them to Cleveland to keep order. One of these weekend warriors, Private Edgar Steinbrecher of the 147th Infantry Regiment, was posted at the West Third Street Bridge. At one point during his sentry duties, he looked over the side of the bridge and noticed what he at first took for a department store dummy floating in the Cuyahoga River. Looking closer, he saw that it wasn't a mannequin at all but part of a human being.

Coroner Gerber and Sergeant Hogan lost no time in declaring that the latest grisly discovery, the lower half of a male torso and two halves of a left leg, was the work of the Butcher. Gerber emphasized the killer's "expert" surgical technique in his press comments.

By July 14 all missing parts of the corpse except for the head had turned up and Gerber was describing the latest victim as a white male, between the ages of 25 and 35, roughly 6 feet tall and 180 pounds. Though the body's fingerprints were intact, checks in local files, in the files of neighboring police agencies, and in the FBI's voluminous collection yielded no match and the victim remained unidentified. No other usable forensics clues were found. As with every previous torso discovery, leads soon petered out.

The investigation slogged on. Merylo and Zalewski spent their time either running down fruitless leads or dressing up as hoboes and hanging around the Run in an effort to flush out the killer. Cowles's "irregular" network of criminal informants and Ness's squad of "Unknowns" continued their efforts, but all to no avail.

Until St. Patrick's Day, 1938.

* * *

On that day, in the small western Ohio town of Bogart just south of Sandusky, a dog happily trotted home with the severed lower leg of woman clutched tightly in its teeth. The local coroner, E.J. Meckstroth, examined the limb and pronounced it "as neat a job of amputation as I ever saw." Local law enforcement contacted Cleveland authorities, who were naturally interested in any stray human body parts that happened to be found anywhere in the state. Within hours of the notification, Lieutenant Cowles and Pathologist Strauss arrived in Sandusky.

Once the attention of Cleveland law enforcement was drawn to western Ohio, it began to focus on Dr. Francis Edward Sweeney, an alcoholic physician and military veteran attempting to dry out in the Sandusky Soldiers and Sailors Home.

Then in his early 40's, Dr. Sweeney was a Cleveland native, born and raised on the edge of Kingsbury Run, the product of immigrant blue-collar roots from which he was determined to escape. After a tour of World War I duty as a supply clerk in the Army's Medical Corps, he attended Western Reserve's School of Pharmacy, earning his certificate in 1922. Two years later he entered St. Louis University's School of Medicine. While visiting his home town during one of his summer vacations, he married Mary Sokol, a nurse at St. Vincent's Charity Hospital. After Sweeney's graduation in 1928, he and his wife returned to Cleveland where he interned at St. Alexis Hospital. In 1929, Dr. Sweeney hung out his own shingle as a general practitioner and surgeon. The future of Sweeney and his family looked promising but it was in that same year that an irreversible downward spiral began for the young doctor.

Sweeney started to drink heavily and over the next few years his behavior grew progressively more erratic and violent. He neglected his practice, often leaving home for several days, leaving no word of his whereabouts. Late in 1933, during one of these absences, Mary Sweeney filed an affidavit stating that she doubted her husband's sanity. This resulted in a short commitment to City Hospital but he was discharged a month later. A second affidavit filed by Mrs. Sweeney was dismissed. Fearing for her own safety and that of her two sons, she moved in with her sister, began using her maiden name, and sued for divorce in the fall of 1934. Sweeney, meanwhile, simply dropped out of sight.

Sometime in 1935 or 1936, Dr. Sweeney came under police scrutiny. Precisely when or how is unclear. Some accounts indicate that one of Ness's "Unknowns," an undercover policewoman with a high-society background whom Ness used as his insider on cases involving Cleveland's rich and famous set, developed Sweeney as a suspect. Other sources suggest that it may have been a criminal informant, possibly one of Cowles' "irregular" network, possibly a completely independent tipster, who provided the lead. What led Ness's undercover agent to suspect Sweeney (if that's how Sweeney actually came under suspicion) or what information the underworld contact passed on (if any such information about Sweeney was actually passed on in this way) is frustratingly vague and unclear. In fact, it's entirely likely given the widespread speculation that the Butcher had been medically trained, that police authorities were simply taking a close look at *all* health care professionals in the area, in which case Sweeney, with his history of mental problems and alcoholism, would naturally have appeared to be a pretty good suspect.

However Sweeney was brought to the attention of Cleveland law enforcement, he was apparently eliminated when it was discovered that he was a patient at the Sandusky veterans' home, presumably an iron-clad alibi. But when the severed leg turned up in March of 1938 so near to Sweeney's institutional residence, Lieutenant Cowles decided to take a closer look at the hard-drinking surgeon.

He discovered that whoever had confirmed Sweeney's alibi had been inexcusably lax. Sweeney was self-committed, which meant he could come and go as he pleased. He had been in *and out* of the Soldiers and Sailors home several times during the period that the murders were occurring.

Cowles also ascertained that the Honor Farm of Ohio's correctional department shared facilities with the veterans' hospital. Investigating further, he made the acquaintance of Alex Archaki, a convicted burglar who was serving out the last part of his term at the honor facility. Archaki admitted to Cowles that he and Dr. Sweeney were acquainted. In fact, it was Archaki who kept Sweeney supplied with liquor during his stay in the hospital. Sweeney paid off these favors by writing prescriptions for barbiturates and other controlled substances for Archaki.

Under Cowles's skillful questioning, Archaki admitted that not only was Sweeney frequently absent from the hospital but that these absences roughly coincided with the estimated times of several of the murders. Whenever Sweeney turned up missing for a few days, a new corpse was discovered shortly after the patient's return.

Finally, Archaki revealed that he had actually known Dr. Sweeney several years earlier. They'd met at a bar in downtown Cleveland some time prior to Archaki's arrest and conviction. Sweeney approached him, bought him a drink, and struck up a conversation. Was Archaki from out-of-town? Did he have a wife or family anywhere in the Cleveland area? How long was he planning to stay in Cleveland? Thinking little of the conversation at the time, it began to seem suspicious to Archaki years later when he and Sweeney crossed paths again in Sandusky and

Archaki noticed that Sweeney's absences from the hospital and the discoveries of new Torso victims seemed so suspiciously coincident. Was it possible that Sweeney was the killer and that he had been qualifying Archaki as a possible victim?

Investigating further, Cowles found that a second round of competency hearings on Dr. Sweeney had been held earlier that year and that county psychiatrists had once more found him sane, causing the sanity complaint to be dismissed.

Cowles and Ness must have been struck by the fact that Sweeney's first competency hearings, in late '33 and early '34, preceded the beginning of the murder cycle by just a few months, while the second round, early in '38, occurred just a few months after the discoveries of the most recent victims, as if to provide a perfect frame within which the murders occurred. Moreover, Sweeney, being a hefty six-footer weighing more than 200 pounds, a surgically trained physician, an alcoholic suspected by his family of deeper-seated psychological problems, and a native Clevelander who'd grown up in the Kingsbury Run neighborhood, fit the Torso Clinic profile of the Mad Butcher in every particular.

Ironically, the severed leg that had caused police attention to focus on Dr. Sweeney turned out to have nothing to do with the Butcher case. It was found to have been the improperly disposed of remains of a perfectly legitimate amputation performed at a nearby hospital.

Nonetheless, Sweeney was now Ness's prime suspect but he knew that he and his staff would have to tread lightly for Dr. Sweeney was a cousin of Congressman Martin Sweeney, the same Martin Sweeney whose criticism of the Butcher investigation during the 1936 election had almost cost Mayor Burton and his personally appointed Safety Director their jobs. The case against Dr. Francis Sweeney would have to be both rock-solid and iron-clad or else it would appear to be nothing more than the politically motivated persecution of an innocent man who had the misfortune to be related to Burton's political nemesis.

As Ness and Cowles pondered what steps could be taken against Dr. Sweeney, another body part was found floating in the Cuyahoga River on April 8, 1938. Coroner Gerber, who was developing into even more of a publicity hound than Ness, announced that the body part, the lower portion of a woman's leg, was only a few days old and was most likely the partial remains of another Butcher victim.

Possibly recalling that the Sandusky discovery had been a false alarm (despite the fact that it had led the police to their best suspect),

Ness asked that some outside authority be consulted for a second opinion, a request that Gerber angrily refused. The examination of human remains was the sole responsibility of *his* agency and he was not about to abrogate it to an independent pathologist at the suggestion of a man whose own department had so miserably failed to catch the killer. The political affiliations and egos of two of the main investigators on the case, Republican Safety Director Ness and Democratic Coroner Gerber, were starting to get in the way of interdepartmental cooperation.

In any case, a few weeks later Gerber's assertions were proven correct when a couple of burlap bags containing a woman's torso, thighs, and one foot were fished out of the Cuyahoga and matched to the earlier discovery. The newest victim's arms and head never turned up and she was never identified.

While Merylo, Zalewski, and the rest of the homicide detail ran down leads on the latest victim, all of which ultimately led nowhere, Ness had Dr. Sweeney placed under continuous surveillance. The word "continuous," however, was less accurate than Ness might have hoped. His "Minute Men," promising though they were, were new to the job, and the more experienced "Unknowns" were small in number (according to Fraley, Ness's secret, independent squad consisted of only three investigators) and unable to mount a large-scale surveillance on their own.

In consequence, Sweeney had no trouble detecting his tails. He delighted in leading them into embarrassing situations and when it suited his purpose had little trouble losing them. On one occasion, he led a tail into a downtown department store and around a blind corner near the elevator banks. When the officer turned the corner, he found Sweeney waiting for him. The doctor smiled, and asked the rookie cop his name. "If we're going to be together so often," said Sweeney, "we might as well be acquainted."

On another occasion, Sweeney led his tail into a bar that catered exclusively to an African-American clientele. The officer sat himself at one end of the bar while Sweeney sat at the other, the twin objects of suspicious attention from the rest of the crowd as the only white customers in the establishment. As the officer tried his best to look unobtrusive, Sweeney arranged to keep him supplied with free drinks.

Aside from the games he played with his police tails, Sweeney seemed to delight in tormenting the higher-ups who were directing the investigation. Lieutenant Cowles began to receive packets of newspaper clippings about the case sent by Sweeney with instructions that they be placed "in my file." He sent Ness a photograph of an empty field with in "X" marked on it along with the notation, "Dig here." Surveillance clearly wasn't working but something had to be shaken loose. Sweeney had to be either clearly identified as the Butcher or clearly eliminated so that the department could move on to more fruitful avenues of investigation.

As Ness pondered his next move, two more bodies were discovered. On August 16, 1938, three men were searching a vacant lot along East Ninth Street for scrap metal. Now the site of the Great Lakes Science Center and the Rock and Roll Hall of Fame, during the Depression years the area was used as an unofficial dump and a source for retrieving discarded material that could be sold for recycling. One of the men thought he saw a coat that still looked salvageable sticking out of the dump. Investigating more closely, he found that it was a patchwork quilt rather than a coat, held down with rocks. He lifted the quilt and found that it had been covering a female torso. He notified police, who mounted a search of the area as a crowd of spectators looked on.

One of the spectators drew the attention of searching police to a heap of garbage from which emanated a terrible stench. Beneath the pile a second skeletal torso was found. Torso 12 was found to be a woman, estimated to have been in her early to mid-30s. Torso 13 belonged to a small-boned male, roughly the same age. Though more of the bodies of these victims were found than was usually the case with the Torso Killer's prey including the head of Torso 12, neither corpse was ever identified. The level of decomposition indicated that the victims had been dead for quite some time and that they may, in fact, have been killed before Torso 11, the woman whose body parts were fished out the Cuyahoga during the previous April.

Ness, smarting from the almost continuous criticism he and his department were taking over the Butcher case, decided that a bold, dramatic action, the kind that had served him so well during his career, was needed to bring things to a head. On Thursday, August 17, just a few minutes past midnight, Ness personally led a raid on a hobo jungle along Canal Road, arresting 38 homeless transients. Roughly simultaneous raids on two other shanty-towns elsewhere in the Run netted an additional 25 arrests. While the transients were being booked into Central Station, the makeshift shanties were demolished. The next day, Ness ordered all traces of the encampments burned.

Publicly, Ness stated that he had mounted the raids primarily to identify possible future Butcher victims, but his main purpose was more likely to prevent them from becoming victims. As Cleveland crime historian John Bellamy put it, "Since [Ness] couldn't find the alligator—the Torso killer—he decided to drain the swamp."

Ironically, considering that Ness had mounted these raids with at least one eye on public relations, the general reaction to the mass arrest of homeless men was anger and shock. Far from preventing their potential murders, Ness seemed to be taking his frustration at his inability to catch the Butcher out on the very people he was supposed to be protecting. This single action probably netted the Safety Director the worst press he ever got in his entire law enforcement career.

But Ness had no time to consider the PR disaster the raids had generated since he was simultaneously planning a second massive police action—nothing less than the intensive search of every single household and building in the Third Precinct. Given the nature of the murders, it seemed obvious that they had to have been committed behind closed doors and, in fact, this had been one of the seven general conclusions reached by the Torso Clinic more than two years earlier. The most likely spot was somewhere in the "Roaring Third." If the killer's "death lab" could be discovered then the Mad Butcher could, in all likelihood, be positively identified. Ness assigned the task to six homicide detectives, including Merylo and Zalewski. Since Ness's position as Director of Public Safety put him in charge of the Fire Department as well as the police force, he was able to partner a fire inspector with each detective. Fire inspectors were empowered to enter buildings at all times without warning and without warrants, and using safety inspections as a pretext to look for the Butcher's murder site was an easy way of getting around the thorny legal questions surrounding search and seizure.

Sometime during this period, Ness also decided that despite the possible political ramifications it was time to pull Dr. Sweeney in and subject him to an intense interrogation, including a polygraph examination. Nevertheless, political considerations couldn't be discounted entirely, so to maintain discretion Ness decided to conduct the interrogation in a suite at the Cleveland Hotel rather than at a police station. The only polygraph machine in the metropolitan area was owned by the suburban force of East Cleveland and, though the East Cleveland Police made it a policy to loan out their machine to neighboring agencies, such a loan could not be made with the secrecy Ness needed. Instead, Ness contacted an old friend from his "Untouchable" days and asked for a favor. The friend was Dr. Leonard Keeler of Northwestern University, who was nothing less than the inventor of the polygraph. The favor was coming to Cleveland with his device and personally conducting a lie detector test on Ness's suspect.

It's not clear exactly when Ness had Sweeney picked up. Some sources say that the interrogation took place as early as May, 1938. At least one source suggests that it might have been even earlier, in April. Others state that it occurred in August, following both the discovery of the two latest bodies and Ness's raids on the hobo jungles in Kingsbury Run and perhaps simultaneously with the door-to-door search of the Roaring Third. Whenever it actually occurred, there is general agreement on *what* occurred.

Sweeney was arrested and brought to the hotel suite in a state of intoxication so extreme that it took three days for him to sober up enough that he could be interviewed. Once Sweeney had managed to crawl out of his booze-induced stupor, Cowles and another detective, Ray Oldag, began questioning him while Ness and Dr. Royal Grossman, a psychiatrist for the Probation Department, looked on. For more than a week, eight hours every day, Cowles and Oldag relentlessly worked on their suspect, an unusually intense grilling even in those pre-Miranda days. Sweeney never broke.

As with everything else connected with his being a suspect, Sweeney seemed to enjoy it. At the end of the week-long interrogation, when told that Dr. Keeler, the foremost polygraph expert in the world, wanted him to submit to an examination, Sweeney readily agreed. After attaching the various sensors to Sweeney, Dr. Keeler ran the suspect through the list of prepared questions at least twice while Ness and the others quietly observed. Upon concluding the examination, Keeler reported his opinions to Ness privately.

"He's your man," said Keeler, "I may as well throw my machine out the window if I say anything else."

Armed with Keeler's assurances, Ness himself took over the interrogation. Confronting Sweeney, he said, "I think you killed those people."

"Think?" retorted Sweeney. "Prove it!"

That, of course, was the problem. However convinced Ness might be by the polygraph results, they were not admissible in court. The only evidence against Sweeney was circumstantial and, while it was persuasive, it was far from conclusive. Moreover, the door-to-door search of the Third Precinct had failed to turn up the "death lab," the discovery of which was Ness's best hope of discovering some physical evidence that he could connect to his suspect. In the end, Ness had no choice. He let Sweeney go.

Sometime during this period, the security Ness had worked so hard to maintain began to break down. Local newspapers began printing reports that the Cleveland Police had a Butcher suspect in custody and expected a break in the case any day. The Cleveland *News* even reported that the suspect was "an ex-doctor." In New York, Walter Winchell (who, ironically, years later, would himself contribute to the mythic stature of Eliot Ness when he signed on as the narrator of *The Untouchables* TV series) even ran an item on the possible solution to the Butcher case in his gossip column. Though Ness never confirmed these reports, some official substantiation was given by Coroner Gerber, who, without naming Sweeney, was quoted as saying, "This man has been a 'hot' suspect for the last two years." While the Safety Director did not join Gerber in confirming the reports and would not do so until two decades later during his conversation with Fraley, the legend of "Ness's Secret Suspect" had taken root.

If Dr. Gerber, loyal Democrat that he was, knew about Sweeney, it was almost certain that Congressman Martin Sweeney, the one man Ness was most anxious to keep out of the loop, also knew.

The whole question of who Ness's suspect was became moot on August 25, 1938, when Dr. Sweeney unexpectedly committed himself to the psychiatric ward of the veteran's hospital in Sandusky. From that day until his death in 1964, Sweeney was an in-patient at a series of VA and state mental hospitals. In essence, he imprisoned himself when Ness, despite his best efforts, was unable to.

Precisely why Sweeney chose to commit himself so soon after the hotel suite interrogation is unclear. If his cousin, Congressman Sweeney, had in fact become aware that he was related to Ness's prime suspect, the commitment may have been part of a deal. If Ness continued his policy of discretion, the Sweeney family would see to it that Cousin Frank would be put where he could do no further harm. And while Ness would likely have been strongly averse to such a proposal, it may under the circumstances have seemed the best possible choice, given the paucity of any substantive proof against the doctor.

In any case, once Dr. Sweeney was institutionalized, the murders stopped. Though the case remained officially open (Detective Merylo, who was also kept out of the small inner circle who knew the identity of "Ness's Secret Suspect," continued to work the case tirelessly right up to his retirement from the police force and beyond), Ness and his staff went on to other concerns and other cases.

* * *

But Dr. Sweeney, presuming that he was in fact the Butcher, managed while comfortably ensconced in a VA mental clinic to claim one last, inadvertent victim. His name was Frank Dolezal, who, while the real murderer may have been lounging in the anonymous security of a government hospital, became noteworthy as the only man ever actually indicted for a Butcher murder.

It apparently started shortly after Sweeney's commitment, when Cuyahoga County Sheriff Martin O'Donnell was persuaded to get his department actively involved in the Butcher case. To that point, the Sheriff's Office had been notable for its near-total absence from almost any aspect of the Butcher investigation. A staunch Democrat and a bitter rival of Ness's, O'Donnell regarded the case as a political hot potato best left for the city cops to juggle. And since all but one of the bodies had been discovered within Cleveland's city limits, he had no official reason to get involved anyway.

Precisely why O'Donnell chose to become so interested that late in the game is unknown, but it is a fact that he was related by marriage to both Congressman Martin Sweeney and Dr. Frank Sweeney. Congressman Sweeney may have decided that, despite Ness's continued discretion, it would be prudent to dig up another suspect, one who could deflect suspicion from his cousin should the doctor ever be publicly exposed. Having influence with the Sheriff's Department that he clearly lacked with the city police, the congressman may have convinced O'Donnell, his in-law and political ally, to help develop such a suspect. This is all speculation, of course, but it does provide a plausible explanation for O'Donnell's sudden and unexpected late entry into a case he'd spent years ducking.

Whether or not Congressman Sweeney was involved in O'Donnell's decision to enter the case, another Democratic Party regular was: former Cleveland Mayor Ray Miller. Part of the machine that had been ousted when Burton's reform administration was elected, it was Miller who put O'Donnell in contact with private investigator Lawrence J. "Pat" Lyons.

Lyons had been closely studying the case and was certain that he could come up with a viable Butcher suspect if he had the backing of official law enforcement. O'Donnell promptly deputized Lyons and assigned him to work full-time on the Butcher case as a special investigator.

Working with two other deputies, Lyons went at the case along classic lines. Since two of the victims, Edward Andrassy and Flo Polillo, had been positively identified and a third, Rose Wallace, had been tentatively identified, Lyons reasoned that anyone who was acquainted with all three was by default a prime suspect. Since in a serial murder case victims are typically strangers to the killer, this wasn't necessarily a fruitful avenue of investigation; but, as imperfectly understood as the phenomenon of the serial killer is now, it was a completely unknown discipline of criminal investigation in the 1930's. Indeed, the term "serial killer" wouldn't even be coined for decades.

Following his belief that there was a connection between the victims and their murderer, Lyons and his partners found that all three victims were frequent customers of the same bar. From this information, they were led to Frank Dolezal, an immigrant bricklayer who also frequented the establishment and was peripherally acquainted with the three known victims. Dolezal had once worked in a slaughterhouse which, the deputies reasoned, might have given him the necessary expertise (recall that the medical experts at the Torso Clinic were reluctant to attribute the killer's surgical acumen to medical training, asserting that he was more likely to be a butcher or a hunter). Dolezal was said to personally possess a full set of butcher knives. Gaining access to an apartment Dolezal had once lived in, Lyons found dark stains on the bottom of the bathtub. He took some scrapings and brought them to his brother, chemist G.V. Lyons, for analysis.

Detective Merylo, who had actually checked out Dolezal some years earlier and had already eliminated him as a suspect, got wind of the county investigation when a drunken Pat Lyons, while eating at a restaurant near the Run, started loudly bragging about his status as the lead investigator on the Butcher case. The owner of the restaurant notified Merylo, who, at first, was inclined to add the drunken deputy to his list of suspects. When the Sheriff's Department learned that municipal police had become aware of Lyons's activities, they decided to pull Dolezal in before Merylo and the city officers could interfere. Deputies arrested Dolezal in his apartment on July 5, 1939, nearly one full year after the most recent discoveries of Torso victims, also seizing four butcher knives they found there as evidence.

Over the next two days, Dolezal was mercilessly interrogated by county detectives. On July 7, O'Donnell announced to the press that Dolezal had confessed to the murder of Flo Polillo, a not altogether accurate announcement. Although Dolezal had admitted killing Polillo, he insisted that he was only protecting himself from a knife attack she had launched at him. Hardly a murder confession.

Publicly, Ness reacted with diplomacy. "The sheriff," he said, "is to be commended for his investigation. The leads he uncovered will, of course, be followed up to see what possible connection the Polillo case may have with any other." He went on to offer the Sheriff's Office full cooperation.

The blunt-spoken Merylo was less complimentary. He publicly declared that he had eliminated Dolezal years earlier. If Dolezal had confessed, it could only be because the sheriff's detectives had coerced the statement.

As if on cue, corroborating evidence started pouring in shortly after the sheriff's press conference. Lyons's chemist brother pronounced the stain found in Dolezal's former apartment to be human blood. Dolezal mysteriously quit that apartment just as Ness was directing his massive search of the area by combined police/firefighter teams. Dolezal had once been Polillo's live-in lover. Two of the four butcher knives confiscated when Dolezal was arrested had suspicious dark stains on them. A prostitute, Lillian Jones, who worked the area made a statement that Dolezal had once attacked her with a knife and that she was only able to escape certain death by leaping from a second-story window. Dolezal himself went on to sign two additional confessions though the details in each confession differed in many important respects, a circumstance which tended to cast doubt on the veracity of any of the confessions. A polygraph examination conducted by the East Cleveland Police seemed to verify Dolezal's guilt, though no questions were asked about the discrepancies in his various statements.

Dolezal was arraigned on one count of first degree murder on July 13, 1939. Almost as soon as formal court proceedings began, the evidence against Dolezal began to fall apart.

A further examination by criminalists at Western Reserve University disclosed that the stains found in Dolezal's old apartment were nothing more than dirt. Merylo uncovered work records that proved Dolezal couldn't have been anywhere near where he said he was in his statements to sheriff's deputies. Dolezal himself was claiming that he had been continually beaten, deprived of food and sleep, and otherwise abused in attempts to get him to confess. The initial arraignment was tossed out on the grounds that Dolezal had been forced to appear without his attorney, Fred Soukap.

On July 21 Dolezal was re-arraigned, this time on the reduced charge of manslaughter since the only evidence against him was his own confession in which he claimed to have killed Polillo in "self-defense". As Dolezal was led away, he wriggled out of the grip of escorting officers, rolled up his shirt sleeves and displayed his heavily bruised arms to the crowded courtroom. "They said they didn't beat me," he shouted.

As Dolezal's guilt became more and more doubtful, O'Donnell started to back-track. Whether or not Dolezal was the Butcher, the sheriff asserted, he had certainly killed Flo Polillo, adding, "At this point, we are only concerned with the Polillo case."

Coroner Gerber, who had staked his reputation on the assertion that one killer was responsible for all the Torso victims, made one of his rare public criticisms of a fellow Democrat. Dolezal's confession to the Polillo killing meant nothing, he said. If Dolezal killed Polillo, then he killed all the other victims as well. If he was innocent of the other Torso deaths, then he was also innocent of Polillo's.

What had started out as a major coup showing up Ness and his staff was turning into a public disaster for O'Donnell and the Sheriff's Department. And it was about to get even more embarrassing.

On August 22, 1939, a few minutes before two a.m., Deputy Hugh Crawford, on jail duty in Cellblock B-4, where Dolezal was the only prisoner, found the county's Butcher suspect hanging from a coat hook in his cell, his neck encircled by a makeshift rope made of cleaning rags. He later claimed that Dolezal was still breathing when he found him.

Calling for help, Crawford was immediately joined by Chief Jailer Archie Burns and Sheriff O'Donnell himself. Cutting Dolezal free, they called for a male nurse who was on duty at the jail and an ambulance. Within five minutes after Crawford discovered the prisoner, emergency medical personnel were administering oxygen and insulin in an effort to revive him, but to no avail. Dolezal was already dead.

Discrepancies in the accounts of sheriff's personnel started showing up almost immediately. Dolezal, who stood at 5 feet 8 inches, hung himself from a hook that was only 5 feet 7 inches from the floor. Crawford had claimed that he had left his post for no more than three minutes to inform some visitors that they would have to leave. The visitors' names were never found on the log and Coroner Gerber insisted that it would have taken at least 12 minutes for Dolezal to die of strangulation. Even Deputy Adolf Schuster, assigned to the jail that night with Crawford, publicly expressed doubt that a man contemplating suicide would have eaten all of his lunch beforehand.

Despite his loyalty to his party, Gerber had no choice but to perform an autopsy on Dolezal and hold an inquest. The autopsy, which Gerber worked on personally along with County Pathologist Strauss and Dr. Harry Goldblatt of Western Reserve Medical School, cast doubt not only on the manner of Dolezal's death but on the veracity of his supposedly "freely given" statements. Dolezal was found to have sustained no less than six broken ribs, three on each side, and while it was impossible to state with certainty exactly when he had suffered these injuries, it was hard to believe, as Dolezal's lawyer lost no time in publicly pointing out, that the hapless immigrant could have worked steadily as a bricklayer with such impairments. The obvious conclusion was that the injuries must have occurred while Dolezal was in custody.

At the inquest, testimony that Dolezal had been continually abused and beaten in an effort to get him to confess was offered. Lillian Jones, the prostitute who had earlier claimed that Dolezal had threatened her with a knife, retracted that statement and now testified that she had been pressured into making the accusation by Pat Lyons. She and her sister, Ruby Jones, also claimed that Lyons had made it clear that county officers intended to get a statement out of Dolezal any way they could. "Dolezal is the right man," Lyons was reported as saying, "and we're going to beat the hell out of him until he confesses."

Gerber was smack dab in the middle of that tiny, proverbial space west of the rock and east of the hard place. Loyal arguably to a fault to the party that had put him in office, he was, nevertheless, like Ness, like Burton, an honest public official, and he took a great deal of professional pride in his work as a forensic investigator. He couldn't simply ignore the evidence and return the verdict his political allies wanted. In the end, he compromised. Dolezal, he declared at the close of the inquest, had died by his own hand but his multiple injuries had been sustained while in the custody of the Sheriff's Office.

Virtually no one who's studied the Mad Butcher case at any length believes Dolezal had anything to do with the murders. For one thing, except for Flo Polillo, he steadfastly denied any involvement in the murders no matter what kind of abuse sheriff's investigators administered. And he claimed to have killed Polillo only in self-defense. For another, Dolezal was a comparatively small man, unlikely to have been able to overpower victims who were, in some cases, bigger than him. Finally, as we now know, serial killers rarely stop of their own volition but no new victims had been discovered since August of 1938.

To the assertion that the killings ended once Dolezal was arrested, Coroner Gerber, hardly one whose agenda included making a political ally like Sheriff O'Donnell look bad, retorted, "The arrest of Dolezal didn't stop the murders. They had already stopped."

No, Dolezal can't be regarded as a serious Butcher candidate, but only as another victim, if not directly of the Butcher then of a law enforcement establishment more concerned with politics than justice.

* * *

The tragic story of Frank Dolezal raises one major question. Why did Ness, if he truly believed Frank Sweeney to be the Butcher, remain silent? Surely he wouldn't have felt obliged to keep any agreement with Sweeney's congressman cousin, presuming there was any such agreement, if it meant the persecution of an innocent man. And if there was no such arrangement, his silence is even more puzzling.

Indeed, Ness's failure to speak up is the main reason many true-crime scholars doubted his confirmation of the "Secret Suspect" story decades later. It simply defied logic for Ness to remain mute in the face of a man he *knew* to be innocent paying for crimes he did not commit.

However, in the years since Ness's cryptic conversation with Fraley about "Gaylord Sundheim," Sweeney has been publicly identified, so we know that there really *was* a "Secret Suspect," that it was not merely an unconfirmable story manufactured by Ness years later.

Which returns us to the original question. If he had a secret suspect, and he did, and he was convinced of that suspect's guilt, and he apparently was, why didn't he say something to help Dolezal?

No one can say for sure now but I personally think that there were several factors leading to Ness's decision, the first of which was that in spite of everything, Ness, at least in 1939, still harbored some lingering doubts about Dr. Sweeney's culpability.

In 1997, during an interview with members of the Cleveland Police Historical Society, Arnold Sagalyn, a special assistant to Ness during the late '30s (some sources state that he was, in fact, one of the elite "Unknowns") and the last surviving member of Ness's staff, verified that Sweeney actually was the so-called "Secret Suspect," but also admitted that Ness was nagged by doubts about Sweeney's guilt. While Sweeney seemed to fit the profile in every particular, Sagalyn said, Ness found it difficult to reconcile Sweeney's guilt with the lack of any conclusive, tangible proof.

Another factor may have been that while there was general agreement that a single multiple murderer was operating in Cleveland during the mid to late '30s, there was never universal agreement about precisely which bodies should be attributed to him. To this day, many discount the first body, the "Lady in the Lake." The presence of formaldehyde in one of the two bodies discovered in August of 1938 caused several Torso investigators to exclude at least one, if not both of those bodies from the Butcher's roster, chalking them up to a funeral home prank rather than murder.

And not everyone agreed that Florence Polillo, the only victim Dolezal claimed as his, should be included. Detective Sergeant Hogan, the chief of homicide, was one of those who insisted, at least at first, that Polillo was not part of the series. There were just enough differences in the circumstances of her death that it was possible that someone other than the Butcher was actually liable for it. And since Dolezal was only admitting responsibility for Polillo's death, Sweeney's and Dolezal's guilt were not mutually exclusive.

If one considers the doubts he still harbored about Sweeney's guilt, the fact that even if Sweeney *was* the Butcher he still could have been innocent of the Polillo murder (the corollary of which was that Dolezal could have been guilty of it even if he *wasn't* the Butcher) and, finally, the possibility that he may have made a commitment to keep Dr. Sweeney's identity a secret, Ness's silence during the Dolezal affair becomes easier to understand.

But even if these factors kept Ness from speaking up in 1939, they raise another question. Why, if he wasn't absolutely convinced of Sweeney's guilt at the time, did he seem so certain of that guilt when he finally broke his silence during the 1956 conversation with Fraley?

The reason alluded to earlier, that Ness simply wanted to be publicly perceived as having solved the mysterious Butcher crimes, is quite likely a good part of the explanation. Indeed, Ness's detractors have used this quite understandable, quite human inclination as an excuse to disregard his claims altogether. But Ness's desire for credit really has nothing to do with the validity of his proposed solution.

Another factor and one which would not have seemed as obvious in 1939 but which would have become more evident with the passage of time, was simply the fact that the murders stopped once Sweeney was safely in the custody of a psychiatric hospital. As Dr. Gerber pointed out, there had been no new murders for nearly a year by the time the Sheriff's Office named Dolezal as a suspect, so Dolezal's arrest clearly wasn't the impetus behind the end of the killings. But Dr. Sweeney entered the VA facility a few scant weeks after the discovery of the last bodies and, over the course of the next several years, as it gradually became apparent that they *were* the last bodies, it must have seemed to Ness and to others who were familiar with Sweeney much more than mere coincidence.

Not that there weren't other victims occasionally put forth as the possible work of the Butcher. Dismemberment murders occurring in Kentucky, Michigan, and Pennsylvania during the early to mid-1940s have all been mentioned and investigated as possibly being the work of the Butcher. It was also suggested that L.A.'s most famous unsolved murder, the "Black Dahlia" case, might have been his responsibility. And while there were those who were quick to attribute such crimes to the Torso Killer (particularly Detective Peter Merylo, who, obsessed with the case as he had become, rarely encountered a dismembered corpse anywhere in the country that he wasn't willing to add to the Butcher's list of victims), no convincing forensic evidence has ever connected any of these crimes to the Cleveland series and most scholars regard them as being the work of totally separate offenders. Which brings us back to the original point. Once Sweeney took himself out of the game, the Torso killings ended. As time went by, that fact alone might have been the single circumstance that Ness found most convincing.

Finally, there was the fact that, over the next two decades, Sweeney kept up a sinister, taunting, one-way correspondence with Ness that seemed deliberately calculated to hint at his guilt without coming right out and admitting it.

Six items of this correspondence still exist, a letter and five post-cards. Each contain obscurely worded messages, apparently intended as inside jokes that Sweeney presumably believed would be clear to Ness. One of the cards has a picture of the Deeds Carillon tower in Dayton, Ohio, pasted on it, a structure remarkable for its resemblance to a knife-blade. Next to it Sweeney wrote a cryptic message that seemed to be a reference to the line from Shakespeare's *Macbeth* about "a dagger I see before me." He signed it "A-Signatur, The-Sweeney Boy, R-member." In another, he pasted a newspaper ad for the book *Handbook for Poisoners* (Rinehart, 1955), adding nothing more than his signature, "F.E. Sweeney, M.D., Your Paranoidal Nemesis." A third depicts two actors (one of whom, ironically enough, is Neville Brand who, a few years later, when *The Untouchables* was adapted for TV, would portray Al Capone opposite Robert Stack's Ness) from the prison film *Riot in Cell Block 11* (Allied Artists, 1954), gripping the bars of their cell door in uncontrolled anger. In still another, he attached an ad for plant seeds, signing himself "The-American Sweeney," a possible reference to the mythical British mass murderer Sweeney Todd. Years later, Ness's wife Elizabeth would recall the feelings of terror the arrival of one of these vaguely threatening missives always generated despite her husband's assurances that they were beyond the writer's reach.

Given Dr. Sweeney's penchant for making fun of his pursuers, the string of taunting cards and letters he sent Ness over the years could be attributed to his sense of, for lack of a better word, mischief. But to Ness, the sinister correspondence would surely have looked like one more circumstance strongly indicative of Sweeney's guilt.

When Ness finally confirmed the rumors of his "Secret Suspect" to Fraley, he refrained from referring to him by name. In addition to giving him a pseudonym, he also gave deliberately false or misleading information. He stated, for example, that his suspect had dropped out of medical school before completing his studies and that he had died in a mental institution two years earlier. Of course, Sweeney had fully qualified as a physician by the late '20s. He was also alive at the time of Ness's conversation with his collaborator and remained so for another eight years. Ness apparently wanted it known that he had actually solved the case widely regarded as his greatest defeat but still seemed to feel some obligation to protect Sweeney's identity. As noted earlier, Ness's reluctance to name his suspect or to give concrete details about him caused many who studied the case to doubt his claims.

Sweeney's real name would finally come to light through the efforts of three different researchers, each pursuing three separate investigations, for three different reasons.

The first was Marilyn Bardsley, who in the early 1970's began researching the case with the intention of turning it into a stage play.

When an article about her appeared in a local paper, she was contacted by Dr. Royal Grossman, the psychiatrist who had been present with Ness and the others during the hotel room interrogation of Sweeney. He confirmed that Ness's tale of a "Secret Suspect" was true. Bardsley later tracked down the long-retired crime lab supervisor, David Cowles, who also confirmed Ness's account. However, both Grossman and Cowles refrained from actually naming the suspect.

A second article many months later resulted in a call from Alex Archaki, the honor prisoner who had been a resident at the Sandusky veterans' home at the same time as Sweeney. He told Bardsley the same story he'd told Lieutenant Cowles four decades earlier. And, unlike Grossman and Cowles, Archaki named names. The man Cowles had been interested in, he told the hopeful playwright, was Dr. Frank Sweeney. Bardsley recontacted Dr. Grossman and Lieutenant Cowles who both reluctantly substantiated Archaki's story. Sweeney had, they both admitted, been the "Secret Suspect."

Although Ms. Bardsley's play never came to fruition, she did eventually write a novel in which the lead character was based on Frank Sweeney. She also wrote two non-fiction books about Eliot Ness and his work on the Butcher case.

In the 1980's, award-winning mystery writer Max Allan Collins, Chester Gould's successor on the *Dick Tracy* comic strip, began a long series of carefully researched historical novels featuring a Depression-era private eye named Nathan Heller. One of the conventions of the hard-boiled P.I. novel is that the hero's best friend is a cop, giving the hero a convenient contact in official law enforcement. Famous examples include Homicide Captain Pat Chambers in Mickey Spillane's Mike Hammer series, DA's Investigator Bernie Ohls in Raymond Chandler's Philip Marlowe series, and Sergeant Dennis Becker on television's *The Rockford Files*. Collins, in developing his Heller series, had the original notion of casting real-life figure Eliot Ness in the Chambers-Ohls-Becker role, partly because he had always been a fan of the Robert Stack TV series, and using Ness as a character would give him an excuse to delve into the real man rather than the TV-created myth. What he found was that there was a lot of interesting material about Ness that he wouldn't be able to use if the legendary lawman was relegated to supporting character status. So he spun Ness off into his own series of novels, the second of which was based on the Butcher case.

One of the places Collins went to research Ness generally and the

Butcher case specifically was the library of the Western Reserve Historical Society in Cleveland which, several years earlier, had been entrusted by Eliot Ness's family with the voluminous scrapbooks chronicling his long police career that the famed crime-fighter had painstakingly compiled over the years. Collins, though an admirer of Ness, was one of those who doubted the stories of the "Secret Suspect," so he was surprised to find, preserved in the scrapbooks along with all the newspaper clippings and photographs, the sinister mailings posted by Sweeney to Ness.

"I did not know what these items were, at first," he later wrote. "But when I realized I was holding missives likely written by the Mad Butcher of Kingsbury Run to Eliot Ness (and saved by him!), I dropped them as if they were on fire; and I did not sleep worth a damn that night...." He now knew not only that the stories of the "Secret Suspect" were true, but also the actual identity of that suspect.

Because Ness, Cowles, Grossman, and the others were so carefully secretive about their investigation, Sweeney had never been named as the prime Torso suspect in any official police report. In 1991 that changed when the Cleveland Police received a request from the LAPD to investigate a possible connection between the Butcher slayings and the murder of Elizabeth Short, the so-called "Black Dahlia." This request had probably been generated by a new wave of public interest in the Short case, possibly induced in part by the publication of James Ellroy's best-selling novel *The Black Dahlia* (Mysterious, 1987). John Fransen, then a sergeant in Cleveland PD's Homicide Unit, was given the assignment.

Fransen knew nothing of Bardsley's research two decades earlier and even if he had the people she had talked to who confirmed Sweeney's identity had passed away in the ensuing 20-odd years. And it's doubtful that he was specifically familiar with Collins's research though he did learn that the cryptic notes allegedly sent to Ness by the "Secret Suspect" had been discovered and were in the care of the Historical Society.

Using those cards and the single letter as a foundation, Sergeant Fransen tackled the case like the trained, experienced homicide detective he was. Knowing where to look and having access to investigative avenues unavailable to civilians like Collins or Bardsley, he was able to discount any connection between the Cleveland and LA cases fairly early in his probe but he did put together a massive file that offered convincing proof that Sweeney was, if not necessarily the Butcher, certainly the fabled "Secret Suspect." Sweeney's name was finally part of the official record.

Within a few years, Arnold Sagalyn, the last surviving member of Ness's team, would, as noted earlier, also confirm Sweeney's identity, which made it irrevocably and irreversibly part of the public record as well.

Which leads us to the last, unanswerable question. Was Ness right? Was Sweeney actually the Mad Butcher?

Speaking only for myself, I think he probably was, though I have to admit to a certain amount of bias. I am, after all, also an admirer of Ness and I'd prefer to think that, if he wasn't quite able to deliver a knockout punch to the Torso Killer, he'd at least managed to win on points. Besides, naming *somebody* as the Butcher provides "closure," a satisfying end of the story, a solution to the mystery. And, all things considered, even factoring out my own pro-Ness prejudice, Sweeney's clearly the best candidate.

But all of the evidence that led Ness and his team to focus on Sweeney was not enough to take to court in 1938 and it would be even less likely to earn a conviction today. Of the two most compelling points indicating his guilt, Sweeney's near-perfect match to the Torso Clinic profile and his failure of the polygraph test, the former is a flimsy circumstance that might apply equally to dozens of other men and the latter is not legal evidence and could never be introduced at trial. There was and is no conclusive evidence proving Sweeney's guilt beyond a reasonable doubt. As long as we're speculating, however, one undeniable fact should be noted here one more time.

The murders stopped.

Once Ness developed a suspect, and that suspect was out of circulation, the murders stopped.

And on the basis of that single point, no matter who the actual killer was, I'm more than willing to mark the case of "The Mad Butcher of Kingsbury Run" in Ness's win column.

FURTHER READING

It's difficult to separate research about the Mad Butcher case from research about Ness's years as Cleveland's Director of Public Safety, the two subjects are so inextricably mixed. But that's not such a bad thing. Ness's time in Cleveland *should* be more widely known. His part in the Capone investigation has transformed him into a pop culture icon but his greatest, longest-lasting contributions to law enforcement were accomplished in Cleveland, not Chicago.

In fact, it's likely that, with the possible exception of William H. Parker in Los Angeles, no police chief of a major metropolitan center had as profound or as enduring an effect on the city he served or the department he led as Eliot Ness. Eighty years later, Cleveland's force is still considered one of the best and one of the cleanest big city police departments in the country, and in an amazingly eventful career, that's Ness's most impressive legacy.

Ness's life after he left the Safety Director's job in 1941 was disappointing. During the war he returned to federal service as the Director of Social Protection, in charge of combating sexually transmitted diseases in the Armed Forces. The post involved, among other things, coordinating local police efforts to curb prostitution in and around US military bases, making him, in effect, America's number one vice cop. This would be the last law enforcement position he would ever hold.

After the war, he entered private business, enjoying some initial success but suffered reverses from which he never completely recovered. A disastrous foray into politics in 1947, when he allowed himself to be persuaded to run for mayor of Cleveland, ended in an embarrassing defeat. His dismal failure to unseat the incumbent, Thomas Burke, an effort into which he had sunk much of his own money, not only tarnished his reputation in the city he had served so well but hastened his business reverses and, since no one wanted to hire a police administrator with "political ambitions," black-balled him from any future positions in law enforcement.

A decade of near-poverty followed ending with Ness's death in 1957 at the age of 54. He passed away just a few weeks before *The Untouchables* appeared in bookstores. He never got a chance to enjoy the mythical status that the book would ultimately confer.

Aside from contemporary newspaper accounts, William Ritt's article "The Head Hunter of Kingsbury Run" is one of the earliest comprehensive looks at the case. It appeared as a chapter in the true-crime anthology *Cleveland Murders* (Duell, 1947) edited by Oliver Weld Bayer as part of the Edgar-winning "Regional Murders" series.

John Bartlow Martin's article "Butcher's Dozen," in the November 1949 issue of *Harper's Magazine*, appeared shortly afterwards as part of a series the magazine was running on unsolved crimes. It was later reprinted in Martin's collection *Butcher's Dozen and Other Murders* (Harper, 1950).

Both articles give a good overview of the case, but Martin's is generally regarded as the more authoritative.

It was Ness's intention, after Oscar Fraley convinced him that his memoirs would make good reading, to follow up his account of the Capone investigation with a sequel describing his Cleveland years. Sadly, his untimely death made this impossible. Left with the famed lawman's scrapbooks and notes made during off-hand conversations, Fraley wrote a solo book about Ness's tenure with Cleveland PD, *Four Against the Mob* (Popular Library, 1961). A very thin volume emphasizing, as the title suggests, Ness's battles with organized crime, its tenth chapter is the first detailed account of Ness's own part in the Butcher investigation, containing Ness's first public confirmation of the "Secret Suspect" rumors and the first description of the hotel room interrogation. Frustratingly skimpy on details, the posthumously written *Four Against the Mob* is still a good general source of information and it's as close as anything gets to a first-hand account by Ness of his service in Cleveland in general and of his investigation into the Torso murders in particular.

Despite its title, Steven Nickel's *Torso* (Blair, 1989), like *Four Against the Mob*, examines Ness's whole career in Cleveland, not just the Kingsbury Run murders. But, where Fraley emphasized Ness's war on racketeers and crooked cops (which is to say it emphasized his obvious successes) and relegated the hunt for the Butcher to a short chapter near the end of the book, Nickel focuses on the Torso case. Well-written and well-researched, it was the first book-length study of the Butcher investigation, and of Ness's part in it. Though clearly one of Ness's admirers, Nickel, apparently not privy to information about Dr. Sweeney, was one of those who expressed doubts about the veracity of Ness's tale of the "Secret Suspect," suggesting that it might perhaps have been "merely a story concocted by Ness to show the world that he had, after all, solved the case."

The first full-fledged biography of Ness, Paul W. Heimel's *Eliot Ness – The Real Story* (Knox, 1997) devotes about a fifth of its length to Ness's years as Cleveland's Safety Director, including detailed accounts of the Butcher case. This was the first and is still one of the few Ness biographies to describe his life post-police work in great detail.

John Stark Bellamy II's *The Maniac in the Bushes* (Gray, 1997) devotes 13 of its 25 chapters to the Butcher case, alternating a Butcher chapter with a chapter about some other historically interesting Cleveland crime or disaster. One of the easiest-to-follow accounts of the case, it's also the first one I've found that mentions Sweeney by name, though he quickly dismisses the mentally unstable physician as a serious suspect. In fact, Bellamy's proposed solution to the case is perhaps the most interesting thing about the book. He questions whether or not there ever was a single Butcher and suggests that there might have been three, four, or even as many as 13 separate murderers, each acting independently of the others. It's an interesting theory and, given the disagreements among investigators at the time over which bodies should and should not be attributed to the Torso Killer, not an unattractive one. His arguments in favor of this position are spirited and well-written though not, in my opinion, altogether convincing.

The single best account of the Butcher investigation, giving equal time to all the investigators including Merylo and Gerber rather than just Ness, is James Jessen Badal's *In the Wake of the Butcher* (Kent State University, 2001). Badal's extraordinarily complete and extremely readable account gives one of the fullest descriptions of how Sweeney was developed as a suspect. He also considers other suspects developed by other investigators, gives one of the best accounts of the Dolezal tragedy, and examines the dismemberment murders committed in other jurisdictions to see how closely they can be connected to the Cleveland series. I'm very surprised that it wasn't at least nominated for a Fact Crime Edgar.

Almost as good is Marilyn Bardsley's *The Kingsbury Run Murders* (Dark Horse Multi-Media, 2001), an e-book that can be found at TruTV's Crime Library website. Bardsley, it will be remembered, was the researcher who first uncovered the name of the long-hidden "Secret Suspect" and her account of the investigation into Sweeney gives a few details not found in Badal's book. Bardsley is also the author of *Eliot Ness – The Man Behind the Myth* (Dark Horse Multi-Media, 2000) which is, except for Heimel's book, the only biography to cover Ness from cradle to grave rather than just giving accounts of his law enforcement career. It also has a fairly complete account of the Butcher case and is also available at the Crime Library website.

THE BUTCHER IN FICTION

Like the story of Jack the Ripper terrorizing and scandalizing a fog-shrouded Victorian London, the story of the Mad Butcher of Kingsbury Run spreading fear throughout a great Midwestern city fighting its way out of the Depression would seem a subject ripe for fictionalization. Yet, curiously, the Butcher's five-year reign of terror was largely ignored by fiction writers for nearly a half century. Then in the 1980's, as the term "serial killer" began to come into common usage with the general public, a torrent of novels, films, stage productions, and television dramas, all using serial killer plots, began to appear. At roughly the same time, Eliot Ness was again at the forefront of public attention thanks to the 1987 Oscar-winning film version of Ness and Fraley's book. As it became more widely known that one of America's most famous detectives, a man credited with jailing the most infamous organized crime figure in history, had also spent years on the trail of an elusive, and particularly gruesome serial killer, the imagination of many fiction writers was captured. In a relatively short period of time the story of Ness and the Butcher has inspired everything from a series of comic books to a musical stage production.

The earliest fictional treatment of the Butcher case was "The Strawberry Teardrop" by Max Allan Collins. The first short story to feature his series private eye, Nate Heller, it appeared in *The Eyes Have It* (Mysterious, 1984), an anthology of hard-boiled P.I. stories edited by Robert J. Randisi. Safety Director Ness is present in his supporting "hero's best friend" role. A few years later Collins expanded "The Strawberry Teardrop" into a novel, *Butcher's Dozen* (Bantam, 1988), excising Heller and moving Ness to center stage. For dramatic purposes, Collins telescopes the time frame and re-orders some events (the Dolezal fiasco, for example, occurs *before* Ness develops the fictionalized Sweeney figure as a suspect, rather than nearly a year after). In a fairly lengthy afterword in which he discusses where he diverged from real life and why, Collins describes finding the Sweeney correspondence while researching the case. He regards *Butcher's Dozen* as one of his best books. I agree. I also think it's perhaps *the* best fictionalization of the case.

The latest TV series version of *The Untouchables*, syndicated to local stations in 1993, ran a two-part episode during its first season apparently based on, or at least inspired by, the Butcher case. The episode, "A Tale of Two Fathers," written by Andrew Mirisch and Richard Chapman, actually took little from the real-life case other than the central situation of pitting Ness against a serial killer. Set in Chicago, during Ness's service as a federal agent intent on nailing Capone, it depicts the unknown murderer as a victimizer of children rather than homeless adult transients. Ness and Capone, concerned parents both, agree to work together to track down the child-predator. Movie buffs will easily recognize the story as an uncredited remake of the classic German crime film, *M* (Foremco, 1931). And since *M* fictionalized the case of German serial killer Peter Kurten (the so-called "Vampire of Dusseldorf "), "A Tale of Two Fathers" has the effect not of dramatizing Ness's actual encounter with a serial killer but of injecting Ness into a real-life case with which he had nothing to do in real-life.

John Peyton Cooke's *Torsos* (Mysterious, 1994), like "The Strawberry Teardrop," relegates Ness to a supporting role, assigning ball-carrier duties to a totally fictional Cleveland homicide detective who is also a closeted homosexual. Cooke speculates that since most of the victims were men, the Butcher may have been targeting gays and in this novel he runs with that theory. In the course of the hero's investigation into the Torso killings, he starts to develop a romantic relationship with an attractive street hustler who may be the Butcher's next target.

The first person to actually conceive of fictionalizing the Butcher case was Marilyn Bardsley, who discovered the identity of the "Secret Suspect" while conducting research for a proposed play based on the case. Her attempt to turn the case into a stage production apparently did not meet with success but she was able to turn it into a novel entitled *Diary of a Serial Killer* (Dark Horse Multimedia, 1996). Told from the point of view of, indeed narrated by, "Frank Sullivan," an alcoholic physician whose cousin is a powerful congressman, the novel purports to be a series of journal entries by Sullivan describing his crimes over a five year period as well as his obsession with the man he regards as his chief nemesis, Eliot Ness. Frank Sullivan, obviously modeled on Francis Sweeney, provides an interesting comparison to another fictional serial-killing M.D., Thomas Harris's Hannibal Lector. Like her two non-fiction books about Ness and the Butcher case, *Diary* is available free of charge as an e-book on the TruTV website.

Bardsley may not have managed to get the story of the Butcher up on stage but a live theatre production that did come to fruition was *In the Shadow of the Terminal Tower* by Midwestern playwright Peter Ullian. It was first performed in 1992 at the Iowa Playwright's Festival as a production of Iowa's University Theatres and, after a multi-state tour, went on to win Ullian two student awards and one professional award (the prestigious Roger L. Stevens prize) from the Kennedy Center for the Performing Arts.

The play caught the attention of the Harold Prince Musical Theater Program in New York, which commissioned a musical adaptation. This version, *Eliot Ness . . . in Cleveland*, with a book by Ullian and music and lyrics by Robert Lindsey Nassif, debuted at the Denver Center for the Performing Arts in 1998.

Artist Brian Michael Bendis, seeing the visual possibilities in the case, turned it into a graphic novel which, for those of you not up on the latest publishing jargon, is basically a comic book on steroids. *Torso* (Image Comics, 2001), illustrated by Bendis from a script by Bendis and Marc Andreyko, was originally serialized in six monthly comic books. The chapters were then collected in a single trade paperback volume, one of a series of crime and suspense comics appearing under the collective title *Jinx*. Like Cooke's similarly titled prose novel, this sequentially illustrated story features a gay homicide detective as one of the major characters.

Award-winning author William Bernhardt's *Nemesis – The Final Case of Eliot Ness* (Ballantine, 2009) is the latest novelization of the case and it's noteworthy for being one of the few, perhaps the first, fictional depiction that actually names Dr. Sweeney instead of giving him a pseudonym. Mr. Bernhardt, a former trial attorney in Oklahoma, best-known for a series of legal thrillers featuring crusading attorney Ben Kincaid, got many positive reviews for *Nemesis*, but coming so late in the long string of fictional treatments of the case, it basically travels an already well-trod path.

Fictional perusals of the Jack the Ripper murders are almost too numerous to count. Given the number of fictionalizations the Torso case has generated in a relatively short time, one wonders whether the Butcher might someday catch up with the Ripper.

TRUTH BENEATH A
TATTERED COAT

London Mysteries

The years following Britain's "Finest Hour" turned out not to have been as rosy as everyone assumed they'd be when the immediate goal of winning the war and defeating the threat of Fascism posed by the three Axis Powers was finally attained.

Rationing, for example, turned out not to be merely a wartime emergency measure but was continued well into the 1950's.

The prosperity that everyone believed would return like magic once the war was over was a long time in coming.

And the level of violent crime was rising to an alarming degree.

One particular crime came to be seen as symbolizing the breakdown in law and order. It wasn't necessarily the worst of the era. It wasn't necessarily the most violent. But it was the one that captured the imaginations of the British public. It inspired an award-winning film which led to a popular TV series that lasted for two decades. It cemented the reputation of one particular policeman, already well-known to the average Londoner as the single most famous cop in the entire United Kingdom and one of the most famous cops in the world. It could be said to have been the crime that, in some ways, led to the development of the police procedural sub-genre in British crime fiction.

It began at about 2:30 PM on Tuesday, 29 April 1947, when a trio of masked bandits armed with pistols rushed into a jewelry and pawnshop at the corner of Charlotte and Tottenham Streets in London's West End, jumped the counter, and demanded the contents of the safe. The director of the shop, Alfred Stock, slammed the safe closed before the robbers could get any of the items stored there. One of the frustrated gunmen began to pistol-whip Stock. Stock's assistant, Bert Keates, standing near the safe, picked up a stool and threw it at his boss's attacker. One of the other robbers cut loose with a shot to stop Keates's interference but it had the effect of drawing more shop assistants from elsewhere in the store, more people than they could reasonably control, even given their firepower. One of the new arrivals set off a burglar alarm.

Deciding that discretion was the better part of valor, the trio of robbers fled the store empty-handed and entered a car that was idling at the curb just outside the front entrance. They started to take off but a truck driver, alerted by the commotion, turned his vehicle in front of them, blocking their way. They abandoned the vehicle and took off on foot but another passerby, Alec de Antiquis, driving past the corner on a motorcycle, also heard the alarm and, seeing the three masked figures attempting to escape, maneuvered around the truck, overtook the fugitives, and pulled in front of them. One of them pulled out his pistol and fired at Antiquis point blank, hitting him in the left temple. The failed robbery had suddenly become capital murder.

Alec de Antiquis, 34 years old, married, with six kids, had opened a motorcycle repair shop after leaving the military. Aside from a service record to be proud of, he had, a short time earlier, run into the road to stop and calm a runaway horse. On another occasion, he'd rushed into a burning building to save a child. Soldier or civilian, he was an uncommonly brave man, who, almost by instinct, acted courageously whenever danger threatened.

Now he was dead at the hand of a cowardly, masked criminal.

Detective Chief Inspector Robert Higgins, commander of the C.I.D. squad at nearby Tottenham Road Police Station, began the investigation. One of his first acts was to notify the officer then in charge of the C.I.D. for the entire West End, who would have ultimate responsibility for the investigation.

The man in charge of the West End that day, Detective Chief Inspector Robert Fabian, was already one of the most famous policemen in Britain. Ten years earlier, he'd tracked down an associate of Jack "Legs" Diamond, who'd crossed the ocean intent on starting a Yankee-style protection racket in England. Nine years earlier, he'd made headlines by tracking down a notorious gang of armed robbers known as "The Mayfair Playboys." Eight years earlier, he'd personally dismantled a terrorist bomb planted in Piccadilly Circus, an act that had earned him the King's Police Medal, at that time the highest award for law enforcement in the entire British Empire. Two years earlier, as commander of the Flying Squad, he'd nailed a pair of con men earning thousands by selling steel ingots but saying they were platinum. One year earlier, he'd been called in by local police to identify the killer of Dagmar Peters, a hitchhiker found strangled on the side of a well-traveled highway in Kent.

Now, because his immediate superior was on holiday, he was temporarily in command of every detective in London's West End and about to take on perhaps the highest-profile case of his career.

But there was little for him to go on. Detective Superintendent Fred Cherill, one of the top fingerprint experts in the world, could find none on the stolen getaway car the robbers had abandoned. Nor did the car yield any other trace evidence.

The world-famous Home Office pathologist, Sir Bernard Spilsbury, was able to pronounce that the victim had died by a gunshot wound and was able to retrieve the slug, but that only confirmed what they already knew.

The Yard's ballistics expert, Mr. Robert Churchill, declared that the slug had been fired from a .320 center-fire revolver, but unless they had a gun to match the slug to that information would do them little good.

But a young man fitting the general description of the three bandits had been seen shortly after the murder hastily entering a building at 191 Tottenham Court Road. A key had been found by the caretaker of that building on one of the steps leading to the upstairs offices. It was found to be the ignition key of the getaway car. The unidentified young man had been part of the gang!

A general search of the building was conducted and a raincoat, similar to a garment worn by one of the robbers, was found rolled up out of sight behind the counter of one of the offices. Inside the coat were a pair of gloves and a scarf, folded into a triangle with the ends knotted together to form a face mask.

Fabian traced the coat to a factory in Leeds and from the factory to a clothing store in the London borough of Deptford. Because wartime rationing was still in force in 1947 and clothes couldn't be purchased without the buyer producing a sufficient number of rationing coupons, Fabian was able to trace the coat to one Thomas Kemp in the Southwark neighborhood of Bermondsey.

At first this seemed to be a dead end since Kemp had no criminal record and, to all appearances, was a hard-working, law-abiding man.

A further check, however, disclosed that while Kemp had no record for law-breaking, his brothers-in-law, Tommy and Harry Jenkins, had quite impressive and violent ones.

Tommy Jenkins's record for violence, in fact, provided him with a perfect alibi for Alec de Antiquis's murder. On the day Antiquis was shot, Tommy was in prison with five years still to run on the eight he'd been sentenced to serve for manslaughter, ironically for killing an innocent bystander who was attempting to thwart his escape from the scene of a smash-and-grab at a London jewelry shop.

But Tommy's 23-year-old younger brother, Harry, was out and about and he was now Bob Fabian's prime suspect.

As Fabian was drawing the net around Harry, the murder gun turned up, found by a boy on the muddy banks of the Thames. An examination by Churchill confirmed that it was the same gun that had fired the fatal shot into Antiquis's skull.

On May 11, Fabian personally arrested Harry. As the younger Jenkins already had two convictions for assaulting cops, in one of which he'd broken a beat constable's jaw, Fabian took along two other detectives for cover.

At the Yard, Harry Jenkins blithely refused to answer questions.

Fabian arranged to have witnesses see if they could identify Jenkins in a police line-up, an "identity parade" in British police jargon, then set about trying to identify the other two members of the robbery gang.

Harry's best friend was Christopher Geraughty, age 21, who had a long criminal record of his own and was almost certainly the second man. A younger hanger-on, Peter Rolt, 17, with a record for shop-breaking, seemed a likely bet for the third. Fabian took steps to locate them.

Meanwhile, witnesses were unable to identify Jenkins and Fabian had been forced to release him. He had him followed. Jenkins soon led police to a pub where he met Geraughty and Rolt. Now Fabian was certain he had the entire gang located. But he was still miles shy of having enough evidence to convince a jury. Still, the three all were acting nervously, as if they knew the noose was tightening.

Fabian had Jenkins pulled in again, this time with his sister, Mrs. Thomas Kemp, who had tried to mislead police about her husband's coat by saying he'd lost it in a bar.

This time Jenkins decided to answer questions, partly to get his sister off the hook for trying to mislead police, but mainly, Fabian was sure, to get himself off the hook for murder.

He'd borrowed the raincoat from his brother-in-law, right enough, but he'd loaned it out to a third party, a parolee named Bill Walsh whom he and his sister both said could probably be found in the nearby community of Southend-on-Sea. Walsh was already wanted for parole violation and was suspected by Detective Inspector Fred Hodge of being involved in another jewelry store robbery that had occurred in West London's Queensway neighborhood on April 25, four days before the Antiquis murder. Hodge reported to Fabian that a reliable informant had fingered Bill Walsh for that crime.

Fabian, Higgins, and Hodge went to the Southend police station to examine the "occurrence books" made by local beat officers during their patrol tours. One officer's notebook disclosed that Walsh had been seen in the company of Chris Geraughty and another party on April 26, one day after the Queensway robbery and three days before the Antiquis murder. Another officer's book revealed that a .455 revolver had been found loaded in some shrubbery.

Fabian put out an all-points bulletin for Walsh, who was located and arrested three days later. Walsh denied either borrowing the coat from Jenkins or participating in the abortive robbery that had led to Antiquis's death. He admitted to casing the shop but that was all. He also copped to the Queensway robbery with Jenkins, Geraughty, and one Michael Joseph Gilliam. He admitted that his partners in that crime might have a grudge against him since he had kept all the swag for himself. This explained why Jenkins was anxious for him to take the fall for the Charlotte Street crime. He and James Geraughty wanted revenge for Walsh's betrayal.

Meanwhile, a second gun had been found on the banks of the Thames a short distance from the spot where the murder gun had been discovered. Ballistics confirmed that this was the gun that had been fired at Stock as he attempted to stop his boss's pistol-whipping. Both guns had been found less than a quarter mile from the home of Jenkins's parents-in-law.

Deciding that Jenkins could not be broken, Fabian had Geraughty pulled in. Under careful questioning, Geraughty admitted to taking part in the Charlotte Street robbery and even admitted that he had been the one who shot Antiquis. He refused to name Jenkins as one of the gang members but he did implicate Rolt.

Rolt was then picked up. He also admitted his part in the crime and, not having the long-standing friendship with Jenkins that Geraughty did, was more than willing to implicate Jenkins.

Now Fabian had all three of them. He arrested Jenkins. On May 19, the trio was indicted. On July 21, the trial at the Old Bailey commenced. Geraughty and Rolt had both admitted their parts in the crime but Geraughty claimed that he had only been trying to scare Antiquis and had no intent to kill, hoping to get off on a manslaughter charge as Harry's brother, Tommy, had years earlier. Harry Jenkins attempted to establish an alibi, claiming that he had been at work and producing eight different witnesses to testify to the truth of this assertion.

At the trial's conclusion, the judge explained that under law if a death occurred during the commission of a felony, that death, even if unintended, was a capital murder, and it didn't matter whose finger was on the trigger; all parties to the felony were equally guilty of the murder. The jury was out for less than an hour. All three of the defendants were found guilty. Geraughty and Jenkins were hanged at Pentonville Prison on September 19. Rolt, because of his youth, was sentenced to be detained "during His Majesty's pleasure."

The Roman comic poet Caeclius Status once observed that, "Wisdom oft' lurks beneath a tattered coat." When Bob Fabian found the tattered coat that broke the Antiquis case he may not have uncovered wisdom but, as far as the jury was concerned, he did uncover the truth.

There was an unexpected epilog to the case that Fabian must have found particularly satisfying.

Three years earlier, when Harry's older brother Tommy and his partner, Ronald Hedley, had killed an innocent bystander as they tried to escape the scene of a crime, Hedley had had his death sentence commuted to life and Tommy Jenkins'd gotten off on manslaughter. The gang Tommy and Harry had led and that Hedley had been part of, had not broken up but had grown and thrived, and gun crime increased in the ensuing years.

But with the executions of Harry Jenkins and Chris Geraughty, the gang almost immediately dissolved and, in the weeks immediately following the hangings, abandoned guns began to turn up all over London, under park bushes, in garbage cans, thrown into the river, etc. The use of firearms suddenly seemed like a liability and, for a little while at least, the incidence of gun crimes dropped.

But, as all enlightened people know, capital punishment isn't a deterrent to crime.

FURTHER READING

My main sources for this article were "The Antiquis Murder," a chapter from Robert Fabian's autobiography, *Fabian of the Yard* (British Book Centre, 1953), and "The Shadow of a Gunman," a chapter from Donald Thomas's history of post-war crime in England, *Villains' Paradise* (Pegasus, 2005).

There are numerous other accounts of the crime for those interested in finding out more. Paul Willetts's *North Soho 999* (Dewi Lewis, 2007) has gotten a number of splendid reviews, drawing comparisons with Truman Capote's *In Cold Blood* (Random, 1966). Regretfully, it has not yet appeared in an American edition and, except for some excerpts available on the 'Net, I was not able to consult it for this article.

Former Scotland Yard Flying Squad Detective Dick Kirby's *The Guv'nors – Ten of Scotland Yard's Greatest Detectives* (Wharncliffe, 2011) is a collection of biographies of some of the best-known of the Met's legendary thief-takers and it includes a splendid chapter on Fabian.

Presumably (and it *is* only a presumption since I haven't read the book, but it seems a reasonable one), there is some mention of the case in the memoirs of other principals in the investigation, such as Robert Higgins's *In the Name of the Law* (Long, 1958) which, like *North Soho 999*, has never appeared in an American edition.

FICTIONAL DEPICTIONS OF THE ANTIQUIS MURDER

The most famous fictionalization of the Antiquis murder, appearing only three years after the actual crime, is undoubtedly that classic filmic valentine to the British bobby, *The Blue Lamp* (Ealing, 1950), in which the brave and sympathetic murder victim was changed from an heroic civilian to an heroic veteran beat cop, Police Constable George Dixon (Jack Warner). The trigger-happy thug who guns Dixon down about halfway through the film is played by Dirk Bogarde in one of his earliest roles. Directed by Basil Dearden from a script by T.E.B. Clarke (according to some sources, a one-time special constable in the Metropolitan Police), Jan Read, Ted Willis, and Alexander Mackendrick, the film won the British Academy of Film and Television Arts (BAFTA) Award for Best British Film. Bernard Lee, best-known as "M" from the James Bond movies, played "Inspector Cherry," an apparent composite of Bob Fabian and Bob Higgins, who tracks down Dixon's killers.

Dixon, who came to epitomize to Britons the ideal of what a British bobby was supposed to be, turned out to be pretty hard to kill. Six years after his unmistakable and incontrovertible on-screen death, he was resurrected for a TV series, *Dixon of Dock Green* (BBC, 1956-76), and spent the next two decades performing a very gentle style of law enforcement. Jack Warner returned as the kindly, avuncular copper, the picture of health, his death at the hands of Bogarde never referred to.

265

Regretfully, as most of the series was broadcast live, very few of the 400-plus episodes still exist but those that do have a nostalgic charm.

The twelfth episode of *Whitehall 1212* (NBC, 1951-52), a radio drama produced with the cooperation of Scotland Yard, was based on the Antiquis case. Broadcast on February 12, 1952, it was titled "The Death of the Innocent Bystander." Antiquis's name was changed to Arthur Freeman for this fictionalized depiction. Each episode of *Whitehall 1212* opened with a simulated tour of the Yard's Black Museum, with the host stopping at a particular exhibit, in the case of this episode an innocuous raincoat, and then tells the story behind it.

A very similar radio series, running at about the same time, is probably better-remembered than *Whitehall 1212*, primarily because of the participation of Orson Welles, who served as the show's host. It was called *The Black Museum* (Syndicated, 1952). This show's version of the Antiquis murder was called "A .32 Caliber Bullet."

After the Antiquis investigation, Bob Fabian was promoted to Detective Superintendent. He retired shortly after the conclusion of the case to write his memoirs, mentioned above. When the pioneering police procedural series *Dragnet* (NBC, 1951-59, 1967-70; ABC, 2003-04) proved an international hit, the BBC was anxious to put out a similar program of its own. Seeing Fabian's autobiography as the vehicle for such a series, they bought the rights and hired American producer John Larkin to oversee production of a series in which each episode would dramatize one of Fabian's cases. Bruce Seton, who bore a close if not uncanny resemblance to the real Fabian, played the lead. The eighth episode, "Murder in Soho," was based on Fabian's investigation into the Antiquis case.

Filmed rather than broadcast live, *Fabian of the Yard* (BBC, 1954-56) was, like *Dragnet*, an international hit, making its hero not only the most famous policeman in England, but arguably the most famous policeman in the whole world, at least for a little while. Bob Fabian was perhaps the first in a long line of real-life cops whose careers would be fictionalized on television, a list that includes, among others, Federal Agent Eliot Ness, NYPD Detective Barney Ruditsky, Newark Narcotics Detective David Toma, London River Police Inspector David "Nick" Nixon, Cook County Sheriff's Homicide Investigator Jack Reed, and LAPD serial killer expert John "Jigsaw John" St. John.

After two years, and thirty-six episodes, there was not enough real life from Fabian's career left to fictionalize, so the BBC replaced the series with the above-mentioned *Dixon of Dock Green*. Thus, Bob Fabian had the ironic experience of being supplanted by a character originally created to be the fictional version of the victim of a murder Fabian himself had solved.

Only on television.

STAMPED TO DEATH

Hobbies, Crafts, & Special Interests

In "The Adventure of the One-Penny Black" (*Great Detective*, April 1933), the very first short story ever written by (and about) Ellery Queen, Queen (the fictional sleuth), faced with a murder case involving philately, makes some comment to the effect that stamp collectors are so obsessive that they would cheerfully murder each other without remorse just to possess a stamp they wanted.

That is perhaps an overly harsh assessment of the character of philatelists. In my limited experience stamp collectors, though quite enthusiastic about their pastime, are generally a friendly, convivial, and honorable group.

Indeed, the instances where the possession of a particular stamp led to murder are rare enough that having such an event attached to a given stamp has the effect of enhancing its value considerably. One can assume this would not be the case if homicide in the interests of stamp acquisition were all that common.

Consider the case of the Hawaiian Missionary.

On 28 May 1963, a stamp dealer named Raymond H. Weill obtained a two cent Hawaiian Missionary for forty-one thousand dollars, to that point, according to some sources, the highest price ever paid for a single stamp. Adjusting for inflation, that would come to nearly three hundred thousand dollars in contemporary terms. Because Hawaiian Missionaries are so incredibly light even when compared to other stamps, weighing in at a mere one two thousandth of an ounce, the price Weill paid for that stamp would figure out to over a billion dollars a pound, more than eight billion a pound in 2014 dollars, making the paper that particular philatelic object was printed on, figured on a pound for pound basis, the most valuable substance on the face of the planet.

What made that particular stamp so valuable? Hawaiian Missionaries are not, after all, particularly attractive. They consist of nothing but a central number denoting the denomination of the stamp surrounded by a standard printer's dingbat with the words "Hawaiian Postage" on the top line and the denomination printed in English on the bottom line. Why should such a plain-looking item command such a price?

Well, rarity for one thing, and historical value for another. Hawaiian Missionaries, precisely because they were printed on such a light, fragile type of paper, what philatelists call "pelure," weren't particularly durable, so there aren't a whole lot of them around.

Moreover, they were the first postage stamps ever issued by the Kingdom of Hawaii while it was still an independent monarchy. As the name applied to them by collectors suggests, they were primarily used by Christian missionaries who came to the Islands in an effort to convert the natives. First issued in 1851, they came in three different denominations: the two cent for newspapers, the five cent for letters to the Pacific Coast of the United States, and the thirteen cent for letters to the US's Atlantic Seaboard. Only about two hundred Hawaiian Missionaries in any denomination have survived to the present day.

Of these, the two cent is the rarest, with only fifteen copies known to exist. And the copy acquired by Weill the only one of that known fifteen still uncanceled. Those two factors alone would push the price up. The stamp had also at different times been part of the collections of Philip von Ferrary and Alfred H. Caspary, two of the best-known and most respected philatelists in the history of the hobby, and having either of their names, let alone both, as part of a stamp's provenance would also boost the price. But what really added to its value was the fate of an owner who predated both Ferrary and Caspary, an avid Parisian philatelist named Gaston Leroux.

To the best of my knowledge, the Gaston Leroux who figures in this chapter is no relation to the pioneering mystery novelist who wrote such crime fiction classics as *The Mystery of the Yellow Room* (Brentano's, 1908) and *The Phantom of the Opera* (Bobbs-Merrill, 1911), but the coincidence is too striking to let it go unmentioned.

The Gaston Leroux about whom I am writing was an independently wealthy collector active in the latter part of the Nineteenth Century.

The Hawaiian Missionary series were only issued until 1856. By 1892, when this story takes place, they had already become scarce enough that they were being avidly sought after by collectors and Leroux had managed to acquire the Holy Grail of Hawaiian Missionaries, the only known uncanceled two cent. He regarded it as the prize of his collection. Indeed, it would be the prize of almost any collection, as any of his friends in the philatelic community could attest.

One particular friend of Leroux's, Hector Giroux, came to covet Leroux's two cent Missionary above all things. He had his own fairly impressive collection of Hawaiian Missionaries but he needed a two cent to complete it. Leroux's two cent, unused and uncanceled, would be just the thing.

But Leroux didn't want to sell. And nothing Giroux could offer would tempt him to change his mind.

When during one visit Leroux refused yet another of Giroux's offers, Giroux in a fit of frustration killed him, stole the stamp, and placed it in his own collection.

The police solved the case fairly quickly, but only because they caught a rare piece of luck right at the start.

When they first arrived on the scene, they were extremely puzzled by the crime. Leroux was well-liked; no one knew of any enemies. The motive did not seem to be robbery, since money, jewelry, and other valuables were left untouched. In fact, no property appeared to be missing at all. Leroux was dead but there was no obvious motive and, consequently, no lead to follow.

The rare piece of luck was that one of the detectives who examined the crime scene was also a stamp collector. Naturally enough, he was aware of Leroux's eminence in the field. He made a point of checking Leroux's collection.

It appeared to be intact but the philatelist cop (and the name of this officer appears to be lost to history; no source I consulted mentions him by name) knew enough to compare the collection to Leroux's written inventory where he found a discrepancy. Not only did a stamp seem to be missing; it was the crown jewel of Leroux's collection.

The stamp-collecting sleuth did some checking and soon found that Leroux's friend Hector Giroux was widely known to have a real yen for that two cent Missionary.

Posing as a stamp collector (which, since he *was* a stamp collector, wasn't much of a stretch as undercover roles go), the cop contrived to get an introduction to Giroux, was invited to his home, and during the visit brought the conversation around to Hawaiian Missionaries.

Like any proud collector, Giroux couldn't resist the urge to show off his latest acquisition. When he did, the cop identified himself, busted Giroux, and brought him in for questioning.

Unable to give a convincing explanation for how he happened to be in possession of a stamp known to be the property of Gaston Leroux, Giroux soon broke down and admitted to killing his friend in a fit of rage after his latest offer was declined, and to taking the stamp afterwards.

He was convicted and executed.

But perhaps he took some satisfaction from the knowledge that the stamp he had coveted for such a long time and possessed for such a short time had had its already considerable value immeasurably enhanced by the crime he committed.

FURTHER READING

Lots of books about stamp collecting will mention the Leroux murder case and the stolen Hawaiian Missionary. It's part of the folklore of philately. For example, Arthur D. Stansfield's *Let's Collect Stamps* (Stamp Collectors Promotion Council, 1938), a well-known pamphlet of information for beginners which has become something of a collector's item itself, includes an account of the case.

I first saw the Leroux murder mentioned in the unsigned article "More Than Child's Play" (*Time*, 7 June 1963), which described Raymond Weill's purchase of the stamp and gave a short account of the criminal case attached to it. Another unsigned article a few months later, "Three Penny Bonanza" (*Life*, 29 November 1963), also described the sale, also gave an account of the murder and, being *Life*, included two pictures of the stamp, one life-sized and the other blown up so it could actually be seen. The pound-for-pound cost analysis was also part of the *Life* article but I did the inflation adjustment myself.

Many different websites devoted to stamp collecting give accounts of the case. The two I found most valuable were "A Philatelic Murder Mystery," a 4 June 2008 blog entry by Daniel Arpin for his arpinphilately.com website, and "Missionaries, Money and Murder," an article about the case written by Frank McAlanon for the stamp2.com website, first posted on 5 May 2003.

THE SHOOFLY

New York Mysteries

It was the morning lineup, a daily event at 240 Centre Street, the headquarters of the NYPD. Indeed, a daily event at most big city departments back in 1934. Selected detectives from all over the Five Boroughs would come down to Centre Street every morning and watch all the offenders who'd been arrested the day before march across a stage and answer some questions put to him or her by the Chief of Detectives or some other high-ranking cop. The idea was that in this way the detectives would get familiar with who was committing crimes in their city.

It was a pretty hit-or-miss system, and sitting through a lineup was regarded as an onerous task to be avoided whenever possible. But it was a task that every detective in the Force had to endure periodically. On this particular day, however, it's likely that every one of the 200 detectives assembled in the auditorium were glad they were there, for they were first-hand witnesses to an event that would become part of NYPD's folklore.

The newly appointed Commissioner of Police happened to drop by just as a scummy little punk named Harry "Pittsburgh Phil" Strauss was parading across the stage as though he owned the place. Not a hair on Strauss's pomaded head was out of place. Not a millimeter of stubble protruded from his perfectly shaved chin. His pearl-gray, snap-brim fedora was stylishly tilted at a jaunty angle. His tailored navy blue business suit fit him like a glove. His expensive Chesterfield overcoat was, with painstakingly contrived casualness, elegantly draped over his shoulders like a cape.

Strauss was a hit man working under Lepke Buchalter in what would eventually come to be referred to by the media as "Murder, Inc." Indeed, according to some sources, he was the most prolific contract killer ever generated by Organized Crime, with a body count comfortably in triple digits. At that point in his career, though every cop in town knew he was a paid assassin and though he'd previously been arrested 17 times, he'd never been convicted of so much as spitting on the sidewalk.

He was in custody that day for the murder of Alvin Sydnor, a black garage attendant he and a colleague, Abe "Kid Twist" Reles, had beaten to death over a personal grudge. Tragically, their grudge wasn't even against Sydnor but against someone else altogether for whom they'd mistaken the hapless working stiff.

It was Strauss's fourth arrest for murder and his eighteenth overall, and like the other seventeen raps, Strauss was going to beat it. He knew it. And so did the new commissioner. And it enraged him.

He was already in a foul mood as it was. There'd been a rash of armed robberies in which several merchants had been shot. The night before he'd kept vigil at the bed of a dying cop who'd intervened in one of those hold-ups. Strauss's smug, nonchalant attitude turned his foul mood into barely contained fury.

"Look at him," the commissioner suddenly thundered. "He's the best-dressed man in the room, yet he's never worked a day in his life!"

Turning to the detectives, he said, "Don't be afraid to muss 'em up. Blood should be smeared all over that velvet collar. Teach 'em to fear arrest. Make 'em fear you."

Warming to his subject, he went on. "When you meet men like Strauss, draw quickly and shoot accurately. Mark 'em up and muss 'em up. Make 'em learn that this town is no place for racketeers and muscle men."

Strauss looked at the Big Apple's new top cop uneasily. Though he'd skate on the Sydnor kill as he had all those other times, he suddenly got the notion that the times, they were a-changin'. And six years later, when he finally rode the lightning on Sing Sing's electric chair, it probably occurred to him that he'd started on the downward slide that led him to the hot seat the same day that new commissioner became infuriated at the sight of the gangster's sartorial splendor.

If the head of a major city police force said something like that today, he'd probably be castigated all over the media. The civil liberties crowd would be up in arms. Ivory-tower academics would be in tears. But in 1934, this sort of publicly stated attitude toward violent, professional hoodlums was a desirable quality in a police chief. Indeed, as the story got out it earned the new commissioner a lot of respect and good will, not only from the public but from the NYPD's rank and file. In spite of his being a shoofly.

In spite of his being *The* Shoofly.

* * *

You don't hear it much anymore, but years ago, particularly in New

York City, "shoofly" was a slang expression for a cop who investigated other cops. A member of what is now called "Internal Affairs" in most large police agencies, though back in the day it had other names.

And the new commissioner, famous for his unshakable honesty and for his visceral hatred of crooked cops, was often referred to by the rest of his department, sometimes derisively, sometimes fearfully, but ultimately with great respect, as not simply a shoofly, but as *The* Shoofly." And, in an amazingly eventful career, he'd go all the way from patrolman to Commissioner of Police for the City of New York, stepping on almost every single rung on his way to the top and sometimes, when the political winds were blowing against him, sliding down a few rungs and having to climb them all over again.

If he despised bad cops, he despised the gangsters whose bribes they accepted just as much. And in his jurisdiction, there was a lot to despise. During the Prohibition and Depression eras, Chicago's mobster activity was getting most of the publicity, but New York was every bit as gangster-ridden as its Midwestern counterpart. While the Windy City may have had Capone, New York had "Lucky" Luciano, Meyer Lanksy, Dutch Schultz, the aforementioned Lepke Buchalter, Arnold "the Brain" Rothstein, Jack "Legs" Diamond, Owney "The Killer" Madden, and a host of others operating not just openly but brazenly. And The Shoofly hated these corrupters as much as he hated the corrupted.

* * *

His name was Lewis J. Valentine and he was born in Brooklyn in 1882, the son of an immigrant Alsatian father and an Irish-American mother. In 1903, five years after Brooklyn was incorporated into the City of New York, he joined the NYPD as a probationary patrolman and spent the next decade pounding foot beats in Brooklyn and Manhattan. He was not, perhaps, the most spectacular officer ever to patrol a post, but he soon gained a reputation for absolute incorruptibility and, when he made sergeant in 1913, Inspector Daniel Costigan, known throughout the Department as "Honest Dan," immediately tagged the young sergeant for his "Confidential Squad," a newly formed unit charged with ferreting out grafters and scam artists in the Department, an embryonic version of what would later become Internal Affairs.

Even the most honest cops generally dislike working Internal Affairs but Valentine hated policemen who dishonored their shields and betrayed their trusts. For him, exposing crooked cops was not an unpleasant job that had to be done. It was a crusade that he genuinely savored.

One of his most notable cases was his investigation of a beat cop named Sharkey, who'd reportedly offered to fix a murder rap for a sailor for the valuable consideration of $300. Posing as a friend of the accused killer, Valentine paid off the graft himself, then arrested the crooked patrolman. Sharkey ended up in Sing Sing. Valentine ended up a lieutenant.

Valentine was unrelenting when it came to getting evidence against crooked cops. In another case he and his partner, Sgt. Floyd Horton, were so emphatic about bringing a reluctant out-of-state witness back to New York to testify in the trial of a corrupt officer that a Connecticut grand jury indicted the two shooflies for kidnapping. In yet another, Valentine forced a suspected grafter to take an emetic in order to force him to upchuck crooked money that Valentine was sure he'd eaten in an effort to hide his culpability.

He served in the unit until 1918. That's when the Tammany Hall crowd won back City Hall. Their new mayor, John F. "Red Mike" Hylan, kicked out all the "good government" reformers and ordered the Confidential Squad disbanded.

For Valentine, there was worse news than simply being reassigned. During his time in the Confidential Squad, he'd clashed with a lieutenant named Richard Enright, the president of NYPD's Lieutenants' Association, over allegations of wrong-doing in the Association's finances. He and Horton were not able to make a case but Enright never forgot the slight. Now under Hylan, the Tammany-friendly Lieutenant Enright had been promoted over all the captains, deputy inspectors, inspectors, etc., to Commissioner of the NYPD. It was tantamount to taking a second lieutenant in the Army and suddenly advancing him to Chairman of the Joint Chiefs of Staff.

Now Enright was at the top of the NYPD pyramid. And Valentine, Horton, and Costigan were at the top of his excremental roster.

Costigan was busted down two grades to captain and given command of a remote, dreary, humdrum precinct in the Bronx. He would ultimately retire after being kicked around by Enright for several years.

Horton retired from the Force the hard way. A lieutenant by this time, he got involved in an off-duty shoot-out with two armed bandits when he intervened in a robbery. Badly wounded, he died a few hours later, but not before writing down the plate number of the gunmen's getaway car. When the two suspects were located based on Horton's information, one was found to have died in the exchange of gunfire with Horton. The other was convicted of Horton's murder. Horton's death should have put him beyond the reach of Enright's spite, but Enright still found a way to exact revenge on the dead hero. Though posthumously awarded the Medal of Honor, NYPD's top award for valor, Horton, due to Enright's influence, was never inducted into the Honor Legion, an organization of decorated NYPD officers.

Meanwhile, Valentine, still only in his 30's with a wife and five kids to support, was years away from being able to retire. Enright assigned him as a relief desk lieutenant, which meant he was assigned to no particular station. As the relief man he could on any given day be assigned to any precinct and he never knew which one from day to day. His main hope for getting off the merry-go-round was the score he'd received on the captains' exam. First on the list, he was almost certain of a promotion. The assignments might not be any better, but if he could hold out 'til he was 41, he'd at least be able to retire on a captain's pension.

Enright, however, deliberately passed him over three times, sending him to the bottom of the list per Civil Service regs.

Valentine, bloodied but unbowed, knew that commissioners changed like the spring flowers. He simply knuckled down and began to study for the next test. But he'd need all his steadfast courage to get past what would undoubtedly become the lowest day of his entire career.

He was working an 8:00AM to 4:00PM shift at a Manhattan precinct when he got a panicked call from his wife, Theresa. She had not been able to awaken their only son, Eddie, that morning. Valentine arranged for an ambulance to rush him to a hospital, where Theresa was told that Eddie had contracted spinal meningitis and couldn't be expected to live more than a few hours. Valentine was called and told that if he wanted to see his son before he died, he'd have to come immediately.

Valentine was faced with a terrible choice. If he left immediately, he could be charged with abandoning his post, just the excuse Enright needed to fire him, leaving him unable to support his wife and their four remaining children. But if he stayed on duty until officially relieved, he'd almost certainly lose his only chance to visit with his son one last time. He did the only thing he could do. A devout Catholic, he sat at his desk and prayed.

Unexpectedly, Valentine's relief showed up two hours early, complaining that things were boring at home and he thought he'd come down to the station to see if anything exciting was going on.

Valentine made it to the hospital in time to see his son once more before he passed. He'd later attribute this to the power of prayer. And perhaps it was. But it's likely that God worked His grace through one or two of Valentine's colleagues who, unbeknownst to their lieutenant, had notified his relief of the terrible family crisis he was facing.

Enright lasted eight years as commissioner and they were dreary years for Valentine. But the department had gone downhill in that time and even Tammany Hall realized what a political liability the NYPD under Enright had become. To get rid of Hylan, and thus Enright, they backed the flamboyant Jimmy Walker, known as "Beau James" for his stylish mode of dress, for mayor. Without Tammany support, Hylan didn't make it past the primary and Walker easily walked away with the general election a few months later. At the suggestion of his mentor, Governor Al Smith, Walker chose George McLaughlin, New York State's Superintendent of Banking, for police commissioner. McLaughlin had no law enforcement experience but owned a well-deserved reputation for honesty and for being a gifted administrator.

McLaughlin restored Valentine's standing in the Civil Service list, and when his long-awaited promotion to captain came through, put him in command of a precinct in Manhattan that had long been a bulwark of Tammany power, specifically instructing Valentine to run it straight. A few months later, McLaughlin summoned him to headquarters a second time and told him he was being promoted to deputy inspector.

In the NYPD, captain was (and is) as high as one could go through civil service. All ranks above captain, from deputy inspector through inspector, deputy chief inspector, assistant chief inspector, bureau chief, and chief inspector, were made by appointment, and all incumbents in those positions served at the pleasure of the commissioner. Valentine's near-immediate jump to deputy inspector was to some degree a vindication after his years in the wilderness. At the same time, he knew that political winds could always shift. Nevertheless, if they shifted now, at least he could never be busted down lower than captain.

Deputy Inspector Valentine was put in charge of a newly organized, Costigan-style Confidential Squad which, in addition to suppressing corruption in the NYPD, conducted major investigations into vice, gambling, and other organized crime activities that were at the root of so much police corruption.

Over the next three years, Valentine's unit conducted over a thousand investigations, exposed hundreds of crooked cops and politicians, and regularly raided Tammany gambling dens and speakeasies that were supposedly under police protection.

Though Walker had been chosen by the Tammany Hall crowd specifically to clean up the NYPD, or more correctly, to make a show of cleaning it up, he was now facing all kinds of heat from his sponsors about the ruckus Valentine was raising. On the one hand, he had to derail Valentine. On the other, he had to try to make it appear that he was doing no such thing or he'd pay for it politically.

Less than a year after appointing him, Walker dismissed McLaughlin, primarily because of his failure to rein in Valentine's squad. Before McLaughlin left, he promoted Valentine to full inspector.

McLaughlin's replacement, Joseph Warren, was a one-time law partner of Walker's, and the mayor assumed he'd play ball. However, despite being specifically instructed by Walker in no uncertain terms of the importance of declawing Valentine, Warren did something no one expected. He showed some guts.

Shortly after assuming office, he summoned Valentine to Headquarters and told him he was being promoted to deputy chief inspector, roughly the NYPD equivalent of a brigadier general.

"Your duties are unchanged," Warren told Valentine. "I like your work."

Warren, like McLaughlin, lasted less than a year.

Walker's third commissioner was Grover Whalen, whose only official position to that point was as New York City's official greeter. Finally, Walker had a police commissioner who knew how to do as he was told.

Whalen's first official acts were to bust Valentine back three grades to captain, send him to a remote precinct in Queens, and to dismantle the Confidential Squad once again.

"You're a fine lot of men," Valentine told all the members of his unit after he got the news, "and I'm proud to have known you. I know you'll be a credit to your commanding officers wherever you are. You were to me."

At his new station, he addressed the men he'd be leading. If they expected him to act bitter about his change of fortune, they were surprised.

"Some people have been spreading rumors that I'm going to quit," he told them. "Get that out of your heads. I've been sent here to do a job, and I'm going to do it. A good cop goes where he's told, and does what he's told. I expect you to do that for me."

This time, Valentine's stint in Purgatory lasted six years. But Walker was weakened and he was about to take a knockout punch

What finally saved Valentine and vanquished "Beau James" was one of those "investigating commissions" that New York City sets up roughly every two decades to expose police corruption. This one, started in 1930, was headed by retired Judge Samuel Seabury, and was specifically charged with looking into collusion between crooked cops and crooked judges in the Magistrate's Court, the petit court in NYC where defendants made their first appearance. The resulting revelations, particularly those made by Valentine himself when called to testify, were earth-shaking and, among other things, forced Jimmy Walker to resign from office in 1932.

Joseph McKee was appointed Acting Mayor but served only two months, losing a special election to another Tammany lackey, Joseph O'Brien, who completed the remainder of Walker's unexpired term. But the Seabury revelations kept on coming and were turning out to be too damaging. O'Brien lost his bid for a full term in 1933 to a reform candidate who arguably became the most beloved chief executive in New York City's history, Fiorello LaGuardia. Running specifically on an anti-Tammany platform, LaGuardia would be reelected in 1937 and 1941, the only self-declared Tammany foe ever to win reelection. Tammany Hall never really recovered.

LaGuardia's first act was to appoint a highly decorated soldier, Major General John O'Ryan, as reform police commissioner. At LaGuardia's direction, O'Ryan plucked Valentine from Siberia and made him his four-star Chief Inspector (a rank now known as "Chief of the Department"), second-in-command of the NYPD. It was probably understood that, for practical purposes, O'Ryan was choosing his own successor.

Chief Valentine's first order to the troops was, "Be good or be gone. The day of influence is over. There is no room in the Department for parasites and drones."

Nine months later, General O'Ryan left and LaGuardia appointed Valentine as his police commissioner. After all the ups and downs in his career, The Shoofly was now the Top Cop, commanding the largest police force in America and probably the largest police force anywhere in the Western Hemisphere.

Valentine wasn't kidding when he told his officers to "Muss 'em up." The dogs of war had been loosed and organized crime figures were no longer immune from NYPD harassment. Luciano was convicted, imprisoned, and eventually deported. Dutch Schultz was actually killed by other gangsters when his arrest and inevitable conviction became imminent. Lepke was convicted of four different murders and executed. Vito Genovese was indicted for murder and fled the country. Owney Madden was driven out of town, taking refuge in the corrupt hamlet of Hot Springs, Arkansas. Many others fled only as far as the other side of the Hudson, just over the state line and thus beyond the limits of Valentine's jurisdiction.

As tough as he was on gangsters, he was even tougher on crooked policemen. During his tenure, he fired over 300 cops, severely chastised over 4000, and fined 8000. Over a hundred crooked cops, faced with exposure, committed suicide. Valentine was unrelenting in his crusade for an honest department.

Taxpayers, he said, pay the salaries of cops and for that reason alone "have the right to expect courtesy and service in return."

Nevertheless, Valentine had a soft spot for cops who tried to do an honest job. Unusually in a department so large, he had an open-door policy, and any beat cop who felt he wasn't getting a fair shake from his immediate supervisors or commanders could count on Valentine's lending him a sympathetic ear.

And when it came to supporting his men, he put his money where his mouth was literally, by letting it be known that he would make personal loans to any cop who was having a tough time making ends meet. Reportedly, officers took him up on this offer several times a week during his entire term of office.

In 1945, after eleven years as commissioner, longer than anyone had ever served to that time and longer than anyone since until the administration of the current incumbent (as this is being written), Ray Kelly, Valentine decided to retire. LaGuardia asked him to stay on and Valentine's popularity with the general public was such that all three of LaGuardia's opponents in the upcoming mayoral election swore they would retain him if he did stay on. But Valentine had already accepted another job, one that paid him almost four times as much as he was getting for running the NYPD.

The producers of *Gang Busters* (CBS, 1935-40, 1948-55; NBC Blue, 1940-48; Mutual, 1955-57), the extraordinarily popular police anthology radio drama, was in need of a host, and the most famous cop in

America (with the possible exception of J. Edgar Hoover, who, unlike Valentine, wasn't really a cop at all but a career bureaucrat with a gift for administration and public relations) had just the kind of authoritative voice that worked splendidly on radio. Valentine spent the next few months as the show's announcer but was soon tempted back into law enforcement.

At the request of General Douglas MacArthur, he became part of the occupation government running Japan after the end of World War II, specifically charged with reorganizing that shattered country's police force. He continued in this job for several months, returning to the States in late 1946.

In December of that year, less than twelve months after his retirement from the NYPD, he died. He'd developed a liver ailment during his time in Japan and was not able to recover after his return home. He did manage to complete the manuscript for his autobiography, which was published posthumously.

Some great police chiefs put a personal stamp on the departments they lead, a stamp that lasts for years after their departure. Bill Parker in Los Angeles, Eliot Ness in Cleveland, Tom Cahill in San Francisco, Lear Reed in Kansas City, MO, all left long-lasting imprints on the cities they served.

Lew Valentine didn't quite do that. In 1949, a few short years after his death, in what seemed like a rerun of the 1930 Seabury investigation (which itself had been preceded by the 1895 Lexow Committee and the 1914 Curran Committee), the Helfand Commission was set up to investigate corruption in the NYPD. In 1972, the Knapp Commission (formed after revelations made by, among others, Frank Serpico, a young cop who, like Valentine, would soon come to be a living symbol of honest law enforcement) was set up for the same purpose. In 1994, it was the Mollen Commission, yet again investigating the same sorts of allegations. As New York and its police force grew and crime conditions changed and the mission evolved, corruption just kept creeping back into the NYPD. It was like a tide, and not even Lew Valentine could hold back the tide back forever.

But he did hold it back during the time he actually led the Department and it could be argued that the conditions later investigated by the Helfan, Knapp, and Mollen Commissions were, perhaps, not nearly as bad as they might have been had Lew Valentine not been standing his post for those eleven years.

He was a tough cop. He was an honest cop. And he demanded that the officers he commanded be the same way. He still sets an example more than sixty years after his death that any police officer should be proud to emulate.

FURTHER READING

Honest Cop (Dutton, 1939) was the first book-length account of The Shoofly's career. Written by Lowell J. Limpus, a reporter for the New York *Daily News*, it's something of a valentine to Valentine, but not necessarily one that was undeserved.

Valentine's own account of his life and career, *Night Stick* (Dial, 1947), was published about a year after his death. It's a surprisingly well-written book, considering Valentine's comparatively limited formal education, in which self-aggrandizing is kept to a minimum.

NYPD – A City and Its Police (Holt, 2000) is a history of the Force by retired Washington, DC, police officer James Lardner and retired Chicago police officer Thomas Reppetto. Given Valentine's importance to the NYPD, it's not surprising that a good portion of the book is devoted to him and his administration of the Department. Lardner and Reppetto don't seem to be particularly sympathetic to any of the men who became NYC's Top Cop, not even to Theodore Roosevelt. With one exception. They do seem to have a somewhat grudging admiration for the plain-speaking Valentine, a man of integrity who, despite achieving high rank, never lost his street cop's heart. *NYPD – A City and Its Police* is a fairly even-handed look at the Department, warts and all (and in the NYPD, there are, frankly, a lot of warts, though there's also a lot of history to be proud of), and since both authors spent their law enforcement careers in other departments, neither of them has an ax to grind. That being the case, their respect for Lew Valentine can be taken as a hard-won, objective conclusion, not a preconceived notion.

Gang Busters – The Crime Fighters of American Broadcasting (OTR Publishing, 2004) by Martin H. Grams, Jr., provided information on Valentine's association with the fabled radio series.

Articles that were helpful in this chapter include "Lew Valentine Muss 'Em Up" by Jay Maeder in the March 29, 1999, issue of the New York *Daily News*; "LaGuardia's Tough and Incorruptible Police Commissioner" by A.G. Sulzberger in the November 11, 2009, issue of the New York *Times*; and "Captain Dan Costigan Asks to be Retired," an unsigned article in the November 13, 1921, issue of the *Times*.

THE FICTIONAL VALENTINE

As far as I've been able to determine, the first fictional character obviously modeled on Lew Valentine appears in a rip-snortingly entertaining cops-n-robbers film called *Bullets or Ballots* (Warners, 1936). The main character is Johnny Blake, an NYPD detective played by Edward G. Robinson, who's rather obviously modeled on real-life headline-making Headquarters sleuth, John "Broadway Johnny" Broderick (a two-fisted copper who took Valentine's "muss 'em up" edict literally). Blake's mentor in the Department, is Captain Dan McLaren (played by Joseph King), a supremely honest cop busted down from high command and placed in charge of a backwater precinct, who is just as obviously modeled on Valentine. When McLaren is suddenly elevated to Commissioner, he immediately initiates an undercover operation against the Mob with Blake as his point man.

More recently, in *Koramatsu – Black Curtain* (Xlibris, 2001), a self-published crime novel by Richard Winston set in post-war Japan, Valentine is again used as a supporting character, this time under his real name (sort of). The hero is Major John Capablanca, an Army CID agent who's an NYPD detective in civilian life. Now, as part of the Occupation force, his assignment is to assist his old boss, Retired Commissioner Valentine, in "democratizing" the Japanese Police. Some inaccurate details suggest that Winston was not as attentive to research as he should have been. Commissioner Valentine's given name is rendered as "Louis" rather than "Lewis," and he is depicted as giving out autographed copies of his autobiography, *Night Stick*, a book that wasn't published 'til after his death.

Both *Bullets or Ballots* and *Koramatsu* cast Valentine in a secondary role. In *The Racket* (RKO, 1951), a remake of an Oscar-nominated silent film, the apparent Valentine figure takes center stage. Robert Mitchum plays an incorruptible police captain who's been kicked around from one precinct to another because of his unyielding opposition to Organized Crime, as represented by Robert Ryan. The backstory of Mitchum's character, Captain Tom McQuigg, sounds too much like Valentine's to be coincidental. However, the city depicted, though not named, seems to be Chicago rather than New York. Further, the McQuigg character in the original, silent film version of this story (Caddo Company, 1928), as played by Thomas Meighan, though unswervingly honest, is not as overtly Valentine-like as Mitchum is in the remake, possibly because Valentine was not yet that well-known nationally. Presumably this is also the case with the 1927 Broadway stage play by Chicago crime journalist Bartlett Cormack, from which both films derive.

Lew Valentine, under his own name, is the main character in a special episode of *Gang Busters* titled "The Honest Cop." First broadcast on December 21, 1946, mere days after Valentine's death, it is described as a "dramatization" of Valentine's career. Given the time between Valentine's death and the broadcast of this episode, scheduled at the last minute in place of the second chapter of a two-part episode that had begun the week before, the script had to be written very quickly and the cast assembled with great haste. Nevertheless, it seems to have been a labor of love. Mayor LaGuardia himself appeared on the show to eulogize his hand-picked police chief, and the Choir of the Benedictine Nuns also performed on the episode.

GUNFIGHTER

Chicago Mysteries

Cops are paid to go in harm's way, to walk down those proverbial mean streets without themselves becoming mean, to run toward the sound of the guns when everyone with sense is running away from them. Consequently, the use of deadly force in the performance of duty is an unpleasant but necessary part of a police officer's professional life.

But it's also the tip of the iceberg.

Most cops will go their entire careers without ever having to fire their weapons except for periodic range qualifications. Even fewer will fire their weapons more than once.

But there are a select few who, though not trigger-happy or kill-crazy, manage to get into three or more gun battles in the course of their career (for some reason, it's almost never two; it's either none, once, or more than twice). For those officers who are involved in multiple armed encounters, many reasons might be at the root. The dangerousness of the jurisdiction in which they work (big cities tend to generate more shootings than suburban or rural areas). The risks inherent in their particular assignment (officers assigned, for example, to NYPD's Stakeout Squad or to LAPD's Special Investigations Section, both of which were set up specifically to target armed criminals in the act of committing a violent crime, naturally get into more shootings). The personality of the individual officer (some cops just have a highly developed sixth sense that enables them to sniff out danger).

In its history, Chicago has had a number of cops who combined all three of those elements, and consequently "saw the elephant" many times in their career. Detective Sylvester "Two-Gun Pete" Washington, who worked in the ultra-dangerous South Side, was involved in over a dozen gun battles and killed nine men in the line of duty (though he always claimed twelve). Captain Frank Pape, the so-called "toughest cop in America," spent twenty years hunting armed bandits in the city-wide Robbery Unit, during which he also killed nine men in over twelve shootings. Both officers have had books written about them. Both may have inspired well-known fictional depictions of their exploits.

But the cop who was in all probability CPD's Top Gun is today remembered by relatively few. Though he's often mentioned in books about Chicago crime, it's as a passing reference; he's never been the main subject of such a work. Yet he, too, was involved in over twelve armed encounters, killing at least a dozen bad guys (and, in all likelihood, fifteen or sixteen, the exact number is uncertain since he was sometimes one of several officers firing). And all of these dangerous exploits occurred during the first eleven years of a distinguished career that lasted nearly forty, while Washington and Pape's shootings were sprinkled throughout their tenure in the Department. By the time he retired, he was the most decorated policeman in CPD's history.

His name was Frank Reynolds.

A second-generation cop, the rugged-looking Irishman joined CPD at the age of 24 following a stint of WW1 military duty as a Naval Gunner's Mate. This was a dangerous time to be a cop in the Windy City. Between 1924, when Reynolds first entered the Department, and 1934, when his last recorded shootout occurred, 129 Windy City policemen were murdered in the performance of their duties, more than one a month on average. By comparison, only 17 Chicago officers died in the line of duty between 2002 and 2012, and this includes four accidental deaths and one heart attack while on undercover duty.

Starting out like all rookies as a uniformed patrolman, he was transferred to plainclothes duty during his first year at the behest of Deputy Chief of Detectives John Stege, who'd known Reynolds as a child. Stege would mentor the young cop during that eventful first decade.

Reynolds's first recorded use of deadly force occurred on Hallowe'en 1927. He and his partner entered a grocery store while it was being robbed at knife-point. The offender, on being challenged by the officers, turned and attacked them. Both officers fired on the robber, killing him.

A few months later, on February 19, 1928, Reynolds was behind the wheel of an unmarked squad car in hot pursuit of a stolen auto. When the suspect vehicle crashed, the thief exited and took off on foot, a gun in his hand. Reynolds and the officer riding shotgun opened fire, bringing him down before he got very far. He died in the hospital, but not before confessing to 25 different armed robberies during the previous months.

Later that same year, Reynolds and other members of his unit arrived at the scene of a pharmacy that had been robbed. The owner had offered no resistance but had been shot down by the bandits anyway after handing over all his cash. Within minutes, Reynolds and his men had traced the offenders to a nearby apartment building. His demand for surrender was met with gunfire and the cops and robbers traded bullets for the next few minutes until the bad guys ran out of ammo and surrendered. After being booked, they confessed to both the murder of the pharmacist and to another murder during the course of a drugstore robbery a week earlier during which they shot and killed a store customer.

In March the following year, Reynolds made the front pages of every paper in town (and in those days Chicago had a lot of papers) for his actions in what the media dubbed "The Moorish Cult Battle."

An Islamic sect known as the Moorish Science Temple, popular with African Americans during the '20's and '30's, was undergoing internal strife following the death of its founder Timothy Drew, known to his followers as "Prophet Noble Drew." An official of the sect, Charles Kirkman, had been selected by the governing board to replace Drew. Three other rivals for the leadership position, one claiming that he had been personally selected by Drew before his death and three others claiming nothing less than that they were the reincarnation of Drew, left the sect to form splinter groups.

The rivalry turned violent when Kirkman was kidnapped by the leader of another faction, Ira Johnson, who styled himself Ria Johnson El. Johnson, one of the three who claimed to be the reincarnation of Drew, had enjoined his followers to arm themselves and resist the interference of police.

The kidnapping was reported by Kirkman's wife, who named Johnson as the offender, and CPD officers arrived at the home of Johnson shortly afterward to investigate. Upon their arrival, they heard a voice inside yell, "The law is here! Get your guns!"

A uniformed patrolman, Stewart McCutcheon, slipped through a window in the back of the house then unlocked the back door to let in Officers George Kleback and Jesse Hults. As they entered, they were met by a fusillade of heavy fire, killing Hults and wounding the other two.

As the fight became general, a call went out to Reynolds, then attending a coroner's hearing, who immediately sped to the scene.

Another officer, William Gallagher, was killed as Johnson and one of his followers, John Stephenson, exited the house on the run, firing blindly to clear their way to a nearby apartment building, where they barricaded themselves.

Upon his arrival, Reynolds posted men at both the front and back entrances of the building and entered by himself.

This sounds foolhardy, but Reynolds was a bachelor with no kids to worry about. In those days, the widows and orphans of fallen cops were left in severe financial straits. The city provided no support whatsoever to the families of slain officers and the only remuneration they could hope for was a pittance paid out from a fund maintained by the Patrolmen's Benevolent Association. Two cops had already fallen in this incident, leaving behind families who would have an enormous difficulty getting along without their main bread winners. Reynolds always took the point in such situations to preserve the men who had wives and children to support.

As Reynolds entered, he spotted Stephenson and ordered him to surrender. Stephenson raised his weapon and Reynolds fired a shot. Stephenson fell, but with a mighty effort pulled himself back to his feet and again raised his revolver to fire. Reynolds squeezed off four more shots, finishing Stephenson off. Johnson was found in hiding in one of the apartments. He gave up without a fight. He later pled guilty to multiple murder charges and was sentenced to life.

For his actions that day, Reynolds was awarded the Lambert Tree Medal, CPD's highest award for valor.

On Valentine's Day, 1930, exactly one year after the infamous Valentine's Day Massacre on the North Side, Reynolds and his partner intervened during the robbery of a cabbie by a passenger. The robber, upon hearing the officers identify themselves as cops, turned and fired at them. They returned fire and killed him. The bandit, later identified as Theodore Murray, was found to be the offender in eight previous armed robberies.

For this action, Reynolds received a "merit promotion" to acting sergeant. An article in the February 19, 1930, edition of the Chicago *Tribune* announcing the promotion said, "Reynolds . . . has eight dead bandits officially to his credit, though his admiring colleagues say the number is in reality eleven."

Sometime in 1930 Reynolds, attempting to apprehend four armed offenders was fired on by one of them. Reynolds returned fire, killing the suspect, later identified as William Churchill. No other details about the encounter survive. Shootouts between police and criminals were common enough that it is likely that Reynolds was involved in several that never even made the papers or at least never made the front page.

By 1933, the nation's headlines were filled with news of John Dillinger, the Midwest bank robber who'd become the most renowned of that class of gangster known as the "motorized bandits," a class that included such celebrated desperados as Charles "Pretty Boy" Floyd, Kate "Ma" Barker and her sons, and Lester "Baby-Face Nelson" Gillis.

Like most of the motorized bandits, Dillinger tended to prey on banks in rural or suburban areas, particularly in Indiana. But between jobs he often used Chicago as a base. Indeed, during just such a sojourn late in 1933, a member of his gang was responsible for the murder of Chicago Police Sgt. William Shanley. This made members of the CPD particularly covetous for their agency be the one to do for the Dillinger group.

Feeling the heat that Dillinger's activities was generating, the Indiana State Police, the CPD, and, after Dillinger'd finally committed a federal offense that allowed the U.S. Government to insert itself into the case, the Chicago Field Office of the FBI all set up special "Dillinger Squads" to bring down the notorious hoodlum.

CPD's Dillinger Squad was led by Captain John Stege, reduced from his rank as Chief of Detectives but still a force to be reckoned with in the Department. As his second-in-command, he chose his long-time protégé Frank Reynolds, the latter's permanent promotion to sergeant having been confirmed earlier that year. The Squad operated 24 hours a day with Reynolds commanding the Night Watch.

Reynolds, with his deadly reputation, was said to be the one cop Dillinger feared. Perhaps to bolster his courage, Dillinger occasionally phoned Reynolds during his watch, tauntingly threatening him. He made similar calls to Captain Matt Leach, who ran the counterpart detail for the Indiana State Police. Interestingly, in fictional depictions of the pursuit of Dillinger, it is Melvin Purvis, Agent-in-Charge of the FBI's Chicago office, and *de facto* head of the Bureau's Dillinger unit, who is the recipient of those calls.

Beset by jealousy and mistrust, the various Dillinger Squads did not cooperate or pool information and when, on July 22, 1934, Dillinger lost a shootout with three FBI agents outside of Chicago's Biograph Theatre, neither Stege, Reynolds, nor any other member of their Squad was informed of the stakeout operation occurring in their city until after the fact.

Nevertheless, though the Squad ultimately had nothing to do with the actual apprehension of Dillinger, they did manage to accomplish some impressive pieces of police work during their short term of existence.

The single most impressive occurred when the Squad was only a few days old. On December 21, 1933, exactly one week after Sgt. Shanley's murder, Stege received an anonymous tip that Dillinger and two of his henchmen, Jack Hamilton (the killer of Shanley) and Harry Pierpont, were hiding out in an apartment in the Rogers Park neighborhood and that they were expecting a visit that night from someone known only as "Mule." Stege and Reynolds, along with all the officers assigned to Reynolds's night watch, arrived at the building at approximately nine o'clock that night. The bulk of the squad, some armed with Tommy guns, guarded the perimeter, while Reynolds and two other detectives approached the entrance to the building. One of the three officers buzzed the suspect apartment, announced through the communicator that he was Mule and was buzzed in. The three cops made their way up the stairs from the lobby to the first floor. Reynolds knocked on the door and heard a voice say, "It's okay. It's the Mule."

The door was opened a crack. Reynolds forced his way in, shoved the man at the door aside, announced he was a policeman, and drew his gun on two men seated in the front room.

One of them was holding a German pistol, either a Luger or a Mauser depending on the account, which he pointed at Reynolds. Reynolds fired before the seated man could get off a shot. Badly wounded, the fugitive managed to get to his feet and fire two shots. Reynolds dropped to his knee and fired three more shots, finishing the suspect off.

He then turned to the second seated man, who also rose to his feet and began firing at Reynolds with his pistol. Reynolds squeezed off his last two shots, killing him, then discarded his empty revolver and drew his back-up piece, a semi-automatic Colt Super .38, and turned to the third man, the one who had opened the door for him.

Reynolds's two partners had been trading shots with that third man, who'd sustained numerous wounds and fallen to the floor but was still attempting to crawl away from the cops while raising his pistol to fire. Reynolds shot him once in the head, ending both his life and the fight.

Stege entered the apartment after the dust settled and the smoke cleared, examined the three corpses and announced that they were Dillinger, Hamilton, and Pierpont. Reynolds was not so sure. Apparently recognizing the three from a bulletin he'd read, but not recalling their names, he told Stege, "These men are Jews."

Reynolds turned out to be right. The three dead men were Louis Katzewitz, Charles Tattlebaum, and Sam Ginsburg, known bank robbers who had escaped from prison six months earlier and were now wanted for four murders, including two cop-killings. They weren't Dillinger or his men but they were dangerous criminals whose deaths made the world a slightly safer place.

For his actions that day, Reynolds was awarded his second Lambert Tree Medal, the first officer in CPD's history to win two of the coveted decorations and still one of only two to accomplish that singular feat.

The Battle of Rogers Park appears to have been the last armed encounter in which Reynolds was ever involved. He would continue to be assigned high-profile investigations. He'd be promoted to lieutenant in 1935 and to captain in 1938 (a particularly difficult position to attain for one who was still some two years shy of his 40th birthday), but there are no accounts of his ever again firing his weapon in combat.

He came very close at least once though, in 1942, when he faced off against a minor functionary in the Democratic Regular Organization ("The Machine") named Eddie Sturch. Sturch had entered a bar one December evening, pulled out a pistol and began ordering the patrons about and shooting the place up. The call went out for CPD's top gun and, in a short time, Captain Reynolds arrived, calmly entered the bar, walked up to the self-important ward heeler and told him who he was. Sturch instantly recognized the name, dropped his gun, fell to his knees, and begged for his life. Against a minor-league pol, however well-armed, Reynolds didn't even need a gun. Just his reputation.

In 1961 he received his final promotion, to the rank of commander and was placed in charge of the New City District Station.

He retired in 1962 upon reaching the mandatory retirement age of 63. In addition to his two Lambert Tree Awards, Reynolds had earned three Hero Awards from the Chicago *Tribune*, fourteen departmental "Creditable Mentions," and ten departmental "Extra Compensations," making him the most decorated officer in the history of the CPD.

In 1969, after having survived so many deadly engagements without so much as a scratch, Reynolds died in a common household accident of injuries sustained after falling down a flight of stairs in his own home.

FURTHER READING

The most comprehensive piece on this little-known hero of law enforcement is a chapter in Paul Kirchner's book, *More of the Deadliest Men Who Ever Lived* (Paladin, 2009), titled simply "Frank J. Reynolds." Kirchner became interested in Reynolds after reading references to him in John Toland's history of the Depression-era "War on Crime," *The Dillinger Days* (Random, 1963), and pored over hundred of microfilms of Chicago newspapers determined to find out more about him.

Reynolds was still alive and still on active duty when Toland interviewed him for his book, and it is perhaps the next best source of information on him. But most books about Dillinger or about the 1930's Midwest crime wave will probably have at least a passing reference to Reynolds. However, some, in an attempt to make Dillinger into a heroic, or at least sympathetic, figure, tend to cast Reynolds in an unflattering light. In *John Dillinger – The Life and Death of America's First Celebrity Criminal* (Da Capo, 2005), for example, author Dary Matera refers to CPD's Dillinger detail as "Chicago's Goon Squad," and describes Frank Reynolds as the unit's "chief assassin."

Similarly, in *Dillinger – The Untold Story* (Indiana University, 2005) by G. Russell Girardin and William Helmer, Katzewitz, Tattlebaum, and Ginsburg, are described as "a trio of minor hoodlums," a description which seems calculated to diminish the accomplishment of Reynolds and his partners. Admittedly the three bandits weren't in Dillinger's league but they had robbed numerous banks at gunpoint, successfully escaped from a secure facility, and killed four people, including two armed, trained policemen. In my view, that removes them from the "minor" category.

The July 27, 1962, issue of *Chicago Police Newsletter*, in an article announcing Reynolds's retirement, provided information about Reynolds's career post-Dillinger Squad.

REYNOLDS IN FICTION

Both of the runners-up for the title of CPD's Top Gun, Detective Sylvester "Two-Gun Pete" Washington and Captain Frank Pape, were very likely the models for famous fictional counterparts.

It's been suggested that Washington and his partner, Joseph "Indian Joe" Geeters, were the inspiration for the cop-heroes of Chester Himes's "Harlem Detective" novels, "Coffin Ed" Johnson and "Gravedigger" Jones. It's a fact that Himes once told an interviewer that a pair of black detectives assigned to Chicago's South Side, who'd been in many fatal gun battles were the models for his heroes. It's also a fact that Washington and Geeters were getting a lot of national coverage in the African-American press via magazines like *Ebony* and *Jet*, so it's not at all unlikely Himes would have heard of them. Finally, Washington and Geeters are the only pair of Chicago cops from that era who fit the description Himes gives. On the other hand, in a different interview, Himes said that the models for his characters were a pair of LAPD detectives, so who's to say?

Frank Pape was, according to multiple sources, the uncredited technical advisor of the Chicago-set TV series *M Squad* (NBC, 1957-60), and star Lee Marvin supposedly modeled his character, Frank Ballinger, on Pape.

But, until recently, it appeared that Frank Reynolds had never been used as grist for any fictioneer's mill. Indeed, some fictional depictions of cases in which he was involved seem to go out of their way to exclude Reynolds. For example, in a recent film about the pursuit of Dillinger, *Public Enemies* (Universal, 2009), after Dillinger is arrested in Arizona and immediately extradited back to Indiana for trial, it is FBI Agent Melvin Purvis (Christian Bale) who meets him. In real life, the Chicago-area cop who met Dillinger at the airport was Frank Reynolds, who's not even depicted in the movie.

But, while researching Reynolds for the article that was my main informational source for this issue's column, Paul Kirchner was seized by the notion that Reynolds may have been the inspiration for the character who is, but for Sherlock Holmes, the most famous detective in fiction.

A cop named Dick Tracy.

Chester Gould, Tracy's creator, never mentioned Reynolds as a model in interviews, insisting that his broad concept was simply pitting a "modern-day, American Sherlock Holmes against Al Capone" (Capone being the obvious model for his first and most frequently recurring villain, the Big Boy). When pressed, he added that the various federal agents who were finally successful in putting Capone away fit rather well into his concept of a modern-day American Holmes. When pressed further, he admitted that Eliot Ness, who got the most ink of any of those G-Men, particularly impressed him.

Further, award-winning mystery novelist Max Allan Collins, a close friend of Gould's during his lifetime and Gould's successor as the writer of the strip, has told me that Gould was particularly *un*impressed with the notoriously corrupt Chicago Police, which seemed so ineffectual against Capone.

Nevertheless, there are a number of reasons to conclude that Kirchner might be on to something.

For one thing, Kirchner, in addition to his non-fiction prose work, is a highly-regarded comics artist in his own right. In fact, mystery fans may be familiar with him as the illustrator of the graphic novel *Murder by Remote Control* (Ballantine, 1986), which was scripted by former Dutch cop turned crime novelist Janwillem van de Wetering. As a professional in both the comics medium and the crime fiction genre, he is presumably familiar with their lore and history. His opinion, then, should at least be regarded as informed, if not infallible.

Second, it's a fact that when Gould sat down and drew the audition strips that he sent off to Chicago *Tribune* editor Joseph Patterson, he made Tracy a city police detective, not a federal investigator.

Finally, Gould also said he wanted his character to be someone who could deal with criminals "via the hot lead route," as he put it. The fact of the matter is that the feds who went after Capone, though their courage and integrity was rock-solid, just weren't involved in very much gun play (TV and movie depictions notwithstanding). Eliot Ness and his squad of dry agents knocked over breweries manned by Capone employees who had strict orders not to resist but to surrender quietly if they were raided. IRS Criminal Investigator Frank Wilson pored over columns of numbers in financial ledgers. The opportunity to deal out hot lead just didn't come up that often.

Frank Reynolds, on the other hand, did deal out hot lead. A lot.

Moreover, of the three CPD top guns mentioned here, Reynolds is the only one who could possibly have been the model for Tracy, since Pape didn't join the Force until 1934, and Washington 'til 1935, while Tracy debuted in the nation's funny pages in 1931.

On the other hand, by 1931, Reynolds had already been involved in several shootouts, had already been awarded his first Lambert Tree Medal, and had already won at least one of the Hero Awards given by the *Tribune*, Gould's own paper.

On balance, I think Kirchner may be right.

THE FIRST SUICIDE BOMBER

Los Angeles Mysteries

"One man's terrorist is another man's freedom fighter."

It's hard to pin down which all-too-glib cynic was responsible for that benighted comment, but it seems to get repeated a lot. If not the exact words, at least the basic gist. Recently, for example, White House correspondent Helen Thomas, the so-called "dean of the Washington Press Corps," in her capacity as an "objective" journalist, publicly expressed those sentiments.

This "moral equivalence" argument, the notion that it all depends on one's perspective, has never really flown with me. Leaving aside the obvious fact that there have been many terrorists who, quite clearly, weren't fighting for freedom at all (such as repressive religious fanatic Osama bin Laden; fascist Giuseppe Valerio Fioravanti, and white supremacist Robert "Dynamite Bob" Chambliss), and many freedom fighters who weren't, even by the broadest possible definition, terrorists (like George Washington, Martin Luther King, Jr., and Mahatma Gandhi), and that the phrase therefore quite clearly confuses means and ends, it seems fundamentally obvious on its face that there are some things are just dead wrong, no matter how righteous the cause. It's just dead wrong to level a couple of high-rise office buildings and kill thousands of people to draw attention to your cause; it's just dead wrong to blow up a train station in the hope of causing maximum casualties among innocent bystanders; and it's just dead wrong to bomb churches where innocent children are worshipping. And if your objective happens to be to end oppression, to spread freedom, or to alleviate poverty and suffering, it's still just dead wrong.

I was reminded of the commonly repeated phrase as I was researching this article, about a little-remembered incident in America's only-slightly-better-remembered first War on Terror.

Yes, that's right. There was another War on Terror, years before the one we're fighting now. It occupied the minds of Americans for the better part of 40 years. It claimed hundreds of American lives.

And it's now all but forgotten.

All but forgotten, I suspect, largely because a lot of the *goals* of the perpetrators of those acts of terror were things that we all now pretty much agree with. Fair play and fair pay for laborers. Eight hour workdays. Safe conditions in the workplace.

And yet the acts of some of those who were fighting for those goals were utterly reprehensible and this should be recalled at least as much as the justice of their cause. American Labor, at that time, was infested from top to bottom with anarchists who, in support of their political philosophy, sincerely believed, much as radical Islamists do today, that violence against innocents was not only necessary but even desirable to bring about their goals.

A few examples illustrate the anarchists' penchant for political terrorism. A pipe bomb thrown at Chicago's Haymarket Rally in 1886 left eight cops dead. 16 sticks of dynamite planted in the Los Angeles *Times* Building in 1910 set off the underground gas lines beneath, destroying the entire structure along with the building next door and killing 21 people, most of them the very laborers the bombers were supposedly trying to help. A suitcase bomb detonated during a Preparedness Day Rally in San Francisco in 1916 left ten people dead. An explosive shrapnel device planted in a wagon on Wall Street one autumn day in 1920, killed more than 38 people, injured another 400 (most of the dead and injured low-paid messengers, stenographers, and clerks), and introduced what would soon be recognized as a brand new criminal weapon, the car bomb (notwithstanding the fact that the vehicle was actually a horse-drawn carriage).

Ordinary people, people who had nothing to do with the issues at stake, felt themselves to be living in a country under siege, a country that could not adequately defend them from the random violence that could strike anywhere at anytime.

That was the state of things in America when, at approximately 11 AM on November 19, 1912, a bizarrely dressed man carrying an odd box marched into the Los Angeles Police Department's Central Station at First and Hill Streets.

He wore a weird hood that covered his entire face with a pair of goggles as eyepieces. His box, covered in cloth and attached to his shoulders by leather straps, rather resembled a hand organ. His left hand was inserted into a hole cut into the left end of the box. Sergeant R.C. Hild, on duty in the main lobby of the station, saw the garishly costumed man as he passed by his desk and asked what he wanted.

"I've got enough dynamite in here to blow us all into eternity," replied the masked man. "I want you to send for the highest official of the

Southern Pacific Railroad."

With that, he entered the outer office of Chief of Police Charles Sebastian and repeated his demand to Clarence E. Snively, Sebastian's executive officer. He intended, he told Snively, to force "the head man" to give in to his demands for better pay and working conditions for employees of the railroad. Snively immediately pretended to make a call to S.P. General Manager Paul Shroup, then told the intruder that Shroup was too busy to come immediately but would leave for police headquarters as soon as possible.

"He'd better hurry," said the masked man. "I'm getting nervous."

Chief Sebastian came out of his private office and spoke to the bomber. Judging the man to be completely serious he decided to evacuate the station and the surrounding buildings.

The area was cordoned off for one block on all sides of headquarters. Trials that were in progress in two courtrooms on the second floor of the station were immediately adjourned and all parties were escorted out of the building to safety. There were two main problems that forestalled a speedy evacuation.

One was how to safely remove the more than 100 prisoners then being held in the main city jail attached to police headquarters. There weren't enough police transport wagons on hand to move so many prisoners at once.

The other was the City Hospital just around the corner from the station. On the previous night a hotel fire had caused the number of patients in the facility to swell. Now all those extra patients had to be taken someplace else very quickly, yet not so quickly that their injuries would be exacerbated.

Two local trolley cars were sent for to supplement the paddy wagons in transporting the prisoners to a safer place of confinement. Extra ambulances from other hospitals assisted in the removal of the patients.

Meanwhile, the mysterious terrorist had not moved from his position in Chief Sebastian's office. A mining engineer named Randel who had been attracted to the scene by all the commotion was persuaded to examine the bomber's device and see if it could actually work.

Randel approached the intruder and accused him of bluffing. In response, the bomber pulled back the cloth covering, opened the top of the box and with his right hand, withdrew a stick of the dynamite and handed it to Randel. The front of the box was glass, and Randel could plainly see that bomber's left hand was clutching a triggering device.

299

Randel took the stick, examined it, and immediately recognized it as genuine but continued to insist that it was fake.

"Light it and see," said the bomber.

Randel's report left no doubt. The device the masked man was holding was a genuine bomb, an "infernal machine" in the parlance of the era. And they had to assume that it worked.

More than hour had passed and the bomber was getting anxious. Sebastian was not going to actually send Paul Shroup in to negotiate labor issues under the shadow of a bomb, but if the terrorist's demands were not met he was likely to make good his threats and destroy police headquarters as well as a good chunk of the surrounding area. It had been against his better judgment to allow Randel into the station, but none of the police officers in the building had the expertise in explosives that Randel had and the terrorist's capability to carry out his threat had to be verified. That verification having been made, Sebastian was not about to put any more civilians in harm's way. Whatever was going to be done from this point would have to be done by cops.

Two officers on the scene immediately stepped up to the plate, Detective Sergeant James Hosick, a fingerprint expert who headed up LAPD's Identification Division, and Samuel L. Browne, Chief Investigator for the Los Angeles County District Attorney's Office, serendipitously at city police headquarters that morning for an interdepartmental meeting.

Hosick, a native of Edinburgh, Scotland, immigrated to the United States at the age of 19 with only fifteen dollars in his pocket. Making his way to California, he worked at a number of different jobs while attending business college. He was persuaded to join the Los Angeles Police where he quickly earned an appointment to the Detective Bureau, becoming a self-taught expert on fingerprints and the Bertillon system. Eventually he was placed in charge of the Department's identification unit and during his tenure in that position turned it into one of the most highly regarded police ID bureaus in the country.

Browne, born and raised in Washington, DC, had been a professional soldier prior to accepting his position as the head of the DA's staff of detectives. As an officer in the US Army, he had garnered a great deal of investigative experience, first while serving in Military Intelligence and later as the chief special agent for General Leonard Wood, the future Army Chief of Staff, during Wood's tenure as military governor of the Philippines. Law enforcement seems to have run in Browne's family.

Back in his home town of Washington, he had a first cousin who was destined to make quite a name for himself in the American police service. The cousin's name was J. Edgar Hoover. Browne is sometimes erroneously credited with designing the standard gunbelt used by American police officers, the so-called "Sam Brown belt," although the actual designer was a British Army officer, Sir Samuel James Browne.

Ironically, the paths of Hosick and Browne had crossed before in another "First War on Terror" case. Two years earlier, DA's Man Browne had been the lead investigator (or at least the lead *official* investigator) into the bombing of the Los Angeles *Times* Building and had developed many of the leads that led to the identification of the bombers, labor activists James and Joseph McNamara. And when William Burns, the world-famous private eye who had been retained by the city to conduct his own investigation, located the McNamaras in the Midwest, it was Sergeant Hosick who was sent east to handle the extradition, an extradition that, though quite legal, became so controversial that Hosick was ultimately forced to defend himself (successfully defend himself) when he was charged with kidnapping.

Assigned to different aspects of the case, Browne and Hosick had not actually worked together during the *Times* investigation. Now, if only for a short time, they would become actual partners.

The law enforcement specialty of long, drawn-out negotiations with hostage-takers or barricaded suspects was a discipline that had yet to be developed. Police work in 1912 was a straightforward, uncomplicated affair, and the plan that Browne and Hosick agreed upon was, in keeping with the times, simple and uncomplicated. They'd simply jump the bomber, overpower him, seize the device, and try to disable it.

Browne approached the bomber and tried to engage him in a conversation. While the masked terrorist was distracted, Hosick snuck up behind him and slugged him over the head with a billy club. Knocked unconscious, the bomber's hold on the device was released, but it apparently had a "dead man's switch" which caused it to detonate.

Browne grabbed the bomb as the fuse began to sputter and burn down toward the dynamite. He ran outside with it, flung it on the ground breaking it apart, and stepped on the fuse in an effort to extinguish it and separate it from the explosive charge before it burned down and set it off. Miraculously, he managed to break the connection and put out the fuse before there was an explosion. The crisis was over.

A little over an hour had passed since the bomber had entered the station and issued his demands.

Now in custody, the suspect, identified as Carl Warr, a common laborer and a self-proclaimed champion of the working man, was immediately given sobriquets like "The Mad Bomber" and "The Human Bomb" by the local press.

San Diego Police reported that Warr had been among those identified as members of the Industrial Workers of the World, the so-called "Wobblies," the most anarchist-minded of the labor organizations springing up during that time. Earlier that year, a month-long series of clashes had occurred between IWW members and local San Diego citizens who had formed a vigilance committee to resist the encroachment of the group. Warr, however, denied that he had ever been to San Diego or that he was a member of the IWW and spokesmen for the organization insisted that Warr was not known to them.

Warr maintained that his act of terrorism was entirely his own idea, not part of a strategy by the IWW or any other organization. He had been upset, he said, by an unsuccessful strike by SP workers the previous year.

"They'd brought a lot of 'scabs' out here," he said. "They overrun the country and take the jobs away from other men. I wanted to see if the company wouldn't treat their men better. That was all I wanted."

Interestingly, according to most accounts, Warr had never been an employee of either Southern Pacific or its "Red Car" trolley subsidiary, Pacific Electric. His apparent motives were, to the degree that the word can be applied to an act of terrorism, completely altruistic.

Which, if you subscribe to the pernicious doctrine of moral equivalence, only goes to show that one man's terrorist is another man's heroic labor activist.

Like hell.

Thoroughly dispirited by his plan's lack of success, Warr eventually pled guilty to endangering human life and spent twelve years in San Quentin.

Browne and Hosick were both decorated for their collaborative act of heroism.

Within a few years, Browne resigned from the DA's Office, briefly became the police chief of Long Beach, California, and established his own private detective agency. Later he got a job as a security officer at Southern California Edison and still later went to work for the LA County Flood Control Board.

Hosick, who had been reading for the law while serving as an LA cop and who had, as noted earlier, successfully acted as his own legal counsel when his extradition of the McNamara brothers led to his being indicted for kidnapping, resigned from the police force after passing the Bar and spent two years as a Deputy District Attorney before starting a successful private practice.

Shortly after the "Mad Bomber" incident, Chief Sebastian resigned from the LAPD upon being elected mayor. One of his first acts was appointing his assistant, Clarence Snively, as his successor. Sebastian's political career did not last long. Admired as a reformer during his tenure as police chief, his mayoral administration became mired in scandal and corruption. He left office after only a year of his four-year term had passed and faded from the public scene. Snively's term as LA's top cop didn't last that much longer than had Sebastian's as mayor. His most memorable act as chief was mounting what now seems a rather quaint anti-smoking campaign aimed at the youth of Los Angeles.

And the affair in which they all played a part almost completely disappeared from public memory, becoming little more than a footnote in the history of America's First War on Terror, a history that is itself recalled by only a select few.

FURTHER READING

My main source of research for this article was contemporary newspaper accounts of the incident. Particularly valuable were "Maniac Commands Police 70 Minutes," an unsigned article from the November 20, 1912, issue of the New York *Times*, and "City Jail Imperiled by Human Bomb," an unsigned article from the November 20, 1912, issue of the Los Angeles *Examiner*. The front-page *Examiner* article includes a photo of Warr wearing his bizarre "super-villain" costume, his homemade bomb clutched in his right hand while his left is inserted into the box, holding the trigger. Though the article is not credited to any writer, the photo was attributed to one of the paper's staff photographers, E.J. Spencer, who had sneaked into the police station and snapped the shot while the siege was in progress.

Biographical information on James Hosick was found in John Steven McGroarty's *Los Angeles from the Mountains to the Sea* (American Historical Society, 1921), a "Who's Who" of prominent Angelenos. "The 'Chief' Left Off the List" by T.R. Houser, an article from the

July-Sept. 2006 issue of *Rap Sheet*, the quarterly newsletter of the Long Beach Police Officers Association, provided most of Sam Browne's biographical details.

Beverly Gage's *The Day Wall Street Exploded* (Oxford University Press, 2009) is, as its title suggests, primarily about the 1920 bombing of New York City's financial center, but to put that incident in historical context, Ms. Gage provides an admirably complete history of what the author calls "America's First Age of Terror," though she makes no mention of Warr's attempt to bomb LA's police headquarters, an indication of just how forgotten Warr's siege has become.

Though it resulted in fewer deaths than the Wall Street incident, the bombing of the Los Angeles *Times* building is perhaps the best-remembered episode in America's first War on Terror, one might almost say the *only* remembered episode. Perhaps this is because, unlike the Wall Street bombing, the *Times* case was actually solved. Perhaps it's because the perpetrators were represented at their trial by none other than Clarence Darrow, whose spirited defense of the McNamara brothers ultimately led to his own indictment for jury tampering. *Deadly Times* (Macadam Cage, 2007) by Lew Irwin and Dwight Williams provided useful details of the Los Angeles *Times* bombing and particularly on the roles played by Browne and Hosick in the subsequent investigation.

"THE MAD BOMBER" IN FICTION

Calling All Cars was a CBS Radio anthology crime drama that ran from 1933 to 1939. Originating out of Los Angeles, and sponsored by the LA-based Rio Grande Petroleum Company, it dramatized real-life cases from a number of West Coast law enforcement agencies, primarily from the Los Angeles Police. Though a network show, it was not broadcast nationwide but only on CBS affiliates in California, Arizona, and Nevada, states where the sponsor's products were sold. One could say that *Calling All Cars* was a regional version of the better-known, nationally broadcast crime anthology *Gang Busters* (NBC, 1935-36, 1940-48; CBS, 1936-40, 1949-55; Mutual, 1955-57), except that *Cars* actually preceded *Gang Busters* by more than two years. So it would be more accurate to say that *Gang Busters* was a national version of *Calling All Cars*.

Many of the tropes that would come to be associated with *Gang Busters* actually originated on *Cars*. For example, New York Police

Commissioner Lew Valentine and New Jersey State Police Superintendent Norman Schwarzkopf both became famous for hosting *Gang Busters*, but before either of them ever got behind the mike, LA Police Chief James Davis (recently portrayed by Colm Feore in the Clint Eastwood film *Changeling*, Universal, 2008) and other West Coast law enforcement officials had already performed similar chores on *Calling All Cars*.

And *Cars* had an even more dramatic opening. LAPD Sergeant Jesse Rosenquist, the Department's chief radio dispatcher, opened each episode with a "Be On the Lookout" alert, describing that episode's crime and its perpetrators just the way actual officers would have heard it if it had been a real police broadcast. Then, at the end of the episode after the criminal was caught, Rosenquist would put out a follow-up, canceling the original alert.

The fourth episode of *Calling All Cars*, "The Human Bomb," was a dramatization of the Warr case that was broadcast on December 20, 1933. Written and directed by series creator William N. Robson, "The Human Bomb" was a well-made, suspenseful half-hour audio drama that depicted the entire event from Warr's entry into the Central Police Station until he was finally subdued by Detectives Browne and Hosick.

Some half-dozen years later, the first filmed version of the Warr bomb threat was released. *Your True Adventure* was a series of fact-based short subjects distributed by Warner Brothers between 1937 and 1939, all of them based on stories submitted by audience members. Responding to a studio publicity blitz, moviegoers were encouraged to write about some exciting true-life incident in which they had been involved and submit it to the studio. Anyone submitting a story that was ultimately used in the series would be paid $500 for the film rights. That story would then be expanded into a full script by renowned journalist Floyd Gibbons, the famous "headline-hunting" war correspondent, who also introduced each film.

The seventh film in the series, *The Human Bomb* (Warners, 1939), written by Gibbons and directed by Joseph Henabery, was a dramatization of the Warr incident. I haven't seen this version but from the information I've been able to gather, the city is unnamed. The bomber, no longer an idealistic humanitarian, isn't trying to extort labor concessions from the head of the railroad, but mere cash. Specifically $200,000.

Although I could not find his name mentioned in any of the reference material I was able to check, I nevertheless infer that the person who submitted the story for this film was photojournalist E.J. Spencer, whose candid shot of Warr had made the front page of the Los Angeles *Examiner* more than a quarter of a century earlier, because the viewpoint character (and, based on a synopsis of the film I was able to track down, the person who comes up with the solution to the dilemma, thus saving the day) is a cameraman for the local paper who happens to be in the building covering another story when the incident breaks.

According to some sources, when Jack Webb was growing up in the Bunker Hill section of Los Angeles, he was an avid fan of *Calling All Cars*, so, years later, when he became a radio performer himself, it was likely that memories of that show were sparked when an a friend on the Los Angeles Police suggested that Webb should try to get a radio series based upon LAPD files on the air.

Webb, of course, became a legend for creating, producing, directing, starring in, and occasionally writing *Dragnet*, the show that grew from that suggestion. And given Webb's fond memories of the earlier show, perhaps it's not too surprising that a few of the real-life cases that were ultimately fictionalized on *Dragnet* had already been given the "based-on-actual-events" treatment on *Calling All Cars*.

The seventh radio episode of *Dragnet*, "The Big Bomb," written by Webb crony James Moser and directed by Webb himself, also dramatized Warr's attempt to blow up police headquarters. Aired on July 21, 1949, it was easily recognizable as deriving from Warr's terrorist act, but was, nevertheless, markedly different from both the *Calling All Cars* version and the *Your True Adventure* version.

Unlike *Calling All Cars*, *Dragnet* was not an anthology, but had continuing characters, so in Webb's version of the Warr case, the show's protagonist, Sergeant Joe Friday, performed the actions that Investigator Browne had performed in real life, while the actions of Sergeant Hosick were performed by Friday's partner, Sergeant Ben Romero (played by Barton Yarborough). And, despite the famous introductory declaration, "the names" weren't the only thing changed "to protect the innocent" in this episode.

In the interim between the actual incident and the premiere of *Dragnet*, the Los Angeles City Hall had been built and the LAPD's headquarters had relocated there. Though the Central Station could still be found at its old spot at First and Hill, it now functioned primarily as a local precinct rather than as the Department's administrative center. So, instead of threatening to blow up the Central Station, the villain's plans in the *Dragnet* version are much more grandiose. Nothing less than blowing up the entire City Hall. Called "Vernon Carney" in this version, he is not wearing some bizarre costume and he no longer has an altruistic political motive. Carney doesn't want justice and fair play for Southern Pacific's employees. Nor, as in the *Your True Adventure* version, does he want money. He just wants his criminal brother released from jail.

Unlike the *Calling All Cars* version, "The Big Bomb" does not depict the entire incident. Joe Friday, off-duty and enjoying some free time, is called in to help with the emergency situation. When he arrives to be briefed, the crisis has already been in progress for some time. The episode is played out in real time as Friday and Romero try several approaches to convince Carney to give up his plan before reluctantly deciding to take direct action.

The episode was very well-received and Webb was apparently quite pleased with it. During this period in *Dragnet*'s history, the show's radio episodes were performed live rather than recorded. "The Big Bomb" became one of only three episodes that Webb thought were worth doing again. The re-performance, with some minor revisions to Moser's script, aired on July 13, 1950.

Later, when the show moved to television, Webb decided to use "The Big Bomb" as the pilot episode. The TV version, usually referred to in a possible tip of the hat to the *Calling All Cars* episode and the Warner Brothers short, as "The Human Bomb," was actually filmed on location in the Los Angeles City Hall. It aired on December 16, 1951. Another future TV legend, Raymond Burr, played Thad Brown, LAPD's real-life Chief of Detectives and a future Chief of Police. In this episode, Brown performs the actions that were taken by Chief Sebastian and his assistant, C.E. Snively, in the actual case. Stacy Harris, who would become a regular member of Webb's stock company of actors, played Carney.

Well-received by critics and viewers alike, the episode was an auspicious beginning for one of the most popular and influential television shows in the history of the medium.

Decades later, another legendary cop show would do its own version. "You Da Bomb," an episode from the eleventh and penultimate season of *NYPD Blue* (ABC, 1993-2005), was written by Matt Olmstead, Nicholas Wooton, and Bill Clark, and directed by John Hyams. First broadcast on February 10, 2004, it has Andy Sipowicz (Dennis Franz) and the rest of the officers of the 15th Precinct contending with a man who walks into the station's detective squadroom, announces that he has a bomb strapped to himself, and that it will be set off in an hour unless a prisoner is released from one of the station's jail cells. The rest of the episode is played out in real time as Andy and his colleagues try to figure out how to resolve the situation without loss of life. Bochco, something of a specialist in TV cop dramas having created or co-created shows like *Delvecchio* (CBS, 1976-77), *Paris* (CBS, 1979-80), *Hill Street Blues* (NBC, 1981-87), *Hooperman* (ABC, 1987-89), and *Brooklyn South* (CBS, 1997-98), has a reputation for making police dramas that are as *unlike* Jack Webb's shows as possible, but this episode was easily recognizable as an uncredited remake of Webb's TV pilot, right down to the show's being played out in real time. And, possibly because the writers had no knowledge of the real-life crime from which the *Dragnet* episode derived, they use the same fictional motive for the crime that Webb's show did, the release of a prisoner. To fill out the full hour, some new plot twists are introduced. The bomber in this version is an unwilling participant. His child has been kidnapped by a vicious Slavic mobster who wants the prisoner, himself an Eastern European gangster, released immediately, lest his identity as a high-level member of the Russian *Mafiya* be uncovered during the booking process. The father has been forced to make the bomb threat to save the life of his little girl.

One wonders if, decades from now, when this particular episode of *NYPD Blue* is largely forgotten, some future cop show will do an uncredited remake of "You Da Bomb."

THE ANGELS YOU LISTEN TO

Academic Mysteries 101

School shootings like those that shocked the world at Columbine High School in Colorado, the Amish School in Nickel Mines, Pennsylvania, or the Masschusetts Institute of Technology, seem to be epidemic. There were at least seven such incidents in the United States during 2012 and another seven in 2013. They've become so routine that most don't get the coverage the Columbine or Nickel Mines massacres did.

Actually, mass murders at schools have been a part of American history since before there even was a United States. The first recorded such incident occurred in 1760 in what is now Franklin County, Pennsylvania.

Nor is it strictly an American phenomenon. The murderous rampage of Thomas Hamilton in 1996 which left sixteen children and one adult dead, occurred at Dunblane Primary School in Scotland. The Erfurt School massacre in 2006 and the Albertville-Realschule massacre in 2009 both occurred in Germany.

But the best-planned school attack, one that was carried out with meticulous military precision probably was the one that occurred in Austin, Texas, on August 1, 1966. As this is being written, we are a bit more than two years away from the fiftieth anniversary of the day Charles Whitman, perched at the top of a clock tower in the center of a busy college campus with a huge arsenal of firearms, ruthlessly slaughtered sixteen people and seriously injured another thirty-one. The scope of the crime and terrifyingly skillful efficiency with which he planned and carried it out, horrified the country. But what really froze everyone's bone marrow was that Charles Whitman seemed like such a nice, wholesome, all-American boy.

There had, of course, been cases of mass murder before in American criminal history. Indeed there had been a highly publicized case just prior to Whitman's rampage. Only a few weeks earlier, Charles Speck had broken into the Chicago apartment shared by nine nursing students, strangled five of them, butchered another three, and overlooked the ninth only because he apparently lost count and didn't notice her missing when she had the presence of mind to hide under a bed. A few years prior to that, during a brutal home invasion in the rural farmlands of Kansas, Richard Hickok and Perry Smith callously murdered Herb Clutter, his wife, his son, and his daughter, after robbing them of forty dollars, a crime immortalized in Truman Capote's true-crime classic, *In Cold Blood* (Random, 1966).

But Speck, Hickok, and Smith were precisely the kind of scum one would expect to be capable of murdering several people at a stroke. All ex-cons, all bearing the garish tattoos that testified to their criminal past, none of them particularly attractive, they were social misfits unable to control their violent impulses, unable to function in legitimate society, regarding all members of that legitimate society as their natural prey. Though the crimes were unbelievably shocking, the kind of people they were verified the public's preconceptions and stereotypes about violent criminals, and in a paradoxical way, made them feel safe. Such obvious outsiders are, after all, easy to spot. They can be guarded against.

But Charles Whitman was something else entirely.

Tall, muscular, blond, and boyishly handsome, he'd become the youngest Eagle Scout in the world at the age of twelve. Years later, he would become a decorated Marine. He'd just made the honor roll at University of Texas in Austin. He had a pretty wife who was crazy about him. And he had no real criminal past to speak of—there'd been a disciplinary problem in the Marines, a misdemeanor poaching conviction, and some traffic tickets, but nothing serious.

Sure he had problems, like we all do. His father was a stern disciplinarian, but so were many in that era. His parents had recently split, but millions of children see their parents' marriages break apart. He was having trouble balancing the demands of his student life, his family life with his wife and the mother who had moved to Austin after her divorce, and the series of part-time jobs he took to help support himself through school, but hundreds of thousands of undergraduates have the same problem balancing the competing elements of their lives.

So his decision to barricade himself at the top of the UT Tower with several high-powered rifles and randomly shoot so many strangers to death did not provide the comfort of easy explanations that Speck's murders or the murders of the Clutter family did.

And make no mistake about it. It was a decision. A cool, calculated, deliberate decision. He was not insane, because too much of the written record he left behind makes it clear that he knew what he was doing was wrong or at least that it would be considered wrong by society, so there was no doubt that he was able to understand the nature of his actions;

and they took place over too long a period, from just after midnight to an hour or so after noon, to be regarded as an irresistible impulse. Indeed, there was nothing impulsive about his actions. They were the result of careful, meticulous planning. Why he made the decision we'll never know for sure. That it *was* a decision is perhaps the only thing about his actions that day that we *can* be sure of.

The idea, in fact, apparently occurred to him several years before he brought it to fruition. He'd enlisted in the Marine Corps in 1959 and was successful enough that he was selected for a special military scholarship program designed to produce commissioned officers conversant in engineering and hard sciences. It was under this program that he first matriculated at the University of Texas in the fall of 1961. Late in 1961 or early in 1962, as he and a friend looked at the tower, Whitman observed that a single sharpshooter could "stand off an army from atop of it before they got to him." He added that he'd like the chance to go to the observation deck and shoot people. Whitman was known as a practical joker and his friend did not take the remarks seriously, but late in the summer of 1966, after Whitman had actually done as he described, the seemingly humorous comments took on a sinister tone.

Charlie, after years of first being raised by stern, even brutal, father, and then being trained by the most rigidly disciplined of America's armed forces, found the freedom of student life a bit too heady and eventually flunked out of the scholarship program, returning to active duty as an enlisted Marine. But military life no longer suited him and, through his father, he pulled some political strings to get an early honorable discharge.

By this time he had already married the former Kathy Leissner, whom he'd met while at UT. She had already graduated and started her career as a high school teacher while Whitman was finishing up his military obligations, so when he re-entered UT as an undergrad, he found himself being supported by his wife.

Whitman found the pressures on him difficult to bear and wrote about this at length in diaries and notes to himself. On two occasions, following his parents' divorce and his mother's move to Austin, he became angry enough at Kathy that he actually struck her. To his credit, he sought help from Dr. Maurice Heatly, a psychiatrist at the student health center. During his consultation, he admitted that he often had the fantasy of "going up on the tower with a deer rifle and shooting people." This did not overly alarm Heatly. Since the tower's construction, many students who sought his help mentioned some morbid fantasy about it, usually involving suicide. Heatly found that students regarded the tower as a "mystic symbol" of the university and, consequently, of the problems of university life.

Moreover, Whitman's comment seemed to be a generalized fantasy. If someone tells his therapist, "I'm going to kill that bastard before the night's out," such a statement, revealing a specific plan of action within a specific timeframe, is taken more seriously than a comment like "I'd like to blow up the whole damned school." Whitman's comment seemed to Heatly to be the second kind.

He did note that Whitman "seemed to be oozing with hostility," but added this: "There was something about him that suggested and expressed the all-American boy." Without realizing it, he'd nailed the single most frightening aspect of Charles Whitman, his seeming wholesomeness.

This was in March of 1966, four months before his murderous rampage. Such conclusive evidence of premeditation is a prosecutor's wet dream.

Just after midnight on the first of August, 1966, he finally began the process of making his fantasy a reality.

The first step was what criminologists and criminal profilers now call "family annihilation." Ostensibly because he wanted to spare those he most loved the suffering that his planned action would cause them, he'd decided to murder his mother and his wife.

He arrived at his mother's apartment at roughly a quarter past twelve and immediately strangled her to death. Then, to make sure she was irredeemably dead, apparently bashed in the back of her skull with some blunt object.

Returning home at around 2 AM, he entered his bedroom where his wife was sound asleep. Stating in a written account that he wanted her to die as "painlessly as possible," he stood over her sleeping body with a hunting knife and stabbed her at least five times. She probably passed from sleep to death without ever waking up.

Two down and fourteen more to go.

The next step was assembling his arsenal.

He was an avid hunter and already owned several of the weapons he would need, including a 6mm Remington bolt action rifle with a 4-power scope sight, which would be his primary murder weapon that day, as well as a .357 Magnum S&W revolver, a 9mm Luger, and the hunting knife he'd used on Kathy. Between 9 AM and 11 AM, he visited a series of hardware stores and gun shops in Austin and purchased a .30 caliber M-1 carbine, a 12-gauge pump action shotgun, and ammo. Packing all his equipment into a military footlocker, he made his way to campus.

He passed through a security checkpoint manned by a campus police officer and presented him with a perfectly legitimate Carrier ID Card issued to people with a frequent need to transport heavy or bulky items on or off campus. Whitman had been issued the ID through his part-time job as a lab assistant at the University. The campus cop issued a loading zone permit allowing Whitman to temporarily park his vehicle in restricted areas. At around 11:30 AM, Whitman entered the tower, carrying his equipment on a dolly. Passing as a janitor, he had no problem getting his cargo onto the elevator, which he rode to the 27th floor. Once there, he pulled the heavy footlocker on its dolly up another three and a half flights of stairs to the observation deck. He'd been there many times before and knew the way perfectly. On the way he passed Edna Townsley manning the observation deck's reception desk and caved in her head with a rifle butt, dragging her body behind a desk to hide it. She was not dead yet, but she would be within a few hours.

Three down. Thirteen to go.

Just as he got the body hidden, a young couple, Don Walden and Cheryl Botts, exited the observation deck, smiled and said hello to Whitman (apparently not alarmed by the sight of a man holding a rifle) and went down the stairs to the elevator. It's not clear why Whitman spared the couple, but it's likely that their very obliviousness to the danger they were in saved them.

The couple probably passed M.J. Gabour, his wife Mary, his sister and brother-in-law Marguerite and William Lamport, and his sons, Mark and Mike, as the family exited the elevator on the 27th floor and Don and Cheryl entered.

The Gabours found the door to the observation deck barricaded by a desk and concluded that the deck was probably temporarily closed for cleaning. Mike and Mark pushed the door open against the barricade to make sure the closing wasn't a mistake and saw Whitman looking out a window. Whitman turned and picked up the 12-gauge he'd bought that morning and fired three times, grievously wounding Mike and killing Mark instantly. Marguerite, standing behind them, caught a pellet of double-ought buckshot in her upper chest and also died immediately. Mary was also wounded several times in the volley and was blinded for life.

Five down. Eleven to go.

Having established control of the 28th floor and access to the observation deck, he fired a shot at Edna Townsley to make sure she was dead (she wasn't yet, but it would make no difference in the long run), then rolled his arsenal through the entry to the deck and prepared to carry out his plan.

He wrapped a white bandana around his forehead as a makeshift sweat band then wedged the dolly against the doorknob of the entryway to the deck, blocking it off from anyone who might try to enter. He was now alone. It was roughly fifteen minutes before noon.

The first weapon he reached for was the 6mm Remington with the telescopic sight. The Gabours' interruption had delayed him for a few minutes and he'd missed a class change that would have maximized the number of people on the square below. But there were still plenty of targets.

His first was Claire Wilson, a freshman in her eighth month of pregnancy. Aiming directly for her abdomen and the unborn son Claire carried there, Whitman slowly squeezed the trigger. The slug fractured her baby's skull, killing him instantly, and caused serious damage to Claire's stomach, colon, and uterus. Her live-in boyfriend, Thomas Eckman, knelt down next to her as she fell and caught the next slug, dying instantly.

Seven down. Nine to go.

Dr. Robert Boyer, a former UT math professor passing through to visit old friends after completing a teaching assignment in Mexico, was the next to die with a bullet in his kidney.

Eight down. Eight to go.

At the same time, many others were being wounded by non-fatal shots. Laying where they fell, they were completely vulnerable to any follow-up shots Whitman might choose to fire. It would later turn out that Whitman never shot anyone twice. If you were hit but survived, you were safe.

But terribly uncomfortable. In addition to the wounds, the heat was punishing that day, especially on the concrete surface of the campus mall. Forced to keep still, many of the wounded would suffer second-degree burns in addition to their gunshot injuries.

East of the tower, exiting the University's Computation Building, Peace Corps trainee Thomas Ashton started toward the Student Union to meet several of his fellow trainees for lunch. Whitman's shot caught him in the left chest. He died some ninety minutes later while doctors fought to save him.

Nine down. Seven to go.

At 11:55 AM , UT Police Officers L.W. Gebert and Jack Rodman (ironically the same officer who had issued Whitman a loading permit twenty minutes earlier) arrived at the 27th floor, dispatched to the tower after reports of the shotgun attack on the Gabour family had been received. Gabour, still conscious, begged them for a gun so he could kill the man who had murdered his family.

At roughly the same time, Austin Police Officer Houston McCoy, on mobile patrol near Lake Austin was dispatched to the campus. McCoy would be one of the key figures in the unfolding drama.

Meanwhile, Whitman continued his attack, popping up from behind the deck's barricade, taking careful aim at a target, squeezing off a shot, then moving to another part of the deck to repeat the process.

From the west side of the deck, Whitman had a clear view of the Drag, a trendy, student-friendly shopping area adjacent to campus. The next fatality was 17-year-old Karen Griffith, a senior at Lanier High School (ironically the very high school Kathy Whitman taught at). Whitman's slug passed through her arm and into her chest cavity, collapsing her left lung. Summer student Thomas Karr, returning to his apartment after completing a Spanish exam, turned toward her as she fell. It may have been his intention to go to her and render aid, but Whitman's slug entered his back before he could. Strong and tough, he lasted an hour before dying on an operating table. The girl he was trying to help lasted even longer, but over the next few days, her remaining lung would slowly lose function. Karen Griffith died a painful death one week after being shot.

Eleven down. Five to go.

It was now a little past noon. McCoy pulled into campus. Fellow APD Officers Billy Speed and Jerry Culp had arrived just before him. McCoy made his way to the third floor of the English building and got there in time to see Billy Speed take a slug in his right shoulder that continued on into the chest cavity. Bystanders, including Culp and a registered nurse named Judith Parsons, pulled Speed out of the line of fire and got him to an ambulance. He died shortly after arriving at the hospital.

Twelve down. Four to go.

Whitman returned to the west side and sighted down at the Drag again. Harry Warchek, a political science instructor at Alpena Community College in Michigan, had returned to UT, his old alma mater, to work on his doctorate. Whitman's slug entered his chest, piercing his heart, spleen, and lungs, and killing the father of six instantly.

Thirteen down. Three to go.

Paul Sontagg and his girlfriend Claudia Rutt, walking near the entrance to the West Mall where the Drag met the campus, heard the shooting and took cover. Paul peeked over the top of the protective barricade and said, "I can see him. This is for real." A bullet entered his mouth a moment later, killing him instantly. Claudia tried to pull him to safety. Whitman aimed his next shot at her. The slug smashed through her left hand before entering her chest. She died of internal bleeding shortly after reaching the hospital.

Fifteen down. One to go.

Moving to the south end of the deck, Whitman made what might have been his best shot of the day. Five hundred yards away, at the intersection of 21st and University Boulevard, a city electrician named Roy Dell Schmidt had just assured his partner, Solon McCown, that they were too far away to be in any danger. A second after he said so, a bullet entered his abdomen. He was pronounced DOA at Brackenridge Hospital's ER.

Sixteen down. But Whitman was by no means finished.

By this time law enforcement officers from a number of agencies were converging on the scene. In addition to campus and city police, there were state troopers and investigators, and at least one US Secret Service agent assigned to guard LBJ whenever he was in his home state, all returning fire from the ground.

At the same time, armed citizens were making their way to the campus, many of them, avid hunters and sportsmen, equipped with better weapons than the police. They also took shooting positions and attempted to pick off Whitman from the ground.

None of them were able to nail him from their positions, though a few came close. But the sustained return fire meant Whitman could no longer take the time to aim and shoot the high-powered, scope-sighted Remington. Its bolt action made it too slow. Switching to the semi-automatic M-1, he began rapid firing into the crowds below, continuing to wound many, but causing no fatalities. By this time, most of his prey had figured out what was going on and had taken cover, but he was still able to continue inflicting damage every time a target presented itself.

At the same time, although there were plenty of lawmen on the scene, there was no coordinated response. The few walkie-talkies available were notoriously unreliable and phone lines were clogged. There was no way for officers to communicate with each other and make plans.

As Austin Police Chief Bob Miles would later put it, "In a situation like this, it all depended on independent action by officers."

Fortunately, the law enforcement community of Austin, and two officers in particular, was up to the challenge.

One was Houston McCoy. Unable to find anyone in authority to tell him what the plan was, he resolved to enter the tower himself and see what could be done.

A tall, self-described "West Texas cowboy," McCoy had been with the APD about five or six years at this point. He knew the killing had to stop. The problem was how to get into the tower without exposing himself to fire.

At the same time, 40-year-old Allen Crum, though not a cop, was deciding on some independent action of his own. A professional soldier for twenty-two years, he had recently retired from the Air Force as a Master Sergeant, where he had been a B52F tail-gunner. Combat-experienced and familiar with guns, Crum was determined to do his part, like so many armed citizens arriving at the campus to help out. From the store he managed in the West Mall of the campus, he waited until he saw the sniper directing his fire towards the south, and ran to the tower's entrance.

There he met APD Officer Jerry Day and Agent W.W. Cowan of the Texas Criminal Intelligence Unit, a division of the state's Department of Public Safety. He volunteered to help. He knew the building, he said, and could guide them to the top. Agent Cowan, armed with his sidearm and a rifle, handed the long gun to Crum. The three made their way to the top floors.

McCoy meanwhile had made his way to the campus police station, where University Police Sergeant A.Y. Barr was assembling a team to enter the tower. McCoy immediately volunteered. A group of five city officers including McCoy and two campus officers was put together. One of the campus officers, William Wilcox, familiar with the underground system of tunnels connecting the various buildings on campus, led the team safely to the tower.

Another APD officer, Ramiro Martinez, was finding his own way to the tower. Off-duty when the massacre began, he immediately phoned headquarters for instructions and was told to report to the scene and assist with traffic control.

The West Texas-born son of migrant farm workers, Ray Martinez had graduated from Austin's police academy in 1961. Married to an East Texas girl of German descent, he was the father of two girls.

Arriving near the west side of campus, Martinez parked his car and tried to find some traffic to direct. There was none. Traffic had already been diverted away by students and other police.

Looking at the bodies spread over the mall, Martinez decided he would be more useful inside the tower than directing non-existent traffic. Making his way behind the cover of buildings to the South Mall, he ran a zigzag pattern across the open square to the building entrance. Once inside, he made an unsuccessful attempt to notify headquarters of his location, but found the phone lines still jammed. He elevatored up to the 27th floor.

APD Officer Jerry Day, State Special Agent W.A. Cowan, and civilian volunteer Allen Crum were already there.

Outside, withering fire from police and armed citizens was keeping Whitman pinned down and he'd been able to inflict no more fatalities and few injuries after the first twenty or so minutes of his attack.

In the meantime, the APD had launched what would be its only coordinated response to Whitman, but it was destined to be unsuccessful. A helicopter attack had already been ruled out, since a hovering helicopter would be too vulnerable to Whitman's rifle fire. But perhaps a sharpshooter firing from a fixed-wing aircraft might end the siege. Part-time Williamson County Sheriff's Deputy Jim Boutwell, a flight instructor at Tim's Airpark outside of town, convinced the APD brass to try. Lieutenant Marion Lee, one of the department's best marksmen was armed with a high-powered rifle and took the passenger seat of a Champion Citabria, a cloth-covered prop plane, while Boutwell took the pilot's seat. They made several passes over the tower, but Lee was unable to get an accurate shot off, while Whitman was able to hit them several times. If he succeeded in bringing the plane down, the air assault would do more harm than good. Boutwell and Lee decided on an honorable retreat.

Martinez decided the time had come to end things and, while the other officers cleared the 27th floor of wounded, started up the stairs to the observation deck. As he started, Crum joined him.

"No sir, buddy," Crum told Martinez, "you are not going by yourself."

By this time, the officers still on the 27th floor were joined by Mc-Coy and the team that had been assembled at campus police HQ.

Day and the others were still busy moving the wounded. Day informed McCoy that Martinez and an armed civilian were already making their way to the deck. McCoy had been hoping to form some sort of plan but events were moving too fast and it was necessary to improvise. He and the others followed Martinez and Crum up the stairs.

Martinez and Crum had moved the heavy desk to enter the reception area where they discovered the dying Edna Townsley and gave what comfort they could.

Crum informed Martinez that if they were going out there he ought to be deputized. Martinez was thunderstruck. He'd assumed Crum was a policeman. Maybe not APD, since he didn't know him, but perhaps a campus cop or some kind of state agent like Cowan. He carried himself with an air of authority (the legacy of two decades of soldiering), he held his weapon professionally. How could he not be a cop? What was a civilian with a rifle doing up here? No time to wonder about that now.

"Consider yourself deputized," said Martinez.

As the other officers entered the reception area, Martinez attempted to open the door to the observation deck but the dolly Whitman had wedged against it kept it shut.

Making a lot more noise than anyone felt comfortable with, Martinez kicked the door open and went out. Fortunately, Whitman's own shots which he was firing at that moment from the northwest corner of the deck, probably masked the sounds of Martinez's entrance.

Reciting the words of the Act of Contrition, the traditional Catholic plea for the forgiveness of sins, Martinez stepped out onto the deck. Whitman, after ninety minutes in complete control of his sniper's perch, was no longer alone.

Crum, still armed with the rifle, took a post at the entryway and aimed his weapon at the southwest corner while Martinez headed to the southeast and then to the northeast. As Martinez turned the corner, Mc-Coy, armed with a twelve-gauge shotgun, entered the deck.

"Your fellow officer might need your help," Crum said to McCoy.

McCoy hurried to join Martinez and back him up. Day followed with a rifle and joined Crum in covering the corners. Inside the reception area, the remaining officers were keeping the windows covered in case the sniper, moving from corner to corner, exposed himself to their fire.

In addition to the threat posed by Whitman, all the officers (including the deputized Crum) then on the deck were in danger from friendly fire, since no one below had any idea that police had made it to the observation deck. Martinez and McCoy crouched low as they made their way around the deck.

Whitman decided to change his position, moving from the northwest corner to the southwest. Inside the reception area, one of the men on McCoy's team, APD Officer Philip Conner, had his rifle aimed at the window between those corners, ready to shoot if Whitman ran past him but Whitman never got that far.

Crum hearing movement that he assumed was the sniper, fired a round into the southwest corner, driving Whitman back to the northwest. Whitman settled into a seated position and took dead aim at the southwest corner, apparently believing that an attack from that corner was about to be mounted.

That was how Martinez saw him when he rounded the northeast corner and crept out to where he could get a look at Whitman. The jutting clock on the wall partially obstructed Martinez's view, but seeing Whitman taking aim at the southwest corner, he thought that Crum might have left his post and was about to be shot. He didn't have time to get into a better, safer shooting position. He brought up his .38 and opened fire.

He emptied all six shots at Whitman. The sniper struggled to bring his carbine to bear but at least one of Martinez's shots had hit, causing him to seize up and fire wildly into the air, unable to get his rifle aimed properly.

McCoy still couldn't see Whitman, but watching where Martinez had fired gave him an idea of the sniper's location. He moved to better firing position and took aim at the brightest part of his target he could see, Whitman's white headband.

The blast of nine double-ought buckshot pellets, each individual pellet slightly wider in diameter than a .32 caliber bullet, smacked into the upper half of Whitman's face. Reflexively, McCoy racked another round into the chamber and fired a second time, this blast hitting the left side of the sniper's head. Whitman started to slump down, out of McCoy's range of sight. If he wasn't dead yet, he soon would be, but at that instant he was still moving.

Martinez, his weapon empty, instinctively grabbed the shotgun out of McCoy's grip and ran toward Whitman, firing a third blast into his upper torso, nearly severing Whitman's left arm from his body.

More than ninety minutes of terror was finally ended.

Some of the aftermath was predictable. There were, inevitably, criticisms of the APD and the UT Campus Police, and calls for the resignation of Chief Miles. Miles responded to the criticism in the best way possible, by documenting everything he could and then making the findings public.

Of course a police force should be ready for anything, but no police force in the history of American law enforcement had ever faced the kind of crime Whitman had unleashed on the campus and city communities. If the response was less well-organized than it could have been, the most salient point to recall was that the law enforcement personnel of Austin, not just Martinez and McCoy, but the whole collection of city, campus, county, state, and federal lawman, rose to the occasion with courage and an inspiring commitment to duty. So, for that matter, did the citizens of Austin. Like the 9/11 attackers, Whitman showed us the worst that humanity can offer, but in doing so, brought out the best.

Whitman's sniper attack, along with the Watts riots that same summer, were among the events that led to police forces across the country setting up tactical teams, like LAPD's SWAT or NYPD's Tactical Patrol Force, to deal with such incidents in a coordinated manner.

Also predictable were the waves of arguments for increased gun control laws, particularly after it became known that Whitman had bought a large part of his arsenal the very morning of his rampage. But, as a military veteran, and a licensed hunter with no real criminal record, there would have been no reason to refuse to sell Whitman those guns, and a waiting period would in all likelihood have done nothing but delay his plans. In any case, his main weapon of murder that day, the scope-sighted Remington rifle, along with the two handguns he brought along for close-in fighting, had already been in his possession for years.

Less predictable was the way the aftermath affected the two officers most responsible for ending Whitman's crimes.

When Chief Miles first got word that Whitman had been killed by officers, the only name he got was "Ramiro Martinez," so the press release read, "ATTEMPTED APPREHENSION MADE BY OFFICER RAMIRO MARTINEZ, PATROLMAN, AUSTIN POLICE DEPT & OTHERS."

McCoy, and not just McCoy, but Day, Cowan, Conner, Crum, and the rest were suddenly "others," while Martinez was the hero of the hour.

By the next day, the Austin *American-Statesman* had run a picture of Martinez on the front page with the caption, "shoots slayer." Martinez's picture was even bigger than Whitman's. Within a week, *Life*, featuring the Whitman story as its cover feature, ran a full page photo spread of Martinez and, as they had done in 1945 with another unassuming, boyishly handsome Texas hero named Audie Murphy, turned the modest young cop into a folk hero. Through it all, Martinez had not talked to a reporter, had not issued a statement, had not sought any publicity whatsoever from the incident. Without his approval or even knowledge, sole credit was being thrust upon him, and McCoy, whose actions were every bit as brave and who, in all likelihood, actually fired the shots that finally ended Whitman's siege, was being ignored.

And the years to come would be far kinder to Martinez than to McCoy. Martinez was promoted to sergeant shortly after his shootout with Whitman and transferred to the Criminal Investigation Division. He enjoyed the work very much but found himself falling farther and farther behind income-wise as APD salaries failed to keep pace with inflation. He finally felt he had to leave police work and resigned in 1968 to open a restaurant. It took only a few weeks for him to realize that he'd made a huge mistake. Law enforcement wasn't just his job, it was his vocation. Unfortunately, a return to APD, at least at his former rank of sergeant/investigator, was impossible according to civil service rules. Instead, he applied for a job with the Texas Department of Public Safety, the umbrella organization covering all of the state's various law enforcement bodies, and became a special agent in the DPS's Narcotics Division. In 1973 he transferred into the most respected and fabled police agency in the Lone Star State, the Texas Rangers. Over the years he gained a reputation as one of the ablest criminal investigators in the state. Retiring from the Rangers in the early '90s, he became a Justice of the Peace in Comal County, Texas. He can look back on a satisfying and fulfilling career in public service.

McCoy also left APD shortly after the Whitman incident and became a flight instructor but was never able to find the peace that Ray Martinez did. Over the years he descended into depression and alcoholism. Diagnosed with post-traumatic stress disorder by VA doctors, he attempted to get disability payments from Austin based on the strain and anxiety he'd suffered in his shootout with Whitman but was unsuccessful. He eked out a living on a Social Security disability allowance of roughly $800 a month and what he made from a CD he recorded about the incident called *Voices from the Tower*. He died late in 2012. In an interview some months before his death he said, "Just be sure to say that I was not the only police officer there that day. It was teamwork."

One incident serves as a microcosmic illustration of the differences in the way their two lives went. When a TV-movie was made dramatizing the incident, Martinez and his wife sued and won an out-of-court settlement because of the distortions made about them. McCoy, who was represented by a fictional character, also sued, lost, and was ordered to pay court costs.

Ray Martinez and Houston McCoy both acted with bravery and determination on that fateful day. Both performed their duty in a manner that they could take pride in.

Ray Martinez deserved every single one of the accolades he's received since the shootout.

But so did Houston McCoy. The thing is Martinez got the accolades. McCoy didn't.

The most predictable part of the aftermath were the attempts, still continuing to this day, to explain the reasons behind Whitman's murderous rampage.

An autopsy discovered a small tumor in his brain. Many assumed that this tumor had simply driven him mad. But a tumor that was so bad that it caused his entire moral compass to go haywire would also have affected his brain functions so much that the level of marksmanship he was able to display that day would not have been possible.

The dysfunctional family he came from was no explanation. He had two brothers with the same background and neither of them became mass murderers.

The pressures of his student life were not particularly remarkable. Undergrads all over the country take heavy course loads, work at part-time jobs, and attempt to carve out a social life out of their crowded schedule.

A particularly spectacular form of "suicide-by-cop?" Probably. The writings he left behind made it clear that he didn't expect to survive. But then we come back to the question, with so much to live for, why did he *want* to commit suicide, and why take so many people with him?

The more horrifying the crime, the more we want to attribute it to sickness rather than evil. But evil exists, and those who don't acknowledge this make themselves more vulnerable to it.

Kinky Friedman, mystery novelist, country/western musician, Texas gubernatorial candidate, and UT alum (some sources indicate that he was actually one of Whitman's dorm roommates) wrote a semi-comic song about the incident called "The Ballad of Charles Whitman." His comments on the demons driving his fellow UT student probably come closer to suggesting a reason than anything anyone else said.

"I'm sure the people who didn't like [the song] thought I was mocking a tragedy or something," he said in a recent magazine piece. "But they didn't listen to the song. It explores the mind of Charles Whitman and what makes these things happen. The question is, 'Why?' Why would somebody do that? He was a straight-A student, an Eagle Scout, a Marine … we're fascinated because there's a little bit of Charlie in us all. We're all capable of terrible acts, and we're all capable of greatness. It's a question of which angels we're listening to, I suppose."

The angels we're listening to. It's as good an explanation as any, and better than most.

FURTHER READING

The first, and still most comprehensive book about the Whitman murders is Gary M. LaVergne's *A Sniper in the Tower* (University of North Texas, 1997), which goes into considerable detail about Whitman's life prior to the murders. To the degree possible, he mentions every single victim, fatal or otherwise, and takes the time to make them all real people, to make the impact Whitman had on the town and the campus palpable and real.

Marlee McLeod's e-book *Charles Whitman – The Texas Tower Sniper* (Court TV, 2005) is not as comprehensive as LaVergne's book, but does provide a good general overview of the case. It's available free of charge at the crimelibrary.com website.

Ramiro Martinez's autobiography *They Call Me Ranger Ray* (Rio Bravo, 2004) covers his entire law enforcement career, not just the events of August 1, 1966, but it does include a first-hand account of his part in bringing Whitman's rampage to an end.

The cover feature in the August 2006 issue of *Texas Monthly* is a whole series of riveting first-hand accounts, gathered by journalist Pamela Colloff, called "96 Minutes."

As with most famous American crimes there are lengthy articles on the Whitman case in both Carl Sifakis's *Encyclopedia of American Crime* (Facts on File, 1982) and Jay Robert Nash's *Encyclopedia of World Crime* (CrimeBooks, 1990).

THE TEXAS SNIPER IN FICTION

Every once in a while, a novel predicts in fiction something that actually comes to pass in real life. Over a century ago, for example, an otherwise obscure writer named Morgan Robertson wrote a book called *Futility* (Mansfield, 1898) about a huge, supposedly unsinkable ocean liner that sinks on its maiden voyage after crashing into an iceberg on a foggy April night. Fourteen years later, on a foggy April night, a huge, supposedly unsinkable ocean liner on it maiden voyage did just that. In descriptions of the vessel, its size, capacity, crew, etc., Robertson was uncannily accurate. The name of the real-life ship was, of course, the *Titanic*. The name of Robertson's fictional ship? The *Titan*.

A more recent example is Tom Clancy's Jack Ryan spy novel, *Debt of Honor* (Putnam, 1994), in which an airliner is used as a bomb to destroy a famous American building. In Clancy's book it's the US Capital, not the World Trade Center, that is leveled, and it's Japanese nationalists, not Islamic terrorists, behind the plot. Nevertheless, the parallels are unsettling, and Clancy's book preceded the actual attack by seven years.

So perhaps it's not so surprising to learn that a paperback original thriller by a writer named Ford Clark anticipates Whitman's crimes. Ted Weeks, the psychopathic sniper in Clark's *The Open Square* (Gold Medal, 1962) is, like Whitman, a military-trained sharpshooter. Like Whitman, he was raised by a perfectionist disciplinarian father. Like Whitman he carries an arsenal of weapons to his perch, along with food, water, hundreds of rounds of ammo, etc.

Ultimately, like Whitman, Weeks is killed and his rampage ended by members of a police force headed by a chief named Miles.

There were a number of "mad sniper" novels and movies that appeared in the wake of the havoc caused by Whitman, but oddly, few had quite as many real-life parallels as the book that anticipated the sniper attacks by four years.

Peter Bogdanovich's first film, *Targets* (Paramount, 1968), for which he wrote the script as well as directed, is about a sniper deliberately patterned on Whitman who mounts his attack on a drive-in movie theater instead of a college campus. An old-time horror movie star, Basil Or-lock (played by old-time horror movie star Boris Karloff) is the one who ends the murders, rather than the police.

Some of the books apparently inspired by, if not directly based on, the Whitman case are Jack Pearl's *A Time to Kill... A Time to Die* (Norton, 1971), Maj Sjowall's and Per Wahloo's *The Abominable Man* (Pantheon, 1972) and its film version *The Man on the Roof* (Svensk Filmindustri, 1977), and George LaFountaine's *Two-Minute Warning* (McCann, 1975) and its identically titled film version (Universal, 1976).

The only fictional depiction that I'm aware of that is based directly on the case is the previously mentioned 1975 NBC TV-movie. Called *The Deadly Tower*, it was written by William Douglas Lawford, and directed by Jerry Jameson, and starred Richard Yniguez as Martinez, and in a casting coup, Kurt Russell, whose career to that point con-sisted of playing precisely the kind of all-American boy that Whitman seemed to be, as Whitman. Released on VHS under the title *Sniper* (not to be confused with the military drama starring Tom Berenger), *The Deadly Tower* is a tremendously exciting, well-acted, well-directed ac-tion drama, expertly depicting the fear and horror Whitman sowed on that day. Moreover, it changed the course of Russell's career, making it possible for him to break out of the wholesome Disney image he'd become shackled with.

What it didn't do was stick particularly close to the facts of the case. Houston McCoy, for example, is not present at all, his place in the dra-ma taken by a fictional character named C.T. Foss, played by Paul Carr, who at the crucial moment aims his shotgun at Whitman but freezes and doesn't fire a single round, leaving it up to Martinez to end things single-handedly. McCoy was known to be very upset about this film.

"They made me look like Gomer Pyle," he said.

Martinez, who at least came off looking heroic, was not pleased with the film either. His wife was depicted as a frail, timid Chicana, who hates her husband's job, rather than the blonde, blue-eyed, robust German-American girl who was always so supportive of his career. And scenes of the racism Martinez had to endure at the hands of his fellow APD officers were, Martinez said, totally fabricated.

As mentioned earlier, both officers sued. Martinez won, or at least muscled the producers into a settlement. McCoy lost.

Why was Martinez built up at the expense of McCoy? Because the film's producer, Antonio Calderon, had an agenda.

"The most positive aspect of this of this picture is that for this first time in the history of television, the subject and hero will be a Chicano," he told one interviewer.

Apparently Calderon had forgotten about TV shows like the swash-buckler *Zorro* (ABC, 1957-59) or the fact-based western series *The Nine Lives of Elfego Baca* (ABC, 1958-60), but be that as it may, he wanted a Latino hero and a Latino who had a non-Latino wife, who didn't chafe under the yoke of racism, or who shared the heroic credit with a West Texas cowboy just wasn't part of the program.

Changing the facts to suit the needs of the story is one thing. Shakespeare did it. John Ford did it. Jack Webb did it. It's almost inevitable when real life is being fictionalized. As Max Allan Collins has said, God's a great storyteller, but a lousy plotter. That's why He created writers.

But changing the facts to suit a political agenda, and, in consequence, depicting a brave man who did his duty well as a man who froze when it came to crunch?

Well, that's something else.

DEATH IMITATES ART

Murder Down Under

One of Donald E. Westlake's Dortmunder novels, *Jimmy the Kid* (Simon & Schuster, 1974), tells the story of a gang of criminals who use a mystery novel as the blueprint for their crime and manage to screw it up to comic effect. With Westlake's typical flair for self-referential humor, the book that Dortmunder and his colleagues use as a guide is a gangster novel by a writer named Richard Stark, who is of course Westlake himself under another persona.

Bill Pronzini's *Undercurrent* (Random, 1973), an early entry in his popular series about a San Francisco private detective whose name we never learn, also uses the device of a criminal gang using the plot of a long-forgotten pulp mystery novel as a model for an actual crime.

In real life, there are several instances of criminals who have based their crimes on plots from crime fiction. The method for securing and immobilizing victims used by the villain of Patricia Cornwell's award-winning debut novel, *Postmortem* (Scribner, 1990), itself based on a real-life serial killer case, was apparently copied by a murderer in Sarasota, Florida, approximately a year after the book's publication.

Similarly, when the film version (United Artists, 1972) of Ed McBain's 87th Precinct novel *Fuzz* (Doubleday, 1968) was shown on network television, two viewers were inspired to imitate the crimes of characters from the book and film who wandered the city at night setting homeless people on fire.

The notion that a fictional crime conceived as a vehicle for entertainment might have been used as the model for a real crime must be nightmarish for any crime writer who has ever had to face such a prospect.

In one early case, the fictional crime used by a mystery writer at the very beginning of his career was actually put into practice before the book for which the crime was devised had even been published. The writer wound up being a witness at the real-life criminal's trial, and in more than one newspaper, accounts of that trial ran simultaneously with serialized installments of the novel.

The writer's name was Arthur William Upfield.

He had been born in 1888 in Gosport, on the south coast of England, the oldest son of James Upfield, a successful businessman. To his father's chagrin, young Arthur showed little aptitude for business. What Arthur wanted to do was write. Indeed, at the age of 12 or 13, he had already completed a 100,000-word novel.

Perhaps Mr. Upfield could be forgiven for not seeing much potential in his son's first literary effort. On the other hand, the fact that such an ambitious project could be brought to completion at such an early age should have been an indication that he had potential, but this was not recognized at the time.

When Arthur was 16, his father got him a position as an apprentice with a real estate firm. Arthur did not prove to have the stuff of which successful estate agents are made. Instead of concentrating on learning the rudiments of his new profession, he set to work on another novel, a blood and thunder thriller about the conquest of Europe by hordes of Asiatic invaders that, in some respects, prefigured Sax Rohmer's Fu Manchu novels which would appear some years later. Diverted by the imaginary Yellow Peril he had created, he failed the required examination for an estate agent's license.

James Upfield had four other sons, all of whom showed more promise than Arthur. He decided to waste no more time on the offspring who had proved such a disappointment. In 1911, he packed young Arthur off to Australia, a destination he had chosen primarily because it seemed far enough away from England that Arthur would never be able to save enough money to return.

Arthur worked at a number of occupations over the next three years. When World War I started in 1914, he entered military service as a member of the Australian Imperial Force and saw combat action at Gallipoli, Egypt, and France. When the Armistice was declared, he returned to England where his family, proud of his Army record and pleased that he'd been able to provide for himself in the years prior to the War, welcomed him with what must have seemed to Arthur an unexpected warmth.

He obtained a safe position as the private secretary to a retired military officer but found that a settled life in his native country was not for him. Within a short time he resigned his position and returned to his adopted land, Australia. For the next few years he wandered the country, working at a variety of jobs. In his spare time, he returned to the profession that his father had so disdained, and wrote.

During the 1920s he managed to sell two novels. The second, *The Barrakee Mystery*, eventually published in the United States as *The Lure of the Bush* (Doubleday, 1965), was a crime novel that featured a most unusual detective, Inspector Napoleon Bonaparte of the Queensland Police. Half-European and half-Aboriginal, Bonaparte was modeled on an educated half-caste named Leon Wood with whom Upfield had formed a close friendship during his wandering days. Wood, known as "Tracker Leon" because he often worked as a police tracker, had been raised at a Christian mission school after being found next to his dead mother as a baby. Upfield appropriated several details of Wood's life in constructing the fictional background of his detective.

Upfield was convinced that Bonaparte was a character who could make his fortune but *The Barrakee Mystery* hadn't been as big a success as he'd hoped.

By 1929, unable to support himself solely from his writing income, Upfield had settled near the tiny village of Murchison in the state of Western Australia and obtained a position as a fence-rider, assigned to a stretch of the 2000-mile Rabbit Proof Fence, built along the eastern border of Western Australia and designed to guard the agricultural output of the state from the verminous rabbits that had been introduced to the continent in the 1850s.

During his tenure as a fence rider, Upfield began plotting his second Bonaparte novel, *The Sands of Windee* (London House, 1959). What Upfield needed was a foolproof method for disposing of the body of a murder victim. One night, gathered around a campfire by the fence with several friends and co-workers, Upfield began a discussion about the best way to eradicate any trace of a murder victim. One of the men suggested simply burning the body several times, grinding whatever bone matter was left into powder, then spreading the ashes and powder to the wind. Upfield agreed that this might suffice and adopted that method in his manuscript.

Another member of the group, known to them all as "Snowy" Rowles, also took note of the method described. Rowles's real name was John Thomas Smith, and before adopting the Rowles persona he'd racked up a fairly impressive police record.

Over the next few months three men, Jim Ryan, George Lloyd, and Louis Carron all mysteriously vanished.

Detective Sergeant Harry Manning of the Western Australian Police was dispatched from Perth to investigate the disappearances. A methodical investigator and an expert tracker, Manning was able to trace at least one of the men, Louis Carron, to a spot where he found the remains of an old campfire. Sifting through the ashes, Manning found several small pieces of skeletal material, a few teeth that appeared to be human, and a gold wedding band with a peculiar flaw.

Manning turned the organic material over to the state pathologist, Dr. W.S. McGillivray, who determined that the skeletal remains were human. With the help of Carron's dentist, McGillivray was able to establish that the teeth found by Manning had belonged to Carron.

In the novel, Bony was able to trace the victim and ultimately to solve the crime, after discovering a small metallic object that had not been destroyed when the body was burned, a trepanning disc that had been surgically implanted into the victim's skull after he'd sustained injuries to his head during military service. In real life, a metallic object that had escaped destruction also proved to be a vital clue. Manning traced the wedding ring to a jeweler in Auckland, New Zealand. The unusual flaw stemmed from the fact that the eighteen carat gold ring had been resized, and soldered with nine carat gold. The error was never corrected and the flaw made the ring unique. The jeweler was able to confirm that that particular ring belonged to Carron.

Eventually, Snowy Rowles was tracked down and arrested. In 1932 he was put on trial for the murder of Carron. Upfield was called as a witness to describe the conversation in which he, Rowles, and others, had discussed methods for disposing of the body of a murder victim.

All Australia was avidly following accounts of the trial. One paper in particular, the *Western Mail*, was providing daily accounts of the trial. The *Mail* had also obtained serialization rights to *The Sands of Windee* so that readers could not only follow the course of the actual trial on a day-to-day basis, but also the fictional story that had inspired the crime.

Rowles, on the basis of the forensic evidence and Upfield's testimony, was convicted and executed.

Upfield's career, bolstered by the publicity he had received through his connection to the infamous crime, began an upswing and within a short time was able to support himself on nothing but his income from the Napoleon Bonaparte novels.

It was hardly the lift Upfield would have wanted for his career but he was a pragmatist, and he took full advantage. In the course of the next three-and-a-half decades, Upfield would become one of the world's most honored mystery writers, and his Bonaparte mysteries would be sold all over the world. And a good part of his success was due to a conversation over a late night campfire that a man with murder in his heart happened to be listening to.

No trace of Ryan or Lloyd was ever found, but Rowles had already been hanged for the murder of Carron, and, as Sam Spade once succinctly noted, they can only hang you once.

FURTHER READING

Upfield was contracted to write a short account of the Rowles case for a small Australian publisher. The original book, a paperback original appearing in 1934, is very difficult to find now. A recent American edition of *The Murchison Murders* (McMillan, 1987) preserves Upfield's account of the case between hard covers and also reprints three articles Upfield wrote for the Australian magazine *Walkabout*.

The most comprehensive book about the Snowy Rowles case is undoubtedly Terry Walker's *Murder on the Rabbit Proof Fence* (Hesperian, 1993). Walker, a long-time Upfield fan, researched the case at length, and his book is regarded as the definitive account.

An article for the November 2002 issue of the Australian magazine *Quadrant*, Rod Moran's "Grasping at the Straws of 'Evidence,'" is actually about another case altogether, the alleged massacre of aboriginal tribesmen by members of the Australian police in the 1920's. Moran spends quite a bit of time describing the Rowles case and the forensic evidence used to convict Rowles, in order to debunk what he regards as an unfounded myth about the so-called "massacre." The article is also available on-line.

THE ROWLES CASE IN FICTION

As noted earlier, *The Sands of Windee* was serialized in an Australian newspaper at the same time Rowles's 1932 trial, having already appeared in book form in the UK in 1931. Oddly, though the Bonaparte novels were quite popular in the United States, there was no American edition of the book for nearly thirty years. Even more oddly, the novel was not published in book form in Australia for nearly thirty years.

Upfield's third Bonaparte novel, *Mr. Jelly's Business*, was serialized in Australian journals in 1933. If Rowles was basing his real-life crime on *The Sands of Windee*, then, in *Mr. Jelly's Business*, Upfield seemed to be returning the favor, using several elements from Rowles's real-life crime for the novel.

It's set in the vicinity of a village similar to Murchison, where Bonaparte, working undercover to investigate a mysterious disappearance, is posing as a fence-rider for Western Australia's Rabbit Inspection Department, the same job Upfield had when Louis Carron and the others dropped out of sight. As in the real-life case, the murderer makes an unsuccessful attempt to hide his crime by burning the body, but just as Detective Sergeant Manning was too clever for the real-life killer, so Detective Inspector Bonaparte is too clever for Upfield's fictional one.

Mr. Jelly's Business appeared in book form in 1937 and six years later, under the title *Murder Down Under* (Doubleday, 1943), it became the first Bonaparte novel to be published in the United States.

In the only short story to feature Inspector Bonaparte, "Wisp of Wool and Disc of Silver" (*Ellery Queen's Mystery Magazine*, December 1979), Upfield recycled both the method of disposing of the body of a murder victim, and the clue by which Bony solves the crime, from *The Sands of Windee*. Constructed as an "inverted mystery," the reader knows who the murderer is before the detective, and sees the murder committed, so that the interest becomes, not figuring out whodunit, but observing the duel of wits between criminal and sleuth (in the manner of an episode of the popular TV series, *Columbo*). As in the novel, Bony identifies the victim by means of a metallic trepanning disk inserted into the victim's skull during surgery. Unlike the somewhat sympathetic killers in the original novel who were declared by Bony to have been "justified" in their actions, the murderer in the short story is a vicious, unrepentant villain. In other words, he was more like Snowy Rowles.

Upfield wrote this story in 1948, and submitted it to *EQMM* for a short story contest the magazine was running that year. For some reason, the file containing the manuscript was misplaced, and the story wasn't published until 1979, a decade and a half after Upfield's death. Upfield probably felt safe reusing so many elements from *The Sands of Windee* because he was submitting the story to an American magazine and, though the Bony series had proved popular in the US, *The Sands of Windee* had not been among the novels reprinted in the States. In fact there would be no American edition of *The Sands of Windee* until 1959. And, rather than being published by Doubleday, Upfield's regular American publisher, that edition would be published by a relatively small press called British Book Centre, which specialized in reprinting British books for US readers.

"Wisp of Wool and Disc of Silver" has been reprinted in *Ellery*

Queen's Crime Cruise Round the World (Doubleday, 1981) edited by Eleanor Sullivan, in *Best Australian Mystery Stories – Dead Witness* (Penguin, 1990) edited by Stephen Knight, and in Upfield's posthumously published short story collection *Up and Down Australia* (Lulu, 2008).

Some two decades after the actual Murchison murders, Upfield used another element of the real-life case for his fifteenth Bonaparte novel, *The New Shoe* (Doubleday, 1951). Fascinated by Sergeant Manning's tracing of Carron's wedding ring (and thus Carron's identity) by its unique resizing flaw, Upfield has Bonaparte trace the identity of an unknown man, whose murdered corpse is found hidden in a lighthouse, by tracing a wedding ring with a similar flaw to the jeweler who made the repair.

In 2009, the Australian Broadcasting Corporation ran a made-for-TV movie titled *3 Acts of Murder* which dramatized the case. Directed by Rowan Woods from a script by Ian David, it starred Robert Menzies as Upfield, Luke Ford as Rowles, and Nicholas Hope as Sergeant Manning. The film aired to good reviews and solid ratings and went on to win one Australian Film Institute award and to be nominated for three others.

It's available on DVD, but only in Australia. Thanks to the 'Net, that's not really a major problem, but if you do get it, you will need an all-region player, since Australian television uses the "Phase Alternating Line" (PAL) mode while American television uses the "National Television System Committee" (NTSC) mode.

A FOOL FOR A CLIENT

Legal Mysteries

He was human sludge. A con man, a thief, an armed robber, an abductor, a violent sexual predator, who never cared a damn about anyone but himself. Yet millions of people all over the world would come to regard him as a victim.

He was actually a man of high intelligence with a creative bent who would write four books in his short life and who, had he turned his talents and mental abilities to legal pursuits, would likely have made a comfortable living. Yet he became a professional criminal who, for a time, was the man most feared by the California public and the man most wanted by California law enforcement.

He died in San Quentin's lethal gas chamber. Yet, as far as is known, he never actually killed anyone. Certainly, he was never charged with or convicted of killing anyone.

And to a large degree, the reason he was executed was not so much because he was guilty of the heinous (if non-lethal) crimes that had landed him on Death Row, though he almost certainly was, but because he was too arrogant to consider the possibility that a professional lawyer might have done a better job of defending him against those charges than he could do himself.

There is an old saying that a lawyer who represents himself has a fool for a client. No one proved the wisdom of that proverbial adage better than Caryl Chessman, the notorious "Red Light Bandit."

In 1921, he was born in St. Joseph, Michigan. Soon after, his family moved to California where Caryl's father, Serl, found work in the film industry.

But when the Depression hit, Serl Chessman lost his movie job and had to support his family by a series of odd jobs. A car accident left Caryl's mother, Hallie, paralyzed from the waist down, and left Caryl with a broken nose that would, in adulthood, give him a tough, rugged, somewhat threatening appearance. The family's financial situation, already stretched by the economic crisis engulfing the entire planet, was exacerbated by the ensuing medical bills. Serl, driven to extremes, unsuccessfully attempted suicide to provide Hallie and Caryl with the financial security that his life insurance would provide. He'd eventually rally to start a successful business.

Caryl, in high school by this time, was beginning his life of crime. He started small, stealing items of negligible value from unlocked homes more for the thrill than from any hope of financial gain. The next step was bike thefts or thefts of sports equipment, items to be shared by other members of the *ad hoc* youth gang he was part of. Eventually, he stole a car, which resulted in his first arrest at the age of 16.

While waiting to be booked at Juvenile Hall, Chessman calmly and easily escaped out of the low-security institution, an act that apparently swelled his self-confidence. He decided to go for bigger things, breaking into a drug store that same night. The police caught him in the act. Now a car thief, an escapee, and a burglar, Caryl Chessman had graduated from minor league delinquent to full-fledged professional outlaw.

He was sent to a rural juvenile facility in Little Tujunga in the San Fernando Valley but escaped again. This time he stayed at large for three days before getting picked up for loitering.

He was then sent to a higher security facility, the state reform school in Whittier, California, but once more escaped after two weeks. Re-arrested within days, he was sent to an even more hard-core juvenile institution, Preston Industrial School, fifty miles north of Stockton. Not a place he could just walk away from. And even if he did break out, he was in the back of beyond with no place to go. The best course to take was to work his way out by being a model inmate. He volunteered for extra chores, made a point of attending church twice a week, and stayed out of trouble, all of which turned a fourteen month sentence into seven.

In a short time, he was under arrest again, once more for car theft as well as credit card fraud, and was back at Preston. This time he did the full fourteen months. As a two-timer, he was not eligible to earn an early release.

18 years old when he got out in 1939, Chessman made a show of trying to go straight, helping out at his father's business, marrying a nice girl from his old high school. He claimed to be attending night school at UCLA and his bride and parents were gratified that Chessman was finally making an effort to better himself.

Actually, rather than going to college, Chessman had organized a gang of stick-up men who'd eventually be dubbed the "Boy Bandits." The nights he was supposedly in class, he and his gang were robbing liquor stores, four or five every week. On one occasion, when police caught them caught red-handed in a stolen car, Chessman and his gang managed to overpower the cops, steal their guns, and use their prowl car as a getaway vehicle.

Spurred by the embarrassment, law enforcement agencies in the Los Angeles area started taking proactive measures to trap the gang. Glendale Police and L.A. County Sheriff's detectives were working together to mount a massive stakeout operation, planting officers in a dozen different liquor stores.

Caught in the act during their next robbery, Chessman and his henchmen attempted to shoot their way clear. Two of the stakeout cops were wounded, as was one of the gangsters. Miraculously no one died. Chessman was now an adult offender.

Charged with thirty-nine different felonies, Chessman bargained for a deal. Turning in the two members of his gang still at large, he was allowed to plead guilty to four counts of robbery and one count of assault with a deadly weapon. He drew sixteen years to life at San Quentin.

"Big Q" was not a place you could easily escape from like Little Tujunga or Whittier, nor was it a place you could earn your way out of by going to church or volunteering for clean-up duty like Preston. The best he could hope to do was make his time comparatively easy. His IQ tested out at 128, in the "very superior" range, and his reading comprehension and written communication skills were impressive. Shortly after his arrival, Chessman was given a job in the prison's education building, teaching reading skills to illiterate inmates. In short order, he was given a job as a clerk to the warden himself. Ultimately, he'd earn a transfer to California's experimental "prison without walls," Chino in San Bernardino County.

Chino was run on the honor system. And a surprisingly large number of the inmates there actually kept their promise, and made no attempt to escape. Caryl Chessman was not one of them.

Blessed with an opportunity to turn his life around in an institution that was dedicated to putting men who'd gone wrong back on the right path, Chessman broke his word and walked out ten weeks after his arrival.

He was caught three weeks later. In those ensuing three weeks, he'd managed with an accomplice to steal a car and to burgle several homes

Chessman wheeled and dealed again, pleading guilty to one charge of burglary in exchange for having the other charges dropped. Five years were added to the sixteen-to-life he'd been serving when he escaped from Chino.

Convicted of multiple felonies and with a record that made him an obvious escape risk, Chessman was sent to California's "Big Max," Folsom Prison, where the worst of the worst did their time.

Chessman decided to play it smart, serving his sentence quietly, making no waves. After three years he had an unblemished disciplinary record and, with a convincing story about how his parents were both suffering from medical problems, he was able to persuade the prison board to let him out early. He was ordered to serve one more year, after which he'd be released on a parole of eleven years. "Twenty-one-to-life" had been shortened to seven. In effect, he'd pulled off yet another escape, this time with the complicity of the California Department of Corrections. By January of 1948, one month after his release, he'd embarked on the crime wave that would make him infamous, yet, ironically, transform him into a sympathetic figure for anti-death-penalty activists all over the world.

He stole a gray, late model Ford, the same kind of vehicle that was being used as a patrol car by many police forces in the Los Angeles area. Less than a week later, he committed the first of the crimes that would earn him the sobriquet "The Red Light Bandit."

Thomas Bartle, a local dentist, was driving on the Pacific Coast Highway with his date, Ann Plaskowitz, after an evening out. A car pulled behind him and shined a red spotlight at him. Believing he must have committed some moving violation without realizing it, Dr. Bartle pulled over. A tall man in a tan uniform walked up to the driver side and asked Bartle for his identification. Bartle pulled his wallet from his pocket, started to slide out his driver's license and suddenly found himself staring down the barrel of a .45 caliber semi-automatic pistol.

"Just give me the money," the *faux* cop demanded. Bartle handed over all his cash, fifteen bucks, then after the gunman fled drove to the nearest California Highway Patrol station to report the robbery.

This was the first of a series of hold-ups following the same pattern. The apparent patrol car, would either pull over a car with a young couple in it or brace a young couple parked in one of the many scenic overlooks to be found along the highway system of the L.A. area and steal their cash. Because of the style of the car, the red spotlight, and the tan, uniform-like clothing of the robber, the couple would believe that they were being approached by a policeman and were thus able to be taken by surprise.

By the third robbery, he varied his M.O. a bit. The victims this time were Jarnigan Lea, a professional military man, and Regina Johnson, the wife of a neighbor of Lea's. Lea had invited Regina, her husband Harry, and their daughter, out for a drive. Harry declined and their daughter was behind in her schoolwork, but Regina, a recovering polio victim who hadn't been able to go out much while her illness crippled her, was encouraged by both Lea and her husband to go ahead.

Chessman, in his phony cop uniform, driving his phony cop car, had added a bandanna mask to his "Red Light Bandit" ensemble. And this time he decided he wanted something more than money.

After forcing Lea to hand over fifty dollars, he ordered Regina out of the car.

"You're coming with me," he said.

Ordering Lea to stay put, he dragged Regina into his car and forced her to orally copulate him. Then, after stealing a five dollar bill from her purse, he shoved her out of the car and drove off.

So far there had been three holdups, and in one of them the woman had been forced to accompany the robber and then sexually attacked. Patrols by both the LAPD and the LA County Sheriff's Office were stepped up. Aside from the viciousness of the crimes, officers of both agencies were incensed that the robber was pretending to be a policeman to accomplish his crimes.

Two days went by without another robbery. Then the car with the makeshift red spotlight approached a vehicle parked high up on Mulholland Drive. Inside were a young college student, Frank Hurlburt, and his date, Mary Alice Meza, a girl he'd met at church.

"Stickup," said Chessman, shoving the barrel of the Colt .45 at Hurlburt. When the undergrad said he had no money, Chessman said, "I'll just take your girl, then." With that, he dragged Mary Alice out of Hurlburt's car and over to his. When she was secure in the front seat, Chessman noticed that Hurlburt had started his car and was driving away at an increased speed. With the frightened Mary Alice seated beside him, Chessman overtook Hurlburt, driving him off the side of the road before he could reach help.

Chessman, with Mary Alice still his prisoner, then drove around the Mulholland Hills for some twenty minutes before finding a place remote and private enough for his purposes. He stopped, and ordered Mary Alice to strip.

Knowing what was on his mind, she protested that she was having her period and proved it by showing him her panties with a Kotex pad inserted. He ordered her to lie down on the back seat, stomach down, and unsuccessfully attempted both anal intercourse and vaginal intercourse from the rear. Mary Alice again protested and told him that she was still a virgin.

Finally, he pulled Mary Alice from the car, forced her onto her knees and, as he had with Regina Johnson, demanded that she orally copulate him. When he was finished, he allowed her to dress and then, unexpectedly, drove her close to her home.

Four robberies, two with sexual violence. And since the two cases involving sexual violence also involved forcing the victims to accompany their attacker at the point of a gun, certain important legal technicalities would ultimately come into play

Three days later, Chessman changed his tactics again. Rather than mugging young couples parked in "lovers' lane" parking spots (and sometimes sexually violating the female), he and an accomplice, later identified as David Knowles, entered a clothing store in Redondo Beach, a suburb of LA, and robbed the cash register of over $200. The owner, Melvin Waisler, and his employee, Joe Lescher, were forced at gunpoint to accompany one of the robbers from the main part of the store to a back room where they were relieved of their wallets, adding another $38 to the robber's take. When Waisler tried to sneak a closer look at one of the robbers, he was clubbed on the head from behind by the other. As with the two female victims who were forced to accompany their attacker, forcing Waisler and Lescher to go from one room to another would turn out to have serious legal implications.

An hour later, LAPD Officers Robert May and John Reardon, cruising near the intersection of Hollywood Boulevard and Vermont Avenue, saw a car that fit the description of the vehicle being used by the "Red Light Bandit."

May and Reardon followed the gray Ford for a few blocks and watched it pull into a gas station on Vermont as if to fill up. Instead of getting gas, the car stopped for a few moments then pulled out, now going in the opposite direction. May and Reardon made a u-turn and continued to follow the Ford. Deciding to stop and identify the driver and passenger, Reardon turned on the red spotlight of his car, and signaled for the Ford to pull over. Instead, the suspect car accelerated. May called in the pursuit on the radio, flipped on the siren, and the chase was on.

By the time the two cars were again passing Hollywood Boulevard, they were going at more than 60 miles per hour. Other police cars were joining the chase or setting up makeshift roadblocks at intersections towards which the cars were heading. Shots were being exchanged between the speeding vehicles.

At the intersection of Vermont and 6th, the occupants of the Ford saw two patrol cars blocking their way. Another car blocked a side street to keep them from turning off. The driver of the Ford, Chessman, tried to make a u-turn but found the street too narrow. Reardon told May to hang on and ended the chase by ramming the Ford. Chessman exited with the intention of shooting it out but fumbled with his Colt and dropped it. Unable to make a fight of it, he took off on foot but was overtaken and tackled by Reardon, who soon had Chessman in cuffs. Officers from the other units had, in the meantime, placed Knowles under arrest.

The car came back stolen. A search turned up a piece of red hair ribbon and a wire shaped into a circle just wide enough to hold something in place over the white spotlight on the driver's side. Could that "something" have been a piece of red cellophane or translucent red cloth? The suspects were taken to the Hollywood Station to be booked.

Detective Lieutenant Colin Forbes, in charge of the "Red Light Bandit" case, was something of an LAPD legend. He was still on active duty despite a bullet lodged near his spine that he'd received during a shootout more than a year earlier. Notified that a suspect who was a close match for his quarry was in custody, he reported to the Hollywood Division the next morning and went over the evidence uncovered by May and Reardon with his two partners, Sergeants Arnold Hubka and Al Goosen. He recognized the hair ribbon as the one Mary Alice said she had been wearing the night of the robbery, which she had apparently lost while forced to service Chessman. Other items, like a penknife and the .45, also matched the description of items carried by the offender.

Forbes started interviewing Chessman. In fairly short order, Chessman copped to the first "Red Light" robbery, then to the robbery of the clothing store in Redondo Beach, then finally to the second "Red Light" robbery. Oddly ignoring chronology, he'd admitted to the first robbery first, the fifth robbery second, and to the second robbery third, but nimbly avoided mentioning the third and fourth crimes, the robbery of Jarnigan Lea and Regina Johnson, and the robbery of Frank Hulbert and Mary Alice Meza. He seemed to be carefully avoiding any mention of the hold-ups in which sexual violence was a factor. Perhaps he hoped that, in their desire to get a quick closure, the police would allow him to admit to the three less serious cases, then simply close out the other two without actually charging him.

That wasn't going to happen. The legal "technicality" that was about to come into play was how the California Penal Code defined kidnapping. You didn't have to take a person that far. You just had to force him or her to go "a substantial distance," specified as being at least fifteen feet, or from one room to another. Regina Johnson had been forced from one car to another. That might count. Waisler and Lescher at the clothing store had been forced from one room into another. That probably did count.

Mary Alice Meza had been forced into a car by the Red Light Bandit, driven around Mulholland Hills for close to a half hour, forced to sexually gratify the Bandit, then finally driven near her home. All told, she'd been held captive for more than three hours.

That definitely counted.

After interviewing him, Forbes and his partners took Chessman for a ride past the sites of the Lea/Johnson and Hulbert/Meza robberies. Chessman's face froze. Forbes, looking at the expression on Chessman's face, knew that Chessman knew why they were driving him past those scenes. And Chessman knew that Forbes knew.

Then they went by the home of Mary Alice. She was in a bad way. As a result of the stress she'd undergone, her face had swollen to twice its normal size, as though she had the mumps. And she was an emotional wreck. Forbes spoke with her, gently persuading her to look out the window. She somehow summoned the strength to do so, immediately identifying Chessman as her abductor.

This was a perfectly legal identification in 1948. It would not fly now, but at the time Forbes was not violating any principle of law at either the state or federal level.

On the way back to the station, Chessman denied having anything to do with the Meza or Johnson attacks. The one who pulled those jobs, he insisted, was a guy named Terranova. In fact, he'd gotten the idea for the red spotlight robberies from Chessman.

Shortly after they returned the station, Jarnigan Lea and Regina Johnson arrived, summoned to make a possible identification. Regina took a look at Chessman and immediately identified him.

"Why did you do those things to me?" she demanded.

Chessman just looked away and refused to answer.

When Chessman's photo appeared in the papers, another crime victim was heard from. Donald McCullough, a sales clerk at a clothing store in Pasadena, called the police and identified Chessman as one of the two men who had robbed the store ten days before the first of the Red Light crimes. Later, shown a photo lineup that included a picture of David Knowles, he unhesitatingly picked him out as the second man. The similarities between this robbery of a suburban clothing store, and the robbery in Redondo Beach, were obvious. Forbes had another positive identification and another charge to add to the list.

When Forbes presented his case against Chessman to the DA's Office, he listed eight counts of robbery, one count of grand theft auto, one count of attempted robbery (he'd never actually gotten any cash from Hurlburt), two counts of forced oral copulation, one count of attempted rape (he hadn't successfully completed vaginal penetration of Mary Alice), and four counts of kidnapping. A total of 17 heavy-duty felonies.

Now the district attorney, William Simpson, and his deputy, J. Miller Leavy, who'd be prosecuting the case, had to make a decision. How hard did they want to come down on Chessman?

Section 209 of the California Penal Code, the so-called "Little Lindbergh Law," dealt with aggravated cases of kidnapping. And, in California, an aggravated case of kidnapping was punishable by death. If you kidnapped a person and held him for ransom, that was an aggravated case. If you kidnapped a person who was under 14 years of age (presuming you weren't a biological or legally adopted parent) that was an aggravated case. And if you kidnapped someone in the course of a robbery and then caused your victim bodily harm, that was an aggravated case.

It might seem draconian to some of you (though, frankly, it doesn't to me) that a kidnapping in which the victim was not actually killed was, under certain circumstances, a capital crime. But you have to put yourself in the historical context to understand. The 1927 kidnapping, murder, and dismemberment of little Marion Parker was still a comparatively recent memory to most Californians. And the 1932 kidnapping of Charles Lindbergh, Jr., was an even more recent memory to Americans everywhere. Leaving those two notorious cases aside, in the 1920's and '30's, kidnapping for ransom was a growth industry among professional criminals. Bank robbery, another growth industry, commonly included taking bank employees or customers along in the getaway cars as hostages. In 1931, for example, 279 kidnappings were reported in the United States. Those cases yielded only 69 convictions.

The U.S. Government responded by passing the "Lindbergh Law," making it a federal offense to transport a kidnap victim across state lines, to use interstate communications systems, such as the US Mail, to deliver ransom demands, etc. Following Congress's example, many state legislatures, including California's, passed their own strong anti-kidnapping statutes, their own "Little Lindbergh Laws." And, apparently as a consequence of these new laws, kidnapping suddenly became a much less popular activity within the criminal community. Ransom kidnappings became much more rare and hostage-taking in the course of a robbery less a matter of routine and more a matter of infrequent desperation. Perhaps the laws were draconian, but they worked.

Did the law apply in these cases?

Melvin Waisler's store was held up, then he was forced from one room to another, robbed of his personal cash and pistol-whipped. In other words, he was kidnapped during a robbery and sustained bodily harm. A clear example of the capital crime of aggravated kidnapping.

But how about Regina and Mary Alice?

Their kidnappings had certainly taken place during the course of a robbery. So the question was did sexual violence constitute bodily harm, *per se*?

The California statute, as it stood in 1948, did not specifically include sexual violence, just "bodily harm." On the other hand, neither did it specifically *exclude* sexual violence. And in any case, whether or not a particular act inflicted on a kidnap victim constituted bodily harm was a question of fact for a jury to decide.

Deputy DA Leavy didn't think a jury would have to make that great a cognitive leap to decide that sexual violence was a form of bodily harm. Particularly given the two victims. Mary Alice was, at 17, still a minor, still a virgin, and was suffering severe physical allergic reactions because of her ordeal, as well as serious emotional disturbances. Regina was a polio victim who was still not fully recovered, and she, too, was suffering from her own psychological problems.

Bodily harm? No doubt about it, Leavy decided. Chessman was just the kind of guy the legislators had in mind when they wrote the statute. He was practically a poster boy for the "Little Lindbergh Law."

At his preliminary hearing, Chessman told the judge that he wanted to represent himself. The judge explained that this was Chessman's right under the Sixth Amendment but it was not recommended. He asked Chessman to reconsider. Chessman insisted. And, as a consequence, he pretty much sealed his fate. From that moment on, though he'd be remarkably successful at holding the Reaper at bay for a time, Chessman was a goner.

Chessman was bound over for trial in Department 42, the courtroom of California Superior Court Judge Charles Fricke. A former prosecutor who'd been particularly distinguished in that field, he'd been an equally distinguished member of the bench for more than 20 years. Fair but unflinchingly firm, Fricke could be counted on to give Chessman precisely the same breaks he would have given Clarence Darrow or William Kuntsler. Which is to say, if Chessman insisted on being his own lawyer, he'd be cut no slack because of his lack of familiarity with courtroom procedure.

On April 29, 1948, the trial began with Judge Fricke asking for any preliminary motions.

Chessman moved that he be disqualified from representing himself on the grounds that he was legally insane and asked to be examined by a board of psychiatrists to determine his mental ability to continue the case.

Fricke denied the motion.

Chessman then moved for a continuance until such time the County Jail could be forced to provide him with the law books, subpoena forms and other legal paraphernalia needed to conduct his defense.

Fricke denied the motion.

"When you are in jail," he told Chessman, "there are bound to be certain limitations on your freedom of movement and ability to work which are incidental to being in jail."

Was it the judge's position, Chessman wanted to know, that a defendant lost certain rights when he or she chose to represent himself?

Not in the least, Fricke replied. But it was simply a fact of life that an attorney was free to do certain things a jail inmate was not. If Chessman wanted those things done, he was free to make use of the services of the Public Defender's Office. If not, he'd have to suffer the limitations any other prisoner would have to suffer.

Chessman then reminded the judge of other motions he had made in writing prior to the beginning date of the trial. The judge replied that they weren't made in the proper manner and were, consequently, denied.

Chessman asked how he could be expected to know courtroom procedure if the judge wasn't going to explain it to him. Fricke rather testily pointed out that his role was to preside over a trial, not conduct a law class. He then once more strongly advised Chessman to get himself a real lawyer.

The next morning, a somewhat embarrassed Chessman requested that a public defender be assigned to him.

"But only as an advisor," he added. "I request that I myself remain counsel of record."

For the rest of the trial, Public Defender Al Matthews would be assigned as Chessman's "second chair." For all the good it did Chessman.

The next step was jury selection, and it was during this process that Chessman made perhaps his greatest error of judgment. The jury that was finally seated consisted of eleven women and one man. Chessman did not object to the seating of so many women, despite the advice of Matthews. One didn't have to be an experienced trial lawyer to realize that a predominantly female jury was unlikely to be sympathetic to an accused sex criminal, but Chessman, in his arrogance, believed he'd be able to more easily charm a jury of women than a jury of men.

The first witness for the prosecution was Regina Johnson, who after walking uncertainly up to the stand because of the residual effects of her polio, positively identified Chessman in a clear if quavering voice. When Chessman got up to cross-examine her, he tried to refer to her attacker as a third party. Regina refused to let him get away with it.

"Did this person state what his intentions were in taking you back to his car?" he would ask.

"No," she would reply. "*You* didn't tell me until after I had gotten into your car."

"How long were you in the other car?" he would ask.

"Which car to you mean by 'the other car?'" she'd reply. "Mr. Lea's car or *your* car?"

"Was this person wearing any rings, a wristwatch, anything like that?"

"*You* were wearing gloves."

Every time Chessman referred to the attacker as "he" or "this person," Regina would invariably refer to the attacker as "you," reinforcing her identification in the minds of the jury over and over again.

The very first witness had, all by herself, practically strapped him into the gas chamber and he still had the testimony of Mary Alice Meza to look forward to.

The next five witnesses for the prosecution included victims of the robberies in which there was no sexual attack, police witnesses, and a medical witness providing forensic evidence of Mary Alice's attack.

This set the stage for Mary Alice herself.

She was a much more timid witness that Regina, but no less effective. She also positively identified Chessman as her attacker and, in a voice so quiet it was often difficult to hear her, described her three-hour ordeal in detail.

Chessman decided not to be as confrontational as he'd been with Regina. Instead, he was outwardly courteous. His questions elicited nothing that really helped his case. But despite his outward show of manners, it was clear that his cross-examination was making Mary Alice extremely uncomfortable, and it was also clear, particularly to the women members of the jury, that Chessman was enjoying her discomfort.

Leavy next called two more police witnesses, then had witness testimony from the preliminary hearing read into the record, then rested.

Chessman's case consisted of a series of alibi witnesses. One of these was his mother, Hallie Chessman, whose long ago, crippling injuries in the car accident had gotten progressively worse. She was now slowly dying of spinal cancer and had to be wheeled into the courtroom in a hospital bed. Literally testifying from her deathbed, she intended to do whatever she could to save her boy, with her last breath if necessary.

But however sympathetic the jury may have found her, they didn't find her credible. And as for the other alibi witnesses, they didn't even find them sympathetic.

Chessman's last witness was himself. Directly examined by his "co-counsel," Al Matthews, he again made one more effort to sell the story of "Terranova," the "other" Red Light Bandit, the one who did the really nasty stuff. He also alleged that he'd been beaten while in custody.

After Chessman rested, Leavy put on a few rebuttal witnesses who cast doubt on Chessman's claims of police brutality. This was followed by closing arguments, and final instructions to the jury by Judge Fricke. The jury then retired to deliberate.

Two hours into the second day of deliberation, one of the jurors sent out a note to Judge Fricke asking if it was possible that a man sentenced to life without the possibility of parole, the only penalty short of death allowed if they found Chessman guilty of the aggravated kidnapping charges, might still be released some day.

Judge Fricke replied that the law could change whenever the legislature decided, that sentences could be commuted, and that pardons could even be given. There was no guarantee that life without parole would actually mean the rest of the defendant's natural life.

This might seem like Fricke was stacking the deck. In fact he was giving an answer that was not only honest, but prescient. David Knowles, Chessman's accomplice in the two clothing store robberies, had already been sentenced to life without parole for for the aggravated kidnapping of Melvin Waisler. He'd be released on parole eleven years later.

After further deliberation, the jury found Chessman guilty of all charges that same day, and recommended the death penalty for the aggravated kidnapping of Regina, the death penalty for the aggravated kidnapping of Mary Alice, and life without parole for the aggravated kidnapping of Waisler.

Judge Fricke thanked the jury, set the date of sentencing, and adjourned.

Court Reporter Ernest Perry went home and directly to bed. He'd been laboring through an intense pain in his chest and needed the rest.

That chest pain would turn out to be more than just a passing minor illness. On June 23, two days before Judge Fricke was to pass sentence, Perry died of a heart attack. This would turn out to be a huge break for Chessman, but, typically, he blew it through his own ignorance and arrogance.

On June 25, the court came to order and Judge Fricke asked if there were any legal reasons why sentence should not be passed. Matthews had advised Chessman as strongly as possible to move for a new trial since Perry had died before completing the final transcript from his shorthand notes. The transcript would be crucial for mounting an appeal.

Instead, Chessman rose to say, "The defendant is absolutely innocent of all charges."

"That is an opinion, not a legal cause," said Fricke. "There being no legal cause, it is the judgment of this court . . . that you, Caryl Chessman, be . . . put to death by administration of lethal gas . . . ."

He then went on to prescribe lesser sentences for the lesser crimes.

After the judge had completed the sentencing process, Chessman rose, reminded the court of Perry's death, and moved for a retrial on the basis that California statutes held that if a court reporter died before transcribing all his notes, a new trial must be held.

"Motion denied," said Fricke. "The statute applies only to civil cases, not criminal cases. Furthermore, since this court has completed sentencing of you, the matter of a new trial has now passed from the jurisdiction of this court to the jurisdiction of the California Supreme Court."

Literally a fatal error. Despite the urgent advice of Matthews, Chessman decided to make a melodramatic proclamation of innocence instead of tending to business. Arrogance and ignorance was turning out to be a lethal combination.

By early July, Chessman was safely lodged in Cell 2455 of San Quentin's Death Row. He was determined to get the death penalty reversed. He would succeed in delaying it longer than any other death row inmate to that point in the history of American jurisprudence but, as with the actual trial, his arrogance and ignorance would continually keep the gold ring of a full reversal out of his reach.

While Chessman was settling in at the Death House, Judge Fricke was trying to figure out how to get the transcript of the trial completed. Prosecutor Leavy suggested that Stanley Fraser, a colleague and former roommate of Ernest Perry, be hired to transcribe Perry's notes. The two men used a similar style of short-hand to record testimony and, when they shared an apartment, would occasionally transcribe for each other. The suggestion was adopted and Perry's shorthand notes were turned over to Fraser. Seven months later, Fraser submitted a preliminary draft to Judge Fricke, who suggested some corrections based on his memory. Once the suggested revisions were included, Fraser submitted a final draft, which was accepted and filed. A copy was sent to Chessman at San Quentin.

Chessman was livid that a transcript was prepared without his knowledge or input. He wrote Fricke a long letter, pointing out 200 errors, based on his memory.

Fricke, using Chessman's letter as a guide, conducted a three-day hearing at which he and Fraser made additional corrections based on Chessman's suggestions. Again, Chessman was not present.

When the revised draft was sent to him, Chessman again hit the ceiling. Why wasn't he present at this hearing?

While the war of the transcript was being waged, Chessman acquired another legal "advisor," respected attorney Rosalie Asher, who coached Chessman on how to file appeals at both the state and federal levels. Under her guidance, Chessman filed a motion with the California Supreme Court to "impeach and correct" the transcript.

The motion was denied.

A few months later, the state supremes completed their automatic review of the death sentence and affirmed it. Back at Department 43,

Judge Fricke set March 28, 1952, as the date of execution.

Chessman petitioned the U.S. Supreme Court to review the state supremes' affirmation. Three days before the execution date, Chessman was granted a stay to give the court time to consider his request. Upon consideration, however, the court refused to review the state decision.

Fricke set June 23 as the new execution date. In the meantime, Chessman filed another appeal to the Ninth U.S. Circuit Court of Appeals. Another stay was granted by the local Federal District Court, through which Chessman had to travel on his way to the Appeals Court. Almost a full year later, the Circuit Court affirmed the District Court ruling, which allowed Chessman to make another try at the U.S. Supreme Court. This bought him another eight months but, once more, the top court ultimately rejected his appeal. By this time it was February of 1954. Another execution date, May 14, 1954, was set. Chessman the amateur lawyer, had remarkably delayed the execution of his sentence for nearly six years, a testament to his drive and energy, if not his legal skill.

To this point, Chessman had been able to get courts to listen to his arguments and grant stays of execution well before the date of execution, but he was running out of sympathetic judges. This time he was not able to find one until sixteen hours before his sentence was scheduled to be carried out. It was Judge Thomas Keating, a California Superior Court Judge for Marin County (where San Quentin was located), who granted a last minute stay to allow Chessman time to make another run at the State Supreme Court regarding the matter of the disputed transcript.

The stay was undoubtedly a huge relief for Chessman and his "legal assistant," Rosalie Asher, but a short-lived one. The state supremes immediately rejected the new petition, and Judge Fricke set yet another new date, July 30, 1954.

While these six years were passing, in addition to all his legal work on his own behalf, Chessman had been writing a book about his ordeal. Through Rosalie Asher, he managed to sell it and in May, two months before Chessman's next date with the gas chamber, it hit the book stores. *Cell 2455 Death Row* (Prentice-Hall, 1954) was an immediate best-seller, largely because of Chessman's impending execution. It was also the vehicle by which Chessman started to gain national and international notoriety. *Cell 2455* was the seed from which the "Chessman the Victim" cult grew.

With the royalties from the book starting to pour in, Chessman was able to hire another lawyer to "assist" him. Ben Rice, a well-known advocate, took much of the load off of Rosalie Asher, who'd been working for Chessman on her own time. Rice had a reputation as a fighter and he'd prove it as he worked to delay the impending execution date once more. Judge Keating, the local Marin County jurist who'd granted Chessman his last stay, had taken a severe public shellacking for interfering in the case, and other judges were reluctant to consider the case in that atmosphere.

But with only a few days left before the sentence was to be carried out, Rice learned that Justice Jesse Carter, one of the members of the State Supreme Court who'd been consistently sympathetic to Chessman's arguments, was on a camping vacation in the Trinity Mountains. Hiring a wilderness guide and renting a donkey (Carter was fishing in an area no jeep could reach), Rice made a determined effort to track him down. After searching for three days, Rice and his guide finally located the judge in a remote spot, frying up the day's catch for dinner. Rice pitched his case. Persuaded that Chessman should have one more chance to argue the matter of the disputed transcript to the U.S. Supreme Court, Carter wrote out a stay of execution and handed it to Rice. With less than a day to spare, Rice got back to Sacramento in time to file the stay and delay the execution yet again.

The US Supreme Court denied the appeal, but "without prejudice," which meant that, if Chessman felt he truly had a point to argue, he could start again at the bottom level of the federal judiciary and work back up. Ben Rice and Rosalie Asher immediately filed an appeal at the Federal District Court in San Francisco from which they had to start to get to the Ninth Circuit, and ultimately back to the U.S. Supreme Court. In the meantime, another execution date, January 15, 1955, had been set and the clock was running again.

Four days before that execution date, the Ninth Circuit postponed the execution indefinitely to give it time to consider the appeal. It looked like the Feds were going to take a closer look at Chessman's case.

A closer look didn't necessarily mean a decision helpful to Chessman. On April 7, 1955, the Ninth Circuit rejected his petition. Now it was on to the U.S. Supreme Court for a second time while yet another execution date, July 15, was set.

On July 5, when the nation's top court agreed to hear Chessman's appeal, U.S. Supreme Court Justice Tom C. Clark granted another stay.

When the Court convened in October, Chessman's case was one of the first heard. Finally, Chessman and his legal assistants had managed, just barely, to put together a winning argument. By vote of 5-4, the Court decided that the trial transcript should not have been certified as complete without all parties, including Chessman, being involved.

Almost two years of legal wrangling between Federal and California courts ensued, but in the end Chessman finally had his way. He was going to go back to Los Angeles to argue against the acceptance of the transcript. If he was able to get a new trial, he would almost certainly beat the death sentence even if he was again convicted of the multiple counts of aggravated kidnapping, because in the intervening nine years the sentencing guidelines had changed.

In the meantime, despite a series of roadblocks put up by the California Department of Corrections, Chessman had written a second book, *Trial by Ordeal* (Prentice-Hall, 1955), less a memoir, as his first book had been, than a lengthy polemic against capital punishment, one that even some opponents of the death penalty found rather shallow. It did not have nearly the success of *Cell 2455 Death Row*, particularly without an impending execution to lend it a sense of urgency. But with the advance he got from his publishers, along with the money he received from selling the film rights to *Cell 2455*, Chessman was able to hire private investigators to aid in his case. They'd uncover a heretofore unknown piece of evidence that should have been all Chessman needed to win.

On September 17, 1957, Chessman was finally back at Department 43, facing one of his old adversaries, Deputy District Attorney J. Miller Leavy. His other adversary, Judge Charles Fricke, had been forced to bow out of the drama. He was in the hospital, undergoing surgery for the throat cancer that would shortly kill him. His place was now taken by Judge Walter Evans.

As he had in the trial, Chessman appeared *pro se*, though his attorneys were present for consultation.

The first witness was Stanley Fraser, who swore that the transcript was a true and accurate rendition of Ernest Perry's notes. He was followed by a series of court reporters and stenography experts, who gave differing testimony as to whether it was possible for one party to accurately transcribe the short-hand notes of another.

Chessman then took the stand himself and pointed out what he believed from his own memory of the trial to be several hundred different errors in Fraser's transcription.

Chessman's most important witness, Dr. James Cryst, who had been Fraser's personal physician from 1947 through 1953, took the stand and testified that Fraser had been an alcoholic during that period and that he had been arrested numerous times for drunk driving, for public drunkenness, and for disorderly conduct while drunk. Dr. Cryst's testimony was followed by Mrs. Eva Hoffman, who owned a liquor store in Fraser's neighborhood and who was able to swear that she had seen him drunk on the street numerous times.

It also came out that Fraser was Prosecutor Leavy's uncle by marriage.

The private eyes Chessman had hired had come through. The evidence of Fraser's alcoholism was a bombshell. The family relationship between the prosecutor and the court reporter was interesting, too, though probably not relevant.

But as had happened so often before, Chessman's arrogance and ignorance tripped him up.

After 42 court days, more than twice as many as the original case had consumed, including three days of jury deliberation, Judge Evans was ready to render a decision.

It was not the one Chessman was expecting. After studying the transcript and considering all the testimony, Judge Evans decided that Perry's notes were, in fact, decipherable; that Fraser was competent to transcribe them accurately; that even if the errors Chessman had pointed out were corrected it would not have made a substantial difference to the final product; that Court Reporter Fraser's being Prosecutor Leavy's uncle was not relevant; that the expert testimony by court reporters and stenographers was pretty evenly divided between those who thought Perry's notes could be translated and those who thought they could not and therefore canceled each other out, leaving nothing to consider; and, most importantly, that Fraser's alcoholism was irrelevant because it had never been shown that Fraser had been drinking *while working on Perry's notes*, nor had it been shown that Fraser's affliction had had a deleterious effect on his professional product.

Chessman had made an amateur's mistake. He had introduced the evidence but he had failed to connect it up. That a self-taught jailhouse lawyer could make such an error was not that hard to believe but what about Ben Rice and Rosalie Asher, Chessman's "second and third chairs?" How had they missed it? Were they so used to playing subordinate roles that this had slipped by them?

However it had been allowed it happen, it had happened. Because of his insistence that his legal advisors portray supporting characters while he cast himself in the lead role, Chessman's apparently Heaven-sent chance to get his case retried and with that retrial, win, lose, or draw, the reward of an almost certain ticket off Death Row, had slipped through his fingers yet again.

A new execution date, October 24, 1959, was set.

Back in his cell, continuing to circumvent the bureaucratic road-blocks set up by the prison authorities, Chessman would complete two more books, *The Face of Justice* (Prentice-Hall, 1957), another memoir about his "unconstitutional victimization," and *The Kid Was a Killer* (Gold Medal, 1960), a crime novel about a prizefigher whose killer instinct enables him to prevail in the ring against far more talented boxers. Neither book was especially well-received.

Meanwhile, he knew that time was starting to run out. His strongest legal argument, that the transcript was faulty, had come to nothing. The standard advice of all courtroom advocates is, "When the facts are against you, pound on the law. When the law's against you pound on the facts."

The law was now against him. And "pounding the facts," in Chessman's case, amounted to little more than the oft-repeated refrain of virtually every defendant ever sentenced to a term of imprisonment.

"Some other guy did it!"

He'd been hinting for years that he knew who the real Red Light Bandit was, the man he'd referred to as "Terranova" at his trial, but insisted that it went against his ethics to inform. That Chessman knew the identity of the real culprit but was willing to go to his death without revealing it because of some misguided code rang false to anyone who recalled that he'd wangled a reduced sentence back in his "Boy Bandit" days by naming the members of his gang who were still at large. Chessman's "facts" simply weren't credible.

So if the law and the facts were both against him, what was he left with?

According to the rest of that old aphorism, "Pound the table."

But if he couldn't get into court anymore, he wouldn't even have a table to pound on.

Two days before his next date with death, U.S. Supreme Court Justice William O. Douglas granted a stay to allow Chessman time to file his request that the Court review the entire case. In other words, if Chessman could actually make a convincing case, the Court would examine his claim that "some other guy did it."

But after examining Chessman's writ, the Court, at least five members of it, was unimpressed. Chessman's assertion that the facts of the case were not as they appeared did not move them. And at the U.S. Supreme Court, pounding the table doesn't count for a lot. The justices denied *certiorari* by a vote of 5-4. Chessman's execution was rescheduled, for the eighth time, for February 19, 1960.

He got one more stay for neither legal nor factual reasons, but for political ones. President Eisenhower was making a state visit to South America, and since Chessman's case had, by this time, become an international *cause célèbre*, the State Department requested a postponement until after the President's trips to Uruguay and Brazil had been completed. Governor Pat Brown granted a 60-day stay.

Judge Clement Nye, now the Presiding Judge at Department 43, immediately set a new date, May 2, 1960, one day longer than the 60-day reprieve Governor Brown had ordered.

Pat Brown was an outspoken opponent of the death penalty but his executive power to commute a death sentence was not as absolute as in other states. In order to do so, he needed majority approval from the State Supreme Court, and such permission had, by a 4-3 vote, already been denied.

But with the 60 days President Eisenhower and the U.S. State Department had given him to play with, Brown decided to make an end run around the supremes by getting the law changed. He requested that the State Senate's Judiciary Committee consider a bill completely abolishing the death penalty in California. The 15-member committee held hearings on the proposal but, in the end, voted it down by an 8-7 vote.

5-4 in the U.S. Supreme Court. 4-3 in the California Supreme Court. 8-7 in the State Senate Judiciary Committee. As the days to his final execution date ticked off, Chessman seemed destined, in the words of Maxwell Smart, to continually "miss it by just that much."

On May 2, Chessman's lawyers desperately tried to find someone who'd grant some kind of last minute reprieve. Another appearance before the state supremes was, in another 4-3 decision, unsuccessful.

Undeterred, they immediately made their way to the offices of U.S. District Court Judge Louis Goodman. He, too, was reluctant. They pleaded for just a short delay in order to have time to present new "evidence" (uncovered by a pair of writers for the popular men's magazine, *Argosy*, which had earlier published excerpts from *Cell 2455 Death Row*) that another party was the real Red Light Bandit. The judge said he would ask the prison for a one-hour delay, just long enough for the lawyers to give him a brief overview of this supposed new evidence, but that was all. He told his secretary to call San Quentin.

But by the time she had found the number and made the call, it was too late. Chessman had already been strapped into the chair. The cyanide pellets had already been dropped into the vat of acid below him. The room was already filling with the poisonous gas that would kill him.

Despite the heroic efforts of his lawyers, time had finally run out for Caryl Chessman. Like a cat, he'd turned out to have only nine lives.

Would that one hour have really made a difference? Doubtful. Few people familiar with the case believed Chessman's assertion that "some other guy did it" because few people familiar with Chessman could believe that anyone so supremely self-involved would really have refused as a point of honor to name the guilty party if there had actually been another party to name.

Which left one to conclude that the "other guy" was a mere chimera. A final, unsuccessful attempt at a grand con.

And, in all the worldwide outrage over the fact that a violent criminal had finally met the end that was prescribed by law, and only after, in the years between conviction and execution, having been given more than a fair chance to get his side heard, the fate of the victims was rarely examined.

I can find no information about what happened to Melvin Waisler. Presumably he continued to enjoy the fruits of a successful business and recovered from the blow on the head he'd received during the robbery of his store.

Regina Johnson eventually recovered almost completely from her polio and to a degree from her attack. Her husband, Harry, 25 years older than the 30-ish Regina, died in the ensuing twelve years. Mrs. Johnson eventually met and fell in love with a nice young fellow named Andy Brennan. In the fullness of time, they married. Andy was, of all things, an officer in the LAPD. He was present at Chessman's execution, representing both his wife and his department.

Mary Alice Meza had no representative at the execution, nor was she present herself since she was a patient in Camarillo State Mental Hospital, where she'd spent eight of the previous twelve years. Ultimately, she'd spend the rest of her life there, plagued 'til the day she died by nightmares about the man who'd so brutalized her back in 1948.

A lot of people believe that Caryl Chessman got a raw deal. Personally, when I remember Mary Alice Meza, I believe that he didn't get punished nearly enough.

FURTHER READING

My main research source for this article was Clark Howard's *The True Story of Caryl Chessman* (Crime Library, 2001). Mr. Howard is, of course, well-known as one of the finest writers of short crime fiction currently practicing. He is also a respected true-crime writer, and has won Edgar nominations in that category for books like *Six Against the Rock* (Dial, 1977) and *Zebra* (Marek, 1979). *True Story* first appeared as an e-book on the Crime Library website, which has since evolved into the TruTV website, dropping Howard's piece in the process. It can still be found on the 'Net, but it takes some digging. It's a straightforward, chronological, compulsively readable account, giving (as is Howard's custom) more time to the victims and to the police investigation, than is usually the case in books like this. I would like to see it more widely available and, since the TruTV site is no longer using it, perhaps Mr. Howard can be persuaded to put it between covers or make it available for Kindle or some other e-book reader. If you can find it, I highly recommend it.

Of course, there are all kinds of books and articles about the Chessman case out there besides Mr. Howard's. Chessman's own books about the case have already been mentioned in the body of this article. Others include, but are not limited to, Milton Machlin's and William Read Woodfield's *Ninth Life* (Putnam, 1961), Frank J. Parker's *Caryl Chessman – The Red Light Bandit* (Burnham, 1975), Theodore Hamm's *Rebel and a Cause* (University of California Press, 2001), and Alan Bisbort's *"When You Read This, They Will Have Killed Me"* (Carroll & Graf, 2006).

CHESSMAN IN FICTION

Convict-turned-novelist Edward Bunker, who like Chessman, had been in and out of prison most of his life, got to know Chessman during one of his stays at San Quentin. His book *Little Boy Blue* (Viking,

1981), the story of a young man as he goes from delinquency to full-bore criminality, escaping from a series of penal institution only to be placed in a series of others, is described as an autobiographical novel, but many of the details of the protagonist's life seem to parallel Chessman's. Perhaps Bunker and Chessman led remarkably similar lives or perhaps Bunker worked some of Chessman's experiences, as well as his own, into the work.

Shane Stevens's *By Reason of Insanity* (Simon & Schuster, 1979) tells the story of a serial killer (though the term had not gained common usage at the time the book first appeared) who believes he is the son of Caryl Chessman. I haven't read the book. People who have seem to either love it or hate it. It's been compared favorably to books like Jim Thompson's *The Killer Inside Me* (Lion, 1952) and Joyce Carol Oates's *Zombie* (Dutton, 1995).

Jack Webb made use of Chessman's criminal career at least twice, and probably three times, for his pioneering radio-TV series *Dragnet* (NBC, 1949-59). "The Red Light Bandit," the sixth episode of the radio series, first broadcast on July 14, 1949, is the most obvious lift. For fictional purposes, Joe Friday enacts the role of Lt. Colin Forbes, as well as Officers Reardon and May. The episode opens with the villain, who has just been paroled, coming to the Police HQ to meet Friday. We learn there is enmity between the two characters because Friday was the one who sent him up. Later, Friday, working the day watch out of Homicide, is assigned when a young girl is kidnapped by a robber, who came up on her and her date, impersonating a policeman, stole money, then took her with him. The girl turns up dead. Friday and his partner track the bad guy down, he is tried, convicted, and executed. Though recognizably deriving from the Chessman case, numerous changes (besides just "the names") are made. The kidnap victim is not just sexually attacked (and despite the taboo nature of this subject matter in 1949, the sexual content of the offense is made clear) but murdered, perhaps to avoid a lengthy explanation about the "Little Lindbergh Law." Interestingly, in the epilog, the criminal is executed rather than awaiting execution. Would that it had been so in real life.

During the radio show's second season, Webb made use of the Red Light Bandit case again in an episode called "The Big Badge," the 47th episode of the radio series, first broadcast on May 4, 1950. Like the bad guy in "The Red Light Bandit," the villain in this episode is impersonating a police officer in order to be able to approach young couples parked in overlooks around Los Angeles, only instead of a red spotlight, he's using a phony badge and is thus known as the "Badge Bandit" instead of the "Red Light Bandit." In this way, Webb was able to take the same set of facts and use them to craft two completely separate and distinct fictional versions.

I haven't been able to find information about whether or not any of the robberies carried out by Chessman's "Boy Bandits" gang in the early '40's took place in Los Angeles proper. Howard's book mentions Glendale and the parts of LA County policed by the Sheriff's Office. But four or five robberies every week, for a total of nearly 40, makes it probable that at least a few might have been within LA's city limits. If that was the case, it seems likely to me that "The Big Dance," the 83rd radio episode of *Dragnet*, from Season 3, might be based on that case. The young punks in this episode, first broadcast on January 18, 1951, are holding up mom-and-pop grocery stores rather than liquor stores and there are only two of them, but other aspects of the case seem to parallel the "Boy Bandits" case fairly closely. If so, that's three different episodes Webb got out of one criminal career. Unlike "The Red Light Bandit" and "The Big Badge," "The Big Dance" was eventually adapted for television after *Dragnet* made the jump from radio to video. The TV version was broadcast on June 25, 1953, the final episode of the second television season.

Cell 2455 Death Row (Columbia, 1955) is the film version of Chessman's first book. Directed by Fred F. Sears from a script by Jack De-Witt, it stars William Campbell as Chessman, redubbed for this movie "Whit" Whittier. Whittier was, of course, Chessman's middle name, and Chessman was known to his friends as "Chess," so it's easy to see where the fictionalized name derived from. Campbell, an up-and-coming actor in 1955 who never quite hit the big time, bore a fairly close resemblance to Chessman, though he lacked the sinister ruggedness that Chessman's broken nose gave him. His biggest role prior to this film was as the young, cocky co-pilot in *The High and the Mighty* (Warners, 1954), opposite John Wayne and Robert Stack. Later he was one of the co-leads in *Cannonball* (syndicated, 1958-59), a popular TV series about long-haul truck drivers. Today he is probably best-remembered for playing the villain in two of the most popular episodes of the original *Star Trek* (NBC, 1966-69), "The Squire of Gothos," first broadcast on January 12, 1967, and "The Trouble with Tribbles," first broadcast on December 29, 1967. Chessman/Whittier as a boy is played by William Campbell's younger brother, Robert, who, as R. Wright Campbell, would go on to become an Oscar-nominated screenwriter and an Edgar-winning mystery novelist.

Kill Me If You Can (NBC, 1977) is a made-for-TV movie dramatizing Chessman's fight for his life. Directed by Buzz Kulik and written by John Gay, it stars Alan Alda, then popular as Hawkeye Pierce on the TV version of *M*A*S*H* (CBS, 1972-83), as Chessman, a performance that earned him an Emmy nomination. Talia Shire plays his tireless attorney, Rosalie Asher.

In 2011, a DVD of *Cell 2455 Death Row* was released by Sony. Oddly, there doesn't seem to be an official DVD or videocassette of *Kill Me If You Can* available, though it can be obtained from private collectors.

MOLE TO MANHUNTER

Irish Mysteries

During the Irish War for Independence, fought during and immediately after World War I, the main targets of Republican partisans were not, as might be expected, members of the British military but members of the British law enforcement establishment. Specifically, members of the Royal Irish Constabulary and the Dublin Metropolitan Police.

As a policeman myself, I'm, at best, ambivalent to this strategy, but I can understand it. The fact is that the main armed force maintaining British rule in Ireland was not the Army but the police. Indeed, the most infamous enemies of the Irish Volunteers during the War for Independence, the notorious Black and Tans, were not a branch of the British Army as is commonly supposed, but the Reserve Force of the RIC. Moreover, if you regard yourself as being at war and the war you have to fight is a guerilla war against an occupying force, cops are, frankly, legitimate military targets.

During World War II, would French resistance fighters, for example, have been wrong to target Gestapo officers or even collaborating Sûreté officers on the grounds that they were cops, not soldiers? Or were members of the Gestapo just as legitimate a target as, say, members of the Wehrmacht, the Waffen-SS, or the Luftwaffe?

I don't mean to suggest that officers in the RIC or the DMP were comparable to the Gestapo. That would be not only fatuous, but terribly unjust. Nevertheless, there's no denying that the British-backed police in Ireland played a role there that was, if not precisely equivalent, at least analogous to the role played by the German-backed police in the occupied nations of Europe. And, if members of the Irish Volunteers, soon to be known as the Irish Republican Army (and known today as the "Old IRA," to distinguish it from later groups using the same name), sincerely believed that their war for independence was justified, then it followed that those British-backed police were legitimate targets.

And targeted they were. In a series of hit-and-run guerilla operations, the steadily demoralized Irish police were being attacked constantly.

But, when you're outnumbered and outgunned as the IRA was, it's just as important, arguably more important, to hit your enemy from the inside. Michael Collins, the Director of Intelligence for the IRA and generally regarded today as being to the Republic of Ireland what George Washington is to the United States, understood this. For this reason, he made a point of actively recruiting double agents from within the ranks of the police. Three such recruits particularly valuable to the Cause were David Neligan, Eamonn "Ned" Broy, and James McNamara (MacNamara according to some sources).

One of those three, Dave Neligan, is the subject of this article.

Neligan was born in 1899 in the village of Templeglantine in County Limerick. His parents were both teachers and Neligan grew up with a better education than was common for young men raised in the rural boroughs of Ireland.

At the age of 18, he applied for a position in the Dublin Metropolitan Police, and was hired as a constable. It doesn't appear that he was led to a career in law enforcement by some sense of vocation. It was just a common career choice for a young man with an above-average education and limited prospects in other professions.

Like virtually all rookie cops, he started out patrolling a beat on the streets of Ireland's capital city. In fairly short order, he won a transfer to the DMP's detective branch, known as the "G" Division to distinguish it from the Force's uniformed divisions, which were lettered "A" though "F." In those days, with the hint of rebellion in the air, the G Division was as much a secret political police as it was a criminal investigative branch. This did not sit well with Neligan, and by 1920, with the War for Independence in full force, he was convinced to resign from the DMP by his brother, an ardent Republican.

Shortly after Neligan returned to County Limerick, he received word that Michael Collins wanted to meet him in Dublin. At that meeting, Collins persuaded Neligan that he could do more for the Republican cause inside the DMP than outside. At his urging, Neligan rejoined the Dublin force and returned to the G Division.

Almost as soon as he rejoined, Neligan, his brother's Republican sympathies known, was recruited by his police superiors as a double agent against the IRA. In effect, Neligan was now a triple agent, ostensibly spying on the partisans for the British, while actually spying on the British for the partisans. His status as the DMP's "inside man" with the IRA gave him access to particularly useful information.

During the following months, Neligan passed vital data along to Collins. Possessed of an excellent memory, he was able to recall codes, passwords, operational secrets, etc., without committing them to paper. This information allowed the Republican forces to stay ahead of the British in terms of intelligence throughout the entire war. Broy and McNamara were exposed and arrested during this time but Neligan was able to keep his activities concealed.

By 1922, the British finally relented and a treaty was signed creating the Irish Free State, less than the fully independent Republic the partisans had hoped for but no longer a subordinate part of the United Kingdom. Neligan had managed to come through the hostilities without his undercover role ever being exposed.

However, the end of the war did not mean the end of armed conflict. The compromise that created the Irish Free State did not sit well with some of the more militant Republican partisans and almost as soon as the War for Independence was concluded, the Irish Civil War began. The Irish Free State had to raise a military force quickly and Neligan was commissioned as a colonel in the Intelligence Branch of the newly formed Irish Regular Army.

The fighting during the Civil War was vicious and unrelenting on both sides, possibly because of the death early in the conflict of Michael Collins, who commanded the Free State forces. Had Collins lived, the respect in which he was held by both sides might have moderated the relentlessness of the fighting and the conflict might have ended quickly, but his death forestalled that possibility.

During the most furious period of combat, Neligan's name was linked to several atrocities alleged to have been committed by the Irish Army. Men under his command were almost certainly involved in such incidents, though whether or not it was with his approval has never been established. Under the principal of "command responsibility" established during the war crimes tribunals that followed World War II, Neligan might have been held legally, if not personally, responsible, but his direct culpability has never been established. In later years, some anti-treaty partisans admitted having doubts about Neligan's personal guilt. It has been suggested that the connecting of Neligan to such incidents as the Ballyseedy and Countess Bridge massacres, during which IRA prisoners were forced to clear minefields and many were killed, was less because of Neligan's actual activities during the Civil War than because of his activities afterwards.

Though the Civil War ended in 1923 with the anti-treaty forces agreeing to a cease-fire, violence in the emerging Free State did not.

Neligan was asked by Free State Justice Minister Kevin O'Higgins to return to the Dublin Metropolitan Police and reorganize its detective branch. Neligan agreed, resigned his military commission and resumed his career with the DMP with the rank of Chief Superintendent. He immediately established a Special Branch within the DMP. Apparently modeled on Scotland Yard's Special Branch, it was responsible for internal national security and domestic counter-intelligence. The rest of the detective branch he reorganized into a regular, urban CID, also modeled along British lines. Neligan and his men got some favorable publicity six weeks after his appointment when his men caught a gang of armed robbers in the very act of raiding a payroll van in a suburb just outside of Dublin. Dublin's newly-made top detective was off to an auspicious start.

In 1925 the DMP was absorbed into the newly formed national police force, the Garda Síochána, and Neligan's "S" Branch, as it came to be known, now had jurisdiction throughout the Free State, while Neligan, still a chief superintendent, now had the responsibility for commanding detective forces all across Ireland.

The Civil War was officially over but many anti-Treaty partisans still actively promoted violence and committed violent acts in the name of their cause. Still others, from both the anti-Treaty and Free State sides, simply turned to violent crime. In the years following Neligan's appointment, some "S" Branch men were killed in armed conflicts and many were wounded. The families of his men were harassed and assaulted. Neligan and his men responded with comparable zeal. Aside from personal animus towards the criminals, they were responsible for protecting their brother officers in the uniformed branches. The Garda, like the British Police, was unarmed, and Neligan's detectives were the only Irish law enforcement officers who could provide an armed response to armed criminals.

As his detectives persevered in their ongoing supression of violent crime, Neligan continued with his new administrative duties. A six-month detective course was established, both in Dublin and at Garda headquarters in Phoenix Park. Armed detective units were deployed throughout the country, answering to the local District Superintendents for administrative purposes, but to Neligan himself operationally.

Meanwhile, Neligan turned his attention to County Leitrim, the most notorious and violent stronghold of the anti-Treaty gangs. The distinction between what was regarded as "ordinary crime" and armed political resistance had become so blurred in Leitrim as to become almost non-existent. Partisans lived in hidden roosts in the hills and mountains surrounding the county's villages. Gangs would descend on the undefended villagers raiding stores for supplies, stealing money, occasionally giving their victims receipts "in the name of the Republic."

In March of 1925, Neligan ordered his second-in-command, Superintendent Finion O'Driscoll, to take charge of a force of twenty "S" Branch detectives and deploy them in the Leitrim town of Drumshambo. Within weeks, dozens of arrests had been made, serious charges filed, and crime previously listed as "unsolved" were cleared. In the nearby town of Ballinamore, a gang of bank robbers walked into a detail of "S" Branch detectives who had been staked out in the bank, lying in wait. In the ensuing gun battle one bank bandit was killed and another wounded. By July, the mountain strongholds had been cleared and the violence ended.

Over the next few years, significant drops in both property crime and crimes against persons were being reported by the Garda, largely as a result of Neligan's efforts. More importantly, the morale of the entire Garda force was on the rise as its members came to realize that they no longer had to submit to threats and intimidation.

But feelings still ran deep. In 1927, Justice Minister O'Higgins, Neligan's mentor and staunchest suporter, was assassinated. Neligan now had no one watching his back in the Government.

By 1932 the sitting Government lost power when the newly formed pro-Republican, anti-Treaty party, Fianna Fáil, was swept into office and its founder, Éamon de Valera, was appointed President of the Executive Council, the Free State's Prime Minister. Neligan knew that the new government would be looking for any excuse to get rid of him and he did not intend to give them that excuse. But events have a way of superceding the best intentions.

Shortly after the election of the new Government, an incident occurred in the County Clare town of Kilrush. Labor disputes had sprung up between local businessman Daniel Ryan and his employees and Ryan's property was put under a 24-hour police guard. On the evening of August 15, 1932, two Republican demonstrators, T.J. Ryan and George Gilmore, suffering from gunshot wounds, were brought to the local hospital by Garda Detectives Myles Muldowney and Patrick Carroll. Muldowney and Carroll had been assigned to the security detail at Daniel Ryan's premises and they charged that Gilmore and T.J. Ryan had attempted to kill them, forcing them to fire in self-defense.

Over the next few days, as investigations proceeded, Muldowney and Carroll continued to insist that they had only acted in self-defense, while Gilmore and T.J. Ryan were just as insistent that the detectives' attack had been unprovoked. When the investigation was concluded, the two Gardaí had been suspended and charges against the two suspects dropped.

The Garda force, and particularly "S" Branch, was aghast. Neligan was particularly upset. Though, on examining the evidence, he was forced to agree that the two detectives had exceeded their authority, he was, nonetheless, also aware that over the course of many months they had been subjected to the most extreme provocation. Many of their brother cops had been killed and maimed. Their families had been insulted and harassed. Their homes had been vandalized. And, since the election of the Fianna Fáil government, this campaign of violence and vituperation had increased. In Neligan's view, the response of Muldowney and Carroll was, if not justified, perfectly understandable. When the two detectives were finally dismissed from the Force some months after the incident, Neligan organized a fund to help them out while they sought new employment.

This was just the opening the new government needed to get Neligan out of the Garda. He and the Garda commissioner, Eoin O'Duffy, were summarily called before the new Justice Minister, James Geoghagen, and ordered to explain why Neligan had set up an unauthorized fund for two disgraced and dismissed employees. Neligan was suspended with pay and ultimately transferred out of the Garda and into an equivalent positon in the Land Commission. A few months later, after another general election strengthened de Valera's majority in the Dáil Éireann, Ireland's parliament, O'Duffy was also fired.

Neligan, for his part, took his punishment without complaint and spent the next 30-odd years serving the Free State, and later the Republic, in the quiet halls of the Land Commission, where, he later said, he was happy just to have an office to himself and no one telling him what to do. He died quietly in 1983.

The work he did organizing the detective branch of the Garda Síochána still bears fruit to this day. Neligan's old "S" Branch is now the Special Detective Unit, still fighting subversion and terrorism according to the model Neligan once set and, in emulation of the armed units Neligan once deployed against violent crooks, now includes an

Emergency Response Unit, the Garda's equivalent of a SWAT team. The rest of Neligan's criminal investigative force, dedicated to non-political crime, still exists today as the Garda's National Bureau of Criminal Investigation. Though he served in the Dublin Metropolitan Police and the Garda for barely a decade, his efforts during the Force's formative years are still seen in the 21st Century.

FURTHER READING

Neligan's own autobiography, *The Spy in the Castle* (MacGibbon & Kee, 1968), has never been published in the US. However, a recent reprint edition put out by a British firm, Prendeville Publishing, has been distributed here by Irish Books and Media, and is available in specialty stores and on Internet sites like Amazon. Irritatingly, as its title implies, it concentrates almost exclusively on Neligan's activities as a double agent for Michael Collins during the War for Independence, and almost not at all on his later work as the Garda's chief of detectives.

Early in his jounalistic career, Dublin newspaperman Conor Brady, editor of *The Irish Times* from 1986 through 2002, wrote *Guardians of the Peace* (Gill and Macmillan Ltd., 1974), a history of the Garda from its founding through the end of World War II. Again, as with *The Spy in the Castle*, it was never published in the US, but a reprint edition put out by Prendeville Publishing is available, through Irish Books and Media, in specialty stores and on the 'Net. It's an excellent source of information about the Garda's early years, and it does include the detailed account of Neligan's years in the Irish police following the War for Independence and the Civil War that Neligan's own book largely leaves out. Brady, always interested in police affairs, is currently a member of the Garda Ombudsman Commission.

Both books are highly recommended.

NELIGAN IN FICTION

Neligan's life is a movie waiting to be made, but for the moment he exists only as a supporting character, and that only as a composite with two other real-life figures.

In the epic film fictionalizing the life of the main figure in Ireland's struggle for independence, *Michael Collins* (Warner Brothers, 1996), written and directed by Neil Jordan, the trio of spies Collins recruits to inflitrate the Irish Police are combined into one single figure. This character comes to a bad end when he is murdered by British forces.

Actually, only James McNamara died an early death and, though he was exposed as a double agent for Collins, I have been able to find no reference to his having been killed by the British or even that his death was a violent one. Apparently, like Neligan, he survived to serve in the Intelligence section of the Irish Regular Army during the Civil War, after the British had already agreed to the creation of an Irish Free State, so if his death was violent, it may have been Irish, not British who killed him. Still, given the times, it's not outside the realm of possibility that McNamara was killed by the British, but I've found no documentation of this.

Even more confusingly, though the character is clearly a composite figure, rather than being given a fictional name, he is called "Ned Broy." Not only wasn't the real-life Ned Broy killed by the British, he, like Dave Neligan, would later rejoin the police after the establishment of the Irish Free State and was serving as Chief Superintendent in command of the Garda's Dublin Metropolitan Division at the same time Neligan was running the Garda's detective force. Later, when Neligan was fired, Broy replaced him as the head of the Special Branch, and within a few months had become Commissioner of the Garda, promoted over several more senior officers who were suspected of being insufficently loyal to de Valera's Fianna Fáil party. Broy served as the head of Ireland's national police for five years.

In effect, Broy replaced Neligan in real life, and then replaced him in fiction.

THE RETURN OF THE CHINATOWN SQUAD

San Francisco Mysteries

The San Francisco Police Department's "Chinatown Squad" was first established late in 1875 in the wake of a vicious Tong War that had claimed four lives. But its real glory years began some forty five years later when Inspector Jack Manion, a veteran detective with more than two decades on the Job, was appointed head of the squad by Police Chief Dan O'Brien.

From then until his retirement in 1946 Manion and his officers enjoyed singular success in reducing, indeed virtually eliminating, violence, forced prostitution, opium trafficking, and other major criminal activities in the twenty-four square blocks that comprised the Golden Gate City's Chinese neighborhood. He never quite managed to eliminate gambling in Chinatown, but he did curtail it. More importantly, the violence that had previously attended gambling was, for practical purposes, non-existent. He left the SFPD having attained the status of legend, not just in his own department, but in all of law enforcement, respected by his colleagues and revered by the residents of Chinatown.

The Squad itself continued along for another decade or so after Manion's departure and was finally officially disbanded in 1955, a victim of its own success.

Any professional military man will tell you that, in time of peace, you should prepare for war. If you assume that once the war is won it will never be necessary to fight another, you will be left unprepared when the next inevitable call to arms comes.

And the presumption that since violence had been chased out of Chinatown it would never return proved to be just as short-sighted.

Roughly a decade after the old Chinatown Squad had been decommissioned, there was a sudden spike in violence in that neighborhood. The community that had been peaceful for so many years was suddenly the site of a series of well-planned, gangland-style hits.

New immigrants, mostly from Hong Kong, were at the root of the violence. Many of the teen-aged boys in those families entering the US from the Crown Colony had often been members of street gangs in their former home. Once in their new country, those gang members organized into the same sorts of associations and began engaging in the same sorts of activities; drug trafficking, petty extortion of legitimate businesses, etc. And, like youth gangs from other ethnic groups, they were very territorial and very ready to use violence to defend what they regarded as their turf.

Inspector John McKenna was a fifteen-year SFPD veteran when he was assigned to the Homicide Detail in 1969. Prior to his transfer, he'd worked in the Bureau of Special Services, SFPD's vice unit, giving him a thorough knowledge of gambling, the major criminal activity in Chinatown even during the peaceful years. As a consequence, he was often assigned cases that originated in Chinatown. Over the next eight years, he developed into the Homicide Detail's go-to guy whenever there was a murder in Chinatown. In effect, he was, within the context of his homicide assignment, a one-man Chinatown Squad.

But in 1977, McKenna's one-man *ad hoc* operation ended and the Chinatown Squad, with McKenna as its head, was officially reestablished as an autonomous unit within the SFPD.

It all started with firecrackers.

Illegal firecrackers were a major source of revenue for Chinatown's gangs and the Fourth of July was, to the firecracker business, what Christmas is to the toy business. The gang with the largest share of the firecracker business was the Ping Boys, so called because they operated out of the Ping Yuen Housing Projects on Pacific Avenue. The Ping Boys managed their firecracker business under the auspices of the massive Wah Ching triad.

A rival group, the Chung Ching Yee, or "Joe Boys" for its founder, former Wah Ching member Joe Fong, decided it was entitled to a share of the Ping Boys' Independence Day profits and made plans to rob them of the proceeds of their business.

It's difficult, almost impossible, to find a convenient parking place in San Francisco and such was the case for the Joe Boys that day. Forced to park some distance from the project and then approach on foot, they were spotted by their intended victims. In the ensuing gun battle, one of the Joe Boys was killed and four others were wounded. Forced to retreat, the Joe Boys nursed their wounds and their grudges and quietly plotted payback.

It was generally believed by the Joe Boys that the man behind their defeat at the hands of the Ping Boys was Wah Ching honcho Michael

Louie, aka "Hot Dog" Louie. At 2:40 AM on Sunday, September 4, 1977, acting on a tip that Louie was having dinner at a local eatery, three Joe Boys, all masked, one armed with a shotgun, another with a pistol, and the third with a submachine gun, entered the Golden Dragon Restaurant on Washington Street.

It was Labor Day weekend and there was a fairly large crowd of diners still in the restaurant despite the late hour. The Joe Boys' information was correct. Hot Dog Louie was there. But, being an experienced gangster with a well-developed survival instinct, he hit the deck as soon as he saw the three gunmen enter. The tourists enjoying a late night meal on a holiday weekend and the waiters working late to earn a few extra bucks, did not.

The Joe Boys opened fire and seconds later five innocent bystanders were dead. Another eleven were wounded. Not a single round fired that night hit Louie, nor any other Wah Ching or Ping Boy.

The reaction of the public and the media was predictable. Gangsters killing gangsters was to be expected but gangsters killing innocent by-standers was an outrage. Serious action was going to have to be taken.

A week after the Golden Dragon Massacre, Joe Boy Yee Michael Lee was killed and a companion wounded, presumably in retaliation for the attack on Hot Dog Louie. Unless something was done, The City was in for a gang war.

SFPD Chief Charles Gain was the man responsible for doing something. One of the few outsiders ever hired as San Francisco's Top Cop, he'd started his law enforcement career on the other side of the San Francisco Bay in Oakland, eventually rising to police chief there. His relationship with the rank-and-file of the OPD was rocky and he ended his tenure there shortly after the local police association gave him a vote of no confidence, with only twenty per cent of the membership voting to support Gain.

Moving to the other side of the country, he became the public safety director in St. Petersburg, Florida. Again he managed to thoroughly alienate his police officers. His abrasive style was so unpopular that he never even got to the point where a confidence vote was held. He was fired before his first year at St. Petersburg was completed.

His knack for alienating the rank and file reached its zenith after he was hired to take over the San Francisco Police. By 1979, when a similar vote was held by the membership of San Francisco's Police Officers' Association, his tally in Oakland would look pretty good by comparison. Only two percent of the POA gave Gain a positive rating, one tenth of what he'd gotten across the Bay. Ninety-eight percent of the POA membership voted "no confidence." Gain may be the only police chief in American law enforcement history to get a "no confidence" vote from two different major city police forces.

But that was all in the future. In 1977, he was still the chief and the public was looking to him to end Chinatown's gang war.

Gain was not a stern and wrathful crime-fighter in the mold of New York's Lew Valentine or Los Angeles's Bill Parker. He was a self-described "law enforcement CEO" whose main interest was less in thwarting criminal activity than it was in building "in-roads" with "communities" and "interest groups" that were important to the political success of his mentor, ultra-liberal Mayor George Moscone.

As a public relations move, he had the Department's police cars repainted from their traditional black-and-white design to baby blue and white, removing the stark, seven-pointed "SFPD" star from the doors, and replacing them with a nice, inoffensive circle that said "Police Services." He removed all law enforcement paraphernalia, including the American flag, from his office, saying that he "liked an office that's a relaxed space, not militarist or tribunal . . . Everywhere I looked it was police, police, police. Why should I be constantly reminded of that?"

Known for favoring Pierre Cardin suits rather than his police blues, one of the few times he appeared publicly in uniform was at the annual Hookers' Ball, where he posed for a picture standing between a professional prostitute and a transvestite.

Everything he did in the supposed interest of "building inroads" to the community seemed deliberately calculated to antagonize the officers under his command. All things considered, it's surprising that he got as much as two per cent.

Be that as it may, in 1977 he *was* the police chief, and letting gun-crazy gangsters get away with murdering tourists in a town where tourism was arguably the major industry, and honest working stiffs in a town with a strong union presence was not going to do Mayor Moscone any good. So he did something no one could have predicted. He reinstituted the Chinatown Squad.

Of course, being more bureaucrat than cop and having no particular sympathy for the culture and lore of the Department he led (indeed, having a self-evident contempt for that culture and lore), Chief Gain couldn't use a name replete with the sense of drama and historical resonance that "Chinatown Squad" had. Instead, the newly reinstituted detail became, in the best politically correct bureaucratic tradition, the "Asian Gang Task Force."

Inspector McKenna, assured by his boss, Lieutenant Dan Murphy, the commander of the Homicide Detail, that he had *carte blanche* as to manpower, overtime, equipment, etc., set about organizing the new unit. Homicide Inspectors John Fotinos, Carl Klotz, Mike Mullane, and Ron Schneider, were all recruited because of their experience in murder investigation, Juvenile Bureau Inspector Dick Gamble for his knowledge of youth gangs, and Inspector Jim Deasy and Officers Fred Mollatt and Tim Simmons of the Intelligence Section for their expertise on organized crime. Officers Paul Bertsch, Bob Bonnet, Leon Crouere, Larry Wong, Marshall Wong, Mickey Giraldi, Fred Lau, and Dave Horton, all assigned to the Central District, which included Chinatown, were recruited for their local knowledge (and the Wongs and Lau, frankly, for their ethnic background; they were the first members of the Chinatown Squad, whatever it was called, to actually be of Chinese descent; Lau would later become SFPD's first Asian-American chief). Officer Dave Foley, assigned to the Northern District, had neither the specialized investigative expertise nor the local neighborhood knowledge of any of the other Task Force members, but McKenna had worked with him back in his Vice days, and respected him as a first-rate cop. His instincts about Foley would be borne out.

One of the few advantages that cops have when investigating gang hits is that sooner or later, in an effort to increase his street cred, someone involved in the murders will talk and someone who's not involved will hear him and pass on what he's heard. Whatever's said may be less than an admission, let alone a confession. It may be no more than a bare hint that the speaker knows something no one else present knows. Nevertheless, it gives law enforcement a foothold on which to start their climb to a solution.

Chinese gangbangers, by contrast, had no such inclination to boast about or even hint at their involvement in acts of violence. For a Chinese contract killer, the success of the hit spoke for itself without the necessity to gild the lily by bragging.

Moreover, even the law-abiding residents of Chinatown, reflecting the tendency of every new group of recent immigrants, were reluctant to speak to the cops. Fearing reprisal and suspicious of authority figures who were not part of their own community, they imprisoned themselves behind a wall of silence.

In the meantime the new unit, stuck in a closet-sized space in the Hall of Justice down the corridor from Homicide, was woefully under-equipped despite the promises of Chief Gain. The tiny office had no office fixtures and, in any event, not enough room even if such fixtures had been made available. McKenna split shifts and assignments, so that the majority of the unit was either resting at home or out on the street following up leads, leaving only a bare minimum in the office.

With the main force out in the field, the gang members started to get intimidated. It seemed there was no place in Chinatown they could go without running into a member of the Task Force.

As one gang member later put it, "Turn a corner, you ran into an-other cop in plainclothes. Like no place safe, you know. Go in the Ping Yuen Bakery, man, you got coffee and cops. Like hang out at the Sun Sing Theater, you got movies and more cops peekin' at you from the aisles. I mean, all the time! Shit, you couldn't even hide out at school. You got teachers, you got fuckin' cops!"

While concentrating on the Golden Dragon case, new Chinatown-related cases were being turned over to the new unit. This boded well for its long-term existence.

The combination of the constant police presence and the fact that some young men were caught up in the youth gangs more or less against their will finally came to fruition when a member of the Joe Boys, Rob-ert Woo, volunteered to act as an informant. He named one of the shoot-ers and by the end of October the Task Force had the names of the other two.

But there was still the thorny problem of getting enough evidence to convict them. There's a lot of distance, often a distance impossible to traverse, between knowing who the bad guys are and being able to prove it in court.

Slowly but surely, however, that evidence was being collected. A crucial aspect of the investigation was the involvement of Chinese-American officers like Fred Lau and a young rookie fresh out of the academy who was briefly assigned to the unit named Heather Fong (who, like Lau, would go on to be Chief of the SFPD, the second Asian-American, and the first woman, to hold that post). Their familiarity with Chinese culture and their facility with Chinese language was essential to the success of the investigation.

The Task Force eventually learned that the mastermind behind the hit was Tom Yu who, though he planned the attack, was not present when it was actually carried out. The triggermen were Peter Ng, Melvin Yu, and Stuart Lin. The drivers of the two getaway cars were Chester Yu and Sai Ying Lee. Various accessories before and after the fact obtained the weapons, dumped the weapons, obtained information on the whereabouts of the intended victim, obtained the cars used the night of the hit, etc. Slowly but surely, the Task Force officers were gathering the evidence needed.

Dan Foley convinced Robert Woo to meet with one of the gunmen, Stuart Lin, while wearing a wire. Meeting at Galileo High School, the two Joe Boys discussed Lin's alibi and Lin made several admissions about his participation in the massacre in the course of the conversation. He'd be the first domino to fall.

Arrested, he confessed his culpability to Officer Dan Foley but said he was acting under duress when he carried a shotgun into the restaurant that night. He described the roles played by the other five offenders: Tom Yu, who orchestrated the attack; Melvin Yu who carried the SMG; Peter Ng who carried the .38; Chester Yu and Sai Ying Lee who drove; and Peter Cheung who obtained the autos used in the hit.

Eventually, everyone except Sai Ying Lee was arrested. Separate trials were conducted for all the defendants. Changes of venues were granted, so that each trial was held in a different California city.

Stuart Lin, who cooperated with police and whose plea of "duress" was, to a degree, believed by the jury was sentenced to 28 years for second-degree murder. While in prison he earned an associate's degree and began work towards a bachelor's. Tom Yu, Melvin Yu, and Peter Ng were all convicted of first degree murder and all received life sentences. Getaway driver Chester Yu, who also cooperated with the police and who led them to the San Francisco Bay dump site in the Peninsula suburbs south of The City, where divers recovered the weapons, was tried as a juvenile, spent two years at the California Youth Authority in Stockton, then moved to another state upon his release. Peter Cheung, who'd stolen the cars used that night, also cooperated fully and also did two years with the CYA. Tony Szeto, who'd dumped the weapons in suburban San Mateo County, was convicted and sentenced to two years at state prison.

Sai Ying Lee, the second driver was never apprehended.

Less than a clean sweep, but the Asian Gangs Task Force had proved its usefulness and became a permanent fixture in the SFPD.

Officer Dan Foley, who'd developed the informants, kept them friendly and obtained Stuart Lin's confession, would eventually be promoted from patrolman to inspector, and then to sergeant/inspector. When John McKenna retired in 1986, Foley would become the commander of the Task Force.

The Joe Boys, their teeth pulled by the multiple convictions, eventually folded. But remaining gangs became stronger in the vacuum created by the demise of the Joe Boys and new gangs would form up. Gang violence in Chinatown would continue, making the Task Force a continuing necessity to the SFPD. It remains a part of the Bureau of Inspectors to this day, as a detail within the Major Crimes Section, which also includes Homicide, Robbery, and Special Investigations.

Jack Manion would be proud to know that his work continues.

FURTHER READING

Kevin J. Mullen's *Chinatown Squad – Policing the Dragon from the Gold Rush to the 21ˢᵗ Century* (Noir Publications, 2008) is a comprehensive history of the relationship between the SFPD and its Chinese community from the earliest days of The City's history to the present. Despite being a relatively recent publication, it's already out of print and copies come very dear. But if you're interested in the subject, it's well worth getting. Its chapter on the Golden Dragon Massacre is what spurred me to write about the incident for *Just the Facts*.

Mullen spent more than a quarter of a century as a San Francisco cop, retiring as a deputy chief in 1986. Described by a colleague as "a Renaissance Man in the Police Department," he would, in retirement, become the SFPD's unofficial historian. In addition to *Chinatown Squad*, Mullen is the author of *The Toughest Gang in Town – Police Stories from Old San Francisco* (Noir Publications, 2005), which won the American Book Award, *Let Justice Be Done – Crime and Politics in Early San Francisco* (University of Nevada, 1989), and *Dangerous Strangers – Minority Newcomers and Criminal Violence in the Urban West, 1850-2000* (Palgrave Macmillan, 2005). The latter book, like *Chinatown Squad*, has much interesting information about law enforcement in that fabled neighborhood.

Brockman Morris, a former journalist for *The Christian Science Monitor*, was both a self-described "close observer of police work in San Francisco from 1970 to 1978," and a frequent diner at the Golden

Dragon. He'd eaten there the night of the massacre and missed witnessing it (and perhaps missed being seriously injured or killed as a consequence) by "a matter of minutes."

On a website he maintains, brockmorris.com, he includes a book-length account of the case, *Bamboo Tigers*, which he posted in 2000. It may be the most complete account of the case available and it's well-written enough that I'm mildly surprised that he had to self-publish it on the 'Net. While Mullen gave a good, concise overview of the case, Morris provided many of the details that Mullen, giving a broader history of the Squad from the 19th Century to the present day, hadn't the room to include.

"America's Most Unlikely Police Chief Strikes Out," an article by Larry Eichel for Knight-Ridder Newspapers, which I found in the July 12, 1979, issue of the St. Petersburg *Independent*, served to put the Golden Dragon investigation in the context of the controversial administration of the SFPD by a chief more interested in "making inroads" than catching criminals.

THE CHINATOWN SQUAD IN FICTION

Year of the Dragon (Simon & Schuster, 1981) by Robert Daley, former NYPD Deputy Commissioner for Public Affairs, opens with an attack on a restaurant in Manhattan's Chinatown, one that is deliberately evocative of the real-life attack on San Francisco's Golden Dragon. In Daley's version, his hero, Captain Arthur Powers, happens to be present, and winds up shooting it out with the gunmen. This leads to his being put in charge of NYPD's Chinatown Precinct. The same scene opens the otherwise not particularly faithful film version of Daley's novel (MGM/UA, 1985), directed by Michael Cimino from a script by Cimino and Oliver Stone, in which the gun-slinging police captain, played by Mickey Rourke, is, for no particular reason that was evident to me, renamed Stanley White.

The rest of the story, in both the novel and the film, does not parallel the real-life Golden Dragon case to any great degree. The main nemesis of the captain (whether he's Powers or White) is a powerful adult mobster seeking to extend the influence of Hong Kong triads to the United States, rather than members of youthful street gangs.

The book is damned good. And the movie isn't nearly as bad as you may have heard, but on the other hand isn't nearly as good as it should have been given the pedigree it has.

While Daley's novel and the subsequent movie version may be the only, comparatively limited, use of the Golden Dragon massacre for fiction, SFPD's Chinatown Squad, particularly during the Manion years, has provided grist for many a fictioneer's mill.

Manion himself (or characters very obviously modeled on him) appears in several San Francisco-set crime novels, including Earl Derr Biggers's *Behind That Curtain* (Bobbs-Merrill, 1928), in which Charlie Chan travels from Honolulu to the City by the Bay, and works closely with the Squad and its head, "Jack Manley"; Joe Gores's *Hammett* (Putnam, 1975), in which Pinkerton operative turned crime novelist Dashiell Hammett returns to the detective profession for one case and works alongside his old friend, the legendary Manion; *The DeValera Deception* (Enigma, 2010) by Michael and Patrick McMenamin, in which a law professor and a lady photojournalist, recruited into British Intelligence by Winston Churchill, enlist Manion to aid in thwarting a threatened *coup d'etat* in the Irish Free State; and James L. Swanson's *The Stuff That Dreams Are Made Of* (AuthorHouse, 2001), in which a crime writer and his wife travel in time back to 1920's San Francisco, where they get involved with none other than Sam Spade himself and cross paths with Manion.

Carleton E. Morse, the legendary script writer for old time radio drama, best-remembered for the soap opera *One Man's Family* (NBC, 1932-59) and the adventure serial *I Love a Mystery* (NBC, NBC Blue, 1939-44), had close ties with the SFPD, developed during his years as a reporter on the San Francisco *Call*. When he started in radio drama, he used those contacts to create several shows based on files from the Department, including *Barbary Coast Nights*, *Killed in Action*, and *To the Best of Their Ability*, which all aired on NBC's Pacific Coast Network. Perhaps the best-remembered of his SFPD radio dramas was *Chinatown Squad*, which ran in 1932. Like the other three SFPD radio dramas created by Morse, *Chinatown Squad* was narrated by William J. Quinn, who was the chief of the SFPD at that time.

In prose fiction, the longest sustained use of SFPD's Chinatown Squad can be found in a series of short stories by another former San Francisco journalist, Sidney Herschel Small. Between 1931 and 1936, Small wrote thirty short stories featuring Jimmy Wentworth, the head of SFPD's Chinatown detail, all of which appeared in the famed pulp magazine *Detective Fiction Weekly*. Wentworth, in contrast to the real-life

Manion, was a youngster, barely a few years past his time as a rookie, who, though American-born, had grown up in China. His main foe in the series was the Fu Manchu-like Kong Gai, who was the evident mastermind behind all crime in San Francisco's Chinese section. Despite Small's use of a "Yellow Peril" type of villain, the Wentworth stories are unusual in that the depiction of Chinese characters is quite respectful and sympathetic. Small, like his character, grew up in China where his parents had business interests, and was familiar with, and respectful of Chinese culture and traditions. While Kong Gai was a villain, it was because he chose that path, not because he was Chinese. Most of the residents on Wentworth's beat were respectable and law-abiding, and one, an old college buddy who was the son of Chinatown's most successful businessman, was Wentworth's closest friend. All thirty of the Wentworth yarns are collected in a handsome hardback volume, *Tong of Terror – The Chinatown Adventures of Jimmy Wentworth* (Battered Silicon Dispatch Box, 2011).

ABOUT THE AUTHOR

Currently a sergeant in the police force of a national railroad, third-generation cop JIM DOHERTY has served American law enforcement at the local, state, and federal levels, policing a wide variety of jurisdictions, from university campuses to military bases, from inner city streets to suburban parks, and has, at one time or another, worked in a dozen different states for seven different police agencies. He has walked foot beats, made undercover drug buys, been assigned to a special task force tracking down a serial sex criminal, and guarded presidents and royalty. Due to his wide background in police work (and his being a lifelong fan of the comic strip), Jim is the current police technical advisor for *DICK TRACY*.

In addition to *JUST THE FACTS: TRUE TALES OF COPS AND CRIMINALS*, Jim is the author of *RAYMOND CHANDLER - MASTER OF AMERICAN NOIR*, a collection of lectures about the famed hard-boiled crime novelist written for Barnes & Noble's series of online literature classes, and numerous short stories featuring a young cop named Dan Sullivan, whose career more or less parallels Jim's. He has won a Spur Award from the Western Writers of America for Best Short Non-Fiction ("Blood for Oil," included in this book), and, as part of "Team Tracy," a Harvey Award for Best Syndicated Newspaper Strip. He's also been a finalist for a Dagger Award from the British Crime Writers Association, and a Macavity Award from Mystery Readers International.

Born and raised in the San Francisco Bay Area, he currently lives in Chicago with his lovely wife, Katy.

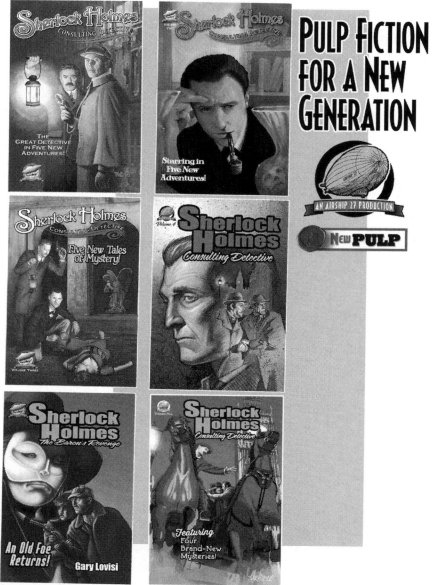